WHO IS I

DISCOVERING OUR TRUE IDENTITY IN JESUS CHRIST AND WHY IT MATTERS!

BOOK I

THE FOUNDATION

Donna M. Rogers

Published by:
Angel of Love & Light Ministries
Tampa, Florida, U.S.A.
www.angeloffaith777.com
Printed in the U.S.A.

ISBN-10:0-9990105-0-6
ISBN-13: 978-0-9990105-0-1

Cover design by James Nesbit

Edited by:

Mary Ann Levy and Ulmpact Publishing Group

Illustrations by Kristen Schipfer-Barrett

TABLE OF CONTENTS

Foreword iii

Acknowledgments vii

Preface xi

Introduction 1

Chapter 1: Where and When Did the Phrase the "Fullness of the Gentiles" Originate According to God's Word? 45

Chapter 2: Abraham is the "Father of Many Nations," so "Who" Are the Twelve Tribes of Israel—the Children of Israel? 55

Chapter 3: The Genealogy of Jesus Christ is rooted in the Abrahamic Covenant 91

Chapter 4: The Prophetic Meaning of Joseph's Dream of the Sun, the Moon and the Eleven Stars Bowing down to Him 105

Chapter 5: Are Abraham's Descendants Jewish or Hebrew? "Who" is a True Jew from God's Perspective? 153

Chapter 6: *Yehôvah*, the God of Abraham, Isaac, and Jacob (Israel) and His Only Begotten Son—Jesus Christ, is the Holy One of Israel 167

Chapter 7: The Word is the Firstborn Over All Creation 171

Chapter 8: God the Father, God the Son, and God the Holy Spirit Are the Same God, Yet They Are Three Distinct Persons in the Godhead 217

Chapter 9: Where Did God the Father Come From? 261

Chapter 10: When Did God (Qualify, Select, and Choose) the Word in His Invisible Image to Be the Firstborn Over All Creation? 275

i

TABLE OF CONTENTS

Chapter 11: Understanding Our True Identity in Christ and Our Purpose as God's Sons and Daughters.. 309

Chapter 12: Why Did the Word Who Was in the Image of the Invisible God Choose to Take the Form of a Bondservant and Come to the Earth in the Likeness of Men?.. 345

Chapter 13: How and When Did *Yehôvah* Call Israel (Jesus) Out of Egypt When He Was a Child?.. 377

Chapter 14: God's Throne is the "Pledge" or "Security" Deposit for the "Covenant" Promises He Gave to Abraham 393

Chapter 15: "Spiritually" Speaking, Israel is Jesus Christ and His Disciples, and "Physically" Speaking, Israel is the Land God Promised to Give Abraham and His Descendants........................ 433

Chapter 16: "Spiritual" Israel is Comprised of Jews from the House of Judah and Former Gentiles from the House of Israel (Jacob/Joseph/Ephraim)... 439

Chapter 17: The Nation of Israel is the First "Physical" Nation in the World God Established as the Firstfruits of His Increase 453

Chapter 18: The Rebirth of the State of Israel on May 14, 1948, is One of the Main Signs of God's Prophetic Time Clock and Authenticates God's Word 481

Epilogue 517

References.. 525

Connect with the Author... 595

About the Author.. 597

FOREWORD

I n this book, Minister Donna Rogers has done a superb job in bringing a clear, simplistic understanding of our Hebraic roots in Christianity. She answers the questions that many Christians may ponder in their mind of why this knowledge is important and is relevant to New Covenant believers.

She answers these thought provoking questions in a way which is laid out perfectly to enhance the reader's mind. This book sets the reader in a position of expectation as she shares revelatory information that many believers in the body of Christ may be hearing for the very first time. You will not be able to put this book down, and after reading this series, you will be fully equipped to be the *bride of Christ* without spot or blemish.

I especially recommend this book to all leaders in the body of Christ because it is a one-stop shop and everything you need to know is presented in chronological order. This book is a "masterpiece" due to the wealth of information it contains which is indisputably based on the whole counsel of God's Word. This material can be used in all areas of teaching and to inform others of the great plan of God.

After reading this series, you will have the total description of what God has in mind for all His children. You will not need to research other books because Minister Donna Rogers has done all the research for you and the "fruits" of her labor of love for God and His people are displayed on each page.

In fact, some readers may be wishing that a book like this was published years ago. Yet this book that many believers have been yearning for has finally come forth for a time such as this, and it is here by the grace of God according to His perfect timing. You will be delighted that you purchased and read this book because your walk with God will never be the same.

To help ease any potential lack of understanding, many of the terms Donna uses in this book such as *Yéshúa,* which is the Hebrew name for our Jewish Messiah Jesus Christ, the commonwealth of Israel, the children of Israel, the House of Israel, the House of Judah, etc., are fully expressed.

Some readers may feel intimidated because of a lack of knowledge when they read this book. However, this is an easy to read book and is written in such a manner that keeps your attention despite the in-depth knowledge of what is being conveyed. As you turn the pages of this book, you, the reader, will be able to feel the heart of the author and understand her passion for the subject. Every page is constructed with you in mind. Read this book with an open mind, as it will challenge many things you have been taught and have already heard.

I thank the Lord Jesus for giving Minister Donna Rogers the revelation and understanding to release this book to all the nations in the world. The hand of the Lord is being revealed in her life and in this book. She has a unique way of stripping away the false teachings and misconceptions of the Scriptures while bringing to light the uncompromised, unadulterated truth of *Yehôvâh's* Holy Word. Get ready for a life-changing experience.

This is only the beginning of what is to come, and you never know what avenues God will open up as a result of this great work. Perhaps a workbook or study guide may follow as a much–needed resource to offer believers a core curriculum to be used to equip the saints for the work of the ministry in a small group setting in churches throughout the nations.

Overseer Jerry S. Mallory
Kingdom Life Builders Int'l Ministries
Valrico, Florida

I am grateful to Almighty YHWH Elohim who sent us a gift in Donna Rogers. Her passion and devotion to Messiah are evident throughout this work to uncover the mystery of Israel scattered to the nations. Those who embark on this life-changing Bible study will come away not only with a new understanding of the God of the Bible and our Messiah but also to our place in the *kingdom of heaven*.

Peter Michael Martinez
Remnant House Ministries

ACKNOWLEDGMENTS

T his series I have penned is a *labor of love* for my Lord and Savior Jesus Christ and the body of Christ.

Jesus Christ is my King, my Lord, my Master, my God, my Savior, my Redeemer, my Healer, my Deliverer, my Father, my Husband, and my very best Friend.

As such, without Jesus Christ, I can do nothing. I have learned nothing compares to the hope I have found in Him for He has captivated my heart and transformed my life with the power of His love! In fact, the more I get to know Him on a personal, intimate basis, the more I realize I cannot live without Him for He is everything to me.

In the first book I wrote for the Lord in 2004 titled, *Shattered Dreams—Wake Up America Before It Is Too Late!,* I candidly shared my testimony which demonstrates the metamorphosis that has taken place in my heart. This occurred when I finally fully yielded to His Lordship in my life and totally submitted myself to the transforming power of the Holy Spirit by placing my faith and trust in the author and finisher of my faith—Jesus Christ.

Since that time, I have learned that *nothing* in this life compares to the promise I have in Him. No one, or nothing else, will satisfy the wonder of His love.

Therefore, I choose to leave the things of this world behind because I have learned that nothing else, or no one else, can compare to His manifest presence in my life.

Thus, I will spend the rest of my life seeking His face to answer the cry of His heart as I dedicate myself to Him, as a living sacrifice, for

His purposes and glory to prevail in and through me, His servant.

On Judgment Day, when all is said and done, I long to hear Him say to me, *"Well done, good and faithful servant; you were faithful over a few things, I will make you ruler over many things. Enter into the joy of your Lord."* (Matthew 25:21, NKJV) (emphasis added).

Until that time, I have three things to do to lead me toward that consummation: Trust steadily in God, hope unswervingly, and love extravagantly—and the best of the three is love.

At this time, I want to extend my heartfelt thanks and gratitude to the following people:

My husband Jimmy who has blessed me beyond measure with his unwavering support and love on our journey together for the past nineteen years. Thank you for helping me so I could answer the call to the ministry God has placed upon my life before the foundation of the world. Jimmy, I want to specifically thank you for taking the time to help me double check the accuracy of each Scripture and reference I used in this series. This was a daunting and very tedious task, to say the least, yet we persevered, and we prevailed together! Thank you, Jesus!

My brilliant and athletic teenage son Dylan for being extremely understanding when I couldn't attend all his sporting events due to my obligations in the ministry including the amount of time I had to devote to writing this book. There were certainly a lot of sporting events due to his involvement with soccer, track, cross-country, and football.

My brilliant and beautiful daughter Kristen Schipfer-Barrett for graciously using the "artistic" and "creative" talents God has blessed her with to help me create most of the illustrations I use in Book #2, Book #3 and Book #4.

My dear friends Susan Jacobson, Cynthia Pinckney, and Dee Rogers for keeping me saturated with prayer during this long, arduous journey for the past three and a half years. Thank you for encouraging me through every major obstacle I encountered. Also, thank you for cheering me on when I felt like giving up because of the intensity of the spiritual warfare involved. You are truly angels God has sent to me, and all of you are truly my sisters in Christ and in life!

I also want to thank and honor my very best friend Patricia Young-Summers who is the one that planted the "seed" of my faith in Christ in the very beginning—well over 30 years ago. We have walked this journey we call life together for so long now; I can't imagine what my life would have become without your friendship and your love.

I thank God for bringing a mighty man of God into my life who is also my spiritual father in Christ—Pastor Jerry Mallory. I was ordained by Pastor Mallory and his lovely wife, Pastor Anne Marie Mallory, under Kingdom Life Builders International Ministries Inc. Thank you for your encouragement, your godly counsel, and the wisdom you have shared with me on my journey to fulfill my God given destiny as a teacher of the gospel. I love, honor, and appreciate you both very much.

Reinhard Bonnke, founder of Christ for All Nations, for selecting, commissioning and releasing me to the nations. I honor and highly respect this mighty General in God's army, and I will forever be grateful to God for giving me the opportunity to be a graduate of

Reinhard Bonnke's School of Evangelism.

James Nesbit who created the incredible, breathtaking cover for this book which brilliantly captured the vision the Lord gave me. James, thank you, for the "masterpiece" you created. May God continue to bless all the work of your hands!

Peter Michael Martinez, founder of Remnant House Ministries. Peter was willing and very gracious not only to read this book but also chose to write a foreword. Thank you, Peter! May God continue to bless your ministry and all the work of your hands in this "kairos" season!

Mary Ann Levy, a sister in Christ, who helped me with the "content" edit for Book 1. Thank you, Mary Ann, for your excellent feedback! I truly appreciate it.

Adorah Tidwell, Communications Director, with Ulmpact Publishing Group for coordinating the final edit for Book 1.

Mary Post, a very dear friend, who did the final editing for Book 2. Thank you, Mary! I enjoyed our chats and collaborating on this project with you.

My neighbor, Connie Nelson, who graciously helped me with the final proofread of this book. Connie, I sincerely thank you for helping me with this endeavor. I appreciate you very much.

PREFACE

This comprehensive, in-depth series of books is an antidote to help curtail the avalanche of false teachings the late and mighty man of God—Steve Hill warned about when he said, *"Just as the ski patrol did in this vision, those who are aware of what's happening must take swift and accurate action. Their weapons of warfare must be aimed at the peaks and the 'avalanche terrain' to dispel the lies. Apostles, prophets, evangelists, pastors, and teachers must be willing to drop spiritual bombs, fire anti-heresy missiles, and even drive into the danger zones armed with explosive truth to confront this potential avalanche."*

Therefore, this series of books will ignite and encourage others, like myself, to launch anti-heresy missiles in an all-out assault to dispel the lies with explosive truth to confront the great apostasy taking place in the body of Christ from pulpits all across the world, especially in America.

Moreover, this series of books will help stem the tide of anti-Semitism, which is rearing its ugly head once again, from happening in the body of Christ. However, this will only happen *if* we understand "who" Israel is, "why" it matters, and in "what" ways this knowledge is extremely relevant to New Covenant believers.

As such, this series of books is "revolutionary" and "transformational" due to the comprehensive, in-depth coverage of the subject matter based on the whole counsel of God's Word and its relevance to the body of Christ for a time such as this.

Also, the amazing prophetic revelation I have received from the Holy Spirit is phenomenal, so I can *spiritually* see the "bigger picture" for God's people to teach, equip, and prepare the body of

Christ for Jesus Christ's second coming which is rapidly approaching.

I have written this series of books in such a manner, so those who have never heard the *gospel of the kingdom* preached, can easily comprehend the basic tenets of our faith in Christ, based on the doctrine of Christ.

In fact, many of the most seasoned believers in Jesus Christ, who comprise the body of Christ, still do not fully comprehend these basic tenets of our faith for this reason: They spend the majority of their lives sitting in church as they listen to a watered-down, compromised version of the *gospel of the kingdom* once delivered to the saints.

It is for this very reason; in this series of books, I will be exposing many false teachings or doctrines. These false teachings which are prevalent in the body of Christ are not according to the uncompromised, unadulterated whole counsel of God's Word. We must make a course correction now. Jesus Christ is coming back soon for a bride who is without spot or blemish, fully mature in Him, and lacking nothing.

As an ordained minister of the gospel, specifically a teacher of the gospel, my primary responsibility is to pledge my total allegiance to God, and minister to Him first and foremost, before I minister to His people.

As a teacher of the gospel, my primary responsibility is to firmly ground God's people in His Word, based on the uncompromised, unadulterated whole counsel of His Word. Also, because of the lateness of the hour, we no longer have the luxury of playing church or being politically correct. There will be a great divide coming into the body of Christ among those who are willing to take a stand on the uncompromised, unadulterated whole counsel of God's Word, versus those who will not—as we are already witnessing.

It begins with the body of Christ answering the thought-provoking questions of "who is Israel?" and "why does it matter?"

Now is the time for God's people to take a stand, and proclaim the true *gospel of the kingdom* that was once delivered to the saints, while there still is time to make a course correction for all eternity.

GOD IS IN THE PROCESS OF ORCHESTRATING AND USHERING IN THE FINAL "REFORMATION" FOR THE BODY OF CHRIST

This series of books is critical for the body of Christ, because we are at the "midnight" hour, and our heavenly Father is in the process of orchestrating and ushering in the final "reformation" for the body of Christ. There is a seismic "shift" coming to the body of Christ which includes, but is not limited to, the following:

❖ God is bringing total "restoration" and "reconciliation" of all things, especially concerning all Israel. All Israel includes both the Jews from the House of Judah and those of us who were formerly Gentiles from the House of Israel. By our faith in our Jewish Messiah, Jesus Christ, we are now grafted into the commonwealth of Israel. In these final hours, we are becoming One New Man in the *physical* earthly realm, as the *fullness of the Gentiles* is coming to fruition.

❖ God is raising up "reformers" who will build up the old waste places and raise up the foundations of many generations, who will be called the "Repairers of the Breach," based on Isaiah Chapter 58, to help facilitate the total "restoration" and "reconciliation" of all Israel.

Again, all Israel includes both the House of Judah and the House of Israel. God established a New Covenant with both the Jews from the House of Judah and those of us who were formerly Gentiles from the House of Israel. See Jeremiah 31:31–33 and Hebrews 8:7–13.

Under the New Covenant God has now put His laws in our mind, and written them on our hearts, instead of on two tablets of stone, by His Holy Spirit who lives in us.

Also, this New Covenant our heavenly Father, *Yehovah,* (Yahweh [YHWH]), established with both houses, was fulfilled (consummated, executed, and ratified [confirmed]) by the precious blood of Jesus Christ, who became the "mediator" between man and our heavenly Father.

Jesus Christ died for the forgiveness of our sins so we could be "restored" and "reconciled" back into "walking" in a covenant relationship with Him and be one body of Christ, under the headship of Jesus Christ, the Chief Cornerstone.

❖ God is calling His people back to the "ancient" path, and to understanding the "root" of the *everlasting* covenant He established with Abraham and his descendants, by "walking" according to the "narrow" path, and the "narrow" way, that leads to life.

Because as it was in the beginning, so it shall be in the end.

As such, our heavenly Father requires His people to be *holy* (sacred, physically pure, morally blameless—consecrated saints) to become His bride who is without spot or blemish (faultless, without blame), because the God we serve is holy.

❖ The Lord is rebuilding the tabernacle of David with unprecedented praise and worship as Israel is "reconciled" and "restored" in all the nations. In mercy the throne will be established; and One will sit on it in truth—in the tabernacle of David, as He judges and seeks justice hastening righteousness (Isaiah 16.5). God is raising up reformers and forerunners who will rebuild and raise up its ruins as in the days of old based on Amos 9:11 and Acts 15:16.

❖ God is beseeching His people to return to the *Highway of Holiness,* based on Isaiah 35:8, which talks about the future glory of Zion. Jesus Christ is coming back for an overcoming, triumphant church. And, it is for this very reason, God's people are called to be "set apart" from the world, and to be consecrated for God's glory and purposes to prevail first in us, then through us, as we carry out the *Great Commission.*

This includes the preaching, and the establishment of God's Kingdom, which will impact the eternal destination of countless souls for all eternity.

❖ God is calling His people to come out of *spiritual,* or *Mystery* Babylon, so we do not share in her sins, and receive her plagues based on Revelation 18:4. Revelation 17:5, talks about *Mystery* Babylon the Great, the Mother of Harlots, and of the abominations of the earth. I will reveal her identity in Book 2, and in Book 3, of this series.

❖ God is shifting the body of Christ back to His "times" and "seasons" based on all the *everlasting* ordinances (statutes) written in the Torah, which are our heavenly Father's instructions for all His people.

This includes our keeping, and observing, all seven of our heavenly Father's holy convocations, based on Leviticus Chapter 23, which are all *everlasting* ordinances.

❖ God is shifting the body of Christ back to being the church depicted in the Book of Acts, where we will "walk" in the "resurrection power" of the Holy Spirit, and do even greater exploits than Jesus, and His early disciples did (Daniel 11:32 and John 14:12).

This shall happen once we receive the "latter rain" the prophet Joel talks about in Joel 2:23, which shall happen when God pours out His Spirit on all flesh, based on Joel 2:28. It will be then that we shall walk in the fullness of His manifest presence as we teach, and preach, the true *gospel of the kingdom* once delivered to the saints.

❖ God is shifting the body of Christ to "function" under the five-fold ministry of Jesus Christ based on Ephesians 4:11.

This Scripture substantiates this indisputable truth: He has given *some* to be apostles, *some* to be prophets, *some* to be evangelists, and *some* to be pastors, and teachers, for the purpose of equipping the saints to do the work of the ministry.

The five-fold ministry of Jesus Christ is established and built upon the foundation of the apostles and the prophets.

❖ God is beseeching His people to repent and return to our first love—Jesus Christ. We must remember from where we have fallen, so we will bear "fruit" worthy of repentance. Otherwise, He will come quickly to remove our lampstand from its place, unless we repent.

❖ God is calling us up to the mountain-top, and beseeching us to get into the "ark" of the New Covenant now! Jesus Christ is the "ark" of the New Covenant, and we must return to our first love, Jesus Christ, who is our place of *refuge* and our *fortress.*

❖ Our heavenly Father *Yehovah* is beseeching those of us from the House of Israel to "walk" in a covenant relationship with Him by "obeying" His commandments found in the Torah.

For the hour is coming, and *now* is, when our heavenly Father is looking for *true* worshipers, who will worship Him in Spirit, according to His truth, based on the whole counsel of His Word.

CONCERNING THE GREAT APOSTASY...

The great apostasy is flourishing from pulpits all across the world, especially in America. As such, it may, or may not, come as a shock to you to realize this truth: Many of the things we have learned at church are not according to God's uncompromised, unadulterated, whole counsel of His Word.

The entire counsel of God's Word, includes both the volume of Moses and the gospel, as written in the New Testament. As such, never before has the need been more critical for God's people to know "why" we believe "what" we believe, and be prepared to back it up with Scripture, based on the whole counsel of His Word.

Therefore, when we study the Word of God, it must be done according to Isaiah 28:10, which says, *"For precept must be upon precept, precept upon precept, Line upon line, line upon line, Here a little, there a little."* (NKJV)

It is for this very reason, in this series of books, I will convey to God's people many things you have not heard before, or been taught about in church, which may be entirely foreign to you.

As you read this series of books, it may seem like I am repeating what I have said in previous chapters for this reason: Many will be hearing some of these truths for the very first time. Thus, while it may seem as though I am repeating myself, I am doing this on purpose.

Also, I am hoping to keep you from having to continually refer to Scriptures discussed in previous chapters which are relevant to the current discussion.

The primary purpose of this series of books is to issue a final wake-up call to the body of Christ, while there is still a small window of opportunity for us to repent, return to God, and turn from our *wicked* ways.

We must return to the "ancient" path which leads to life before it is too late for all eternity to make a course correction. Unfortunately, many believers in the body of Christ have *unknowingly* broken the *everlasting* covenants (plural) with God due to our ignorance of what His Word says, based on the whole counsel of His Word, and because we do not understand our "Hebraic" roots in Christianity. As such, we—God's people, have broken the *everlasting* covenants (plural), Jesus Christ died to fulfill (consummate, execute, and ratify [confirm]) with His precious blood.

Therefore, we must sincerely repent of our sins, and turn back to God with all our heart, soul, mind, and strength, which will be evidenced by us "walking" in His ways according to the whole counsel of His Word.

True repentance must take place, so we will be in the proper condition to "accept" and "receive" His forgiveness for breaking covenant with Him. Tragically, many who profess they are His, even though their hearts are far from Him, shall perish from a lack of knowledge.

Also, based on the present circumstances we find ourselves faced with, God wants His people to be so grieved by the "spiritual," "moral," and "ethical" decay in our lives, and in our society, it will compel us to take action.

We must awaken, arise, and become the "salt" and the "light" He has called us to be, as we establish His *laws*, His *righteousness*, His *justice,* and His *judgments* on the earth, as it is in heaven.

However, before the body of Christ can arise and become God's change agents in the earth like Nehemiah was, we must first be willing to humble ourselves before God to take an inventory of our true *spiritual* condition on an individual basis.

Then we *must* come back into alignment with His Word by "walking" and "living" according to His commandments, as we are convicted, and led by His Holy Spirit, to do so.

This series of books is extremely comprehensive, and detailed, based on the whole counsel of God's Word. As such, this set of books is to be read very slowly and be meditated upon, as you seek the Holy Spirit concerning God's truth the Lord has placed upon my heart for a time such as this, to teach to His people.

On that account, as an ordained minister of the gospel, and a teacher in the body of Christ, based on First Corinthians 12:28, and Ephesians 4:11, my primary responsibility is to teach God's people the uncompromised, unadulterated whole counsel of His Word.

As such, I must lead them to Jesus Christ, rather than to myself, their pastor, priest, or rabbi.

Jesus Christ, who is the author and finisher of our faith, said it best in Matthew 15:8–10, when He called the multitudes to Him as He clearly addresses what the "root" cause of the great apostasy is.

He admonished us to "hear" and to "understand," as He said, *"These people DRAW NEAR TO Me with their MOUTH, And HONOR Me with their LIPS, But THEIR HEART is FAR from Me. And in VAIN they WORSHIP Me, Teaching as DOCTRINES the COMMANDMENTS of MEN.' When He had called the multitude to Himself, He said to them, 'HEAR and UNDERSTAND...'"* (NKJV) (emphasis added).

The "root" cause of the great apostasy is this: Because we have left our first love—Jesus Christ and our hearts are far from Him, we do not obey His and our heavenly Father's commandments. Hence, we are worshiping our heavenly Father and our Lord and Savior Jesus Christ in vain because we are following the "commandments," "traditions," and "doctrines" of men. These false "commandments," "traditions," and "doctrines" of men are being taught by false apostles, prophets, evangelists, pastors, and teachers who have infiltrated the body of Christ.

A lot of the false "commandments," "traditions," and "doctrine" of men that are being taught in the body of Christ by our leaders is being done by their ignorance based on what they were "indoctrinated" with at Seminary or at Bible colleges. Also, some of them are deceived by what they were taught to believe by their mentors which was based on what was handed down throughout the generations by our early church fathers.

Or, it based on their compliance to usher us into the One World "Harlot" Religious System through the "interfaith" or "ecumenical" movements that many mainline well-known evangelical leaders are involved with. I will address this in-depth in Book 2 of this series.

I can assure you based on my mandate from God as a teacher of His Word, I have written this series of books with the fear of the Lord, and with trembling. James 3:1 says, *"My brethren, let not many of you become TEACHERS, knowing that we shall RECEIVE a STRICTER JUDGMENT."* (NKJV) (emphasis added).

Furthermore, many believers in the body of Christ are not adequately prepared or equipped, for what lies ahead as we are entering into unchartered territory, times of great change, and challenges in the season ahead, like we have never seen, or experienced before.

Therefore, there is *nothing* more important in this hour than this: We must get our houses in order "spiritually," "mentally," and "physically" speaking, in this exact order. God is our *only* hope of surviving the days ahead, so we shall overcome until the very end, of either our physical life or the return of Jesus Christ occurs.

THIS IS ONE MESSAGE TO GOD'S END-TIME CHURCH, YET FOUR BOOKS ARE NECESSARY

I have broken down this comprehensive, in-depth teaching into four different books, based on the content of what I am covering.

They build upon each other. And, it is for this very reason; Book #2 will start at Chapter 19, rather than Chapter 1; Book #3 (Volume I) will start at Chapter 37, rather than Chapter 1; and Book #3 (Volume II) will start at Chapter 57, rather than Chapter 1 as indicated below and on the following page:

BOOK #1

Title: *Who is Israel? Discovering Our True Identity in Jesus Christ and Why it Matters!*

Subtitle: *The Foundation*

Scope of Book #1: Foreword; Acknowledgements; Preface; Introduction; Chapters 1 through 18; Epilogue; References; Connect with the Author; and About the Author.

BOOK #2

Title: *Who is Israel? Discovering Our True Identity in Jesus Christ and Why it Matters!*

Subtitle: *The Root*

Scope of Book #2: Introduction; Chapters 19 through 36; Epilogue, References; Connect with the Author, and About the Author.

BOOK #3 (Volume I)

Title: *Who is Israel? Discovering Our True Identity in Jesus Christ and Why it Matters!*

Subtitle: *The Branches and the Fruit*

Scope of Book #3 (Volume I): Introduction; Chapters 37 through 56; References; Connect with the Author; and About the Author.

BOOK #3 (Volume II)

Title: *Who is Israel? Discovering Our True Identity in Jesus Christ and Why it Matters!*

Subtitle: *The Branches and the Fruit*

Scope of Book #3 (Volume II): Introduction; Chapters 57 through 70; Epilogue; References; Connect with the Author; and About the Author.

Again, it is of utmost importance that all four books are read in sequence because God's people *must* understand the "big picture" to fully comprehend what the entire Bible proclaims. Furthermore, we must understand what His Spirit is saying to His church for a time such as this, for this reason: We are fast approaching the "midnight" hour ushering in the second coming of Jesus Christ.

I had to break down this critical message to the body of Christ into four separate books because this message would have been too large to have been published as one book.

The Lord insisted I use Scripture in context, based on the whole counsel of His Word, to back up everything I am proclaiming and teaching. Hence, because I use entire passages of Scripture to substantiate what I am saying, this book is significantly larger as a result.

Moreover, I have provided the Hebrew and Greek definitions with the corresponding *Strong's Lexicon* number of "key" words based on many "key" passages of Scripture. In most cases, the original Hebrew, or Greek meanings of "key" words, profoundly change what is said, or implied.

As such, throughout this series of books, I have put the Hebrew or Greek words, and their corresponding truncated meanings, for certain "key" words, in highlighted brackets, in gray, so you, the reader, can fully understand what is said.

Therefore, when you come to select passages of Scripture where I have taken the liberty of doing this, please read the entire Scripture *without* the Hebrew, or Greek meaning first, so you can understand what it means in context.

Then go back, and slowly, and deliberately, read the Scripture with the appropriate Hebrew, or Greek meaning, so you can meditate on the definition, and fully comprehend what is being said, based on the original Hebrew, or Greek meaning.

Also, I have put the full meaning of all these Hebrew and Greek words, and their associated meanings, in the reference appendix at the back of each book, for those of you who wish to do a more in-depth study of the Hebrew and Greek meanings of certain "key" words.

Furthermore, throughout this series of books, I have chosen to use all caps for "key" words, or portions of Scripture, for this reason: I cannot highlight "key" portions of Scripture in a different color like many teachers do when they present a slide presentation.

Teachers use a different color to draw the attention of the reader to focus on what is being said, or to set apart a portion of the text in a Scripture. I apologize in advance if my decision to capitalize certain words or "key" portions of Scripture offends you in any way. I hope and pray you will focus on the message I must convey, rather than the method I chose to utilize to deliver the message.

WHY I CHOSE TO USE ENTIRE PASSAGES OF SCRIPTURE IN CONTEXT

The Lord wanted me to use Scripture to back up everything I am proclaiming and teaching for the following reasons:

❖ First, the Lord revealed to me this unfortunate truth: Many of His people do not know Him, or what His Word says because many believers in the body of Christ do not take the time to read His Word for themselves. Because if we knew what His Word said, and we truly comprehended both the "goodness" and the "severity" of the God we serve, then we would not be "walking" and "living" in the manner we are currently doing.

As such, when we just reference the Scriptures in our writings, most people will not take the time to look up what God's Word is saying.

Furthermore, we cannot assume God's people know the Word of God for themselves, because God's people are perishing from a lack of knowledge based on the whole counsel of His Word, and who we truly are in Christ.

Unfortunately, as a result, many people in the body of Christ are deceived, and being led astray, by the apostate teachings that are flourishing like never before.

And, as a result, many believers are being held captive, and being used by the tormentor of our souls—Satan, to do his bidding.

❖ Second, as we read the Word of God our minds will be renewed, and our hearts will be cleansed, with the washing of His uncompromised, unadulterated Word.

❖ Third, as we read the Word of God, the Holy Spirit will convict us of any sin in our lives. So we can repent, return to God, and come into alignment based on the whole counsel of His Word before it is too late to make a course correction for all eternity.

❖ Fourth, so the body of Christ will return to "walking" and "living" according to the whole counsel of God's Word and we will no longer break "covenant" with our heavenly Father, and be "cut off" from being His people. Based on the great apostasy which is flourishing like never before, many in the body of Christ, on our present course, shall perish for all eternity, if we do not repent, and make an immediate course correction now. The truth is if Jesus came back now, the vast majority of believers would not be going with Him because they practice "lawlessness" and do not "obey" His Word.

WHY DID THE LORD CALL ME TO WRITE THESE SERIES OF BOOKS FOR HIS PEOPLE?

Jesus Christ is coming back soon with His eyes blazing with fire, and He will judge, and make war, as He pours out the *wrath of God* Almighty on the *unrepentant* wicked inhabitants on the earth.

Unfortunately, this will include those who do not know God and those who do not "obey" the gospel of our Lord. These shall be punished with *everlasting* destruction from the presence of the Lord and from the glory of His power (2 Thessalonians 1:8-9).

Tragically, the vast majority of believers in the body of Christ on our present course will perish due to a lack of knowledge of God's uncompromised, unadulterated whole counsel of His Word. They have been led astray by all the false "commandments," "traditions," and "doctrines" of men. As a result, the vast majority of believers do not "keep" or "obey" the gospel of our Lord which is firmly established on the doctrine of Christ.

Again, the doctrine of Christ includes our heavenly Father's instructions (the Law) written in the Torah by His servant Moses and the gospel in the New Testament. Do you realize that at least 50 percent of the New Testament Scriptures come from the Old Testament based on our heavenly Father's instructions written in the Torah? Why does this matter?

Because at the brightness of Jesus' second coming God will "consume" and "destroy" those who not know Him or keep the gospel of our Lord which is based on the doctrine of Christ.

At this same time, He will also bring His faithful remnant into *everlasting* salvation, as we enter the *kingdom of heaven*. His saints are those who "keep" the commandments of God and have the faith of Jesus Christ (Revelation 14:12). We must keep the commandments of God and have the testimony of Jesus Christ—both are required.

Therefore, now is the time for us, His bride, to make ourselves ready so we will be arrayed in fine white linen, without spot or blemish.

Hence, it is imperative that Jesus' disciples know the whole truth, and nothing but His truth, based on the full counsel of His Word, regardless of whether or not we are babes in Christ or mature believers. Because of the lateness of the hour, we no longer have the luxury of time to drink the milk of His Word for this reason: The imminent return of Jesus Christ is shorter than most people realize.

Now is the time the body of Christ *must* come to the unity of the faith, and of the knowledge of the Son of God, to a perfect man, to the measure of the stature of the fullness of Christ, based on the doctrine of Christ. We are now in the "kairos" season of the *fullness of the Gentiles*. The word "kairos" is an ancient Greek word meaning the "right" or "opportune" moment based on God's "appointed" time.

As such, we *must* no longer be children, tossed to and fro, and carried away with every wind of doctrine, by the trickery of men based on the cunning craftiness of deceitful plotting.

Because of the apostate teachings, and the lies taught by the false prophets and teachers that have infiltrated the body of Christ, God's people are being led straight to the slaughter. Also, we are reaping God's curses, rather than His blessings—because many believers in the body of Christ have broken "covenant" with our heavenly Father. We have been "erroneously" taught that the Old Covenant is now obsolete and Jesus did away with the law. Hence, we are not doing the will of our heavenly Father because we are practicing "lawlessness."

Thus, it is critical the body of Christ is taught *only* God's truth in love, so we may grow up in all things into Him, who is the head of His body—Jesus Christ—the Chief Cornerstone.

Now is the time, and there can be no more delay. We must repent, and make a course correction now. It begins with us returning to our first love—Jesus Christ, for the *kingdom of heaven* is indeed at hand, and our redemption draws nigh!

INTRODUCTION

Before we begin our quest to discover "who" Israel is, and "why" it matters, if you have not read the Preface section of this book yet, please take the time to do so now, because it conveys valuable information you, the reader, must know about in advance. The Preface sets the stage for understanding the full scope of this book, and this series of books. Also, it will help you know why I chose to use the "format," or the "method," I will use throughout this series, concerning select passages of Scripture.

Now let's begin our journey to discover "who" Israel is, and "why" it matters.

"Who is Israel?" is the question most of us in the body of Christ, must define before we can fully understand the fundamental purpose of the entire Bible. The whole Bible is God's inspired Word, and His instructions, detailing His plan of "redemption," "reconciliation," and "restoration" from the Book of Genesis to the Book of Revelation, for all His chosen people.

God's "chosen" people have various names. Some of these names include but are not limited to: the *Saints*; His *elect*; His *royal* priesthood; His *holy* nation; the body of Christ; His Ekklēsia; the Church; the children of Israel, the Israelites; the twelve tribes of Israel; and the *bride of Christ.*

All these various names refer to God's "faithful" remnant. These are those who have placed their faith and trust in our heavenly Father's only *begotten* Son, Jesus Christ. Some variations of Jesus' Hebrew name [1] [2] are as follows: *Y'hoshûa, Yâhshua, Yêshûa, Yâshshua,*

1

Y'hoshûa' or *Yĕhowshuwa,* who is the Holy One of Israel.

I will cover the different variations of Jesus' name in Chapter 8 of this book since there are many depending on what translation of the Bible a person may use.

However, since this series of books is a gift for the body of Christ, I will use the name of Jesus Christ, which Christendom is most familiar.

Also, many people today assume when Israel is mentioned in the Bible, or in the news, it refers only to the Jewish people, or the physical nation of Israel, located in the Middle East.

Furthermore, many Christians proclaim the body of Christ must stand with Israel; however, for the most part, we do not even know the "why" behind the truth of this statement.

It is my hope and prayer by the time you finish reading this entire book; you will know the truth of not only "who" Israel is, but also, "who" God's chosen people are.

Equally important, it is my hope and prayer you will know your true identity in Christ for this reason: God, our Creator, and our heavenly Father, predestined you for a specific, unique purpose, *before* the foundation of the world.

Therefore, it is up to you to fulfill your "eternal" destiny for His glory and His purposes to prevail while you are still living on planet earth. Paul, a preacher, an apostle, and a teacher of the Gentiles proclaims this truth in Second Timothy 1:8–11, which says the following:

> *"Therefore do not be ashamed of the testimony of our Lord, nor of me His prisoner, but SHARE with me in the SUFFERINGS for the GOSPEL according to the POWER of GOD, who has SAVED us and CALLED us with a HOLY CALLING, not according to our works, but according to HIS OWN PURPOSE and GRACE which was given to us in Christ Jesus before TIME BEGAN, but has NOW BEEN REVEALED by the APPEARING of our SAVIOR JESUS CHRIST, who has abolished DEATH and brought LIFE and IMMORTALITY to light through the GOSPEL, to which I was appointed a preacher, an apostle, and a teacher of the Gentiles."* (2 Tim. 1:8–11, NKJV) (emphasis added).

Moreover, what I am about to convey in this series of books is not "replacement theology." Those who teach "replacement theology" proclaim the Jews are no longer God's chosen people, because they crucified Jesus, and did not believe He was or is the Son of God.

As such, any Jew who receives Jesus Christ as their Lord and Savior is as much of the body of Christ, as those of us who were formerly Gentiles, who have now been grafted into the commonwealth of Israel, by our faith in Jesus Christ.

Therefore, as you read this series of books, unless I indicate otherwise, when I refer to the Jews from the House of Judah, I am talking about those Jews who have received Jesus Christ as their Lord and Savior.

Unfortunately, there are many evangelical Christians who are unknowingly opposing Israel, and the Jewish people, because of anti-Semitism, which is on the rise once again. And, some anti-Semitism from Christians may stem from the fact that *some* Jews reject Jesus Christ as being their Messiah.

While it may be true *some* of the Jewish people do not believe in Jesus Christ, one of the main reasons why this is the case is because according to Romans 11:1–24, God has *spiritually* blinded them on purpose due to their hardened hearts, and their unbelief. He did this to offer salvation to the Gentiles, who are pagan, heathen people, who are out of covenant with God. In fact, God is already removing the *spiritual* blindness off of His Jewish people because the *fullness of the Gentiles* is at hand.

Furthermore, even though Martin Luther, John Calvin, Huldrych Zwingli and other early Protestant Reformers were used significantly by God to bring "reformation" to His church; they never did bring about a total transformation. Because if they had, it would have resulted in a complete "restoration" and "reconciliation" of both the Jews from House of Judah and former Gentiles from the House of Israel for this reason: Our heavenly Father, *Yehôvah,* established a New Covenant with both houses.

In fact, this is one of the primary reasons why Jesus Christ shed His precious blood at Calvary, and He became the "mediator" of the New Covenant. It was to "restore" and "reconcile" all the children of

Israel, back to "walking" in a covenant relationship with our heavenly Father, *Yehovah,* (Yahweh [YHWH])—the God of Abraham, Isaac, and Jacob, who is the Holy One of Israel.

Therefore, when I refer to both houses becoming One New Man, I am referring to the Jews from the House of Judah, and those of us who were formerly Gentiles from the House of Israel. Those of us who were formerly Gentiles have now been grafted into the commonwealth of Israel by our faith in Jesus Christ.

As a matter of fact, by the precious blood of Jesus Christ, our heavenly Father, *Yehovah,* established a New Covenant with both houses. As such, all Israel would become one "house," one "kingdom," and One New Man, until we all come to the unity of the faith, and of the knowledge of the Son of God, to a perfect man, to the measure of the stature of the fullness of Christ.

When all the "faithful" remnant of the children of Israel—from all twelve tribes of Israel, becomes "one" in the unity of our faith in Jesus Christ, based on the doctrine of Christ, then we will *literally* become One New Man in the *physical* earthly realm.

Hence, this will result in both Jew and Gentile becoming "one" in the body of Christ. In fact, this will be the testimony of the two final witnesses we read about in the Book of Revelation, *spiritually* speaking, which must take place before Jesus will return.

Yet the body of Christ is still a "house" and a "kingdom" divided against itself based on the whole counsel of God's *eternal* Word. There is only one Redeemer; one Spirit; one God, and Father of all; one faith; one baptism; one hope; one kingdom; one law; one custom; and one body of Christ, which is supposed to be under the headship of the Chief Cornerstone—Jesus Christ.

And, it is for this very reason, in this hour God is "raising up" a new breed of "pioneers" and "reformers" who will finish the work of those who went before us. God is answering the prayers and honoring the *righteous* works of the great heroes of the faith. These great men and women of God have crossed over into their Promised Land, on the other side of the Jordan River, to partake of *everlasting* life in the *kingdom of heaven.*

Those who went before us, and sacrificed their lives, fortunes, and sacred honor for "a cause greater than themselves," live on through us, God's people, who were born for a time such as this, and alive in this final generation, at the end of *this* age.

In fact, God preordained that we would complete the work our ancestors in the faith started long ago, for His *eternal* purposes and glory to prevail. The apostle Paul substantiates this truth in Hebrews 11:39–40, which proclaims, *"And all these, having obtained a good TESTIMONY through FAITH, did not RECEIVE the PROMISE, God having provided something BETTER FOR US, that THEY should not be MADE PERFECT APART FROM US."* (NKJV) (emphasis added).

Moreover, we are heirs to all the "covenant" promises God gave to them and their descendants as well. Also, we have the privilege and the awesome honor, as well as the daunting responsibility, of co-laboring with our Warrior King. As such, this final generation may very well witness the fulfillment of everything ever spoken from the mouths of the "Prophets of Old!" What God has spoken through His prophets will come to fruition. The *Lord of Heaven's Armies* shall go forth on His chariots of fire to make the kingdoms of this world, become the kingdoms of our Lord and of His Christ, in and through us, His people.

Furthermore, most "reformation" movements throughout the *synergy of the ages*, including those that are now underway, have one major flaw which is this: They still seek to "exclude," or "exalt" above the other, either the Jews from the House of Judah, or those of us who were formerly Gentiles from the House of Israel (Jacob/Joseph/Ephraim), even though a "faithful" remnant from both houses are God's "chosen" people.

Both the Jews from the House of Judah and those of us who were formerly Gentiles from the House of Israel, who have now been grafted into the commonwealth of Israel by our faith in Jesus Christ, are His *royal* priesthood and His *holy* nation! We are His own "special" people, so we may proclaim the praises of Him who has called us out of darkness into His marvelous light. Jesus Christ is the "mediator" between God and all His people from both the House of Judah and the House of Israel for this reason: *Yehôváh,* our heavenly Father, established a New Covenant with both houses.

A "FAITHFUL" REMNANT OF ALL ISRAEL SHALL BE SAVED

After the *fullness of the Gentiles* reaches its zenith, which according to the leading missionary organizations is expected to come to fruition in 2016–2017, it will be then; God will remove the *spiritual* blindness off of His Jewish people, so all the "faithful" remnant of Israel shall be saved. The following Scriptures substantiate this truth:

> *"But Israel shall be SAVED by the Lord With an everlasting SALVATION; You shall not be ashamed or disgraced Forever and ever."* (Isa. 45:17, NKJV) (emphasis added).

> *"And it shall come to pass That whoever CALLS on the NAME of the LORD shall be SAVED. For in MOUNT ZION and in JERUSALEM there shall be DELIVERANCE, As the Lord has said, Among the REMNANT whom the LORD CALLS."* (Joel 2:32, NKJV) (emphasis added).

Furthermore, it is my hope and prayer, after you read all four books in this series of books I have written, you will fully understand "who" Israel is, and "why" it matters.

I also hope and pray the body of Christ will understand and know who we are in Christ from a "Hebraic" perspective, based on the whole counsel of God's Word, especially since we are now entering the time of the *fullness of the Gentiles.*

In a nutshell, the entire Bible concerns God's "Covenant of Marriage" to His bride, which includes all twelve tribes of Israel, not just the Jews from the House of Judah. Moreover, based on Ephesians 1:3–6, God's plan of redemption He decreed and established *before* the foundation of the world, is that a "remnant" of Israel shall be saved! Therefore, the entire Bible is about one thing—Israel. Ephesians 1:3–6, says the following:

> *"Blessed be the God and Father of our LORD Jesus Christ, who has blessed us with every SPIRITUAL BLESSING in the HEAVENLY PLACES in Christ, just as He CHOSE us in Him before the FOUNDATION of the WORLD, that we should be HOLY and without BLAME before Him in LOVE, having PREDESTINED us to ADOPTION AS SONS by JESUS CHRIST to HIMSELF, according to the GOOD PLEASURE of His WILL, to the praise of the glory of His GRACE, by which He made us ACCEPTED in the BELOVED."* (Eph. 1:3–6, NKJV) (emphasis added).

And, it is for this very reason, God sacrificed Jesus Christ, His only *begotten* Son for us. John 3:16, proclaims, *"For God so LOVED the WORLD* [including its inhabitants] *that He gave His only BEGOTTEN SON, that whoever BELIEVES in Him should not PERISH but have everlasting LIFE."* (NKJV) (emphasis added).

Moreover, in Isaiah 49:5–9, our heavenly Father, *Yehovah,* is talking about His only *begotten* Son, Jesus Christ, whom He has given to us as a "covenant" and a "light" to the Gentiles. He would be *Yehovah's* salvation to the ends of the earth, which includes restoring the earth, causing us to inherit the desolate heritages, restoring the preserved ones of Israel, and "raising up" the tribes of Jacob. As you read Isaiah 49:5–9, as Jesus' disciples, this applies to us. Therefore, take the time to read all of Isaiah 49 for yourselves. Isaiah 49:5–9, says the following:

9

"And now the LORD [Yehovah] says, who FORMED ME from the WOMB to be His SERVANT, To bring Jacob [Israel] back to Him, So that ISRAEL is GATHERED to Him (For I shall be glorious in the eyes of the LORD, And My God shall be My strength), Indeed He says, 'It is too small a thing that You should be My Servant to RAISE UP the TRIBES of JACOB, And to RESTORE the PRESERVED ONES of ISRAEL; I will also give you as a LIGHT to the GENTILES, That You should be My SALVATION to the ENDS of the EARTH.'" (Isa. 49:5–6, NKJV) (emphasis added).

"Thus says the LORD [Yehovah], the REDEEMER of ISRAEL, their HOLY ONE, To Him whom man despises, To Him whom the nation abhors, To the Servant of rulers: 'Kings shall see and arise, Princes also shall worship, Because of the LORD [Yehovah] who is faithful, the Holy One of Israel; And He has CHOSEN you.'" (Isa. 49:7, NKJV) (emphasis added).

"Thus says the LORD: In an ACCEPTABLE TIME I have heard You, And in the DAY of SALVATION I have helped You; I will PRESERVE you and GIVE you as a COVENANT to the PEOPLE, To RESTORE the EARTH, To cause them to INHERIT the DESOLATE HERITAGES; That You may say to the prisoners, 'Go forth,' To those who are in darkness, 'Show yourselves.'" (Isa. 49:8–9, NKJV) (emphasis added).

Also, Jesus Christ is the "ark" of the New Covenant which He fulfilled (consummated, executed, and ratified [confirmed]) with His precious blood. Now instead of having external laws *Yehŏ̄vah's* people could not keep beforehand, we are now filled with His Holy Spirit who dwells in the heart of every blood-bought believer.

The Holy Spirit gives us God's grace and power that enables us to keep His laws. Under the New Covenant, God has now put His laws in our mind and written them on our hearts, instead of on two tablets of stone.

Furthermore, all of God's instructions, based on the whole counsel of God's Word, are built on all of His *everlasting* covenants (plural), He has established with mankind, and all creation, throughout the *synergy of the ages.*

And, all of God's covenants (plural) are about one thing which is this: The total "restoration" and "reconciliation" of all things. All these things God shall "restore" and "reconcile" will be accomplished through His people who "walk" according to the terms and conditions of His "Marriage Covenant" to His bride—His "faithful" remnant in the body of Christ.

His "faithful" remnant includes both the Jews from the House of Judah and those of us who were formerly Gentiles from the House of Israel (Jacob/Joseph/Ephraim), who have now been grafted into the commonwealth of Israel, by our faith in Jesus Christ.

In other words, His "faithful" remnant are those believers in the body of Christ, who have placed their faith and trust in their *spiritual* well-being in our Jewish Messiah, and Redeemer, Jesus

11

Christ, the only *begotten* Son of *Yehovah*, our heavenly Father, and *Elohiym,* our Creator.

His "faithful" remnant also "obeys" the commandments of God, based on the doctrine of Christ.

GOD'S EVERLASTING COVENANTS WERE ALL "CONFIRMED" BY THE BLOOD OF JESUS CHRIST AND ARE STILL VALID FOR NEW COVENANT BELIEVERS

All of God's *everlasting* covenants (plural), He has established as *El Elyon* (the *Most High God*), and as *El Olam* (the *Everlasting God*), [3] with mankind and all creation throughout the *synergy of the ages,* were "confirmed" (ratified) by the blood of Jesus Christ.

Equally important to point out is this fact: Since we are citizens of Israel, because we who *were* once Gentiles in the flesh have now been grafted into the commonwealth of Israel by our faith in Jesus Christ—our Jewish Messiah, then we are subject to the same "laws" and "customs" Israel, more specifically, the Jews from the House of Judah follow.

By the time you read this series of books, you will know beyond a shadow of a doubt, this critical truth: God has only one "law" and one "custom" for all His people under the New Covenant He established with both the House of Judah and the House of Israel.

Now I will substantiate based on Ephesians 2:11–13 this fact: All of God's people who have placed our faith and trust in Jesus Christ, who is our Lord and Savior, are heirs to the "covenants of promise." The word "covenant" has an "s" on the end of it, meaning there is more than one *everlasting* covenant. Ephesians 2:11–13, says the following:

> *"Therefore remember that you, once **GENTILES*** [G1484: ***ethnos:*** a *race* (as of the same *habit*), that is, a *tribe;* specifically a *foreign* (*non-Jewish*) pagan, heathen people or nation] *IN THE FLESH—who are called Uncircumcision by what is called the Circumcision made in the flesh by hands— that at THAT TIME you were WITHOUT Christ, being ALIENS from the **COMMONWEALTH*** [G4174: ***politeia:*** *citizenship,* concretely a *community, freedom*] *of ISRAEL and STRANGERS from the **COVENANTS*** [(plural) G1242: ***diatheke:*** a *disposition,* that is, (specifically) a contract (especially a devisory will); covenant] *of PROMISE, having no hope and without God in the world. But NOW in Christ Jesus, you who ONCE were FAR OFF have been brought NEAR by the BLOOD of CHRIST."*
> (Eph. 2:11–13, NKJV) (emphasis added).

THERE IS NO SUCH THING AS A "GENTILE" BELIEVER IN CHRIST

In Ephesians 2:11–13, the apostle Paul specifically says, we were *once* Gentiles in the flesh, but *now,* in Christ Jesus, we who *once* were far off have been brought near by the blood of Christ.

13

Therefore, there is *no* such thing as a "Gentile" believer in Christ, because of the word "Gentile" in the Greek means: A heathen, pagan, nation of people, who are out of covenant with God.

As such, those who are Gentiles have the following "fruit," or "attributes" associated with them:

❖ They do not have or "obey" God's law. Therefore, they are out of covenant with God, for God does not "justify" the "hearers" of the law. Rather, God "justifies" the "doers" of the law, who show the work of the law written in their hearts, based on Romans 2:12–16.

❖ They are "idolatrous" based on First Corinthians 12:1–3.

❖ They are "uncircumcised" in their hearts and are without Christ. Therefore, they are aliens from the commonwealth of Israel, and strangers from the covenants (plural—not just the New Covenant) of promise, having no hope, and without God in the world, based on Ephesians 2:11–13.

❖ They know about God, but do not glorify Him, or give Him thanks. Therefore, they are futile in their thoughts, and their foolish hearts are darkened. As such, the *wrath of God* is against them due to their "ungodliness," and "unrighteousness," since they suppress the truth in "unrighteousness," based on Romans 1:18–23.

❖ They are wicked and have given themselves up to

"uncleanness," based on the lusts of their hearts, and they have exchanged the truth of God for a lie. As such, they worship the created, rather than the Creator. Moreover, they "practice" evil and wicked things, and they "approve" of those who do the same, based on Romans 1:24–32.

❖ They are dead in their trespasses and sins, and they "walk" according to the ways of this world, based on the dictates of the *prince of the power of the air* (Satan), whose Spirit—the "Spirit of Antichrist," accomplishes his work through the *sons of disobedience.* As such, they conduct themselves according to the lusts of their flesh and of their mind and are still *children of wrath,* based on Ephesians 2:1–3.

Therefore, disciples of Jesus Christ are no longer Gentiles as substantiated by the apostle Paul in Galatians 3:28–29, which says, *"There is neither JEW nor GREEK* [Gentile], *there is neither SLAVE nor FREE, there is neither MALE nor FEMALE; for you are ALL ONE in CHRIST JESUS. And if you are CHRIST'S, then you are ABRAHAM'S SEED, and HEIRS according to the PROMISE."* (NKJV) (emphasis added).

Furthermore, since we are heirs according to the promise because we are of Abraham's "seed," we as believers in Jesus Christ must know what the promises are God gave to Abraham when He established the *everlasting* covenant with Abraham and his descendants.

Moreover, we must know what Abraham and his descendants had to do to "receive" these covenant promises from God as well, based on

15

their faith in God, which was evidenced by their obedience.

In Book 2 of this series, which is subtitled, "The Root," I will fully convey "what" the *Abrahamic* Covenant is, and "how" it is still applicable to New Covenant believers.

Unfortunately, many of God's people are *unknowingly* breaking this *everlasting* covenant our heavenly Father, *Yehôvâh,* established with Abraham, due to our ignorance of the whole counsel of God's Word, and a lack of understanding concerning our "Hebraic" roots in Christianity. Notice I did not say our "Jewish" roots in Christianity because Abraham was not Jewish; he was Hebrew, which I will cover in Chapter 5 of this book.

Furthermore, once we understand "who" Israel is, and we know about the *Abrahamic* Covenant and its relevance to New Covenant believers, then we must answer the question, "why does it matter?"

Therefore, in Book 3 and Book 4 of this series, which is subtitled, "The Branches and the Fruit," I will teach God's people what the Lord has placed upon my heart for such a time as this. This teaching is based on the whole counsel of His Word, for His people are perishing from a lack of knowledge based on the apostate teachings prevalent in the body of Christ.

In Book 3 and Book 4, I will be exposing many of the false teachings which are prevalent in the body of Christ based on the "traditions," "customs," and "doctrine" of men. Many have exchanged the truth of God's Word for a lie, and worshiped and served the creature, rather than the Creator, because we have been deceived, and led astray. And, one of the many things we are deceived about is concerning "who" Israel is.

Also, it is one thing for us to seek to understand and answer the question, "who is Israel?" However, we must also know the relevance of "why" this matters, and in "what" ways this is relevant and applicable to New Covenant believers.

In other words, what good is it for God's people to have knowledge of His Word, *if* we do not seek to "apply" it to the way we live our lives, which *should* be according to the whole counsel of His Word?

Before most believers in the body of Christ will "apply" God's knowledge and wisdom to the way we live our lives, first we must know "why" it is relevant and necessary for us to do so.

Therefore, until the body of Christ knows beyond a shadow of a doubt "who" Israel is based on the whole counsel of God's Word, and its relevance to New Covenant believers, most are going to continue to believe the Old Testament was written only for the Jews from the House of Judah.

This "mindset" is contrary to God's Word, especially since God established a New Covenant with both houses!

The same holds true for those who believe and teach the end-time Scriptures were written for only the Jews because the Church will be "raptured" off the earth before most of the end-time signs come to pass—because *"it is written…"*

17

AS IN THE DAYS OF NOAH, SO IT SHALL BE WHEN THE SON OF MAN RETURNS

As a matter of fact, Jesus told us in the days preceding His second coming; it would be just like in the *days of Noah*—where people were eating, drinking, marrying, and being caught up in the things of this world. Then, suddenly the flood came, and except for Noah and his family, the raging waters from the flood swept them all away as God "destroyed" and "consumed" the wicked, *unrepentant* inhabitants from the face of the earth.

Therefore, the only ones who were "left behind" were a righteous remnant—a total of eight people which signified a "new" beginning. And indeed, it was!

In fact, after the flood took place during the *days of Noah*, God used a rainbow as the "sign" of the *everlasting* covenant He established with the earth, and with every living creature of all flesh that is on the earth. Based on this covenant, God promised that never again would all flesh be "cut off" by the waters of the flood, and never again shall there be a flood to destroy the earth.

Then it would come to pass God made another *everlasting* covenant with Abraham and his descendants—the Israelites, or the children of Israel, who are from all twelve tribes of Israel, which is still in effect to *this* very day!

Hence, all the *everlasting* covenants (plural), God has established with mankind and all creation throughout the *synergy of the ages,*

18

are still in effect. They build on one another. And, they were all ratified by blood, which was shed from either an animal or from a human being, until the final sacrifice of the precious blood Jesus Christ shed on the cross at Calvary, is the *only* blood sacrifice that has "redeemed" all creation for all time forevermore.

In other words, the blood of Jesus Christ fulfilled (consummated, executed, and ratified [confirmed]) all the *everlasting* covenants (plural), God has established with mankind and creation throughout the *synergy of the ages.*

WHAT IS A COVENANT?

Before we progress any further, I need to define what a covenant is. The word "covenant" is referenced 315 times in the Bible and is a written contract (compact), which is sealed (ratified) in blood. The agreement is all-inclusive—everything that belongs to one party belongs to the other party as well. Therefore, all covenants are an oath, pledge, or promise that is "legally" binding.

According to *Strong's Hebrew Lexicon* #H1285, the word "covenant" as used in the Old Testament, is the Hebrew word "bĕriyth" (pronounced "ber-eeth'"), which means: In the sense of *cutting* (like H1254), and is a *compact* made by passing between *pieces* of flesh.

In addition, the word "covenant" means the following: (1) covenant, alliance, or pledge between men; (2) treaty, alliance, or league (man to man); (3) constitution or ordinance (monarch to subjects); (4) agreement or pledge (man to man); (5) alliance (of friendship); (6) alliance (of marriage) between God and man; (7) covenant (divine ordinance with signs or pledges); (8) phrases: (a) covenant making; (b) covenant keeping; and (c) covenant violation.

Whereas, according to *Strong's Greek Lexicon* #G1242, the word "covenant" as used in the New Testament, is synonymous with the word "testament." It is the Greek word "diatheke" (pronounced "dee-ath-ay'-kay"), which is from G1303, which means: Disposition, that is, (specifically) a contract (especially a *devisory will*); covenant or testament.

Therefore, the definition of a "covenant" God establishes with mankind, or creation is a solemn, binding, legal agreement, or promise, sealed with blood between two or more parties. Also, God's *everlasting* covenants (plural) have either "blessings" associated with "keeping" the covenant; or "curses" associated with it for "breaking" the covenant.

Since a "covenant" is a written compact, or contract, between God and His people, then as disciples of Jesus Christ we are expected to know the terms and conditions of "walking" in a covenant relationship with our heavenly Father, *Yehôvâh,* once we come to the saving knowledge of His only *begotten* Son, Jesus Christ, *after* we become saved.

As such, when mankind "chooses" to trespass and rebel against God's covenants (plural), we cannot expect God will allow men to break His covenants, which is according to His *laws,* His *ordinances,*

His *statutes*, and His *judgments*, without reaping the consequences for doing so!

Moreover, even though each covenant God established with mankind and creation was for different purposes, and established through different individuals throughout the *synergy of the ages,* together, they solidify *Yehôvȧh's* "eternal" purposes which shall come to pass, because He has determined the end from the beginning.

As such, His "eternal" plan will unfold according to the good pleasure of His will, to the praise of His glory and of His grace, by which He made us accepted in His beloved Son, Jesus Christ.

It is for this very reason; God views all His *everlasting* covenants (plural), He has established throughout the *synergy of the ages,* as "one" *everlasting* covenant for all His people, and for all time. God views time from an *eternal* perspective, which has no beginning, or end. As such, God operates out of time as we know it.

Therefore, even though there are multiple *everlasting* covenants (plural), *Yehôvȧh* has established throughout the *synergy of the ages* of mankind's existence, collectively they are interwoven with one another for this reason: Together, they fulfill *Yehôvȧh's eternal* plan of "redemption," "restoration," and "reconciliation" of the entire world.

The synergy which is created as a result of all God's *everlasting* covenants produces a greater effect than each covenant by itself could ever achieve. As such, if you do not believe this is true, then the next time you see a rainbow in the sky think about this fact: The

Noahic Covenant remains in effect despite the fact Jesus Christ became the "mediator" of the New Covenant, and "ratified" (confirmed) it, with His precious blood.

SOME OF GOD'S EVERLASTING COVENANTS

All of God's *everlasting* covenants were fulfilled (consummated, executed, ratified [confirmed]) by the precious blood of Jesus Christ, who became, and is, the "mediator" between God and man under the New Covenant. Therefore, all the following *everlasting* covenants (plural), are still in effect:

❖ *Yehôvâh's* covenant with "the Day" and with "the Night" based on Jeremiah 33:19–26, which I will cover in-depth in Chapter 13 of this book. Also, I will go into this in more detail in Chapter 52 of Book 3.

❖ The "Covenant of Marriage" which God defined between a man and a woman at the beginning of time based on Genesis 2:24–25.

❖ The *seventh* day Sabbath, which is not only the fourth commandment of the Ten Commandments we are commanded to keep, it is also a "perpetual" covenant *Yehôvâh* has established throughout all generations for the children of Israel *forever* based on Exodus 31:16–17. The word "perpetual" as used in Exodus 31:16–17, is the Hebrew word "ôlâm" (pronounced "o-lawm'"), which means:

22

Properly *concealed*, that is, the *vanishing* point; generally, time *out of mind* (past or future), that is, (practically) *eternity*; and is from the beginning of the world and is without end.

The word "forever" means from the beginning of the world and is without end for all eternity, which I will cover this fact in-depth in Chapter 58 of Book 3.

In case you are wondering, this commandment to keep the *seventh* day Sabbath is reiterated in the New Testament. I will cover this fact in-depth in Chapter 58 of Book 3.

In Chapters 58 and 66 of Book 3, I will fully convey how this one "perpetual" covenant alone, distinguishes between those believers who are truly God's covenant people, versus those who are "worshiping" Him in vain. As such, this is one of the things that will "set apart" those who will receive the "mark of God," rather than the "mark of the beast," *spiritually*, speaking.

In addition, in Chapter 2 of this book, and in Chapters 44, 58, 66, and 69 of Book 3, I will cover this truth: The "mark of God" is placed on the foreheads of the children of Israel from all twelve tribes of Israel, not just on the foreheads of the Jews, from the tribe, or the House of Judah.

These 144,000 are the "faithful" remnant from all twelve tribes of Israel who will still be alive and remain (survive), the tribulation period until the *physical* second coming of Jesus Christ. This triumphant, overcoming regiment of God's warriors is the *bride of Christ*. The *bride of Christ* will be supernaturally protected during the tribulation period because they are part of the *firstfruits* wave offering to God, and to the Lamb.

As such, they will be "redeemed" from the earth, from amongst men, *after* the *first* resurrection of the dead in Christ takes place, which happens on the *last* day of planet earth, and not before!

I cover this fact in detail in Chapter 67 of Book 3, and I will elaborate on this indisputable truth in previous chapters of all four books as well.

God will supernaturally protect these 144,000 "faithful" remnant from all twelve tribes of Israel, who will still be alive and remain (survive) the tribulation period. They will witness with their own eyes, the return of Jesus Christ, because they are "sealed" with the "mark of God" on their foreheads. I will cover this subject in-depth in Chapter 66, of Book 3.

A couple of reasons "why" these 144,000 "faithful" remnant, who are from all twelve tribes of Israel, have the "seal of the living God" on their foreheads, is as follows:

- ❖ First, they have kept the *seventh* day Sabbath, and all of God's Sabbaths (plural). In fact, God's Sabbaths are a "sign" (mark or evidence), He is our God, and we are His "covenant" people.

❖ Second, they have kept the rest of our heavenly
Father's seven holy convocations listed in Leviticus
Chapter 23. God's seven holy convocations are all
everlasting ordinances (statutes), God "decreed" and
"established" *before* the foundation of the world
which is still valid for all eternity. And, it is for this
very reason; I will cover all of our heavenly Father's
seven holy convocations in Chapters 57–59 of Book 3.

As such, if we are of the "opinion" it does not matter to God
"when" and "how" we worship Him—I can assure you He is a
jealous God based on what He tells us in Exodus 20:5. And, it
is for this very reason, the first four commandments of the
Ten Commandments, details from God's perspective, "how"
we are to honor Him, serve Him, and worship Him to
demonstrate our love for Him.

In fact, our heavenly Father specifically tells His people
"how" "when" and in "what" ways we are to worship and serve
Him so that He will be our God, and we will be His people.

It is for this very reason, our heavenly Father has specifically
detailed His will according to His *eternal* Word, and He
specifically says we are to keep His Sabbaths (plural) at His
"appointed" times. His Sabbaths include the *seventh* day
Sabbath, the Jews from the House of Judah, have been
keeping "religiously" for thousands of years.

As a matter of fact, God's *seventh* day Sabbath is the very first
"holy convocation" out of seven, God commands us to honor

and keep. This is based on Leviticus Chapter 23, which lists the feasts of the Lord as being His feasts.

God specifically says to us, His people, in Leviticus 23:3, *"Six days shall work be done, but the SEVENTH DAY is a SABBATH of SOLEMN REST, a HOLY CONVOCATION. You shall do NO WORK on it; it is the SABBATH of the LORD in all your DWELLINGS."* (NKJV) (emphasis added).

This truth is so critical for God's "faithful" remnant to understand; I have devoted Chapter 58 of Book 3, to adequately convey this indisputable truth, which is based on the whole counsel of God's Word.

❖ The "Covenant of Salt" which is based on Leviticus 2:13; Numbers 18:19; and Second Chronicles 13:5. This "Covenant of Salt" is an *everlasting* ordinance forever.

❖ The "Covenant of Love" which Jesus ratified with His blood under the New Covenant. Furthermore, Jesus reiterated the importance of us loving God first, and then one another, in the New Testament when He explicitly tells us all the law, and the prophets, hang on these two commandments. However, the "Covenant of Love" was first established under the *first* covenant. This is according to the following Scriptures: Exodus 20:6; Leviticus 19:18; Leviticus 19:34; Deuteronomy 5:10; and Deuteronomy 7:7–9; Nehemiah 1:5; Isaiah 56:6; and Ezekiel 16:8.

26

The following Scriptures should drive home this point: These commandments which were given to us by our heavenly Father in the Torah under the *first* covenant, are all reiterated in the New Testament as well.

> *"You shall LOVE the LORD YOUR GOD with all your HEART, with all your SOUL, and with all your STRENGTH."* (Deut. 6:5, NKJV) (emphasis added).

> *"Jesus said to him, 'You shall LOVE the LORD YOUR GOD with all your HEART, with all your SOUL, and with all your MIND.'"* (Matt. 22:37, NKJV) (emphasis added).

> *"You shall not take vengeance, nor bear any grudge against the children of your people, but you shall LOVE your NEIGHBOR as YOURSELF: I am the Lord."* (Lev. 19:18, NKJV) (emphasis added).

> *"And the second is like it: 'You shall LOVE your NEIGHBOR as YOURSELF.'"* (Matt. 22:39, NKJV) (emphasis added).

Therefore, the Ten Commandments that were first established in the Old Testament, under the *first* covenant, as written in the Torah by God's servant Moses, are all reiterated in the New Testament and are still in effect under the New Covenant. As such, this commandment to love God with all our mind, heart, soul, and strength, and to love one another, is why "love" essentially fulfills the *essence* of the law, only *if* we "walk" in love according to the *Spirit of Grace,* rather than the flesh.

Otherwise, we will be judged according to the law! I will cover this indisputable truth in Chapter 56 of Book 3.

❖ The "Covenant of Peace" was established in the Old Testament, based on the following Scriptures: Numbers 25:12; Joshua 9:15; First Kings 3:15; Job 5:23; Isaiah 54:1; Isaiah 54:10; Ezekiel 34:25; Ezekiel 37:26; and Malachi 2:5. It is also referenced in Hebrews 13:20 in the New Testament.

❖ The "Covenant of Circumcision" is the "sign" of the *everlasting* covenant God established with Abraham—the "Father of Many Nations," and his descendants, we in Christendom refer to as the *Abrahamic* Covenant.

This covenant is an *everlasting* covenant. And, this *same* covenant resulted in the *first* covenant God established through His servant Moses, for all twelve tribes of Israel, when the law was given at the base of Mount Sinai, during the very first Feast of Weeks (*Shavuot* in Hebrew), otherwise referred to as *Pentecost* in the ancient Greek. I will cover this in-depth in Chapters 19 and 20 of Book 2. Also, Stephen, who was addressing the call of Abraham, refers to this "Covenant of Circumcision" in Acts 7:8, which is in the New Testament.

In fact, under the New Covenant, this "Covenant of Circumcision" now refers to disciples of Jesus Christ being "circumcised" in our hearts, based on Romans 2:29, and many other Scriptures I will cover in Chapter 22 of Book 2.

❖ The *Mosaic* covenant, Christendom refers to as the Old Covenant, or the *first* covenant, is the Law of Moses, God first established at the base of Mount Sinai through His servant Moses.

This covenant was established with all twelve tribes of Israel, including those who were not there on *that* particular day, during the very first Feast of Weeks (*Pentecost* or *Shavuot*).

Many people refer to this *first* covenant God established with the children of Israel as the "Old" Covenant based on *only* one Scripture in the entire Bible. This is based on Hebrews 8:13, which says, *"In that, He says, 'A NEW covenant,' He has made the first OBSOLETE. Now what is becoming obsolete and growing old is ready to vanish away."* (NKJV) (emphasis added).

Concerning the Scriptures found in the Book of Hebrews, *some* scholars believe this statement was made by the apostle Paul, because traditionally the apostle Paul was thought to be the author of the Book of Hebrews. In fact, the original King James Version of the Bible titled the work, "The Epistle of Paul the Apostle to the Hebrews."

It is for this very reason, throughout this series of books; I will refer to the writings in the Book of Hebrews to be that of the apostle Paul. However, there are *some* scholars who do not believe Paul is the author of the Book of Hebrews for this reason: The difference in the writing style when compared to what he wrote in First Thessalonians, Galatians, Philippians, Philemon, First and Second Corinthians, and Romans.

Nevertheless, this statement made in Hebrews 8:13, presumably by the apostle Paul, has resulted in many believers in the body of Christ taking this statement made by him out of context for this reason: Hebrews Chapter 8, is talking about the "order of the priesthood."

What has become "obsolete" is the "order of the priesthood" according to the *order of Aaron,* because Jesus Christ became our Great High Priest under the *order of Melchizedek.*

In addition, Jesus Christ is the "mediator" between God and man under the New Covenant for this reason: He shed His precious blood on the cross at Calvary for the forgiveness of our sins in order to "restore" and "reconcile" us back into "walking" in a covenant relationship with our heavenly Father.

Because of this growing practice of believers in the body of Christ taking Scripture out of context, and basing our doctrine mostly on what the apostle Paul says as being "the" final authority on a matter, this inaccurate application of Scripture needs to be addressed. There are many believers who do <u>not</u> seek to understand what our heavenly Father said, what Jesus said, and what the rest of the early disciples said.

As a result, many believers are being led astray from the *gospel of the kingdom* once delivered to the saints.

It is for this very reason; the Holy Spirit has placed it upon my heart, to deal with some of the most controversial statements made by the apostle Paul.

In fact, some of the things written in the epistles by the apostle Paul are hard to understand, which "untaught" and "unstable" people twist to their own destruction, as they do with the rest of the Scriptures.

Some of these statements, *if* taken out of context based on the whole counsel of God's Word, at first glance, seem to contradict what was said by our heavenly Father, and our Lord and Savior Jesus Christ, who should be the final authority concerning His *eternal* Word!

Therefore, I will cover these controversial statements made by the apostle Paul in-depth in Chapters 49–51 of Book 3.

Many believers are cherry-picking select passages of Scripture they agree with while discarding the rest.

Our doctrine must be based on the whole counsel of God's Word—which is the doctrine of Christ.

31

THE NEW COVENANT "RENEWED," "RESTORED," AND "REBUILT" THE FIRST COVENANT

If you take the time to perform a word search in the Bible using the word "old," with respect to the word "covenant," you will *only* find one Scripture in Hebrews 8:13, that infers the *first* covenant is old.

Then based on *only* this one Scripture, many believers say the *first* covenant is now obsolete when this is not true at all. It is for this very reason, in Chapter 40 of Book 3, I will cover what the New Covenant is, and in Chapter 41, I will cover what the primary differences between the *first* Covenant, and the New Covenant, are.

A more accurate description of what we in Christendom say is the "Old Covenant" is the *first* covenant, because when Jesus Christ shed His precious blood and established the New Covenant, He essentially "renewed" (confirmed) the *first* covenant, where *some* things are now obsolete.

Not all things our heavenly Father, *Yehôvah,* instructed us to do, which are in accordance with the *first* covenant, have passed away. As a matter of fact, the *first* covenant, in particular, the Law of Moses, *Yehôvah* chose Moses to be the "mediator" of in the Old Testament, are the terms and conditions of disciples of Jesus Christ "walking" in a covenant relationship with our heavenly Father, *Yehôvah,* after we become saved by faith through grace.

This is one of the reasons why *the Word,* who became the Son of Man in the Person of Jesus Christ, was sent to the earth by our heavenly Father to fulfill (consummate, execute, and ratify [confirm]) all our heavenly Father's *everlasting* covenants (plural), with His precious blood.

Therefore, except for the sacrificial system used for the atonement of sins, the blood, the "order of the priesthood" that offered the sacrifice, the "mediator" of the covenant, and *some* of the ceremonial requirements, the instructions God gave to all the children of Israel found in the Torah, are still applicable to New Covenant believers.

Especially since God has now put His laws, which Jesus did not abolish, in our mind, and has written them on our hearts, instead of on two tablets of stone, under the New Covenant!

Again, I will cover the primary differences between the *first* covenant (Old Covenant), and the New Covenant, in detail in Chapters 41–47 of Book 3.

❖ The *Davidic* Covenant. This covenant the Lord established with King David, is still in effect and will cease to exist when we see the sun, moon, and the stars no longer giving their light, which all the end-time Scriptures talk about. I cover this indisputable fact in Chapters 13 and 16 of this book, and I will cover this in-depth in Chapter 69 of Book 3.

All these *everlasting* covenants (plural), God has established with mankind, and all creation throughout the *synergy of the ages* is one of the reasons why Jesus Christ came to the earth the first time to fulfill (consummate, execute, and ratify [confirm]) with His precious blood. And, it is for this very reason; He became the "mediator" of the New Covenant.

These same *everlasting* covenants (plural), will be totally fulfilled and "confirmed" once again when Jesus Christ appears a second time. Jesus' second coming will occur, to the very "day" and the very "hour," according to our heavenly Father's feasts/holy convocations, which shall commence during the fall, according to God's "appointed" times and seasons, based on our Creator's calendar.

THE BIBLE UNVEILS THE GREATEST LOVE STORY EVER TOLD AND IS ALL ABOUT ISRAEL

The Bible, from the Book of Genesis to the Book of Revelation, is a written historical account which details the beginning and the end of all history, from God's perspective, because all history is His story!

Also, the Bible unveils the greatest love story ever told, concerning God's betrothal to His bride—His "faithful" remnant in the body of Christ, which includes all twelve tribes of Israel.

Furthermore, *spiritually* speaking, on the tree (cross) at Calvary, Jesus Christ joined the two "houses" or two "kingdoms" which is comprised of both the House of Judah, and the House of Israel (Jacob/Joseph/Ephraim), which became One New Man from the two "houses," or two "kingdoms," based on Ephesians 2:14–16.

As such, until the One New Man in Christ from the two "houses," or two "kingdoms," manifests itself as "one" body of Christ completely in the *physical* earthly realm, the body of Christ continues to be a "house" and a "kingdom" divided against itself, because we do not know "who" we are in Christ, or "why" we have been left on the earth.

In these final hours, the "midnight" hour, the Lord is calling His people to repent and return to the "ancient" path.

God is in the process of restoring all things He has spoken through His holy prophets since the world began, so He may send Jesus Christ to appear a second time.

However, before Jesus returns, God is orchestrating the greatest move ever since time began and is in the process of bringing the total "restoration" and "reconciliation" to all things, especially in regards to Israel. This is substantiated in Acts 3:19–22, which says the following:

> "*REPENT* [7] [G3340: *metanoeō*: to *think differently or afterwards, that is, reconsider* (morally to feel compunction)] *therefore and be CONVERTED* [8] [G1994: *epistrephō*: to cause to return to the worship of the true God and to the love and obedience of God], *that YOUR SINS may be BLOTTED OUT, so that TIMES of REFRESHING may come from the PRESENCE of the LORD, and that He may SEND Jesus Christ, who was preached to you before, whom HEAVEN must RECEIVE until the TIMES of RESTORATION of all THINGS, which God has*

35

Who is Israel? Discovering our True Identity in Jesus Christ and Why it Matters! The Foundation

> *SPOKEN by the MOUTH of ALL His HOLY PROPHETS SINCE the WORLD BEGAN. For Moses truly said to the fathers, 'The Lord your God will raise up for you a Prophet like me from your brethren. Him you shall hear in all things, whatever He says to you.'"* (Acts 3:19–22, NKJV) (emphasis added).

Yes, indeed! We live in the most exciting time in all history, and we were born for a time such as this.

God is in the process of orchestrating the greatest move of all time by bringing the total "restoration" and "reconciliation" to all Israel, so He can send Jesus Christ, whom heaven must receive *until* the times of the restoration of all things spoken by the "Prophets of Old" is accomplished.

As such, based on Acts 3:19–22, our heavenly Father will not send Jesus for His bride *until* the times of the restoration of all, not some, things take place!

However, it is evident by all the different denominations in the body of Christ; this has not yet come to fruition.

One of the main reasons why the body of Christ remains a "house" or a "kingdom" divided against itself, is because God's people do not know about all the *everlasting* covenants (plural), God has established with His people.

All these *everlasting* covenants culminate with the New Covenant, Jesus Christ ratified (executed), with His precious blood.

Donna M. Rogers

WE NEED TO UNDERSTAND THE GOSPEL OF THE "KINGDOM"

To understand the *gospel of the kingdom*, we need to read and understand the beginning of the book (the Bible), specifically in Genesis 1:26–28, when we were given our main "mandate" by God, our Creator, who created an "eternal" soul for every male, or female, who would ever be "conceived" in their mother's womb, *before* one of our days on the earth ever came to be.

In Chapter 11 of this book, I will address this subject in-depth concerning our "kingdom" mandate to take dominion for God's glory and eternal purposes to prevail, as we make His enemies His footstool, and all the nations of the world His inheritance.

It begins with God's people understanding our true identity in Christ Jesus, and understanding our "kingdom" mandate to fulfill God's *eternal* destiny as we, His sons and daughters, fulfill our destiny, which He preordained since the foundation of the world, before one of our days on the earth ever came to be!

Moreover, we can only achieve this mandate to take "dominion" and "subdue" every living creature for the purpose of establishing His Kingdom on the earth as it is in heaven, as we disciple the nations. This "mandate" can only be accomplished by us abiding in God's manifest presence, and being endued with power from on high.

Only then do we have the hope of establishing His *laws*, His *righteousness*, His *justice*, and His *judgments* as we "subdue" and take "dominion" over the enemy, while we are still living on the

37

earth, for God's Kingdom purposes and glory to prevail, in and through us, His sons and daughters.

However, for the subject at hand, this is what the *gospel of the kingdom* means: We are to "rule" and "reign" on the earth as it is in heaven, as we abide in Jesus Christ through the Holy Spirit, and seek God's will for our lives—our purpose of "why" He created us in the first place.

Then we must "do" only what our heavenly Father tells us to do, which will happen when we "obey" His Voice and His Word. It is only then can we hope to establish God's will on the earth as it is in heaven, while we still live on the earth, and fulfill our destiny as His sons and daughters before we die a physical death.

The apostle Peter outlines what the *kingdom of God* looks like as he was preaching the "good news" to Cornelius' household in Acts 10:34–43, which says the following:

> *"Then Peter opened his mouth and said: 'In truth, I perceive that God shows no partiality. But in every NATION whoever FEARS Him and WORKS RIGHTEOUSNESS is ACCEPTED by Him. The WORD which GOD SENT to the CHILDREN of ISRAEL, preaching peace through Jesus Christ—He is Lord of all—that word you know, which was proclaimed throughout all Judea, and began from Galilee after the baptism which John preached: how God anointed JESUS of NAZARETH with the HOLY SPIRIT and with POWER, who went about DOING*

GOOD and HEALING all who were OPPRESSED by the DEVIL, for God was with Him.'" (Acts 10:34–38, NKJV) (emphasis added).

"And we are WITNESSES of all THINGS which He did both in the land of the Jews and in Jerusalem, whom they KILLED by hanging on a tree. Him [Jesus] God [Yehóvâh, our heavenly Father] RAISED UP on the third DAY, and SHOWED Him OPENLY, not to all the PEOPLE, but to WITNESSES chosen BEFORE by God, even to us WHO ATE and DRANK with Him after He AROSE from the DEAD. And He COMMANDED us to PREACH to the PEOPLE, and to TESTIFY that it is He who was ordained by God to be JUDGE of the LIVING and the DEAD. To Him all the PROPHETS WITNESS that, through His NAME, whoever believes IN (9) *[G1519: eis: reached or have entered into the point or purpose of a place, time or result] Him will receive REMISSION* (10) *[G859: aphesis: freedom or pardon; forgiveness deliverance and liberty] of SINS."* (Acts 10:39–43, NKJV) (emphasis added).

As such, our "purpose" or "mandate" is to be conformed into the image of Christ and do what Jesus did during His earthly ministry. Hence, we should be like Jesus concerning what we "think," "say," and "do," so we will fulfill our God-given purpose and our eternal destiny.

But first, we must receive His "anointing" and His "resurrection power" from on high, that we have freely been given based on the

39

atoning work Jesus did for us on the cross at Calvary for the remission of our sins.

This is what the *gospel of the kingdom* is all about! The *kingdom of God* is "in" us once we believe by faith and put our trust in Jesus Christ, as our Lord and Savior, for everything we could possibly need or desire.

This is substantiated in Luke 17:20–21, which says the following:

> *"Now when He* [Jesus] *was asked by the Pharisees WHEN the KINGDOM of GOD would COME, He answered them and said, 'The KINGDOM of GOD does not COME with OBSERVATION; nor will they say, 'See here!' or 'See there!' For indeed, the KINGDOM of GOD is WITHIN you.'"* (Luke 17:20–21, NKJV) (emphasis added).

Do not dismiss the significance of this truth: Luke 17:21, says, *"For indeed, the KINGDOM of GOD is WITHIN you."* (NKJV) (emphasis added).

In other words, the *kingdom of God* is the "invisible" Spirit of the living God (the Holy Spirit), who lives in the heart of every true disciple of Jesus Christ!

The *kingdom of God* will only manifest on the earth as it is in heaven, based on what you "choose" to do in order for you to establish God's kingdom "rule" and "reign" on the earth while you still live on planet earth!

Donna M. Rogers

GOD'S PEOPLE ARE TO ESTABLISH AND MANIFEST GOD'S "KINGDOM" WHILE WE ARE STILL LIVING ON THE EARTH

The *kingdom of God* is manifested on the earth as it is in heaven when God's people "walk" in the fullness of God's grace, power, and authority we have *already* been given. Jesus Christ came to the earth the first time to "seek" and to "save" that *which* was lost, due to the first Adam's transgression. Jesus Christ "redeemed," "restored," and "reconciled" all things, *spiritually* speaking, by His death, resurrection, and ascension into heaven.

However, as I will convey later in Book 2 like Abraham did before *the Word* became flesh, we "activate" and we will "experience" the *physical* manifestation of the *kingdom of God* on the earth, as it is in heaven, by our faith. We must "believe" to "receive" the covenant promises of God found in His Word.

Therefore, when God's people truly believe "what," God's Word says is true in our hearts, only then will we "walk" in accordance with God's Word.

Only then will we seek to take "dominion" and "subdue" every living creature on the earth, for God's purpose and glory to prevail, while we are still living on the earth. Yet the reality of this will only take place *if* God's people abide in Jesus Christ, and we submit ourselves to the *sanctification* process of the Holy Spirit. Then God's people will be doing even greater exploits than Jesus, and His early disciples did, as illustrated in the Book of Acts when they received God's "dunamis" ([miraculous] power, might, and strength) from on high!

41

This is the only way a lost and dying world will see God before Jesus comes back the second time. They will "see" and "experience" the living God based on what His people "do" rather than by what we say!

Also, before we can "do" the will of our heavenly Father, first we need to find out what *Yehovah*, our heavenly Father, is trying to accomplish, in and through us, His people. We find out what our heavenly Father's good, perfect, and pleasing will is through prayer and abiding in His manifest presence. This will only happen *if* we cultivate a personal, intimate relationship with our heavenly Father, and our Redeemer and King, Jesus Christ, who is the Holy One of Israel.

Furthermore, this will result in us understanding our "Hebraic" roots in Christianity, so the "faithful" remnant from all twelve tribes of Israel shall be saved.

Contrary to what is taught, not all believers in the body of Christ are the *bride of Christ,* based on *some* of the following reasons: The *bride of Christ* has arrayed herself in fine white linen, without spot or blemish—which are the "righteous" acts of the saints, based on Revelation 19:8. Also, she is ready and eagerly waiting for her bridegroom's return. Moreover, the *bride of Christ* is the "faithful" remnant who "obeys" God's Voice and His Word, and "keeps" His *everlasting* covenants (plural), so He shall be our God, and we shall be His "covenant" people.

Again, God's people are indeed perishing from a lack of knowledge which is based on our ignorance of the whole counsel of God's

Word. As a result, His people are *unknowingly* breaking "covenant" with our heavenly Father, and His only *begotten* Son, Jesus Christ, when this is one of the main reasons why *the Word,* was sent to the earth as the Son of Man in the Person of Jesus Christ, in the first place.

It was so mankind could be "restored" and "reconciled" back into "walking" in a covenant relationship with our heavenly Father, which both houses—the House of Judah and the House of Israel, broke due to their *spiritual* harlotry.

God's people will return to God and "walk" in a covenant relationship with our heavenly Father, only by knowing our true identity in Christ Jesus, and who we truly are as His sons and daughters. And last, but certainly not least, we must know "who" Israel is and "why" it matters!

Therefore, the primary purpose of this series of books is to help equip God's people, so we can make ourselves ready to be the *bride of Christ*—without spot or blemish. We must awaken, arise, and prepare the way for the return of Jesus Christ because the eternal destination of countless souls is at stake for all eternity!

However, before we can prepare others for the return of the Lord, God's people must first know who we are in Christ, and who we are as God's sons and daughters. Then we must repent and return to the "ancient" path which leads to life. This path is very narrow, and few find it!

Finding this "narrow" path and traversing it, requires God's people to crucify their flesh and die to themselves!

In addition, God's people must understand the "root" of His *everlasting* covenant, He established with Abraham and his descendants. This is the only way we will *properly* "disciple" the nations.

Then God's people *must* arise to help bring in the end-time harvest of souls—for the fields are ripe for harvesting, but the laborers are few.

Now let's begin our journey to discover the answers to all these profound questions based on what God's Word actually says, rather than based on the "theories" and the "doctrines" of men.

We will begin this quest to understand our true identity in Christ, by defining what is meant by the term the *fullness of the Gentiles,* and discovering "where" and "when" this phrase originated based on God's Word in Chapter 1. We must also understand "why" this knowledge is "relevant" to New Covenant believers.

The *fullness of the Gentiles* is reaching its zenith in this "kairos" season which will usher in the return of Jesus Christ, our conquering King, who is coming back for a bride fully mature in Him and lacking nothing.

Donna M. Rogers

CHAPTER 1

WHERE AND WHEN DID THE PHRASE THE "FULLNESS OF THE GENTILES" ORIGINATE ACCORDING TO GOD'S WORD?

To determine who Israel is, based on the twelve tribes of Israel, we need to go back to the beginning based on the written records of the Old Testament. The nation of Israel began as one kingdom. However, after King Solomon died, the children of Israel became divided into two kingdoms—the House of Judah and the House of Israel.

From the very beginning, *Yehovah* planned to reunite the Jews from the House of Judah and those of us who were formerly Gentiles, who have now been grafted into the commonwealth of Israel by our faith in Jesus Christ. More specifically we, who comprise the House of Israel (Jacob/Joseph/Ephraim), are the ten tribes of Israel who broke covenant with *Yehovah* and became scattered all over the earth.

As a matter of fact, over two thousand years ago, at the time when the early disciples were turning the world upside down with the *gospel of the kingdom,* James addressed the twelve tribes of Israel in James 1:1–3, which says the following: *"James, a bondservant of God and of the Lord Jesus Christ, to the TWELVE TRIBES which are SCATTERED ABROAD: Greetings. My brethren, count it all joy when you fall into various trials, knowing that the testing of your faith produces patience."* (NKJV) (emphasis added).

45

Furthermore, the twelve tribes of Israel are still scattered over the earth, and will continue to be until Jesus Christ's second appearing, when He will send His angels forth (which are His reapers) to gather His elect from the four winds, from the farthest part of the earth to the farthest part of heaven. However, before this happens, the *fullness of the Gentiles* must reach its zenith. This is made possible only by *Yehôváh's* plan of redemption, offered to all mankind through His only *begotten* Son, Jesus Christ.

Therefore, we will now discover when *Yehôváh's* plan concerning the *fullness of the Gentiles* began according to His Word. It begins at the death bed scene of the patriarch Jacob, the son of Isaac, whose name was changed to Israel after he wrestled with God and prevailed. Jacob, the grandson of Abraham, called forth all his sons to give them his final blessing.

However, before Jacob blessed his own sons, he first blessed Joseph's sons, his grandsons Manasseh and Ephraim. Yes, indeed! Joseph was still the apple of his daddy's eye for in Genesis 48:21–22 below, Jacob (Israel) tells Joseph he is giving him one portion above his brothers.

> *"Then Israel [Jacob] said to Joseph, 'Behold, I am dying, but God will be with you and bring you back to the LAND of YOUR FATHERS. Moreover I have given to you ONE PORTION ABOVE YOUR BROTHERS, which I took from the hand of the Amorite with my sword and my bow.'"* (Gen. 48:21–22, NKJV) (emphasis added).

46

Therefore, Jacob's blessing would not be complete without blessing Joseph's children Manasseh and Ephraim, even though there is no indication Jacob blessed any of his other grandchildren. We need to carefully examine what took place when Jacob blessed Joseph's sons because this is when the *fullness of the Gentiles* would be prophetically decreed. It was to take place through Ephraim, rather than Manasseh, who *should* have received the double-portion blessings as the *firstborn* son.

However, this should not surprise us, because it was Jacob after all who tricked his father, Isaac, into giving him the *firstborn* son's blessing shortly before his death, which was supposed to go to Esau who despised and sold his "birthright" for a bowl of stew.

Now let's see what happens as Jacob's beloved son, Joseph, gathers his sons Manasseh and Ephraim to receive their blessings from Jacob (Israel). This is long before Moses is sent by *Yehôva̓h* to lead the Hebrew people out of Egypt from their enslavement of Pharaoh, who did not know Joseph. The Book of Exodus records Israel's birth as a nation when the Hebrew people made their exodus out of Egypt.

In Genesis 48:1–4, Jacob (Israel) tells Joseph, *Yehôva̓h* appeared to him at Luz, in the land of Canaan, and blessed him, by saying He would make Jacob fruitful, multiply him, make him a "multitude" of people, and give the land of Canaan to his descendants after him, as an *everlasting* possession. Genesis 48:1–4, says the following:

> *"Now it came to pass after these things that Joseph*
> *was told, 'Indeed your father is sick'; and he took with*
> *him his two sons, Manasseh and Ephraim. And Jacob*

*was told, 'Look, your son Joseph is coming to you'; and Israel strengthened himself and sat up on the bed. Then Jacob said to Joseph: 'God Almighty appeared to me at Luz in the land of Canaan and blessed me, and said to me, 'Behold, I will make you FRUITFUL and MULTIPLY you, and I will make of you a **MULTITUDE** (1) [H6951: qâhâl: assemblage; assembly, company, congregation, multitude] of PEOPLE, and GIVE this LAND to YOUR DESCENDANTS after you as an **EVERLASTING** (2) [H5769: 'ôlâm: properly concealed, perpetual, at any time, (beginning of the) world (+ without end); eternity] POSSESSION.' "* (Gen. 48:1–4, NKJV) (emphasis added).

Then in Genesis 48:5–7, Jacob tells Joseph his two sons, Ephraim and Manasseh, are his as Reuben and Simeon are. Then Jacob (Israel) tells Joseph any offspring he has after them shall be his and will be called by the name of their brothers in their inheritance. In other words, Jacob is giving Joseph two shares as an inheritance in the Promised Land by taking Joseph's sons Ephraim and Manasseh as his own. Any other offspring Joseph may have in the future will be called by the name of their brothers—the children of Israel. This is talking about Joseph's *spiritual* descendants, because Joseph had no more children, even though the Bible tells us he had grandchildren from his sons Manasseh and Ephraim. Genesis 48:5–7, says the following:

"And now YOUR TWO SONS, Ephraim and Manasseh, who were born to you in the land of Egypt

48

before I came to you in Egypt, ARE MINE; as Reuben and Simeon, THEY SHALL BE MINE. Your OFFSPRING WHOM YOU BEGET after THEM shall be YOURS; they will be CALLED by the NAME of their BROTHERS in their INHERITANCE. But as for me, when I came from Padan, Rachel died beside me in the land of Canaan on the way, when there was but a little distance to go to Ephrath; and I buried her there on the way to Ephrath (that is, Bethlehem)." (Gen. 48:5–7, NKJV) (emphasis added).

Now let's see what Jacob (Israel) says as he bestows his blessing on Ephraim and Manasseh. This pivotal scene takes place in Genesis 48:18–20, when Joseph's second born son, Ephraim, received the double-portion blessing from Jacob instead of the *firstborn* son Manasseh. And, since Ephraim received the double-portion blessing that usually goes to the *firstborn* son, the name Ephraim means "doubly fruitful."

In addition, as substantiated in this Scripture, Jacob was aware of what he was doing when he blessed Ephraim instead of Manasseh. In other words, it was not done in error! Moreover, Jacob not only prophesied that Ephraim's heirs would one day become the *fullness of the Gentiles,* but he also set them *before* the tribe of Manasseh. Genesis 48:18–20, says the following:

"And Joseph said to his father, 'Not so, my father, for this ONE is the FIRSTBORN; put your right hand on his head,' BUT his FATHER refused and said, 'I KNOW, my son, I KNOW. He [Manasseh] also shall

49

> *become a people, and he also shall be great; but truly his YOUNGER BROTHER* [Ephraim] *shall be GREATER than he, and his descendants shall become a **MULTITUDE*** [H4393: *mělo': fulness* (literally or figuratively)] *of **NATIONS*** [H1471: *gôy:* a foreign *nation*; hence a *Gentile*; nation of heathen people].' *So he blessed them that day, saying, 'By you Israel will bless, saying, 'May God make you as Ephraim and as Manasseh!' And thus he* [Jacob (Israel)] *SET Ephraim before Manasseh."* (Gen. 48:18–20, NKJV) (emphasis added).

Hence, the term the *fullness of the Gentiles* was birthed based on Genesis 48:18–20. In addition, take the time to read the account of Jacob's last words to all his sons—the twelve tribes of Israel, to understand what shall befall us, the descendants of Abraham, Isaac, and Jacob (Israel), in these last days.

This account begins in Genesis Chapter 49, in which Jacob called his sons and said, *"Gather together, that I may tell you what shall BEFALL you in the LAST DAYS."* (NKJV) (emphasis added).

Therefore, for us to understand what will happen at the end of days, we must understand what God decreed from the very beginning through His servants, the prophets.

This is based on Amos 3:7, which states, *"Surely the Lord God does NOTHING, Unless He REVEALS His SECRET to His SERVANTS the PROPHETS."* (NKJV) (emphasis added).

However, for the subject at hand, you will particularly want to pay close attention concerning what Jacob (Israel) prophesied about his son Judah, based on Genesis 49:8–12, which says the following:

> *"Judah, you are he whom YOUR BROTHERS shall PRAISE; YOUR HAND shall be on the NECK of your ENEMIES; Your FATHER'S CHILDREN shall BOW DOWN before you. Judah is a LION'S WHELP; From the prey, my son, YOU HAVE GONE UP. He bows down, he lies down as a LION; And as a LION, who shall rouse him? The SCEPTER shall not DEPART from JUDAH, nor a LAWGIVER from between his feet, Until **SHILOH*** (5)* [H7886: shíylóh: tranquil, Shiloh, an epithet of the Messiah] COMES; And to Him shall be the OBEDIENCE of the PEOPLE."* (Gen. 49:8–10, NKJV) (emphasis added).

> *"Binding his donkey to the vine, And his donkey's colt to the choice vine, He WASHED his GARMENTS in WINE, And his CLOTHES in the BLOOD of GRAPES. His eyes are darker than wine, And his teeth whiter than milk."* (Gen. 49:11–12, NKJV) (emphasis added).

Based on Genesis 49:8–12, when Jacob (Israel) issued this prophetic decree and blessed his son Judah, he was also prophetically decreeing and prophesying about Jesus Christ, who is the Lion of the *tribe of Judah,* and the *Root of David.* This is based on Revelation 5:5, which says the following: *"...Do not weep. Behold, the LION of the TRIBE of JUDAH, the ROOT of DAVID, has prevailed to open the scroll and to loose its seven seals."* (NKJV) (emphasis added).

It came to pass that Jesus Christ has indeed ascended into heaven and is now seated at the right hand of His heavenly Father whose children shall all bow down before Him—as every knee bows, and every tongue confesses, Jesus Christ is the *King of kings and the Lord of lords.*

Moreover, based on what Jacob stated when he specifically said, *"...Your FATHER'S CHILDREN shall BOW DOWN before you..."* (emphasis mine), Jacob is referring to the ultimate fulfillment of Joseph's dream which was about his mother, father, and brothers who would all bow down to him for this reason: Joseph is a prophetic shadow picture of Jesus Christ.

Joseph's dream is based on Genesis 37:9, which says, *"Then he dreamed still another dream and told it to his brothers, and said, 'Look, I have dreamed another dream. And this time, the SUN, the MOON, and the eleven STARS bowed down to me.'"* (NKJV) (emphasis added).

In addition, concerning what Jacob prophetically decreed about our Messiah in Genesis 49:8–10, the "scepter" shall not depart from Judah, nor, will God's laws be abolished, because the Lawgiver now lives on the inside of us by His Holy Spirit.

God's laws shall be upheld until Shiloh (our Messiah) comes back to the earth and to Him shall be the total "obedience" of the people. When Jesus Christ sets up His millennial kingdom on the earth after the one thousand years is over, it will be then Jesus will strike the nations, and rule them with a rod (scepter) of iron.

In the next chapter, we will continue our journey to understand "who" Israel is from a "Hebraic" perspective based on the Word of God, which is the result of the *everlasting* covenant God established with Abraham—the "Father of Many Nations."

Who is Israel? Discovering our True Identity in Jesus Christ and Why it Matters! The Foundation

CHAPTER 2

ABRAHAM IS THE "FATHER OF MANY NATIONS," SO "WHO" ARE THE TWELVE TRIBES OF ISRAEL—THE CHILDREN OF ISRAEL?

One of the *everlasting* covenants we need to know about that God established with all His people is the Abrahamic Covenant. This covenant is still in effect for those of us who *were* formerly Gentiles, which have now been grafted into the commonwealth of Israel, by our faith in Jesus Christ.

Those of us who *were* formerly Gentiles are from the House of Israel (Jacob/Joseph/Ephraim). We are the ten tribes of Israel which comprised the *northern* kingdom of Israel, after the death of King Solomon. Whereas, the Jews from the House of Judah comprised the *southern* kingdom of Israel.

Our heavenly Father, *Yehovah,* decreed and established a plan of "redemption," "restoration," and "reconciliation," *before* the foundation of the world, to ensure all Israel shall be saved.

All Israel includes a "faithful" remnant of Jews from the House of Judah and a "faithful" remnant of those of us who were formerly Gentiles from the House of Israel (Jacob/Joseph/Ephraim).

We shall be saved according to the election of grace as His *royal* priesthood and a *holy* nation. It was for this very reason; our "Passover Lamb" was slain *before* the foundation of the world. This is as substantiated in Revelation 13:8, which says, *"ALL who DWELL on the EARTH will WORSHIP him* [the dragon (Satan) who gave authority to the beast and the beast (the Antichrist and his Kingdom) based on Revelation 13:4], *whose NAMES have NOT been WRITTEN in the BOOK of LIFE of the LAMB slain from the FOUNDATION of the WORLD."* (NKJV) (emphasis added).

Therefore, when the *fullness of the Gentiles* comes to fruition, *before* Jesus Christ appears the second time, it will be then *Yehôvah* shall send out His angels to gather all the children of Israel—His elect, from the ends of the earth, to the ends of the heavens, and bring them into "the" Promised Land—the *kingdom of heaven.* We will remain in the *kingdom of heaven* for one thousand years, until the *new* heaven and the *new* earth is created based on Revelation 21:1.

However, before this happens, those who have died in Christ will be resurrected in the *first* resurrection, before those who are still alive and remain (survive) the tribulation period will be "caught up" (raptured), based on First Thessalonians 4:13–18. This is when the *first* resurrection of the dead takes place, which is based on Revelation 20:5–6.

In the meanwhile, until Jesus Christ returns the second time, our heavenly Father, *Yehôvah,* has been in the process of joining all twelve tribes of Israel into one *holy* nation, one *royal* priesthood, *physically* speaking. This is while we are still living in the land (on the earth), by us standing on the *holy* mountain of Israel—the rock—who is Jesus Christ, the Chief Cornerstone of His Church (Ekklēsía).

We are now entering the dispensation of the *fullness of the times* the apostle Paul speaks about in Ephesians 1:10, where he specifically says, *"...He might GATHER TOGETHER in ONE all THINGS in Christ, both which are in HEAVEN and which are on EARTH—in Him."* (NKJV) (emphasis added).

On the cross at Calvary over two thousand years ago, Jesus Christ already made both the House of Judah, and the House of Israel— One New Man in Him, *spiritually* speaking. In addition, the One New Man is referring to our individual salvation where we have become a "new" creation in Christ, based on Second Corinthians 5:17, *if* we walk according to the Spirit.

It also refers to us "collectively" becoming One New Man, as God's Ekklēsía—"one" body of Christ, who is a *holy* nation, and a *royal* priesthood, and is *supposed* to be under the headship of Jesus Christ, the Chief Cornerstone. This is based on the following Scriptures: Exodus 19:6; First Peter 2:9; First Corinthians 12:12; and Galatians 3:28-29.

Therefore, our heavenly Father's eternal plan of "restoration" and "reconciliation" will be *totally* fulfilled when He unites His body in a "unity of the faith" based on the uncompromised, unadulterated whole counsel of His Word, which is firmly established on the doctrine of Christ.

This new move of God which is currently underway is for all His children from both the House of Judah, and the House of Israel— all twelve tribes of Israel, not just the Jews from the tribe of Judah.

Our heavenly Father's eternal plan for the "restoration" and "reconciliation" of all Israel is unfolding before our very eyes. He is in the process of *physically* uniting all His covenant people into one "house," one "kingdom," and One New Man in the *physical* earthly realm.

God's plan of "restoration" and "reconciliation" of the entire world, including its inhabitants, will be achieved because there are *no* "ifs" in God's eternal plan, for His *eternal* Word shall accomplish the very thing for which He has sent it! As such, the execution of His eternal plan shall be totally fulfilled in Christ Jesus, our Jewish Messiah, and those who follow in the footsteps of our King.

Just prior to the second return of Jesus Christ that which was spoken by the prophet Ezekiel, based on Ezekiel 37:21–23, will be totally fulfilled. Then the children of Israel will no longer be divided into two "nations," nor, shall we ever be divided into two "kingdoms" again, because this will usher in the return of Jesus Christ. As such, this is one fulfillment of the two witnesses the Book of Revelation speaks about, *spiritually* speaking. Ezekiel 37:21–23, says the following:

> *"Then say to them, 'Thus says the Lord GOD: 'Surely I will take the children of Israel from AMONG the NATIONS, wherever they have GONE, and will GATHER THEM from every side and BRING THEM into their own LAND; and I will make them ONE NATION in the LAND, on the MOUNTAINS of ISRAEL; and ONE KING shall be KING over THEM all; they shall NO LONGER be TWO NATIONS, nor shall they ever be DIVIDED into TWO KINGDOMS*

> *again. They shall not DEFILE THEMSELVES*
> *anymore with their IDOLS, nor with their*
> *DETESTABLE THINGS, nor with any of their*
> *TRANSGRESSIONS; but I will DELIVER them from*
> *all their DWELLING PLACES in which they have*
> *SINNED, and will CLEANSE them. THEN they shall*
> *be My PEOPLE, and I will be their God.'"* (Ezek.
> 37:21–23, NKJV) (emphasis added).

Like many other Scriptures found in the Bible, Ezekiel 37:21–23, has a dual fulfillment and meaning. In addition, some Scriptures have multiple fulfillments in history.

Therefore, one meaning of this Scripture is referring to our heavenly Father, *Yehovah,* bringing back His chosen people from both the House of Judah and the House of Israel (Jacob/Joseph/Ephraim), to the *physical* nation of Israel. The *literal* nation of Israel is the very first nation of the world, the Lord established for His chosen people—the Hebrew people.

Our heavenly Father, *Yehovah,* has indeed brought many of His children back to the Promised Land, on the mountains of Israel, to the *physical* nation of Israel located in the Middle East. As "tens of thousands" of God's covenant people have been led by the Spirit to make their pilgrimage to the land of Israel.

However, *spiritually* speaking, the phrase "the mountains of Israel" is referring to His bride coming up to His *holy* mountain in the *heavenly* realm, which we will do as we praise, worship, and pray in the Spirit, and we enter the *Holy of Holies,* as we seek the face of the One who has captivated our hearts. Yet Ezekiel 37:21-23, is also referring to the *spiritual* nation of Israel—the body of Christ—God's Hebrew people. We have entered into a "covenant" relationship with our heavenly Father, *Yehóvah,* by placing our faith and trust in our Jewish Messiah—our Lord and Savior Jesus Christ—who is the Holy One of Israel. Jesus is also the "mediator" of the New Covenant. As such, we are the Israelites and God's Hebrew children, and by the time you finish reading this entire book, you will know beyond a shadow of a doubt, what I am proclaiming is true.

It is for this very reason, the apostle Paul, who was of Jewish descent by birth, says to us in Second Corinthians 11:22, *"Are they HEBREWS? So am I. Are they ISRAELITES? So am I. Are they the SEED of ABRAHAM? So am I."* (NKJV) (emphasis added).

Therefore, so are New Covenant believers, who are the *bride of Christ,* for we are God's "faithful" remnant. We are the Israelites! We are God's Hebrew people who have crossed over into a "newness" of life in Christ, because we have died to our sins, and we have been resurrected as a "new" creation in Him!

We serve the same God Abraham worshiped, served, and obeyed—*El Elyon* (the *Most High God*), and *El Olam* (the *Everlasting God*), who is also the God of Abraham, Isaac, and Jacob (Israel)! He is the same *everlasting* God who sent *the Word* to the earth as the Son of Man in the Person of Jesus Christ, who is the "mediator" of the New Covenant our heavenly Father, *Yehóvah,* established with both the House of Judah and the House of Israel.

As such, all who place their faith and trust in our Jewish Messiah—

60

Jesus Christ, who was sent to the earth the first time to "restore" and "reconcile" us back into "walking" in a covenant relationship with our heavenly Father, *Yehovah,* have now been grafted into the commonwealth of Israel.

DISCIPLES OF JESUS CHRIST, SPIRITUALLY SPEAKING, ARE THE "SEED" OF ABRAHAM AND "HEIRS" OF THE COVENANT PROMISES

Therefore, *spiritually* speaking, we are from the "seed" of Abraham and "heirs" according to the covenant promises which are all fulfilled in Christ. This is substantiated by the apostle Paul when he says to us in Galatians 3:16, *"Now to ABRAHAM and his SEED were the PROMISES made. He does not say, 'And to seeds,' as of many, but as of one, 'And to YOUR SEED,' WHO is CHRIST."* (NKJV) (emphasis added).

Also, see Psalm 105:6; Acts 3:25; Romans 4:13; Romans 4:16; and Romans 11:1.

Now let's refocus our attention on what the apostle Paul says to us in Second Corinthians 11:22, which says the following:

> *"Are they* **HEBREWS** [1] [2] **[G1445: *Hebraios:* a *Hebraean* or Jew; G1443: *Eber: Eber,* a patriarch]**? *So am I. Are they* **ISRAELITES** [3] [4] **[G2475: *Israelites:* an Israelite, that is, a descendant of Israel (literally or figuratively); G2474: *Israel:* the adopted name of Jacob, including his descendants (literally or**

61

figuratively)]*? So am I. Are they the SEED of ABRAHAM? So am I.*" (2 Cor. 11:22, NKJV)

Therefore, based on the Greek meaning of the word "Hebrew" a Hebrew is one who is called a "Hebraean" or a "Jew" and are descendants of the patriarch Ebner. Whereas, based on the Greek meaning of the word "Israelites," an Israelite is a descendant of Israel, either *literally,* or *figuratively,* and is the "adoptive" name of Jacob the patriarch, including his *literal,* or *figurative,* descendants.

If you are like me and have an inquiring mind, you are probably asking yourself the following question: "Who is a Hebraean that is a descendant of the patriarch Ebner, who is also related to the patriarch Jacob?" I will fully answer this question in Chapter 5 of this book.

For now, let's continue to dig a little deeper concerning the Greek meaning of the word "Hebrew" so we can understand the full significance of what the apostle Paul said to us in Second Corinthians 11:22, where he uses both the word "Hebrews" and "Israelites" which is referring to those who are from the "seed" of Abraham.

Thayer's Greek Lexicon further defines the Greek meaning of the word "Hebrew" as follows:

1. Any one of the *Jewish* or *Israelitish* nations.

2. In a narrower sense, those who live in Palestine and use the language of the country.

3. All Jewish Christians, whether they spoke Aramaic or Greek.

Moreover, we have been taught to believe a Jew is someone who has the following attributes:

1. An adherent of Judaism as a religion, or culture.

2. A member of the widely dispersed people originally descended from the ancient Hebrews and sharing an ethnic heritage based on Judaism.

3. A native, or inhabitant, of the ancient kingdom of Judah.

THE JEWS ARE DESCENDANTS OF JUDAH, JACOB'S FOURTH BORN SON

Now I want to share with you this compelling article titled, "The Bible Distinction between 'The House of Israel' and 'The House of Judah'" by F. F. Bosworth I was led to during my research for this book. [5]

Based on what Bosworth wrote you would be amazed. My commentary is highlighted and in brackets for clarification purposes only. In this article, Bosworth states the following:

❖ According to biblical history, there were no "Jews" known as such, until about fifteen centuries *after* Abraham was born, and until six hundred years after the death of Moses.

Who is Israel? Discovering our True Identity in Jesus Christ and Why it Matters! The Foundation

- ❖ The Hebrew people were not Jews, because of Judah, from whom the Jews descended, was not yet born. [In Chapter 5 of this book I will cover this fact: Abraham, Isaac, and Jacob were not Jewish. They are Hebrews. I will also cover in this same chapter "who" a *true* Jew is from God's perspective].

- ❖ This racial type of remnant we know as the Jews are only a small portion of the descendants of Judah, who was only one of the twelve sons of Jacob. There are no Jews among any of the descendants of Jacob's other eleven sons.

- ❖ From Judah, the fourth son of Jacob, are descended the Jews—the word "Jew" being simply an abbreviation of the name "Judah." A glance at the genealogy will show that it is impossible for Abraham, Isaac, and Jacob, to have been Jews. Only the descendants of Judah—those coming *after* him, could be called by his name—not his ancestors.

- ❖ The Bible tells us the Jews would be "few in numbers" based on Ezekiel 5:3, but it tells us Israel would be as the *sands of the sea* for "multitudes" based on Hosea 1:10.

- ❖ The term "Jew" was never used until more than a thousand years after Abraham. It appears for the first time in Second Kings Chapter 16, where we are told the *King of Israel*, together with the *King of Assyria*, made war against the *King of Judah*. [In the NKJV the word "Jews" first appears in Second Kings 25:25].

64

- ❖ In Genesis 49:10, it tells us Judah represents the "scepter" family. Whereas, in First Chronicles 5:2, we are told the "birthright" belongs to Joseph.

- ❖ Unless we see the distinction between the House of Israel, and the House of Judah, from the time of the division, till the final and glorious reunion of the two houses, which will take place at the end of the "latter days," the prophecies concerning Israel cannot be understood based on Ezekiel 38. [Amen. Hence, one of the purposes of this series of books.]

- ❖ God divided the Abrahamic promises among Jacob's twelve sons, and when He said through Jacob, Ephraim's "seed" shall become a "multitude of nations," He was not referring to the Jews, who never have, or ever will be, "a multitude of nations!" Rather, God was speaking to the "birthright" heirs.

The "nation" and a "company of nations" promised in Genesis 35:11, was a "birthright" blessing to be fulfilled in the "last days" before Christ's return, based on Genesis 49:1, to Joseph, and his descendants, based on First Chronicles 5:1, none of which are Jews.

Moreover, in Jeremiah 31:9, God said, *"Ephraim is My firstborn,"* and in Genesis 48:19, Jacob said of Ephraim, *"His seed shall become a multitude of nations"* which is just the opposite of what was said of Judah— *"He shall become a remnant."*

Therefore, this promise to Israel was not to Judah and is proven by this fact: Judah has never been a "multitude of nations," and never will be. [I already covered this in detail in Chapter 1 when I explained where the term the *fullness of the Gentiles* originated based on Jacob (Israel) blessing Joseph's two sons—Ephraim and Manasseh shortly before his death.] [end of excerpt]

THE JEWS ARE FROM THE TRIBE OF JUDAH

When the nation of Israel was split into two kingdoms after the death of King Solomon, the "Jews" were associated with the *southern* kingdom of Israel—the tribe of Judah, the *one* and *only* tribe *Yehovah* said He would give to Solomon's son, Rehoboam, for the sake of King David, and Jerusalem, which *Yehovah* had chosen.

This is substantiated in First Kings 11:9–13. In addition, *Yehovah* warned Solomon to repent and return to Him twice, but he did not listen. Therefore, *Yehovah* told Solomon in advance He would tear the kingdom away from him after his death, and give it to Solomon's servant Jeroboam, instead of his son, Rehoboam. First Kings 11:9–13, says the following:

> *"So the LORD became angry with Solomon, BECAUSE his heart had turned from the LORD God of Israel, who had APPEARED to HIM TWICE, and had COMMANDED him CONCERNING this THING, that he should not GO AFTER other GODS; BUT he did*

not KEEP what the LORD had COMMANDED. Therefore the LORD said to Solomon, 'BECAUSE you have DONE THIS, and HAVE not KEPT My **COVENANT** [6] *[H1285: bᵉrîyth: a compact (made by passing between pieces of flesh)] and My* **STATUTES** [7] *[H2708: chûqqâh: appointed, custom, manner or ordinance], which I have COMMANDED you, I will surely TEAR the KINGDOM AWAY from you and GIVE IT to your servant [Jeroboam]. Nevertheless, I will not DO IT in YOUR DAYS, for the SAKE of your father David; I will TEAR IT OUT of the HAND of YOUR SON [Rehoboam]. However I will not TEAR AWAY the WHOLE KINGDOM; I will give ONE TRIBE [the tribe of Judah] to your son [Rehoboam] for the SAKE of My SERVANT DAVID, and for the SAKE of JERUSALEM which I have CHOSEN.'"* (1 Kings 11:9–13, NKJV) (emphasis added).

Therefore, shortly after the Lord had given Solomon the bad news, because he did not keep His "covenant," or His "statutes," we are told in First Kings 11:30–39, *Yehôvâh* sent His prophet, *Ahijah the Shilonite,* to prophetically decree the following: Solomon's servant Jeroboam, would be given ten of the twelve tribes of Israel to rule over which would later become the *northern* kingdom of Israel— the House of Israel (Jacob/Joseph/Ephraim). However, this did not happen until *after* the death of King Solomon. First Kings 11:30–39, says the following:

> *"Then Ahijah took hold of the new garment that was on him, and TORE IT into TWELVE PIECES. And he*

said to Jeroboam, 'Take for yourself *TEN PIECES*, for thus says the L<small>ORD</small>, the God of Israel: 'Behold, I will *TEAR* the *KINGDOM OUT* of the *HAND* of *SOLOMON* and will give *TEN TRIBES* to you [Jeroboam] *(but he* [Rehoboam Solomon's son] *shall have ONE TRIBE for the SAKE of My SERVANT DAVID, and for the SAKE of JERUSALEM, the city which I have chosen out of all the tribes of Israel), BECAUSE they have FORSAKEN Me, and WORSHIPED Ashtoreth the goddess of the Sidonians, Chemosh the god of the Moabites, and Milcom the god of the people of Ammon, and have not WALKED in My WAYS to do what is RIGHT in My EYES and KEEP My STATUTES* [(7)] [H2708: *chûqqâh*: appointed, *custom, manner* or *ordinance*] *and My JUDGMENTS* [(8)] [H4941: *mishpâṭ*: verdict (favorable or unfavorable pronounced judicially, especially a *sentence* or formal decree of divine *law*; including a particular *right*, or *privilege* (statutory or customary), or even a *style*: based on a ceremony or custom, manner of law, ordinance, or sentence], *as did his father David.'"* (1 Kings 11:30-33, NKJV) (emphasis added).

"However I will not take the WHOLE KINGDOM OUT of HIS HAND, because I have made him [Solomon] *RULER all the DAYS of his LIFE for the SAKE of My SERVANT DAVID, whom I chose BECAUSE he KEPT My COMMANDMENTS* [(9)]

[**H4687**: *mitsvah:* a *command*, whether human or divine (collectively the Law); (which was) commanded; law, ordinance, precept] *and My* ***STATUTES*** [7] [**H2708**: *chûqqâh*].*" (1 Kings 11:34, NKJV) (emphasis added).

"But I will take the KINGDOM OUT of HIS SON'S HAND [Rehoboam] *and give it to you* [Jeroboam]— *TEN TRIBES. And to his* [Solomon's] *son* [Rehoboam] *I will give ONE TRIBE* [the tribe of Judah], *that My SERVANT DAVID may always have a LAMP before Me in JERUSALEM, the city which I have chosen for Myself, to put My name there."* (1 Kings 11:35-36, NKJV) (emphasis added).

"So I will take you, and you shall reign over all your heart desires, and you shall be KING over ISRAEL. Then it shall be, if you HEED all that I COMMAND you, WALK in My WAYS, and DO what is RIGHT in My SIGHT, to KEEP My ***STATUTES*** [7] *and My* ***COMMANDMENTS****,* [9] *as My servant David did, then I will be with you and build for you an enduring house, as I built for David, and will give Israel to you. And I will AFFLICT the DESCENDANTS of DAVID BECAUSE of this, BUT not FOREVER."* (1 Kings 11:37-39, NKJV) (emphasis added).

Do not dismiss this fact: Based on First Kings 11:37-39, God said He would afflict the descendants of David—the Jews from the House of Judah. Why would God purposely do this?

God did this because Solomon did not heed all God commanded him by walking in His ways, and doing what was right in His sight, by keeping His statutes, and His commandments, like his father King David, did.

Thus, the people under Solomon's reign followed in his footsteps. Moreover, the primary reason why God tore the kingdom out of the hand of Solomon during his son's reign was for this reason: Solomon and the children of Israel forsook the Lord and worshiped the false gods of the pagan nations instead.

However, God did not tear the kingdom out of the hand of King Solomon until after his death, and his son, Rehoboam, became king. In fact, what God had promised He would do because of their apostasy did not come to pass until the Israelites revolted against Rehoboam in First Kings Chapter 12.

Rehoboam did not listen to the wise advice the elders had given him regarding excessive taxation of the Israelites. Instead, Rehoboam consulted with the young men who had grown up with him, and he acted on their wicked advice, inciting the rebellion of the Israelites to overthrow their current king.

THE TWELVE TRIBES OF ISRAEL WERE DIVIDED INTO TWO "KINGDOMS" AFTER KING SOLOMON'S DEATH

To determine which tribes ended up comprising the *southern* kingdom of Israel under the leadership of Solomon's son Rehoboam—from the *house of David,* we need to look at First

70

Kings 12:20–24, which says the following:

> *"Now it came to pass when all Israel heard that Jeroboam had come back, they sent for him and called him to the congregation, and made him king over all Israel. There was NONE who followed the HOUSE of DAVID, BUT the TRIBE of JUDAH ONLY. And when Rehoboam came to Jerusalem, he assembled all the HOUSE of JUDAH with the TRIBE of BENJAMIN, one hundred and eighty thousand chosen men who were warriors, to fight against the HOUSE of ISRAEL* [the ten remaining tribes of Israel], *that he might restore the kingdom to Rehoboam the son of Solomon. BUT the WORD of GOD came to Shemaiah the man of God, saying, 'Speak to Rehoboam the son of Solomon, king of Judah, to all the House of Judah and Benjamin, and to the rest of the people, saying, 'Thus says the LORD: 'YOU shall not GO UP nor FIGHT AGAINST your BRETHREN the CHILDREN of ISRAEL. Let every man return to his house, for this THING is from Me.' Therefore they OBEYED the WORD of the LORD, and turned back, according to the WORD of the LORD."*
> (1 Kings 12:20–24, NKJV) (emphasis added).

Also, take note of this fact: Even though *Yehovah* said only one tribe would remain under Rehoboam's reign, we are told two tribes—the *tribe of Judah,* and the *tribe of Benjamin* ended up comprising the *southern* kingdom of Israel, under the reign of Rehoboam, Solomon's son. However, like everything else, *Yehovah* foreknew what the people would do, and is why He told Jeroboam to take ten

71

tribes for himself. *Yehôvȧh* knew the *tribe of Benjamin* would take sides with the *tribe of Judah*. Therefore, Israel was divided into two "kingdoms" based on First Kings 12:20–24, because God acted on what He told Solomon would happen during his son's reign if he didn't repent, and heed what the Lord had commanded him.

ISRAEL IS SPLIT INTO TWO "KINGDOMS"

The two "kingdoms" of Israel, with their corresponding tribes, *after* the death of King Solomon, are listed below:

Northern Kingdom: The House of Israel (Jacob/Joseph/Ephraim)

1.   The tribe of Asher
2.   The tribe of Reuben
3.   The tribe of Gad
4.   The tribe of Naphtali
5.   The tribe of Dan
6.   The tribe of Simeon
7.   The tribe of Levi*
8.   The tribe of Issachar
9.   The tribe of Zebulun
10. The tribe of Joseph (Manasseh and Ephraim)

Southern Kingdom: The House of Judah

1.   The tribe of Judah
2.   The tribe of Benjamin

*Based on Joshua 14:3–5 below, the Levites have no inheritance of the land God promised Abraham, and it also specifically says, *"For the CHILDREN of JOSEPH were two TRIBES: Manasseh and Ephraim."* (NKJV) (emphasis added).

> *"For Moses had given the INHERITANCE of the TWO TRIBES and the half-tribe on the other side of the Jordan; but to the LEVITES he had given NO INHERITANCE among them. For the CHILDREN of JOSEPH were TWO TRIBES: Manasseh and Ephraim. And they gave NO PART to the LEVITES in the LAND, except CITIES to DWELL in, with their COMMON-LANDS for their LIVESTOCK and their PROPERTY. As the LORD had commanded Moses, so the CHILDREN of ISRAEL did; and they DIVIDED the LAND."* (Josh. 14:3–5, NKJV) (emphasis added).

Therefore, concerning the Levites, the *Levitical* priesthood, having no inheritance of the land, this is because of many reasons. I will cover this in-depth in Chapter 43 of Book 3.

The *Levitical* priesthood, established under the *order of Aaron,* still exists. However, the *order of the priesthood* is now under the *order of Melchizedek,* rather than the *order of Aaron,* because under the New Covenant, Jesus Christ is our Great High Priest from the *order of Melchizedek.*

This is based on Exodus 29:9, which specifically says concerning the *Levitical* priesthood, *"...The PRIESTHOOD shall be theirs for a* **PERPETUAL** (10) [H5769: *'ōlâm*: perpetual, at any time, (beginning of the) world (+ without end); eternity] ___STATUTE___ ⁽⁷⁾ [H2708: *chúqqáh:* appointed, *custom, manner* or *ordinance*]." (NKJV) (emphasis added).

Therefore, the *order of the Priesthood,* God first established under the *first* covenant in the Old Testament under the *order of Aaron,* has now changed to the *order of Melchizedek,* under the New Covenant. This is based on Hebrews 7:11 below:

> *"Therefore, if PERFECTION were through the LEVITICAL PRIESTHOOD (for under it the people received the law), what further need was there that another PRIEST SHOULD RISE ACCORDING to the ORDER of MELCHIZEDEK, and not be called ACCORDING to the ORDER of AARON?"* (Heb. 7:11, NKJV) (emphasis added).

Now let's refocus our attention on what happened to the twelve tribes of Israel that were divided into two kingdoms *after* the death of King Solomon.

Eventually, the ten tribes of Israel were defeated by Assyria, and they were scattered into all the nations of the world.

Whereas, the *Judean* Kingdom, was carried away to Babylon under the reign of Nebuchadnezzar, *king of Babylon,* for seventy years as prophesied by the prophets Jeremiah and Daniel, in Jeremiah 29:10, and Daniel 9:2, respectively. Therefore, to understand what may have happened to all twelve tribes of Israel throughout the

74

synergy of the ages, we need to look at the back of the Bible in the Book of Revelation.

In Revelation 7:1–8, it says only a total of 144,000 from all the twelve tribes of Israel—not just the Jews from the *tribe of Judah,* are sealed with the "seal of the living God."

This is *before* the angels can harm the earth, sea, or trees during the tribulation period which will happen *before* they are "redeemed" from the earth from amongst men.

This is substantiated in Revelation 7:1–8, which says the following:

> *"After these things I saw four angels standing at the four corners of the earth, holding the four winds of the earth, that the wind should not blow on the earth, on the sea, or on any tree. Then I saw another ANGEL ASCENDING from the EAST, having the SEAL of the LIVING GOD. And he cried with a loud voice to the four angels to whom it was granted to HARM the EARTH and the SEA, saying, 'Do not HARM the EARTH, the SEA, or the TREES till we have SEALED the SERVANTS of our GOD on their FOREHEADS.' And I heard the NUMBER of those who were SEALED. One hundred and forty-four thousand [144,000] of all the TRIBES of the CHILDREN of ISRAEL were sealed: of the TRIBE of JUDAH twelve thousand were sealed; of the TRIBE of REUBEN twelve thousand were sealed; of the TRIBE of GAD twelve thousand were sealed; of the TRIBE of*

> *ASHER twelve thousand were sealed; of the TRIBE of NAPHTALI twelve thousand were sealed; of the TRIBE of MANASSEH twelve thousand were sealed; of the TRIBE of SIMEON twelve thousand were sealed; of the TRIBE of LEVI twelve thousand were sealed; of the TRIBE of ISSACHAR twelve thousand were sealed; of the TRIBE of ZEBULUN twelve thousand were sealed; of the TRIBE of JOSEPH twelve thousand were sealed; of the TRIBE of BENJAMIN twelve thousand were sealed."* (Rev. 7:1–8, NKJV) (emphasis added).

Do not dismiss the significance based on Revelation 7:1–8, the children of Israel from all twelve tribes of Israel, twelve thousand from each tribe, are sealed with the "seal of the living God."

I will cover what the "seal of the living God" is, and who receives it, in Chapter 66 of Book 3. This subject is so critical for God's people to know about, I have devoted an entire chapter to convey the truth about the *spiritual* "mark of God," versus the *spiritual* "mark of the beast."

Now let's refocus our attention on the twelve tribes of Israel, who are categorized into twelve different tribes, according to Jacob's twelve sons, who are the "patriarchs" of the twelve tribes of Israel.

What is very interesting to take notice of is this fact: The twelve tribes of Israel listed in Revelation 7:1–8, are not the same as those who are identified as Jacob's sons in Genesis 35:22–26, which says the following:

"...Now the SONS of JACOB were TWELVE: the sons of Leah were REUBEN, Jacob's firstborn, and SIMEON, LEVI, JUDAH, ISSACHAR, and ZEBULUN; the sons of Rachel were JOSEPH and BENJAMIN; the sons of Bilhah, Rachel's maidservant, were DAN and NAPHTALI; and the sons of Zilpah, Leah's maidservant, were GAD and ASHER. These were the SONS of JACOB who were born to him in Padan Aram." (Gen. 35:22–26, NKJV) (emphasis added).

As such, based on the chart below, which tribe of Israel is missing in Revelation 7:1–8?

	Jacob's 12 sons based on Genesis 35:22–26	The 12 tribes of Israel based on Revelation 7:1–8
1	Judah	Judah
2	Reuben	Reuben
3	Gad	Gad
4	Asher	Asher
5	Naphtali	Naphtali
6	Dan	Manasseh
7	Simeon	Simeon
8	Levi	Levi
9	Issachar	Issachar
10	Zebulun	Zebulun
11	Joseph	Joseph
12	Benjamin	Benjamin

The answer is—Dan! The *tribe of Dan* is excluded from the twelve tribes of Israel, which are sealed with the "seal of the living God," based on Revelation 7:1–8.

The patriarch Jacob (Israel) prophesied in advance what would happen to his son Dan, in the latter days, based on Genesis 49:16–17, which says, *"Dan shall judge his people As one of the tribes of Israel. Dan shall be a SERPENT by the way, a VIPER by the path, That bites the horse's heels So that its rider shall fall backward."* (NKJV) (emphasis added).

So, the next question we need to answer is this: What happened to the *tribe of Dan,* and why is it not listed in Revelation 7:1–8?

Read the Book of Judges, specifically Chapters 17 and 18, to fully understand how the *tribe of Dan* swore by the false gods, and chased after the false idols of the land, and thus, they were destroyed.

In fact, Amos 8:14, sums up what happened to the *tribe of Dan*, or anyone else, who follows the sin of Samaria. Amos 8:14 proclaims the following:

> *"Those who SWEAR BY the SIN of SAMARIA, Who say, 'As your god lives, O Dan!' And, 'As the way of Beersheba lives!' They shall FALL and NEVER RISE AGAIN."* (Amos 8:14, NKJV) (emphasis added).

Moreover, the prophet Micah talks about the transgression of Jacob and the sins of the House of Israel. Micah 1:5, says the following:

78

"All this is for the TRANSGRESSION of JACOB And for the SINS of the HOUSE of ISRAEL. What is the TRANSGRESSION of JACOB? Is it not SAMARIA? And what are the HIGH PLACES of JUDAH? Are THEY not JERUSALEM?" (Micah 1:5, NKJV) (emphasis added).

EPHRAIM IS THE "STICK" OF THE HOUSE OF JOSEPH; MORE COMMONLY REFERRED TO AS THE HOUSE OF ISRAEL

According to Revelation 7:1–8, as illustrated by the chart on page 77, the *tribe of Dan* was replaced with the *tribe of Manasseh*, yet we do not see the *tribe of Ephraim* listed.

So, we must ask ourselves why this is the case, based on this fact: Ephraim, Joseph's *second* born son, received the double-portion blessing from the patriarch Jacob (Israel), instead of Joseph's *firstborn* son, Manasseh.

Remember Joseph's dream? He dreamt his mother, father, and his eleven brothers would all bow down to him. This is based on Genesis 37:9, which says, *"Then he dreamed still another dream and told it to his brothers, and said, 'Look, I have dreamed another dream. And this time, the SUN, the MOON, and the eleven STARS bowed down to me.'"* (NKJV) (emphasis added).

The reason why the *tribe of Ephraim* is not listed individually, yet the *tribe of Manasseh* is listed as part of the ten tribes of Israel

79

(which comprised the *northern* kingdom), is because Ephraim is the "stick" of the House of Joseph, more commonly referred to as the House of Israel.

THE HOUSE OF JUDAH IS THE OTHER STICK

The House of Judah is the other stick, which the Lord will join as one stick, one kingdom, and One New Man in His hand, so a "faithful" remnant of all Israel shall be saved. This is based on the following Scriptures:

> *"As for you, son of man, take a STICK for yourself and write on it: 'For JUDAH and for the CHILDREN of ISRAEL, his companions.' Then take ANOTHER STICK and write on it, 'For JOSEPH, the STICK of EPHRAIM, and for all the HOUSE of ISRAEL, his companions.'"* (Ezek. 37:16, NKJV) (emphasis added).

> *"Say to them, 'Thus says the Lord God: 'Surely I will take the STICK of JOSEPH, which is in the HAND of EPHRAIM, and the TRIBES of ISRAEL, his companions; and I will JOIN THEM with it, with the STICK of JUDAH, and make them ONE STICK, and they will be ONE in My HAND.''"* (Ezek. 37:19, NKJV) (emphasis added).

> *"In those days the HOUSE of JUDAH shall WALK*

*with the HOUSE of ISRAEL, and they shall COME
TOGETHER OUT of the LAND of the NORTH to
the land that I have GIVEN as an INHERITANCE to
YOUR FATHERS."* (Jer. 3:18, NKJV) (emphasis
added).

In other words, Ephraim is comprised of all ten tribes of Israel,
which comprised the *northern* kingdom of Israel, *after* the death of
King Solomon.

Yet it should also include the *tribe of Benjamin,* from the *southern*
kingdom of Israel, for the following reason: Since Joseph is a
prophetic shadow picture of Jesus Christ, and Jesus Christ is from
the *tribe of Judah,* then the *tribe of Judah* would remain "separate,"
and "set apart," from the House of Joseph, until Jesus Christ joined
both houses on the cross at Calvary, *spiritually* speaking.

Jesus Christ is from the one tribe, the *tribe of Judah,* based on what
Yehovah said in First Kings 12:20–24, that would remain under the
House of David.

As such, this is why Jesus Christ's genealogy specifically says in
Matthew 1:1, *"The BOOK of the GENEALOGY of Jesus Christ, the
SON of DAVID, the Son of Abraham..."* (NKJV) (emphasis added).

Hence, those descendants who are referred to as the "Son of
David," are specifically the Jews, from the *tribe of Judah,* which also
includes the children of Israel from the *tribe of Benjamin.*

Both the *tribe of Judah* and the *tribe of Benjamin* remained loyal to
each other because of the bond of love and friendship between

Jonathan and David when they established a covenant with each other based on First Samuel 18:3.

Whereas, those descendants who are referred to as the "Son of Abraham," are those of us who *were* formerly Gentiles from the House of Israel (Jacob/Joseph/Ephraim), who have now been grafted into the commonwealth of Israel by our faith in Jesus Christ.

In other words, we are the *spiritual* descendants who are from the remaining ten tribes of Israel, which were scattered all over the earth, as it is to *this* very day.

Therefore, both houses—the House of Judah, and the House of Israel would play an instrumental role leading up to the birth of our Jewish Messiah, Jesus Christ. This is why Jesus' genealogy says He is both the "Son of David" and the "Son of Abraham."

Moreover, the following would come to pass: Both houses—the House of Judah, and the House of Israel would be offered a New Covenant, in and through, Jesus Christ, so a "faithful" remnant of all Israel shall be saved!

This was and is God's "eternal" plan of salvation for all the children of Israel, despite their *spiritual* harlotry—which was committed against *Yehôvah* by both houses!

All twelve tribes of Israel—both houses, committed *spiritual* harlotry against *Yehôvah*. As such, He rendered His judgment on both the House of Israel (Jacob/Joseph/Ephraim) and the House of Judah, throughout the *synergy of the ages*. This truth is substantiated in the following Scriptures:

> *"'For the HOUSE of ISRAEL and the HOUSE of JUDAH Have dealt very TREACHEROUSLY with Me,' says the Lord."* (Jer. 5:11, NKJV) (emphasis added).

> *"They have TURNED BACK to the* **INIQUITIES** [11] [H5771: *'ávón: perversity*, that is, (moral) *evil:* fault, iniquity, mischief, punishment (of iniquity), sin] *of their FOREFATHERS who refused to HEAR My WORDS, and they have gone after OTHER GODS to SERVE THEM; the HOUSE of ISRAEL and the HOUSE of JUDAH have BROKEN My* **COVENANT** [6] [H1285: *b'riyth*: a *compact* (made by passing between *pieces* of flesh)] *which I made with their FATHERS* [Abraham, Isaac, and Jacob]."* (Jer. 11:10, NKJV) (emphasis added).

> *"For the Lord of hosts, who planted you, has pronounced DOOM against you for the EVIL of the HOUSE of ISRAEL and of the HOUSE of JUDAH, which they have DONE against THEMSELVES to provoke Me to ANGER in OFFERING INCENSE to BAAL."* (Jer. 11:17, NKJV) (emphasis added).

> *"'For as the sash clings to the waist of a man, so I have caused the whole HOUSE of ISRAEL and the whole HOUSE of JUDAH to cling to Me,' says the Lord, 'that they may BECOME My people, for RENOWN, for PRAISE, and for GLORY; BUT they would not HEAR.'"* (Jer. 13:11, NKJV) (emphasis added).

"'Behold, the days are coming,' says the Lord, 'that I will sow the HOUSE of ISRAEL and the HOUSE of JUDAH with the SEED of MAN and the SEED of BEAST.'" (Jer. 31:27, NKJV) (emphasis added).

*"Then He said to me, 'The **INIQUITY** [11] [H5771: 'āvôn: perversity, that is, (moral) evil: fault, iniquity, mischief, punishment (of iniquity), sin] of the HOUSE of ISRAEL and JUDAH is exceedingly GREAT, and the LAND is full of BLOODSHED, and the CITY full of PERVERSITY; for they say, 'The Lord has FORSAKEN the LAND, and the Lord DOES not SEE!'"* (Ezek. 9:9, NKJV) (emphasis added).

[God's Charge Against Ephraim] "Ephraim has encircled Me with LIES, And the HOUSE of ISRAEL with DECEIT; But JUDAH still WALKS with GOD, Even with the Holy One who is FAITHFUL." (Hos. 11:12, NKJV) (emphasis added).

Now read Hosea 11:12 again, and understand this is a "now" word for those of us who were formerly Gentiles, from the House of Israel, who have now have been grafted into the commonwealth of Israel, by our faith in Jesus Christ.

The reason why the House of Israel is filled with deceit even though the Jews from the House of Judah still walks with God is because we do not know the Torah, let alone walk according to it. This is due to the false teachings in the body of Christ. As a result, we totally disregard our heavenly Father's instructions written in the Torah because we have been erroneously taught the Old Covenant is now obsolete. To the contrary! In fact, God's law written in the Torah is what converts our soul and makes us fully mature in Christ lacking nothing.

MANY BELIEVERS FROM THE HOUSE OF ISRAEL DO NOT WALK IN A "COVENANT" RELATIONSHIP WITH OUR HEAVENLY FATHER BECAUSE WE ARE "DECEIVED"

Unfortunately, for the most part, those of us who are from the House of Israel do not walk in a "covenant" relationship with our heavenly Father, *Yehôvah*.

Yet the Jews from the House of Judah walk in a covenant relationship with Him for this reason: The Jews from the House of Judah "keep" God's *everlasting* covenants (plural), which includes His *everlasting* ordinances, statutes, and judgments.

This also includes "keeping" and "observing" God's seven holy convocations based on Leviticus 23, which is a result of the *everlasting* covenant God established with Abraham and his descendants.

The primary reason why those of us who are from the House of Israel do not "walk" in a covenant relationship with our heavenly Father is because we have been led "astray" and are "deceived" about "who" Israel is! We are deceived about who Israel is because we do not understand our "Hebraic" roots in Christianity.

THE BODY OF CHRIST IS ISRAEL!

We constantly talk and preach about the "Church" and "Israel" as if they are two separate entities because we do not understand our "Hebraic" roots in Christianity—or who we are in Christ.

We do not grasp what the fundamental purpose of the Bible is in its entirety.

The main reason we have been led "astray," and are "deceived," is for this reason: The House of Israel is not properly "discipled," and we do not understand all of God's *everlasting* covenants (plural), especially concerning what the New Covenant truly is.

And, it is for this very reason; I have devoted Chapter 40 of Book 3, to cover what the New Covenant is in detail.

If we are to come back to the "ancient" path, we must understand the "root" of the *everlasting* covenant established by God with Abraham and his descendants.

Then God's people, from the House of Israel, must know and understand our "Hebraic" roots in Christianity. This is the only way we can preach, hear, and walk according to the *gospel of the kingdom* that was once delivered to the saints.

Again, *the Word* was sent to the earth the first time as the Son of Man in the Person of Jesus Christ, by our heavenly Father, *Yehôvâh,* to be the "mediator" of the New Covenant for both the House of Judah, and the House of Israel, which Jesus Christ fulfilled (consummated, executed, ratified [confirmed]) with His precious blood.

As such, we now have no legitimate excuse for not keeping God's law. Jesus did not do away with God's law on the cross at Calvary.

In fact, under the New Covenant, God has now put His laws in our mind, and written them on our hearts, instead of on two tablets of stone, because our Lawgiver now lives in us through His Holy Spirit.

The Holy Spirit gives us God's grace and power to obey God's laws. Therefore, the same power that raised Christ from the grave is living in every blood-bought disciple of Jesus Christ!

IN THESE FINAL HOURS GOD IS "RESTORING" AND "RECONCILING" BOTH THE HOUSE OF JUDAH AND THE HOUSE OF ISRAEL SO A "FAITHFUL" REMNANT OF ISRAEL SHALL BE SAVED

We are fast approaching the "midnight" hour, which will usher in the return of Jesus Christ. Our heavenly Father, *Yehôvah,* is in the process of fully "restoring" and "reconciling" both the House of Judah, and the House of Israel, into "One New Man" in the *physical,* earthly realm. God is doing this, so a "faithful" remnant of Israel shall be saved based on the following Scriptures:

> *"And it shall COME TO PASS That just as you were a CURSE AMONG the NATIONS, O HOUSE of JUDAH and HOUSE of ISRAEL, So I will SAVE you,*

and you shall be a BLESSING. Do not fear, Let your hands be strong." (Zech. 8:13, NKJV) (emphasis added).

"I will strengthen the HOUSE of JUDAH, And I will save the HOUSE of JOSEPH. I will bring them back, BECAUSE I have MERCY on them. They shall be as though I had not CAST them ASIDE; For I am the LORD their God, And I will hear them." (Zech. 10:6, NKJV) (emphasis added).

[The Remnant of Israel Saved] *"At the same time,' says the Lord, 'I will be the God of all the FAMILIES of ISRAEL, and they shall be My PEOPLE.'"* (Jer. 31:1, NKJV) (emphasis added).

"But Israel shall be SAVED by the Lord With an everlasting SALVATION; You shall not be ASHAMED or DISGRACED forever and ever." (Isa. 45:17, NKJV) (emphasis added).

For further understanding, read all of Zechariah Chapter 10, which talks about the full restoration of both the House of Judah and the House of Israel.

It is because of God's mercy He will strengthen the House of Judah and save the House of Joseph and bring them back as one stick in His hand as we become One New Man in the *physical* earthly realm. This must happen before our heavenly Father will send Jesus Christ for His bride.

GOD IS RAISING UP A "BRANCH OF HIS RIGHTEOUSNESS" THAT SHALL "EXECUTE" HIS *JUSTICE,* HIS *RIGHTEOUSNESS,* AND HIS *JUDGMENTS,* IN THE EARTH

In this hour, our heavenly Father, *Yehôvah,* is looking for those who will worship Him, in both Spirit, and in truth. This is based on John 4:23, which says, *"But the HOUR is COMING, and NOW is, when the true WORSHIPERS will WORSHIP the FATHER in SPIRIT and TRUTH; for the FATHER is SEEKING such to WORSHIP Him."* (NKJV) (emphasis added).

As such, our heavenly Father is expecting His people, to be a "branch of His righteousness," who shall "execute" His *justice,* His *righteousness,* and His *judgments,* in the earth until Shiloh (Jesus) comes back.

Therefore, we must continually offer ourselves as a "living sacrifice" as His *royal* priesthood and a *holy* nation.

I will cover this fact in-depth in Chapters 60–62 of Book 3, regarding the true meaning of the *Parable of the Wise and Foolish Virgins,* Jesus talks about in Matthew Chapter 25. For only the *wise* virgins will be "known" or "chosen" as the *bride of Christ!*

As we are already witnessing, just before the second coming of Jesus Christ happens, God is indeed "raising up" to David, a "branch of righteousness," who will "execute" God's *judgments,* and His *righteousness,* in the earth as it is in heaven. This is based on Jeremiah 33:14–18, which says the following:

> *"'Behold, the days are coming,' says the LORD, 'that I will perform that GOOD THING which I have PROMISED to the HOUSE of ISRAEL and to the HOUSE of JUDAH: 'In those days and at that time I will cause to GROW UP to David a BRANCH of RIGHTEOUSNESS; He shall execute JUDGMENT and RIGHTEOUSNESS in the EARTH. In those days JUDAH will be SAVED, And JERUSALEM will DWELL safely. And this is the NAME by which she will be called: THE LORD OUR RIGHTEOUSNESS.' For thus says the LORD: 'David shall never lack a MAN to SIT on the THRONE of the HOUSE of ISRAEL; nor shall the PRIESTS, the LEVITES, lack a MAN to offer BURNT OFFERINGS before Me, to kindle grain offerings, and to SACRIFICE continually.'"* (Jer. 33:14–18, NKJV) (emphasis added).

And last, but certainly not least, God will accomplish this through those who will honor His *everlasting* covenants (plural), *Yehovah* established with both Abraham, and King David, which is why Jesus Christ's genealogy will include a "faithful" remnant who are descendants of both houses!

Therefore, in Chapter 3, we will take an in-depth look at why Jesus Christ's genealogy begins with Abraham, rather than Adam, or Seth.

CHAPTER 3

THE GENEALOGY OF JESUS CHRIST IS ROOTED IN THE ABRAHAMIC COVENANT

According to biblical history, the genealogy of Jesus Christ begins with Abraham, because of the *everlasting* covenant God established with him. Forty-two *generations* later, Jesus was born from the "seed" of the woman as proclaimed by God in the very beginning. This is based on Genesis 3:15, which says, *"And I will put **ENMITY*** [(1)] **[H342: *'êybâh: hostility:* hatred]** *Between YOU and the WOMAN, And between YOUR SEED and HER SEED; He shall bruise your head, And you shall bruise His heel."* (NKJV) (emphasis added).

In addition, Matthew 1:17, substantiates this truth as it proclaims, *"So all the GENERATIONS from Abraham to David are FOURTEEN GENERATIONS, from David until the captivity in Babylon are FOURTEEN GENERATIONS, and from the captivity in Babylon until the CHRIST are FOURTEEN GENERATIONS."* (NKJV) (emphasis added).

Moreover, the number eight, as used in the Bible, means a "new beginning," and this is what God orchestrated through Noah, and his family when God wiped out all the *unrepentant* wicked inhabitants off the face of the earth with the flood.

Therefore, the "new beginning" for all mankind, and creation, was made possible by Noah's *righteousness* by which he "condemned" the world, and became the heir of the *righteousness* which is according to "faith" based on Hebrews 11:7. As such, it is not a coincidence the total number of survivors who were alive and remained (survived) the flood, were a total of eight people.

This is based on Genesis 6:18 and Second Peter 2:4–10. Pay attention to Second Peter 2:4–10, which is a Scripture in the New Testament. It is also a "now" word for those who choose to walk in *unrighteousness*, particularly to those who are false teachers in the body of Christ. Genesis 6:18 and Second Peter 2:4–10, says the following:

> *"But I will establish My COVENANT with you* [Noah]*; and you shall go into the ark—you, your sons, your wife, and your sons' wives with you."* (Gen. 6:18, NKJV) (emphasis added).

> *"For if God did not SPARE the ANGELS WHO SINNED, but CAST THEM DOWN TO HELL and DELIVERED THEM INTO CHAINS OF DARKNESS, to be RESERVED for JUDGMENT; and did not SPARE the ANCIENT WORLD, but SAVED Noah, ONE of EIGHT PEOPLE, a PREACHER of RIGHTEOUSNESS, bringing in the FLOOD on the WORLD of the UNGODLY; and turning the cities of Sodom and Gomorrah into ashes, CONDEMNED them to DESTRUCTION, making them an EXAMPLE to those who AFTERWARD would LIVE UNGODLY; and delivered RIGHTEOUS LOT, who was OPPRESSED by the FILTHY CONDUCT of the WICKED (for that righteous man, dwelling among*

them, TORMENTED his RIGHTEOUS SOUL from day to day by SEEING and HEARING their LAWLESS deeds)— then the Lord knows how to DELIVER the GODLY OUT of TEMPTATIONS and to RESERVE the UNJUST under PUNISHMENT for the DAY of JUDGMENT, and especially those who WALK ACCORDING to the FLESH in the LUST of UNCLEANNESS and DESPISE AUTHORITY. They are presumptuous, self-willed." (2 Pet. 2:4–10, NKJV) (emphasis added).

There are those who are "presumptuous" and think the God of the Old Testament is not the same God of the New Testament. Many believers are of the "opinion" God has suddenly changed His mind since we live in the twenty-first century. As such, they think what He said at the beginning of the Bible is no longer relevant. Yet this "mindset" is contrary to His "eternal" Word which does not change, and it shall never pass away!

For God's "eternal" Word miraculously weaves all the different prophecies and Scriptures together in perfect harmony with one another. Therefore, we must study the whole counsel of God's Word by following the "how to" instructions found in Isaiah 28:10, which says, *"For precept must be upon precept, precept upon precept, line upon line, line upon line, here a little, there a little."* (NKJV)

In addition, Bible prophecy details history in advance, because history is His Story, and God knows the end from the beginning. Therefore, if God said it, then it shall come to pass because *"it is written…"*

Who is Israel? Discovering our True Identity in Jesus Christ and Why it Matters! The Foundation

Now let's refocus our attention on the genealogy of Jesus Christ. This is based on Matthew 1:1–16, which says the following:

> *"The BOOK of the GENEALOGY of JESUS CHRIST, the SON of DAVID, the SON of ABRAHAM: Abraham begot ISAAC, Isaac begot JACOB, and JACOB begot JUDAH and his BROTHERS [the patriarchs of the twelve tribes of Israel]. Judah begot Perez and Zerah by TAMAR, Perez begot Hezron, and Hezron begot Ram. Ram begot Amminadab, Amminadab begot Nahshon, and Nahshon begot Salmon. Salmon begot Boaz by RAHAB, Boaz begot Obed by RUTH, Obed begot Jesse, and Jesse begot DAVID the KING. David the king begot Solomon by her who had been the WIFE of URIAH [Bathsheba]..."* (Matt. 1:1–6, NKJV) (emphasis added).

> *"Solomon begot Rehoboam, Rehoboam begot Abijah, and Abijah begot Asa. Asa begot Jehoshaphat, Jehoshaphat begot Joram, and Joram begot Uzziah. Uzziah begot Jotham, Jotham begot Ahaz, and Ahaz begot Hezekiah. Hezekiah begot Manasseh, Manasseh begot Amon, and Amon begot Josiah. Josiah begot Jeconiah and his brothers about the time they were carried away to Babylon."* (Matt. 1:7–11, NKJV) (emphasis added).

> *"And after they were brought to Babylon, Jeconiah begot Shealtiel, and Shealtiel begot Zerubbabel.*

Zerubbabel begot Abiud, Abiud begot Eliakim, and Eliakim begot Azor. Azor begot Zadok, Zadok begot Achim, and Achim begot Eliud. Eliud begot Eleazar, Eleazar begot Matthan, and Matthan begot Jacob. And Jacob begot Joseph the husband of MARY, of whom was born JESUS who is called Christ." (Matt. 1:12–16, NKJV) (emphasis added).

Notice based on Jesus' genealogy, as detailed in Matthew 1:1–16, it does not begin with Adam or with Seth. Why? Because God established with Noah and his family a "new beginning" for all mankind and creation when He killed all the *unrepentant* wicked inhabitants off the face of the earth with the flood.

It is for this very reason, the genealogy of Jesus Christ, the "Son of David," and the "Son of Abraham," starts with Abraham, Isaac, and Jacob, which is based on the *everlasting* covenant God established with Abraham and his descendants referred to as the *Abrahamic* covenant.

In addition, God also established an *everlasting* covenant with King David, which would result in Jesus Christ being the *firstborn* "Son of David," and the *firstborn* "Son of Abraham," *spiritually* speaking.

Therefore, Jesus Christ would bring forth other "spiritual" descendants, who would place their faith and trust in Him. As such, *Yehôvah* would have many sons and daughters who would be "spiritual" descendants of both Abraham and King David.

Moreover, *Yehôvah* pledged His throne to protect, defend, and uphold the *Abrahamic* covenant. And, as long as the sun, moon, and stars give their light, until the heavens and this earth passes away, the covenant *Yehôvah* established with King David is still valid as well.

Also, worth mentioning at this time is this fact: God made an exception when He chose to list women in Jesus' genealogy in Matthew 1:1–16, because usually only select sons are mentioned in the genealogies listed in the Bible.

Yet God chose to list women who were instrumental in His "eternal" plan to ensure the *spiritual* lineage resulting in the birth of His only *begotten* Son, Jesus Christ, would indeed come to pass. This is based on Genesis 3:15, which says, *"And I will put **ENMITY** (1) [H342: 'éybah: hostility: hatred] Between YOU and THE WOMAN, And between YOUR SEED and HER SEED; He shall bruise your head, And you shall bruise His heel."* (NKJV) (emphasis added).

It is for this very reason; God specifically lists Tamar, Rahab, Ruth, Bathsheba—the *wife of Uriah*, and Mary, who was highly favored by God, who conceived and gave birth to Jesus when the Holy Spirit overshadowed her.

Share this with anyone who tells you God does not permit women to be used in ministry, especially given the fact the apostle Paul says to us in Galatians 3:28-29, *"There is neither JEW nor GREEK [Gentile], there is neither SLAVE nor FREE, there is neither MALE nor FEMALE; for you are all ONE in CHRIST JESUS. And if you are CHRIST'S, then you are ABRAHAM'S SEED, and HEIRS according to the PROMISE."* (NKJV) (emphasis added).

In addition, we need to take a closer look at Jesus' genealogy once again as detailed in Matthew 1:1–3 below. Do not dismiss the significance that Judah, the *fourth* born son, is listed as the *firstborn* of Jacob's sons in Jesus' genealogy instead of Reuben who was Jacob's *firstborn* son, followed by Jacob's *second* born son Simeon, and Jacob's *third* born son Levi.

> *"The BOOK of the GENEALOGY of Jesus Christ, the SON of DAVID, the SON of ABRAHAM: Abraham begot ISAAC, Isaac begot JACOB, and Jacob begot JUDAH and his BROTHERS* [the patriarchs of the twelve tribes of Israel]. *JUDAH begot PEREZ and Zerah by Tamar..."* (Matt. 1:1–3, NKJV) (emphasis added).

Why is Judah, the only son of Jacob that is specifically listed in Jesus' genealogy? The answer is given to us in Genesis Chapter 49, when Jacob called his sons and said, *"Gather together, that I may tell you what shall BEFALL you in the LAST DAYS..."* (NKJV) (emphasis added).

Jacob specifically said of Reuben, his *firstborn* son, in Genesis 49:3–4, *"Reuben, you are my firstborn, My might and the beginning of my strength, The excellency of dignity and the excellency of power. UNSTABLE AS WATER, you shall not EXCEL, Because you went up to your FATHER'S BED; Then you DEFILED it—He went up to my couch."* (NKJV) (emphasis added).

Moreover, Jacob specifically said to both Simeon and Levi, who both forfeited their "birthright" by their *unrighteous* works (deeds), in Genesis 49:5–7, the following:

97

> *"Simeon and Levi are brothers; INSTRUMENTS of CRUELTY are in their dwelling place. Let not MY SOUL enter THEIR COUNCIL; Let not MY HONOR be UNITED to their ASSEMBLY; For in their ANGER they SLEW a MAN, And in their self-will they hamstrung an ox. CURSED be their ANGER, for it is FIERCE; And their WRATH, for it is CRUEL! I will DIVIDE them in Jacob And SCATTER them in ISRAEL."* (Gen. 49:5–7, NKJV) (emphasis added).

We must also remember Joseph's dream where his eleven brothers were bowing down to him in Genesis 37:9, which says, *"Then he dreamed still another dream and told it to his brothers, and said, 'Look, I have dreamed another dream. And this time, the SUN, the MOON, and the eleven STARS bowed down to me.'"* (NKJV) (emphasis added).

What Jacob prophesied to Judah in Genesis 49:8–12, would be a partial fulfillment of Joseph's dream that his mother, father, and brothers would all bow down to him for this reason: Joseph was a prophetic shadow picture of Jesus Christ!

The ultimate fulfillment of this dream will happen just before the return of Jesus Christ when the sun, the moon, and the stars no longer give their light based on the *everlasting* covenant God established with King David. Now pay close attention to the words spoken from the patriarch Jacob, whose name was changed to Israel, as he prophetically declares the revelation of Jesus Christ, our Jewish Messiah, who would come through the *tribe of Judah* by what was spoken over Jacob's *fourth* born son, Judah, in Genesis 49:8–12 below:

> *"JUDAH, you are he whom YOUR BROTHERS shall PRAISE; YOUR HAND shall be on the NECK OF YOUR ENEMIES; Your FATHER'S CHILDREN shall BOW DOWN before YOU. Judah is a LION'S WHELP; From the prey, my son, YOU HAVE GONE UP. He bows down, he lies down as a LION; And as a LION, who shall rouse him? The SCEPTER shall not DEPART from JUDAH, Nor a LAWGIVER from between his feet, Until SHILOH* (2) [H7886: shîylôh: tranquil; Shiloh, an epithet of the Messiah] *COMES; And to Him shall be the OBEDIENCE of the PEOPLE."* (Gen. 49:8–10, NKJV) (emphasis added).

> *"Binding his donkey to the vine, And his donkey's colt to the choice vine, He WASHED His GARMENTS in WINE, And His CLOTHES in the BLOOD of GRAPES. His eyes are darker than wine, And his teeth whiter than milk."* (Gen. 49:11–12, NKJV) (emphasis added).

In addition, in Matthew 1:1–6, which details Jesus' genealogy, notice it specifically says in Matthew 1:3, *"Judah begot PEREZ and Zerah by TAMAR..."* (NKJV) (emphasis added).

As such, this seemingly scandalous union between Judah and Tamar did eventually result in the birth of King David with whom God made an *everlasting* covenant, which would be fulfilled by Jesus Christ in His first and second coming.

Also, worth mentioning is this revelation the Holy Spirit gave me which is this: Since Judah is the *fourth* born son of Jacob and he is the only son of Jacob listed in Jesus' genealogy, the symbolic meaning of the number four is made up of three and one (3+1=4); therefore, it denotes and marks that which follows the revelation of God concerning the Godhead, namely His "creative" works.

God is known by His "creative" works, which can be seen. Hence, the apostle Paul substantiates this fact in Ephesians 3:8–12, which says the following:

> *"To me, who am less than the least of all the saints, this grace was given, that I should preach among the Gentiles the unsearchable riches of Christ, and to make all see what is the fellowship of the mystery, which FROM the BEGINNING of the AGES* (3) [G165: *aiōn*: an *age*; by extension *perpetuity* (also past); by implication the *world* from the beginning of the world which began and is without end; eternal, forevermore] *has been HIDDEN in God who CREATED* (4) [G2936: *ktizō*: to *fabricate*, that is, *found* (*form* originally); create, Creator, make] *all THINGS through JESUS CHRIST; to the intent that NOW the manifold WISDOM of GOD might be made KNOWN by the CHURCH* (5) [G1577: *ekklēsia*: a *calling out*, that is, (concretely) a popular *meeting*, especially a religious *congregation* (Jewish *synagogue*, or Christian community of members on earth or saints in heaven or both); assembly] *to the PRINCIPALITIES and POWERS in the heavenly*

*places ACCORDING to the **ETERNAL** [3]* [G165: *aiōn*]
*PURPOSE WHICH HE ACCOMPLISHED in CHRIST
JESUS OUR LORD, in whom we have boldness and
access with confidence through faith in Him."* (Eph.
3:8–12, NKJV) (emphasis added).

Therefore, my dear sisters and brothers in Christ, let's ponder the
following questions:

❖ Who is the *firstborn* over all creation and the image of the
"Invisible" God based on Colossians 1:15?

❖ Who is our heavenly Father's *firstborn* and only *begotten*
Son, who was conceived by the Holy Spirit, and born of a
woman named Mary, for she was a virgin, and highly favored
by God based on Matthew 1:25?

❖ Who is the *firstborn* of those whom He foreknew, He also
predestined to be conformed to the image of His Son so that
He might be the *firstborn* among many brethren based on
Romans 8:29?

❖ Who is the *head* of the body of Christ—His Ekklēsía, who is
the beginning, and He is also the *firstborn* from the dead, so
that in all things, He may have preeminence based on
Colossians 1:18?

❖ Who is the *firstborn* to the general assembly and His Ekklēsía
of those who are registered in heaven to God the Judge of all
and the spirits of just men made perfect based on Hebrews
12:23?

Who is Israel? Discovering our True Identity in Jesus Christ and Why it Matters! The Foundation

- ❖ Who is the faithful witness, the *firstborn* from the dead, and the ruler over the kings of the earth based on Revelation 1:5?

- ❖ Who has our heavenly Father, *Yehôvah,* made as His *firstborn,* the highest of the kings of the earth which is based on Psalm 89:27?

The answer is *the Word* who, according to John 1:1, was with God from the very beginning, and is God. The *eternal* Word is the *firstborn* over all creation, and He is in the image of the "invisible" God whom our heavenly Father, *Yehôvah,* sent to the earth as the Son of Man in the Person of Jesus Christ, who is our Lord and Savior!

This is how our heavenly Father, *Yehôvah,* will accomplish His "eternal" plan of "redemption," "reconciliation," and "restoration" for the entire world, including its inhabitants, throughout the *synergy of the ages.* This will be according to all His *everlasting* covenants (plural), He has established with mankind, and creation, according to His "eternal" Word.

Our heavenly Father would send *the Word* to the earth as the Son of Man in the Person of Jesus Christ for this reason: He would fulfill (consummate, execute, and ratify [confirm]) the testimony of His heavenly Father written in the Torah with His precious blood.

In summary, we may be the final generation that will "see" and "experience" the total fulfillment of everything our heavenly Father has "decreed" and "established" since the foundation of the world, He has already accomplished in the *spiritual,* heavenly realm!

102

As such, this final generation was "predestined" and "preordained" by our heavenly Father to be born for a time such as this. This final generation will be used by Him for His "eternal" purposes and His "eternal" glory to prevail, so we may fulfill His "eternal" destiny in the *physical* earthly realm. He will use His people to make the nations of the world His inheritance, and His enemies His footstool, because *"it is written..."*

Hallelujah! What an exciting time it is to be alive and be used by God for "a cause greater than ourselves!"

In Chapter 4, I will convey how the prophetic dream God gave to Joseph of the sun, the moon, and the *eleven* stars bowing down to him, would culminate into the ultimate fulfillment of God's promise to both Abraham and King David. This is based on His *everlasting* covenants (plural) *Yehôvâh* established with them. Both of these *everlasting* covenants (plural) are still in effect and will be until the sun, the moon, and the stars no longer give their light when the heavens and this earth shall pass away ushering in the second coming of Jesus Christ.

Who is Israel? Discovering our True Identity in Jesus Christ and Why it Matters! The Foundation

CHAPTER 4

THE PROPHETIC MEANING OF JOSEPH'S DREAM OF THE SUN, THE MOON, AND THE ELEVEN STARS BOWING DOWN TO HIM

J oseph was a dreamer! Yet his experience for many years was a "contradiction" to what God had shown him in a dream as a young lad. This dream would ultimately result in Joseph saving God's people during a time of severe famine. However, there is much more to this prophetic dream Joseph was given by God; we need to understand.

Therefore, in this chapter, I will convey several different meanings of this prophetic dream Joseph was given by God as a young boy.

According to Genesis 37:9, we are told Joseph dreamed still another dream and told it to his brothers. Moreover, I will convey the total fulfillment of this dream, which is based on the *everlasting* covenant God established with King David, which shall fulfill the following Scriptures:

> *"Once I have SWORN by My HOLINESS; I will not LIE to David: his SEED shall ENDURE FOREVER, And his THRONE as the SUN before Me; It shall be ESTABLISHED forever like the MOON, Even like the faithful witness in the sky." Selah* (Psalm 89:35–37, NKJV) (emphasis added).

> *"I have SWORN by MYSELF; The WORD has gone OUT of My MOUTH in RIGHTEOUSNESS, And*

105

> shall *not* RETURN, That to Me *every* KNEE shall
> BOW, *Every* TONGUE shall TAKE an OATH." (Isa.
> 45:23, NKJV) (emphasis added).

> *"For it is written: 'As I live, says the Lord, Every KNEE
> shall BOW to Me, And every TONGUE shall
> CONFESS to God.'"* (Rom. 14:11, NKJV) (emphasis
> added).

Now let's begin our journey to understand what this prophetic
dream Joseph had, as detailed in Genesis 37:9 below, means to us as
New Covenant believers in Jesus Christ.

> *"Then he dreamed still another dream and told it to*
> *his brothers, and said, 'Look, I have dreamed another*
> *dream. And this time, the* **SUN** (1) [H8121: **shemesh**:
> to be *brilliant*; the *sun*; by implication the *east*], *the*
> **MOON** (2) (3) [H3394: **yârêach**: literally the moon;
> H3391: **yerach:** signification; a *lunation*, that is,
> *month*], *and the eleven* **STARS** (4) [H3556: **kôkâb**: a
> star in the sense of *rolling* or *blazing*; or figuratively a
> prince] *BOWED DOWN to me.'"* (Gen. 37:9, NKJV)
> (emphasis added).

While this passage of Scripture is referring to the *physical* sun,
moon, and stars in the *heavenly* realm, the sun, and the moon, in
Joseph's dream is symbolic of his mother Rachel, and his father
Jacob, as we are clearly told in Genesis 37:10–11. Moreover, the
eleven stars are symbolic for Joseph's eleven brothers from the
twelve tribes of Israel. Joseph did not include himself because he

had the dream. Keep in mind Joseph is a prophetic shadow picture of Jesus Christ. Genesis 37:10–11, says the following:

> *"So he told it to his father and his brothers; and his father rebuked him and said to him, 'What is this dream that you have dreamed? Shall your MOTHER* [Rachel] *and I* [Jacob] *and YOUR BROTHERS* [symbolic of the eleven stars] *indeed come to BOW DOWN to the EARTH before you?' And his brothers envied him, but his father kept the matter in mind."* (Gen. 37:10–11, NKJV) (emphasis added).

Therefore, we need to determine which parent is symbolic of the moon, and which parent is symbolic of the sun, because based on Genesis 37:10–11, Jacob interprets Joseph's dream to include his eleven brothers—represented by the eleven stars, Jacob, Joseph's father, and Rachel, Joseph's mother.

In addition, we know based on the following Scriptures, Joseph's brothers did *literally* bow down to Joseph when he was governor of Egypt, and he was selling food during the famine.

> *"Now Joseph was governor over the land; and it was he who SOLD to all the people of the land. And Joseph's BROTHERS came and BOWED DOWN before him with their FACES to the EARTH."* (Gen. 42:6, NKJV) (emphasis added).

> *"And when Joseph came home, they brought him the present which was in their hand into the house, and BOWED DOWN before him to the EARTH."* (Gen.

107

43:26, NKJV) (emphasis added).

And, we are told in Genesis 47:31, his father, Israel (Jacob), bowed himself on the head of the bed when Jacob asked Joseph to swear to him that he would not bury him in Egypt and Joseph responded, *"I will do as you have said."*

In Joseph's dream, he said his father, his mother, and his eleven brothers would bow down to him. Yet the Bible only gives the account of his brothers and his father *literally* bowing down to him, while his mother, who had already died, did not. Therefore, there must be a *spiritual* fulfillment of Joseph's dream we need to understand, and indeed there is.

THE SYMBOLIC MEANING OF THE GREAT "SIGN" OF A WOMAN IN HEAVEN BASED ON REVELATION 12:1–2

In order to determine which parent the sun, and the moon, is symbolic of in Joseph's dream, we need to look in the Book of Revelation, written by the apostle John, who describes his vision of a great sign in heaven of a woman. Revelation 12:1–2, says the following:

> *"Now a GREAT SIGN appeared in HEAVEN: a* **WOMAN** (5) [G1135: *gunē: a woman*; specifically a *wife*; the *Bethulah* constellation; Virgo—the virgin], *clothed with the* **SUN** (6) (7) [G2246: *hēlios*: the *sun*; by implication *light:* + east G138: to *take for oneself*, that

108

is, to *prefer*] *with the* **MOON** [8] [9] [G4582: *selēnē:* selas (*brilliancy;* the idea of *attractiveness* G138: to *take for oneself,* that is, to *prefer*] *under her* **FEET** [10] [G4228: *pous:* "foot" or footstool], *and on her* **HEAD** [11] [G2776: *kephalē:* (in the sense of *seizing*); the *head* (as the part most readily *taken* hold of)] *a* **GARLAND** [12] [G4735: *stephanos:* a badge of royalty or crown] *of TWELVE* **STARS** [13] [G792: *astēr:* a star (as *strown* over the sky)]. *Then being with child, she cried out in labor and in pain to give birth."* (Rev. 12:1–2, NKJV) (emphasis added).

Again, while this passage of Scripture in Revelation 12:1–2, is referring to the *physical* sun, moon, and the stars in the heavenly realm that are in constellations *E'lōhim* created, the "woman" in this Scripture represents Israel, who is married to the Creator of the heavens and the earth.

The word "sun" as used in this Scripture represents Jesus Christ— who is the *Bright and Morning Star,* which rises in the *physical* earthly realm from the East. In fact, we are told in Matthew 2:2, and Matthew 2:9, the wise men saw His star in the East.

When Jesus Christ comes back for His bride, Matthew 24:27 says, *"For as the lightning comes from the EAST and flashes to the west, so also will the coming of the Son of Man be."* (NKJV)(emphasis added).

This is when Jesus will make the whole earth His "footstool" based on Isaiah 66:1. The word "footstool" is the Greek meaning of the word "feet" as used in Revelation 12:1–2.

Who is Israel? Discovering our True Identity in Jesus Christ and Why it Matters! The Foundation

The twelve stars represent Jesus' disciples—the children of Israel, who were birthed from The Prince of the twelve tribes of Israel, who is our Jewish Messiah.

Jesus' disciples are clothed with the glory of God, our heavenly Father, and our Lord and Savior Jesus Christ, who is a "sun," and a "shield," and the head of His Ekklēsía (the Church). This is based on the following Scriptures:

> *"For the Lord God is a SUN and SHIELD; The Lord will give grace and glory; No good thing will He withhold From those who walk uprightly."* (Psalm 84:11, NKJV) (emphasis added).

> *"That they may know from the RISING of the SUN to its SETTING That there is none besides Me. I AM the LORD, and there is no other..."* (Isa. 45:6, NKJV) (emphasis added).

> *"The SUN shall no longer be your light by day, Nor for brightness shall the MOON give light to you; But the LORD will be to you an everlasting LIGHT, And your God YOUR GLORY."* (Isa. 60:19, NKJV) (emphasis added).

> *"'For from the RISING of the SUN, even to its GOING DOWN, My NAME shall be GREAT among the Gentiles; In every place incense shall be offered to My name, And a pure offering; For My NAME shall be GREAT among the NATIONS,' Says the Lord of*

110

hosts. "(Mal. 1:11, NKJV) (emphasis added).

"But to you who FEAR My NAME the SUN of RIGHTEOUSNESS shall ARISE With HEALING in His WINGS; And you shall go out And grow fat like stall-fed calves. " (Mal. 4:2 NKJV) (emphasis added).

"Then the RIGHTEOUS will SHINE FORTH as the SUN in the KINGDOM of their Father. He who has ears to hear, let him hear!" (Matt. 13:43, NKJV) (emphasis added).

"And He [Jesus] *was transfigured before them. His FACE shone like the SUN, and His CLOTHES became as WHITE as the LIGHT. "* (Matt. 17:2, NKJV) (emphasis added).

"He [Jesus] *had in His right hand seven stars, out of His mouth went a sharp two-edged sword, and His COUNTENANCE was like the SUN SHINING in its strength. "* (Rev. 1:16, NKJV) (emphasis added).

"The city had no need of the SUN or of the MOON to shine in it, for the GLORY of God ILLUMINATED it. The Lamb is its LIGHT. " (Rev. 21:23, NKJV) (emphasis added).

"There shall be no night there: They need no LAMP nor LIGHT of the SUN, for the LORD God gives them LIGHT. And they shall reign forever and ever. " (Rev. 22:5, NKJV) (emphasis added).

Who is Israel? Discovering our True Identity in Jesus Christ and Why it Matters! The Foundation

Now let's refocus our attention on the woman depicted in Revelation 12:1–2, specifically concerning the garland, which is a crown of twelve stars encircling the woman's head. This crown of twelve stars is symbolic of the twelve tribes of Israel.

And, since the woman is symbolic of Israel then her head is symbolic of the headship of Jesus Christ, who is the Chief Cornerstone of His Ekklēsía.

In addition, the twelve stars encircling the woman's head represents the twelve gates of this great city—the holy Jerusalem—the Lamb's wife. These twelve gates are symbolic of the twelve tribes of the children of Israel. This is substantiated in Revelation 21:12–13.

The twelve stars encircling the woman's head are also symbolic of the wall of the city, which had twelve foundations, and on them were the names of the twelve apostles of the Lamb. This is based on Revelation 21:14–27.

This holy city we read about in Revelation 21, is called the "New Jerusalem," and refers to *spiritual* Israel, who is the Lamb's wife. *Spiritual* Israel is built on the foundation of the apostles, and the prophets, Jesus Christ Himself being the Chief Cornerstone. This is based on Ephesians 2:20.

The moon, which is located at the feet of the woman who is symbolic of Israel, as depicted in Revelation 12:1–2, has a deep prophetic meaning as well, which I will convey later on in this chapter. In the meanwhile, we need to go back to the beginning. In the *Garden of Eden* after the fall took place, God said in Genesis

112

3:15, He would put enmity (hatred) between the serpent, and the woman, and between *his* "seed" and *her* "seed."

It would eventually come to pass, Jesus Christ shall bruise the serpent's head, even though the serpent shall bruise His heel, and the heel of Jesus' disciples too!

However, the "good news" is this: In Psalm 91:13, we are told God's people, who are the children of Israel, "*...shall tread upon the lion and the cobra, the young lion and the serpent you shall trample underfoot!*" Hallelujah!

So, why do I say the serpent shall bruise the heel of Jesus' disciples as well?

First, before God changed Jacob's name to Israel, his name personified his former identity as a "heel-catcher" which means the following: A supplanter which is used to describe one who comes behind and catches the heel of his adversary. The definition of a supplanter is as follows:

1. Take the place of; displace, or set aside.
2. Take the place of; by unfair methods, or by treacherous means.
3. Remove from its position; get rid of; oust.

As a matter of fact, as I will cover in-depth in Book 2, Jacob came out of his mother's womb holding onto Esau's heel. Then it would come to pass, Jacob talked Esau into forfeiting his "birthright" as a *firstborn* son, in exchange for a bowl of stew in order to satisfy the hunger of his flesh. Jacob then tricked his father, Isaac, with his mother's blessing, and help, into giving him the double-portion blessing, which is usually bestowed to the *firstborn* son, which in this case was Esau.

Thus, this enmity (hatred) between the descendants of Jacob and the descendants of Esau (the Arab and Muslim people who practice Islam) has been brewing since the beginning of time.

In fact, I cover this in detail in Chapters 26 and 27 of Book 2, so we can fully understand this truth: It was God who orchestrated the beginning of the enmity (hatred) between the descendants of Esau, and Jacob (Israel), while they were still in their mother's womb when God birthed two nations!

As such, this *ancient* "jealousy" and "hatred" between Ishmael and Isaac, then in the next generation between Isaac's two sons, Esau and Jacob, and their descendants, will continue until Jesus Christ returns.

Hence, the descendants of Ishmael and Esau, will seek "revenge" and "retribution" from the descendants of Isaac and Jacob, because they truly believe their "birthright" as God's "chosen" people was stolen from them, even though they do **not** worship the God of Abraham, Isaac, and Jacob (Israel) in any way, shape, or form!

Therefore, they will seek to bruise the heel or lift up their heel, against the descendants of Abraham, Isaac, and Jacob (Israel). And, we are already witnessing this happening on a global basis as the descendants of Ishmael and Esau—those who practice "radical"

Islam seeks to annihilate the descendants of Abraham, Isaac, and Jacob (Israel) by beheading the infidels.

The latest ploy of the enemy to "deceive" the world into thinking that the descendants of Ishmael and Isaac, and Esau and Jacob, are "worshiping" and "serving" the same God is this lie: There are three "Abrahamic" faiths. Unfortunately, many Christians are embracing this lie as truth!

I am very concerned about President Trump, and other Christians, who may be "deceived" into believing the lie that there are three "Abrahamic" faiths. In fact, on May 4, 2017, it was reported during President Trump's first foreign trip he was planning to visit the "symbolic" homes (Saudi Arabia, Israel, and the Vatican) of the three "Abrahamic" faiths (Islam, Judaism, and Christianity), as he makes a plea for global unity.

Satan and his minions are using this lie that there are three "Abrahamic" faiths in order to twist the truth and validate why there should be no problem with adherents of Islam, Judaism, and Christianity coming together for the sake of peace and unity. While it is true Ishmael was a "physical" descendant of Abraham; he is not a "spiritual" descendant of Abraham. Nor, is Islam the faith Abraham practiced or embraced!

And last, but certainly not least, Allah is not the God of Abraham, Isaac, and Jacob (Israel) either. I will substantiate this fact, later in this chapter. I have devoted Chapter 32 of Book 2, to convey in-depth, this critical truth: Disciples of Jesus Christ should witness to the Muslim and Arab people who adhere to the Islam religion. Yet we must *never* come into agreement with them by "practicing" Chrislam, or by becoming involved with the interfaith movement currently gaining momentum which is ushering in the One World "Harlot" Religious System.

The second reason why I state the serpent shall bruise the heel of Jesus' disciples as well is for this reason: Immediately after Revelation 12:1–2, which I have already covered in this chapter, the very next passage of Scripture in Revelation 12:3–4, is talking about Satan, who will bruise the heel of Jesus Christ and His disciples.

In the Scripture below, I have taken the liberty to highlight, and put in brackets, the *symbolic* meaning of certain "key" words. Revelation 12:3–4, says the following:

> *"And another SIGN appeared in heaven: behold, a great, fiery red DRAGON* [Satan] *having seven HEADS* [kingdoms] *and ten HORNS* [kings], *and seven DIADEMS* [crowns] *on his HEADS. His TAIL drew a third of the STARS of HEAVEN and threw THEM to the EARTH. And the DRAGON stood before the WOMAN who was ready to give BIRTH, to DEVOUR her Child* [Jesus] *as soon as it was BORN."* (Rev. 12:3–4, NKJV) (emphasis added).

We are told in Revelation 12:4, the dragon stood before the woman who was ready to give birth, and he would attempt to devour her Child as soon as it was born. This did indeed come to pass based on Matthew 2:13, where we are told after Jesus Christ was born, King

Herod, who was a prophetic shadow picture of Satan, and was being used by him, sought to find the young Child to destroy Him. However, the Angel of the Lord appeared to Joseph in a dream, telling him to arise, and take the young Child, and His mother Mary, and flee to Egypt.

Since Satan could not devour Jesus Christ when He was born, he patiently waited until the "appointed" time, when Satan would use one of Jesus' disciples to betray Him, which would lead to His death. This is what happened when Judas betrayed Jesus. In John 13:18, Jesus said, *"I do not speak concerning all of you. I know whom I have chosen; but that the SCRIPTURE MAY BE FULFILLED, 'He who eats bread with Me has LIFTED UP HIS HEEL AGAINST Me.'"* (NKJV) (emphasis added).

We are specifically told in Luke 22:3, Satan entered Judas, surnamed Iscariot, who was numbered among the twelve disciples.

Therefore, worth mentioning at this time is this fact: If Satan entered into the heart of Judas who walked closely with Jesus, and he used Judas for his evil purposes to prevail, then Satan can and will use Christians to do his bidding in order to perpetrate evil.

This is why it is vital for us to closely examine, on a daily basis, the "secret" intents and motives of our heart, and we must pray for God to uproot anything in our heart, which shall cause us to become defiled, and open the door to Satan.

In fact, we should pray daily, Psalm 51:10, which says, *"Create in me a CLEAN HEART, O God, And, RENEW a STEADFAST SPIRIT, within me."* (NKJV) (emphasis added).

Thus, even though Satan did indeed use Judas to betray Jesus, God's "eternal" plan was not thwarted by the enemy. God allowed Satan to use Judas, whose heart was not right in the first place, in order for Scripture to be fulfilled. This act of betrayal by Judas would result in Jesus Christ being crucified because this was the will of the Father.

Read all of Isaiah Chapter 53 which talks about what Jesus went through when He suffered for us all. However, I want to focus your attention on Isaiah 53:10–11, which says the following:

> *"But it was the LORD's GOOD PLAN to CRUSH him [Jesus] and CAUSE HIM GRIEF. Yet when HIS LIFE is made an OFFERING for SIN, he [Jesus] will have MANY DESCENDANTS. He will ENJOY a LONG LIFE [eternally, speaking], and the LORD's GOOD PLAN will PROSPER in HIS HANDS. When he SEES all that is ACCOMPLISHED BY HIS ANGUISH, he will be SATISFIED. And BECAUSE of HIS EXPERIENCE, my RIGHTEOUS SERVANT will make it POSSIBLE FOR MANY TO BE COUNTED RIGHTEOUS, for he will BEAR all their SINS."* (Isa. 53:10–11, NLT) (emphasis added).

Therefore, the next time you tell God to use you as a "living sacrifice" in order for His "eternal" purposes to prevail, remember a servant is not greater than His Master. Like Jesus, when God chooses to crush us, which will result in the anguish of our soul, then our experience as His righteous servant, will make it possible for many to be counted righteous.

As the apostle Paul proclaims in First Corinthians 2:7–9, had the rulers of this age known the "hidden" Wisdom of God (which the Book of Enoch talks about), that God ordained *before* the ages for our glory, then they would not have crucified the Lord of Glory for this reason: Jesus Christ crushed the head of the serpent forevermore, when He conquered death and rose from the grave! Hallelujah!

Now let's refocus our attention on the Child we read about in the Book of Revelation. We all know the "Child" in Revelation 12:3–4, and in Revelation 12:5–6, is referring to *the Word* who was sent to the earth as the Son of Man in the Person of Jesus Christ, because of the promise God gave to Abraham. Revelation 12:5–6, says the following:

> *"She bore a male Child* [Jesus Christ] *who was to RULE all NATIONS with a rod of iron. And her Child was CAUGHT UP to God and His throne. Then the woman* [Israel] *fled into the wilderness, where she has a place prepared by God, that they should feed her there one thousand two hundred and sixty days."*
> (Rev. 12:5–6, NKJV) (emphasis added).

One of the promises God gave to Abraham was this: Through his "seed" he would surely become a great and mighty nation, and all the nations of the earth shall be blessed in him. This is substantiated by the apostle Paul in Galatians 3:16, which says, *"Now to Abraham and his Seed were the PROMISES made. He does not say, 'And to seeds* [plural]*,' as of many, but as of one, 'And to your Seed,' WHO is CHRIST."* (NKJV) (emphasis added).

In review, the woman clothed with the sun in Revelation 12:1–2, represents Israel who is Jesus Christ, and His disciples. However, the sun in Joseph's dream is symbolic of Joseph's father, Jacob, whose name was changed to Israel, which means "he will rule as God," and whose lineage led to the birth of Jesus Christ, who does indeed "rule as God."

THE MOON IN JOSEPH'S DREAM IS SYMBOLIC OF RACHEL AND LEAH—THE TWO WOMEN WHO BUILT THE HOUSE OF ISRAEL

Joseph's mother Rachel, who died *after* giving birth to Benjamin, and his stepmother Leah, are symbolized by the moon in Joseph's dream in Genesis 37:9, and in Revelation 12:1–2, for the following two reasons:

First, Joseph's mother represents the "seed" of the woman who would birth the House of Israel. This would eventually lead to the birth of Jesus Christ through the "seed" of His mother, Mary, who would give birth to God's only *begotten* Son—Jesus Christ.

And, this would fulfill Genesis 3:15, which says, *"And I will put ENMITY Between you and the woman, And between YOUR SEED and HER SEED; He shall bruise your head, And you shall bruise His heel."* (NKJV) (emphasis added).

We must also remember Joseph was a prophetic shadow picture of Jesus Christ in so many ways. He was given this prophetic dream, which would culminate in the total fulfillment of God's promise to Abraham, he would be the "Father of Many Nations," and through his "seed," all the peoples of the earth would be blessed.

However, without God bringing forth the beginning of this promise to Abraham through the "fruit" of Sarah's womb, then Isaac, the *Son of the Promise,* would never have been born. And, if Isaac had not been born, then Jacob would not have been born. If Jacob had not been born, there would be no twelve tribes of Israel, whose lineage brought forth King David, and Jesus Christ, who is the "Son of David" and the "Son of Abraham."

Again, this truth is substantiated in Jesus' genealogy in Matthew 1:1–2, which says, *"The Book of the Genealogy of Jesus Christ, the Son of David, the Son of Abraham: Abraham begot Isaac, Isaac begot Jacob, and Jacob begot Judah and his brothers...."* (NKJV) (emphasis added).

Second, in the sight of God, Rachel and Leah were the two women who birthed the House of Israel, even though Jacob had a total of four wives who had given him sons and a daughter. This is based on Ruth 4:11–12, which says the following:

> *"And all the people who were at the gate, and the elders, said, 'We are witnesses. The LORD make the woman who is coming to your house like RACHEL*

> and *LEAH, the TWO who BUILT the HOUSE of ISRAEL; and may you prosper in Ephrathah and be famous in Bethlehem. May your house be like the house of Perez, whom Tamar bore to Judah, because of the offspring which the LORD will give you from this young woman.*'" (Ruth 4:11–12, NKJV) (emphasis added).

Moreover, the reason for Rachel and Leah, being the only two wives of Jacob's four wives, who are credited with building the House of Israel, is for this reason: They are the only wives for whom Jacob paid the required "bride-price," as required by their father Laban, in order to marry his daughters!

We are told in Genesis 31:41, Jacob was in Laban's house for twenty years and he worked a total of fourteen years for their father Laban to marry Leah and Rachel. This fulfilled the requirement of God's law in Exodus 22:16–17 below:

> "*If a man entices a VIRGIN who is not BETROTHED, and LIES WITH HER, he shall surely PAY the BRIDE-PRICE for her to be his WIFE. If her father utterly refuses to give her to him, he shall PAY MONEY according to the BRIDE-PRICE of VIRGINS.*" (Exod. 22:16–17, NKJV) (emphasis added).

As such, Jacob worked for seven years to marry Leah, when he was tricked by her father Laban, into thinking he was getting Rachel as his wife whom he loved. Therefore, Jacob was required to work another seven years, to marry Rachel! Based on the Greek meaning of the word "moon" as used in Revelation 12:1–2, which is the Greek word "selēnē" which means: Brilliancy; the idea of attractiveness; to take for oneself, that is, to prefer. It is not a coincidence Jacob preferred Rachel, over Leah, because of her attractiveness.

Therefore, Jacob was willing to serve her father Laban, for a total of fourteen years, to take Rachel as his bride, because of the great love he had for her.

Speaking of the great love a man has for his bride that would compel him to do anything to take her as his wife—this is one of the reasons why Jesus Christ was willing to shed His precious blood at Calvary. He was willing to give His life, which was the "bride-price" required in order to redeem (purchase) His beloved bride, as set forth by His Father, *Yehovah,* based on Exodus 22:16–17.

Now let's refocus our attention on this woman, who is symbolic for Israel, which we are told about in Revelation 12:1–2.

In Galatians 4:22–29, the apostle Paul elaborates on "who" this woman—Israel is, *spiritually* speaking, which is depicted in Revelation 12:1–2.

Also, in this same Scripture, we are told about Abraham's two sons. Ishmael was the *firstborn* son, who was born to Hagar, Sarah's bondservant, which means a female *slave,* or *servant.*

Whereas, Isaac is Abraham's *second* born son, whom Sarah conceived, well past childbearing age, because God's Spirit made this miracle come to pass. Therefore, Isaac is the *Son of the*

Promise, who was born to Sarah, who is a "free woman," because she was a citizen of Israel and "legitimately" Abraham's wife in the sight of God, based on their "Covenant of Marriage."

Because Abraham grew impatient waiting for God's "timing" concerning His promise to give him a son as an heir, he slept with Hagar and took her as his wife.

In fact, this promise from God to Abraham concerning a son who would be his heir, who would come from his own body, took so long to come to pass; Abraham forgot about this critical fact: God had already told him "how" this promise for a son would come to pass.

This promise would come to pass by Sarah, not Hagar, bearing him a son. This is based on Genesis 17:19, when God said to Abraham, *"No, Sarah your wife shall BEAR you a SON, and you shall call his name Isaac; I will establish My COVENANT with him for an everlasting COVENANT, and with his descendants after him."* (NKJV) (emphasis added).

Like all of us, Abraham and Sarah allowed their circumstances, and their emotions, based on what they "saw" and "felt" to almost thwart the plan of God for their lives.

This led them to succumb to "unbelief" and "doubt" concerning the "timing" of *when* God would bring to pass this promise for a son as an heir.

After all who could blame them? Abraham was getting older with each passing day, and Sarah was way past menopause. Therefore, her equipment for bearing children was not working any longer!

So, they took matters into their own hands, and used the *works of their flesh* to help God along, because they did not understand this critical truth: The promises of God which are truly from Him can only be birthed by the *Spirit of the living God,* rather than by the works of the flesh.

In other words, God's Spirit would have to heal and restore Sarah completely, so she could conceive and give birth to the *Son of the Promise*—Isaac, which would be from the "fruit" of her womb.

In fact, in Genesis 18:10, God specifically said, *"I will certainly return to you according to the TIME OF LIFE and behold, SARAH YOUR WIFE shall have a SON."* (NKJV) (emphasis added).

Therefore, Isaac would be the *Son of the Promise;* God would choose as His vessel in order to establish His *everlasting* covenant with Abraham and his descendants, who would come forth throughout the *synergy of the ages.*

God would "establish" this promise to Abraham and his descendants through the *first* covenant with all the children of Israel when the law was given at the base of Mount Sinai. And, it would eventually come to pass that God would "renew," "restore, and "rebuild" this *first* covenant when His Son fulfilled the New Covenant by His precious blood that was shed at Calvary.

And, it is for this very reason, why we are told in Galatians 4:22–29, this truth: Both of Abraham's sons—Ishmael and Isaac, represents two different covenants (plural), God has established for all His people. In the next section, we will discover these two women—Hagar and Sarah and their two sons—Ishmael and Isaac are "symbolic" of the two different covenants that God established with His people.

HAGAR, WHO BORE ISHMAEL, AND SARAH, WHO BORE ISAAC, REPRESENT TWO DIFFERENT COVENANTS

Abraham's son, Ishmael, is symbolic for the Old Covenant Moses established with the children of Israel at the base of Mount Sinai which represents "bondage" to the *letter of the law.*

Whereas, Abraham's son, Isaac—the *Son of the Promise,* is symbolic of the New Covenant, where we have been set free from "the curse" we would have received for not keeping the *letter of the law.* Under the New Covenant, we are now under the *law of Christ,* as we are led by His *Spirit of Grace* which is from above.

This is what the apostle Paul is speaking of in Romans 7:6, when he says to us, *"But now we have been DELIVERED from the LAW, having DIED to what we were HELD by* [our sin and bondages]*, so that we should SERVE in the NEWNESS of the SPIRIT and not in the OLDNESS of the LETTER* [of the law]*. "* (NKJV) (emphasis added).

As such, the "New Jerusalem" is *spiritual* Israel, which resides in the heart of every true disciple of Jesus Christ. Now let's closely examine

126

what the apostle Paul writes concerning "who" these women, Hagar and Sarah represent, *spiritually* speaking. They are "symbolic" of the two different covenants. This is based on Galatians 4:22–29, which says the following:

> *"For it is written that Abraham had two SONS: the one by a BONDWOMAN* [Hagar]*, the other by a FREEWOMAN* [Sarah]*. But he* [Ishmael] *who was of the BONDWOMAN* [Hagar] *was BORN ACCORDING to the FLESH, and he* [Isaac] *of the FREEWOMAN* [Sarah] *through PROMISE, WHICH THINGS ARE SYMBOLIC. For these are the TWO COVENANTS: the ONE from MOUNT SINAI which gives BIRTH to BONDAGE, which is HAGAR—for this HAGAR is MOUNT SINAI in ARABIA, and corresponds to JERUSALEM which NOW is, and is in BONDAGE with her children—but the JERUSALEM above is FREE, which is the MOTHER of us all* [Sarah]*. For it is written: 'Rejoice, O barren, You who do not bear! Break forth and shout, You who are not in labor! For the desolate has many more children Than she who has a husband.'"* (Gal. 4:22–27, NKJV) (emphasis added).

> *"Now we, BRETHREN, as ISAAC was, are CHILDREN of PROMISE. But, as he who was born ACCORDING to the FLESH* [Ishmael/Esau and their descendants=Islam] *then PERSECUTED him* [Isaac and his descendants] *who was born ACCORDING to the SPIRIT, even so it is NOW."* (Gal. 4:28–29, NKJV)

Do not dismiss the significance of what the apostle Paul is conveying in Galatians 4:22–27, concerning the Jerusalem that is free, and is the "Mother" of us all, who is from above—referring to the *heavenly* realm, concerning those things that are born according to the Spirit.

The "Mother" of us all is Sarah, Abraham's wife, based on Genesis 17:16, which proclaims, *"And I will bless her* [Sarah] *and also give you a son* [Isaac] *by her; then I will bless her, and she shall be a MOTHER of NATIONS; kings of peoples shall be from her."* (NKJV) (emphasis added).

Sarah is the "Mother" of us all through the "fruit" of her womb, when she finally gave birth to Isaac, the *Son of the Promise,* who was born according to the Spirit, based on one of the promises God gave to Abraham after He established His *everlasting* covenant with him.

Another interesting thing to take notice of based on Galatians 4:28–29, is this: The moon under the feet of the woman in Revelation 12:1–2, is symbolic of Islam's god Allah, because the Arab and Muslim people who practice Islam are "worshiping" the created, rather than the Creator. The Allah of Islam is the moon god of ancient pagan Arabia. [14]

Therefore, it is not a coincidence we are told in Galatians 4:23–25, Ishmael was born from the bondwoman Hagar, according to the flesh, who represents the "covenant" from Mount Sinai which gives birth to bondage. In addition, we are specifically told, Hagar is Mount Sinai in Arabia, and this Hagar also corresponds to

128

Jerusalem, which now is in bondage with her children. As such, this is one of the reasons why the Arab nations are seeking to take control of Jerusalem with the formation of a "Palestinian" state, as they continuously come against God's "covenant" people—the Jews from the House of Judah.

The Jews from the House of Judah are still in bondage until God removes their *spiritual* blindness and they receive the "revelation" Jesus Christ is their Messiah they are waiting for.

Now let's refocus our attention on this woman who is symbolic of Israel, which is depicted in Revelation 12:1–2. She is clothed with the sun from the glory of God, as the woman who is Israel "worships" *E'lōhim*, God, our Creator, who is *Yehôvah*, the *only* true God, and His Son, Jesus Christ, whom He sent.

Yet what is ironic is this fact: Many believers in the body of Christ, due to our ignorance of the whole counsel of God's Word, and failure to understand our "Hebraic" roots in Christianity, are still in bondage, because many are *unknowingly* "worshiping" the false "sun" god Baal, by practicing some of the "traditions," "customs," and "doctrines" of men.

Some of these "traditions," "customs," and "doctrines" of men include holidays such as Easter and Christmas. In fact, you will not find Easter or Christmas in the Bible because God did not establish or sanction these holidays that were instituted by the Roman Catholic Church long ago.

The origins of these holidays that we dearly love to celebrate started when pagans who were out of covenant with God "worshiped" the *false* "sun" god Baal. As I will cover in-depth in Book 3, this is one of the reasons why the Roman Catholic Church changed God's *seventh* day Sabbath from the *seventh* day of the week to Sunday, the *first* day of the week. The other reason they did this was to substitute Easter in lieu of keeping Passover because of anti-Semitism.

As far as Christmas is concerned, Baal was born on December 25th. This particular date is also the birthday of many other false gods, but it is certainly not the birthday of our Lord and Savior Jesus Christ! I will substantiate this fact in Chapter 63 of Book 3.

As such, when Constantine, and the Roman Catholic Church, instituted these holidays in lieu of our heavenly Father's feasts/holy convocations based on Leviticus 23, this was a *partial* fulfillment of Daniel 7:25, which came to pass when they changed God's "times" and "seasons" during the *Council of Nicaea* in AD 325.

Unfortunately, most denominations still follow this apostasy, because they were birthed from the "Protestant Reformation," that was not entirely successful in their quest to break free from the control of the Roman Catholic Church. In fact, the majority of these denominations still adhere to the doctrine of the Roman Catholic Church, rather than the doctrine of Christ, which is based on the whole counsel of God's Word.

The "Protestant Reformation" was a widespread, theological revolt, which took place in Europe, exactly 500 years ago. This "reformation" was initiated by Martin Luther and continued by John Calvin, and Huldrych.

All these men and many others fought valiantly against the abuses and totalitarian control of the Roman Catholic Church. Unfortunately, for the most part, the body of Christ still adheres to the doctrine of the "mother" Church, whose doctrine "supplants" the Word of God. The word "supplants" means: to replace.

It is for this very reason; I will cover in detail in Chapters 57–59 of Book 3, our heavenly Father's appointed "times" and "seasons," that only God has the authority, and the right, to establish, or to change. They are intricately linked to our heavenly Father's seven holy convocations (holidays), we are commanded to keep based on the Word of God, rather than based on the "customs," "traditions," and "doctrines" of men.

Moreover, keeping our heavenly Father's seven holy convocations based on Leviticus Chapter 23, which are all *everlasting* ordinances, has a direct correlation concerning who the "wise" virgins are in the *Parable of the Wise and Foolish Virgins,* Jesus talks about in Matthew 25. I will cover this in-depth in Chapters 60–62 of Book 3.

The "doctrine" of the Roman Catholic Church, not only "supersedes" and "exalts" itself above the Word of God, it directly "opposes" the Word of God for this reason: The "doctrine" of the Roman Catholic Church is against Christ (Antichrist) and is rooted in the occult. In fact, the Roman Catholic Church many moons ago—birthed Islam. I will cover this fact in Chapter 32 of Book 2.

In the Hebrew year of 5777 (2017) as we commemorate the 500th anniversary of the Protestant Reformation, God is "raising up" a new breed of "reformers" who will finally take an ax to sever the "root" which has resulted in the great apostasy we have inherited from our early church fathers. This new breed of "reformers" will completely finish the "reformation" which was started by Martin Luther, and continued by John Calvin, and Huldrych.

However, there is one major difference between this new breed of "reformers" God is "raising up" for a time such as this—they are not anti-Semitic like the aforementioned reformers were. This is a fact, and I encourage you to do your own research on this subject like I have.

As such, this new breed of "reformers" God is "raising up" as He is orchestrating this final "reformation" for the body of Christ will be "Repairers of the Breach," based on Isaiah Chapter 58. They will be called "Repairers of the Breach," because they will help facilitate the total "restoration" and "reconciliation" of all Israel so that we will become the One New Man in the *physical* earthly realm.

Again, all Israel includes both the Jews from the House of Judah and those of us who were formerly Gentiles from the House of Israel (Jacob, Joseph, Ephraim), who have now been grafted into the commonwealth of Israel by our faith in our Jewish Messiah, Jesus Christ.

"ONE" JERUSALEM IS STILL IN BONDAGE

Now let's refocus our attention on Galatians 4:22–27, which tells us there is one Jerusalem who is still caught up in their bondage. This refers to those who "say" they are believers in Jesus Christ, but they are still sinning and reaping the consequences of their bondage to the things of this world. We are *supposed* to die to our bondages and the things of this world, by picking up our crosses daily, and crucifying our flesh, once we receive Jesus as our Lord and Savior.

Another meaning of this Jerusalem, who is still caught up in their bondage, also refers to *physical* Jerusalem, which is the capital of the state of Israel, located in the Middle East. The land, which is supposed to be much larger than what currently defines the state of Israel, is one of the promises God gave to Abraham based on the *everlasting* covenant He established with him. This Jerusalem will never have peace until Jesus Christ comes back to the earth.

Currently, we are witnessing the beginning of the fulfillment of Zechariah 12:1–14, which addresses the coming deliverance of the Jews from the House of Judah now that the *fullness of the Gentiles* is coming to fruition.

This Scripture details *some* of the circumstances concerning Israel's future (the land of Israel promised to Abraham and his descendants). We are witnessing many nations seeking to come against Israel based on the "crafty counsel" of the United Nations, the Council on Foreign Relations, the Trilateral Commission, and the Vatican, to name *some* of the organizations in this coalition that seeks to take back international control of Jerusalem from the Israelites as it is to *this* very day.

God is using Jerusalem as a lure for many nations seeking to gather against it and claim it as their own. In doing so, these nations are going against God Almighty Himself based on the *everlasting* covenant He established with Abraham that *El Elyon* (the *Most High God*), and *El Olam* (the *Everlasting God*), swore by Himself to protect, defend, and uphold.

The Scriptures which are listed on this page and the following page detail *some* aspects of the final siege against the people of Jerusalem who are predominately the Jews from the House of Judah.

These Scriptures also talk about God removing the *spiritual* blindness off of His Jewish people, as substantiated by the apostle Paul in Romans 11:25. Again, we are witnessing God removing the *spiritual* blindness off of His Jewish people in this "kairos" season because the *fullness of the Gentiles* is at hand. This is how late the hour is!

In addition, these Scriptures were *partially* fulfilled during the *Six-Day War,* when Israel prevailed and received the spoils of war—Jerusalem, because of God's miraculous intervention.

Therefore, against all the odds—the Jews from the House of Judah—were victorious in battle against the surrounding Arab nations, who sought to annihilate the Jewish people. Yet the Scripture listed below, and the Scriptures on the next page shall have a total fulfillment at the end of *this* age.

> *"The burden of the word of the LORD against Israel. Thus says the LORD, who stretches out the heavens, lays the foundation of the earth, and forms the spirit of man within him: 'Behold, I will make JERUSALEM*

a CUP of DRUNKENNESS to all the SURROUNDING peoples, WHEN they lay SIEGE against JUDAH and JERUSALEM. And it shall happen in that DAY that I will make JERUSALEM a very heavy stone for all PEOPLES; all who would HEAVE IT AWAY will surely BE CUT IN PIECES, though all NATIONS of the EARTH are gathered against it. In that DAY,' says the LORD, 'I will strike EVERY HORSE with CONFUSION, and its RIDER with MADNESS; I will OPEN My EYES on the HOUSE of JUDAH, and will STRIKE every HORSE of the PEOPLES with BLINDNESS. And the GOVERNORS of JUDAH shall say in their heart, 'The inhabitants of Jerusalem are my strength in the LORD of HOSTS, their God.' In that DAY I will make the GOVERNORS of JUDAH like a firepan in the woodpile, and like a fiery torch in the sheaves; they shall DEVOUR all the SURROUNDING peoples on the right hand and on the left, but JERUSALEM shall be INHABITED again in her own place—JERUSALEM.'" (Zech. 12:1–6, NKJV) (emphasis added).

"The LORD will SAVE the TENTS of JUDAH first, so that the GLORY of the HOUSE of DAVID and the GLORY of the INHABITANTS of JERUSALEM shall not become greater than that of Judah. In that DAY the LORD will defend the INHABITANTS of JERUSALEM; the one who is feeble among them in that day shall be like David, and the HOUSE of DAVID shall be like GOD, like the Angel of the LORD

before them. It shall be in that DAY that I will SEEK to DESTROY all the NATIONS that come against JERUSALEM." (Zech. 12:7–9, NKJV) (emphasis added).

The word "tents" as used in Zechariah 12:7–9, where we are specifically told the Lord will save the "tents of Judah" first, is the Hebrew word "'o̅hel" (pronounced "o'-hel"), which according to *Strong's Hebrew Lexicon* #H168, is from H166, which means: A tent (as *clearly* conspicuous from a distance) covering, (dwelling) (place), home, tabernacle or tent.

In other words, God's Spirit will be poured out like never before, and He will remove the *spiritual* blindness off of the Orthodox Jews from the House of Judah, and they will receive the revelation that Jesus Christ is the Messiah they have been waiting for all this time.

This will happen when they are forced to cry out to *Yeho̅va̅h* to save them from their enemies who desire to annihilate them during the Antichrist's "rule" and "reign" of terror, which shall take place during the tribulation period.

They will finally receive Jesus as their Lord and Savior. Thus, the Lord shall save the "tents of Judah" first, so the glory of the House of David shall be like God—as the Angel of the Lord before them.

Therefore, God's Spirit shall tabernacle with them once again, because their bodies, rather than a *physical* temple, shall become the dwelling place for God's Holy Spirit. In addition, they will be covered, or protected, by God until the hour of His indignation has passed against all the nations that have come up to destroy Jerusalem and her inhabitants. This is one of the reasons why the *tribe of Judah* will be among the first of the remaining twelve tribes of Israel to receive the "seal of the living God" on their foreheads during the tribulation period.

A "faithful" remnant from all twelve tribes of Israel will be sealed on their foreheads with the "mark of God," and they will be supernaturally protected until they are redeemed from the earth from amongst men.

"SPIRITUAL" JERUSALEM IS FREE

The other Jerusalem that is free came through the "fruit" of Sarah's womb with the birth of Isaac, the *Son of the Promise,* based on God's promise to Abraham.

This *spiritual* Jerusalem which is free—resides in the "hearts" of all *true* disciples of Jesus Christ. When we pray for the peace of Jerusalem, as we are commanded to do, we are also praying for ourselves, because *spiritual* Jerusalem resides in the hearts of Jesus' disciples. I cover this fact in Chapter 69 of Book 3.

Yes, indeed! *Spiritual* Israel and *spiritual* Jerusalem is the Lamb's wife and refers to those who "keep" the commandments of God and have faith in Jesus Christ. This fact is substantiated in Revelation 12:17 and Revelation 14:12. Keeping the commandments of God includes our heavenly Father's instructions written in the Torah, which is the testimony of Jesus Christ. Both are required in order to "walk" in a covenant relationship with Abraham's God—*Yehòvah* (Yahweh [YHWH]).

In addition, the *bride of Christ* signifies those of us who have humbled and submitted ourselves to God's refining fire. We also "obey" His Word and His Voice.

Therefore, we have washed our wedding garments with the cleansing water of His Word. As a result, we will be arrayed in fine, white linen, without spot or blemish.

UNDERSTANDING OUR HERITAGE AS THE CHILDREN OF ISRAEL

Jacob had a total of twelve sons—who are the patriarchs of the twelve tribes of Israel. This is substantiated in Genesis 35:22–26, which says the following:

> *"Now the SONS of JACOB were TWELVE: the sons of Leah were REUBEN, Jacob's firstborn, and SIMEON, LEVI, JUDAH, ISSACHAR, and ZEBULUN; the sons of Rachel were JOSEPH and BENJAMIN; the sons of Bilhah, Rachel's maidservant, were DAN and NAPHTALI; and the sons of Zilpah, Leah's maidservant, were GAD and ASHER. These were the sons of Jacob who were born to him in Padan Aram."* (Gen. 35:22–26, NKJV) (emphasis added).

In addition, we know Abraham begot Ishmael, which represents bondage through the flesh from his union with Hagar. It also represents *physical* Jerusalem who is still in bondage with her children.

Whereas, Abraham begot Isaac, the *Son of the Promise,* from his union with Sarah who would be the son God would establish the *everlasting* covenant with.

This covenant is symbolic of *spiritual* Jerusalem, or the "New Jerusalem," which is from above in the *heavenly* realm. Therefore, the "New Jerusalem" is Israel, *spiritually* speaking.

Then Isaac begot Esau, which represents bondage to the world. Esau despised and sold his "birthright," as the *firstborn* son to satisfy his flesh.

Whereas, Jacob represents freedom from bondage to the world, when he wrestled with God and prevailed, and only then was his name changed to Israel, which means "he will rule as God."

How many of us are like Jacob, and we had to wrestle with God in order to learn obedience so we could establish God's "rule" and "reign" on the earth as His children, once we were set free from the bondage which used to enslave us, before we came to the saving knowledge of Jesus Christ?

The truth is this: God cannot use us to set others who are still caught in bondage free, until we overcome our bondage by His grace, through faith, as we receive His power from above. As such, there is a *big* difference between being a believer in Jesus Christ, versus "walking" and "living" as His disciple. Again, even the demons believe in Jesus Christ, and they tremble in that knowledge!

Now let's continue to discover the legacy the patriarch Jacob and his posterity (descendants) left behind, as we seek to learn about our heritage as the children of Israel.

We need to understand the chain of events that would eventually result in the birth of our Lord and Savior Jesus Christ.

Our legacy began with Abraham, Isaac, and Jacob (Israel). However, Jacob is the patriarch of his twelve sons who are the "princes" of the twelve tribes of Israel. Jacob's four wives bore His twelve sons.

Yet only Rachel and Leah are referred to as building the House of Israel, which is substantiated in Ruth 4:11–12.

The twelve sons of Jacob are as follows by order of their birth:

According to Genesis 29:31–35, Leah, Jacob's *first* wife, he did not love, gave birth to Reuben, Simeon, Levi, and Judah.

Then based on Genesis 30:3–8, Rachel, Jacob's *second* wife he loved, was barren, so she offered her maidservant Bilhah, to Jacob, as his wife, for the purpose of bearing children. Rachel became jealous of her sister Leah, who had already given Jacob four sons. Therefore, Jacob complied, and, as a result, Bilhah gave birth to Dan and Naphtali.

Then according to Genesis 30:9–13, when Leah realized she stopped bearing children, she offered Jacob her maidservant Zilpah and gave her to Jacob as a wife. Zilpah then bore a son name Gad followed by Asher.

In Genesis 30:17–21, God blessed Leah again, and she bore Jacob, a fifth son and named him Issachar. Then she conceived again, and bore Jacob, a sixth son, and named him Zebulun. And, at last, a girl was born, and they named her Dinah.

Finally, in Genesis 30:22–24, Rachel, the wife whom Jacob loved, and he worked a total of fourteen years for, conceived, and bore Jacob, his beloved son, Joseph.

It wasn't until *after* God renamed Jacob's name to Israel, Rachel died shortly after giving birth to Benjamin, which is detailed in Genesis 35:16–19. Rachel named her son, Ben-Oni, which means "son of my sorrow." However, his father Jacob called him, Benjamin, which means "son of the right hand."

Wow! Here we have Jacob whose name was changed by God to Israel meaning "he will rule as God."

And, now we have Jacob, the patriarch, changing his son's name to Benjamin, which means "son of the right hand."

How prophetic is it that the name of Jacob, which was changed to Israel, and the name of Ben-Oni, which was changed to Benjamin, is prophetically declaring the "rule" and "reign" of Jesus Christ?

Jesus does indeed "rule as God," and is the Son who is now seated at

141

the right hand of *Yehovah,* His heavenly Father, whose throne is in the *heavenly* temple located on Mount Zion—the *city of the living God,* in the *heavenly* Jerusalem. This is based on Hebrews 12:22.

Now we need to take a closer look at what God told Jacob, when He changed his name to Israel, in Genesis 35:9–15, which says the following:

> *"Then God APPEARED to **JACOB*** (15) [H3290: *Ya'aqob: heel catcher* (that is, Supplanter); *Jaakob, the Israelitish* patriarch] *again, when he came from Padan Aram, and blessed him. And God said to him, 'Your name is Jacob; YOUR NAME shall not be called Jacob ANYMORE, but **ISRAEL*** (16) [H3478: *Yisra'el: he will rule* as *God; Jisrael,* a symbolical name of Jacob; also (typically) of his posterity (descendants)]; *shall be your name.' So He called his name **ISRAEL**.* (16) *Also God said to him: 'I am God Almighty. Be fruitful and multiply; a NATION and a COMPANY of NATIONS shall PROCEED from you, and KINGS shall come from your BODY. The LAND which I gave Abraham and Isaac I give to you; and to YOUR DESCENDANTS after you I give this LAND.' Then God WENT UP from him in the PLACE where He talked with him. So Jacob SET UP a PILLAR* [a prayer altar] *in the PLACE where he talked with Him, a pillar of stone; and he poured a drink offering on it, and he poured oil on it. And Jacob called the name of the PLACE where God spoke with him, **BETHEL*** (17)

[H1008: *Bêyth-'êl: house of God; Beth-El*, a place in Palestine]. *"* (Gen. 35:9–15, NKJV) (emphasis added).

I will now unveil the fullness of the *spiritual* prophetic meaning of Joseph's dream based on Genesis 37:9.

JESUS CHRIST, FROM THE TRIBE OF JUDAH, CAME FROM THE LINEAGE OF JACOB'S, FOURTH BORN SON, JUDAH

It was Judah, the *fourth born* son of Jacob, through whom "the" *Son of the Promise*—Jesus Christ came. It was not Joseph, even though Joseph was a prophetic shadow picture of Jesus Christ.

And, since Joseph was a prophetic shadow picture of Jesus Christ, the dream that Joseph was given by God of his eleven brothers, his mother, and his father all bowing down to him has a *spiritual* fulfillment which is this: Jesus' mother Mary and his earthly father Joseph and his eleven remaining disciples will all bow down to Him when the sun, the moon, and the stars no longer give their light when this earth passes away at His second coming. In fact, as Isaiah 45:23 and Romans 14:11 proclaims—*every* knee shall bow down to Him, and *every* tongue shall confess to God and take an oath.

Concerning God's divine destiny that Joseph did fulfill, it was by God's divine providence that Joseph was appointed—second-in-command—to Pharaoh, the *King of Egypt*. Despite all that Joseph suffered, if it had not been for his unwavering devotion to the God of his father, Jacob, the nation of Israel would have perished from the famine (as predicted in Pharaoh's dream).

And, if that had happened, then Jesus Christ could not have been born through the "seed" of Abraham so that all the nations of the world would be blessed.

Therefore, Joseph saved God's people, just like Jesus Christ would later do, when He became God's only *begotten* Son when the Holy Spirit overshadowed a virgin girl, named Mary, who was highly favored by God.

It was only by *the Word* being manifested in a body of flesh and blood, was it possible for *the Word* to become the Son of Man in the Person of Jesus Christ.

Only then could Jesus *literally* become our sacrificial "Passover Lamb" who was and is without spot or blemish.

Our heavenly Father chose to sacrifice His beloved Son for the redemption of our sins and to "restore" and "reconcile" us back into "walking" in a covenant relationship with Him.

As such, like Joseph, the next time you are suffering for His name's sake, remember by doing so, God is preparing you to help save souls from *everlasting* damnation.

We can do this by sharing, and more importantly, "demonstrating" the testimony of Jesus Christ to a lost and dying world.

Based on Second Peter 3:9, God is not slack concerning His promise, and His will for our lives is this: We will be longsuffering as

He is toward us, so no one should perish, but all come to repentance so they may be saved.

WE WILL "REAP" GOD'S PROMISES ONLY THROUGH THE "SPIRITUAL" SEED WE "SOW"

What God wants His people to realize is this important truth: It is only by the *spiritual* "seeds" we sow in our lives, the promises of God will come to pass by His Spirit.

We will never "reap" God's promises by the works of our flesh. Yet this does not mean nothing is required of us because "faith" without works is dead. All the promises of God can only be received based on how willing we are to "submit" to and "obey" the Holy Spirit, who will always guide us into all truth, based on the whole counsel of God's *eternal* Word.

This truth is evident in the lineage of Jesus Christ in this regard: The *firstborn* son, who would normally receive the double-portion blessing, came to pass *only* through the "seed" of the *Son of the Promise* based on the following examples:

❖ Abraham begot Ishmael and Isaac, yet it was through the *spiritual* "seed" of Abraham's *second born* son, Isaac, the promises God gave to Abraham would come to pass.

❖ Then Isaac begot Esau and Jacob, yet it was through the *spiritual* "seed" of Isaac's *second born* son, Jacob, the promises God gave to Abraham would come to pass.

145

❖ Then Jacob begot twelve sons, yet it was through the *spiritual* "seed" of Jacob's *fourth* born son, Judah, the promises God gave to Abraham would come to pass, which would eventually result in the birth of Jesus Christ who is from the *tribe of Judah.*

❖ And, let us not forget, it was only as a result of Jacob giving Joseph's *second* born son, Ephraim, the *firstborn* blessing, instead of Joseph's *firstborn* son Manasseh, the promises God gave to Abraham are still coming to pass. This is based on Jeremiah 31:9, which says the following:

> *"They shall come with WEEPING, And with SUPPLICATIONS I will LEAD them. I will cause them to WALK by the RIVERS of WATERS* [the Word of God whose Holy Spirit lives in us]*, In a straight way in which they shall not STUMBLE; For I am a Father to ISRAEL, And EPHRAIM is My FIRSTBORN."* (Jer. 31:9, NKJV) (emphasis added).

THE TRIBE OF EPHRAIM/THE HOUSE OF JOSEPH IS THE HOUSE OF ISRAEL

As you already know, Ephraim, Joseph's *second* born son, was given the *firstborn* double-portion blessing by the patriarch Jacob (Israel), instead of Manasseh, Joseph's *firstborn* son.

146

Jacob said in Genesis 48:5–7, that Ephraim and Manasseh will be called by the name of their brothers, and share in their inheritance, as the twelve tribes of Israel. As I have already conveyed, Manasseh is listed as one of the twelve tribes of Israel in Revelation 7:1–8, yet Ephraim is not.

Again, the *tribe of Ephraim,* the House of Joseph, and the House of Israel are synonymous—they all mean the same thing.

Therefore, the House of Israel (Jacob/Joseph/Ephraim), must include the ten lost tribes of Israel for this reason: God's Word says the *tribe of Benjamin* joined with the *tribe of Judah* to comprise the *southern* kingdom, referred to as the House of Judah, *after* the death of King Solomon. This is based on First Kings 12:20–24.

Hence, the House of Israel (Jacob/Joseph/Ephraim) includes the ten *northern* tribes of Israel who were taken into captivity by Assyria in 722 BC that *Yehôvah* scattered to the four corners of the earth.

In fact, the House of Israel is the "lost sheep" Jesus refers to in the following Scriptures:

> *"These twelve Jesus SENT OUT and COMMANDED them, saying: 'Do not GO into the WAY of the GENTILES, and do not ENTER a CITY of the SAMARITANS. But GO rather to the LOST SHEEP of the HOUSE of ISRAEL.'"* (Matt. 10:5–6, NKJV) (emphasis added).

> *"But He [Jesus] answered and said, 'I was not SENT except to the LOST SHEEP of the HOUSE of*

147

ISRAEL.'" (Matt. 15:24, NKJV) (emphasis added).

"And OTHER SHEEP I have which are not of this FOLD [(18)] [**G833: *aulē*** a *yard* (as open to the *wind*); by implication a *mansion:* court]*; THEM ALSO I MUST BRING, and THEY WILL HEAR MY VOICE; and there will be ONE FLOCK and ONE SHEPHERD."* (John 10:16, NKJV) (emphasis added).

When Jesus said these things, He was speaking to His disciples who were all Jewish from the House of Judah.

Therefore, the "lost sheep" Jesus refers to in these Scriptures, is from the House of Israel—the *tribe of Ephraim,* which is the stick of the House of Joseph—the ten lost tribes of Israel.

As such, the "lost sheep" of the House of Israel are Israelites, but they are not Jews.

From a Jewish perspective, being non-Jews, they could be considered Gentiles based on the definition of what a Gentile is. A Gentile is a foreign (non-Jewish) nation of people who are considered to practice pagan "traditions" and "customs," who are out of covenant with God. Therefore, they are lost.

However, viewed from an Israelite perspective they are not Gentiles, but fellow Israelites. No one can dispute that all Jews are Israelites, yet in this case, not all Israelites are Jews.

On the cross at Calvary, Jesus Christ, *spiritually* speaking, joined as

148

one "house," and one "kingdom," both the House of Israel (Jacob/Joseph/Ephraim), who are the ten lost tribes of Israel, and the House of Judah (the *tribe of Judah* and the *tribe of Benjamin*).

Therefore, in Christ, both houses are now one "kingdom," one "house," and one "stick" in God's hand, *spiritually* speaking.

The full manifestation of this taking place in the *physical* earthly realm is now underway, and being orchestrated by God as He is uniting both "houses" and "kingdoms" into One New Man under the headship of Jesus Christ. In fact, this is one fulfillment of the two witnesses the Book of Revelation speaks about, *spiritually* speaking, which must take place before Jesus Christ will return.

Jesus will appear a second time when the times of restoration of all things, which God has spoken by the mouth of all his holy prophets since the world began is accomplished—and not before.

THE TRUE MEANING OF THE "PRODIGAL" SON

The next time you read about the *Parable of the Lost Son* in Luke 15:11–32, you will know the "prodigal" son represents the "lost sheep" from the House of Israel for this reason: The "prodigal" son was lost in the world, and living according to the world, just like the Gentiles do, because they are out of covenant with God.

Whereas, the "prodigal" son's brother, who was angry with his father, because of his father's overwhelming joy when the "prodigal" son came back to him, represents the Jews from House of Judah. Of course, the father of both sons in this parable represents *Yehôvah,* our heavenly Father.

In this hour, God is beckoning His "prodigals" from the House of Israel to return to Him and worship Him with all our mind, heart, soul, and strength, like the Jews from the House of Judah still do. We need to worship Him in Spirit, according to His truth, so we will "walk" with Him in a covenant relationship, based on the whole counsel of His "eternal" Word.

In addition, the older son in this parable represents the Jews from the House of Judah, because they are still trying to earn their *righteousness* in God's sight, by keeping the *letter of the law* perfectly. They do not understand the finished work of Jesus Christ on the cross for they are still *spiritually* blinded by God until the *fullness of the Gentiles* comes to fruition.

This is one of the reasons why *the Word* was sent to the earth as the Son of Man in the Person of Jesus Christ. Because based on the written historical records of the Old Testament, despite the children of Israel's best intentions to keep God's law, they could not no matter how hard they tried.

In fact, no one, other than Zacharias, and his wife Elizabeth, parents of John the Baptist, was *righteous* before God by walking in all the commandments, and ordinances of the Lord, blamelessly based on Luke 1:5–6.

Even Zacharias, due to his unbelief, was struck mute, and unable to speak, when the angel Gabriel told him about the son, his wife

Elizabeth would finally conceive, which is based on Luke 1:19–20.

Hence, this is one of the reasons why our heavenly Father, *Yehôvah,* sent *the Word* to the earth as the Son of Man in the Person of Jesus Christ, who is a Jew from the *tribe of Judah.* On the cross at Calvary, Jesus set us free from "the curse" we would receive by not keeping the *letter of the law.*

Under the New Covenant *true* "circumcision" is not merely obeying the letter of the law, God has now put in our mind and written on the tablets of our hearts.

Rather, *true* "circumcision" results in a "changed" heart, produced by the Holy Spirit as we submit our will to the *sanctification* process, and we become "transformed" by the power of God's love.

As a result, we will "obey" God's Voice, and keep His covenant, because we love the Lord our God, with all our heart, mind, soul, and strength.

Hence, when we bear "fruit" worthy of repentance, and we love one another, the world will know we are disciples of Jesus Christ, and we serve *Yehôvah,* the God of Abraham, Isaac, and Jacob, who is the Holy One of Israel.

In the next chapter, I will substantiate Abraham was not Jewish—he was Hebrew. This is necessary to adequately identify "who" Israel is, and "why" we must understand our "Hebraic" roots in Christianity.

Who is Israel? Discovering our True Identity in Jesus Christ and Why it Matters! The Foundation

CHAPTER 5

ARE ABRAHAM'S DESCENDANTS JEWISH OR HEBREW? "WHO" IS A TRUE JEW FROM GOD'S PERSPECTIVE?

The *everlasting* covenant God established with Abraham was not just for the Jews from the House of Judah. Rather, it is for all of God's Hebrew people referred to as the Israelites, or the children of Israel, from all twelve tribes of Israel, especially since Abraham was not a Jew. Rather, Abraham was a Hebrew based on Genesis 14:13 below:

> *"Then one who had escaped came and told Abram the* ***HEBREW*** [(1)] [H5680: 'ibriy: an Eberite (that is, Hebrew) or descendant of Eber], *for he dwelt by the terebinth trees of Mamre the Amorite, brother of Eshcol and brother of Aner; and they were allies with Abram."* (Gen. 14:13, NKJV) (emphasis added).

In addition, the word "Hebrew" in Aramaic is the word "'ibriy" (pronounced "ib-ree'"), which comes from the root word "abar" which means: To "Cross Over" or to "Pass Over" *spiritually* and *behaviorally* speaking. [(2)]

Therefore, the word "Hebrew" carries the following connotations:

❖ Separated.

❖ The other side, those who live on the other side.

153

❖ Independent, stateless, not the subjects of any human ruler, foreign to all worldly nations.

❖ Migratory, beyond, "that which is beyond."

❖ Sojourner on the earth, one who is "passing through," "passer through" (as distinct from a "settler" in the land or "resident" of the nations).

❖ Descending either "behaviorally" or "genetically" from Ever (Eber), following the path of Abraham, living according to the separatist (holy) instructions of Abraham's Elohim, Yahweh (YHWH).

So, the next question we must answer is this: "Who are the descendants of Eber?"

We are told the answer to this question in Genesis 10:21–22, which proclaims, *"And children were born also to Shem, the FATHER of all the CHILDREN of EBER, the brother of Japheth the elder. The sons of Shem were Elam, Asshur, Arphaxad, Lud, and Aram."* (NKJV) (emphasis added).

All of Shem's descendants are listed in Genesis 11:10–26. However, let's get right to the point which is this: It was Abram, the Hebrew, with whom God established an *everlasting* covenant with He swore by Himself, because He could swear no higher than Himself, to protect, defend, and uphold for Abraham and his descendants, forevermore. Abram is a direct descendant of Shem, Noah's son, as substantiated in Genesis 11:24–26, which says, *"Nahor lived twenty-*

154

nine years, and begot Terah. After he begot Terah, Nahor lived one hundred and nineteen years, and begot sons and daughters. Now Terah lived seventy years, and begot ABRAM, Nahor, and Haran." (NKJV) (emphasis added).

Therefore, Abraham, Isaac, and Jacob were Hebrew not Jewish.

As a matter of fact, when God sent Moses, who was also a Hebrew, to deliver His people the Israelites—the Hebrew people, from their bondage in Egypt at the hands of Pharaoh, based on one of the promises God gave to Abraham in Exodus 5:2 below, Pharaoh asked Moses the following question:

> *"And, Pharaoh said, 'Who is the LORD, that I should obey His voice to let ISRAEL* (3) *[H3478: Yisrā'ēl he will rule as God, Jisrael, a symbolical name of Jacob; also (typically) of his posterity] go? I do not know the LORD, nor will I let ISRAEL* (3) *go.' "* (Exod. 5:2, NKJV) (emphasis added).

Notice the word "Israel" is used twice in this passage of Scripture. This is long before the Hebrew children—the Israelites, would begin their long journey to take possession of the Promised Land God had promised Abraham would be given to him and his descendants as a result of the *everlasting* covenant *Yehôvȧh* established with him.

Therefore, one meaning of the name "Israel" is used to describe God's chosen people, the Hebrew people, who would be ruled by Jesus Christ, who is Israel. Because the word "Israel" in Hebrew is

"Yisra'el" (pronounced "yis-raw-ale'"), which means: "He will rule as God."

As such, my dear sisters and brothers in Christ, who is our *King of kings and Lord of lords* who rules as God? The answer is Jesus Christ.

In addition, the word "Israel" is a *symbolical* name of Jacob and refers to his posterity (his descendants). Therefore, how do God's people—His Hebrew people, who have crossed over into eternal life the moment we place our faith and trust in Jesus Christ our "Passover Lamb," "rule" and "reign" with God on the earth as it is in heaven? We "rule" and "reign" with God by abiding in Jesus Christ through the Holy Spirit and seeking our heavenly Father's will just as Jesus did.

Then we are to establish His Kingdom on the earth, as it is in heaven, by being "obedient" and "doing" only what our heavenly Father tells us to do, as we listen to the Holy Spirit which will always be in alignment with His Word.

Now let's see what Moses and Aaron said to Pharaoh in response to his question, *"Who is the LORD?"* Their response is found in Exodus 5:3, when they said to Pharaoh, *"The God of the **HEBREWS*** ⁽¹⁾ [H5680: *'ibriy*: an *Eberite* (that is, Hebrew) or descendant of Eber] *has met with us. Please, let us go three days' journey into the desert and sacrifice to the LORD our God, lest He fall upon us with pestilence or with the sword."* (NKJV) (emphasis added).

Therefore, *Yehovah* is the God of His Hebrew children who are the *spiritual* descendants (posterity) of Abraham, Isaac, and Jacob (Israel), whose lineage resulted in the birth of Jesus Christ based on the *everlasting* covenant *Yehovah* established with Abraham and his descendants.

Again, it is for this very reason, Jesus Christ's genealogy says in Matthew 1:1–2, *"The Book of the Genealogy of Jesus Christ, the Son of David, the Son of Abraham: Abraham begot ISAAC, Isaac begot JACOB* [whose name was changed to Israel], *and Jacob begot JUDAH and his BROTHERS* [who are the patriarchs of the twelve tribes of Israel]. *"*(NKJV) (emphasis added).

Jacob is the patriarch of his twelve sons who are the "princes" of the twelve tribes of Israel. His name was changed by God from Jacob to Israel at Peniel. Jacob *literally* saw God face-to-face when he struggled with God and with men, yet he prevailed. This truth is substantiated in Genesis 32:28 and Genesis 32:30, which says the following:

> *"And He said, 'Your name shall NO longer be called* **JACOB** [4] [H3290: *Ya'aqob*: *heel catcher* (that is, Supplanter); Jaakob, the *Israelitish* patriarch], *but* **ISRAEL** [3] [H3478: *Yisra'el*: *he will rule* as *God*; *Jisrael*, a symbolical name of Jacob; also (typically) of his posterity (descendants)]; *for you have struggled with God and with men, and have prevailed.'* *"*(Gen. 32:28, NKJV) (emphasis added).
>
> *"So Jacob called the name of the place* **PENIEL** [5] [H6439: *P'niy'el*: *the face of God*; and is a place East

of Jordan]: *'For I have SEEN God FACE to FACE, and my LIFE is PRESERVED.'"* (Gen. 32:30, NKJV) (emphasis added).

Now you have a brief understanding of why our heavenly Father, *Yehóvah,* is calling those of us who were formerly Gentiles, who have now been grafted into the commonwealth of Israel by our faith in Jesus Christ, to understand our "Hebraic" roots in Christianity.

We must return to the "ancient" path which leads to life, and to the *gospel of the kingdom* that was once delivered to the saints.

As such, our heavenly Father, *Yehóvah,* is not calling us to understand our "Jewish" roots in Christianity. Nor, is He calling us to become Jews by practicing Judaism.

Rather, our heavenly Father, *Yehóvah,* is calling His people to come out of *spiritual* or *mystery* Babylon. One facet of *spiritual* or *mystery* Babylon is based on men's "opinions" that are a result of us eating from the "tree of the knowledge of good and evil" rather than us eating from God's Word which is the "tree of life" who is Jesus Christ.

This includes us no longer walking according to the "traditions," "customs," and "doctrines" of men we have inherited from our early church fathers.

Moreover, for us to understand what the *gospel of the kingdom* is, we need to read, study, and heed the whole counsel of God's Word because the Old Testament is the New Testament concealed, and the New Testament is the Old Testament revealed.

Again, Jesus, His disciples, and the apostle Paul taught only from the Old Testament, because the New Testament was not written until much later. For the most part, the body of Christ teaches from and studies only the New Testament, except for the Book of Revelation.

Most people in the body of Christ avoid teaching, reading, and studying the Book of Revelation like a plague. However, this is the *only* book of the Bible that God says we will be blessed if we read it, heed it, and keep what is written in it. This is based on Revelation 1:3, which proclaims, *"Blessed is he who READS and those who HEAR [heed] the words of this PROPHECY, and KEEP those THINGS which are WRITTEN in it; for the TIME is NEAR."* (NKJV) (emphasis added).

The Book of Revelation contains Jesus' final instructions to all seven types of churches that existed throughout the *synergy of the ages*, but His testimony is especially relevant to His end-time Church.

Therefore, contrary to what most believers in the body of Christ are taught, one of the reasons Jesus Christ came to earth the first time was to fulfill (consummate, execute, and ratify [confirm]) the Old Covenant, or the Law of Moses, with His precious blood.

The essence of the New Covenant, which are the terms and conditions of "walking" in a covenant relationship with *Yehôvah*, our heavenly Father, and His Son, Jesus Christ, is based on Hebrews

8:10, which says, *"For this is the COVENANT that I will make with the HOUSE of ISRAEL after those days,' says the LORD: 'I will PUT My LAWS in their MIND and WRITE them on their HEARTS; and I will be their God, and they shall be My people.'"* (NKJV) (emphasis added).

Furthermore, you will want to read this excellent article I came across as I was doing my research titled, *Two Houses of Israel.* The following excerpt from this article tells us where the term "Jew" came from, which will be the primary topic in the next chapter. [6]

> *"The fulfillment of the breakup of the House of Israel occurred in 722 BCE. The House of Judah continued for another 136 years until they were taken away captive to Babylon in 585 BCE. This shows that the House of Israel ceased to exist in 722 BCE. Judah returned to the land after their captivity in Babylon, yet Israel has not returned. After the House of Judah's return from Babylon, they continued as a kingdom and became the sole representative of all the remaining descendants of Jacob. It was after the dispersion and return of Judah that the term 'Jew' began to be used to apply to all Israelites."* [end of excerpt]

Next, we shall discover, from God's perspective, *who* He defines as being a true Jew according to His Word. For His perspective is all that matters and what He says according to His *eternal* Word should be the final authority concerning any matter for true disciples of Jesus Christ.

Listen to what the apostle Paul says to us in Romans 2:28–29 below, of who a true Jew is in God's sight.

> *"For you are not a TRUE Jew just because you were BORN of JEWISH PARENTS or because you have gone through the CEREMONY of CIRCUMCISION. No, a TRUE Jew is ONE whose HEART is RIGHT with God. And true CIRCUMCISION is not MERELY OBEYING the LETTER of the LAW; rather, it is a CHANGE of HEART PRODUCED by the SPIRIT. And a PERSON with a CHANGED HEART seeks PRAISE from God, not from PEOPLE."* (Rom. 2:28–29, NLT) (emphasis added).

Therefore, based on Romans 2:28–29, from God's perspective, a true Jew has the following attributes:

1. One whose heart is right with God.

2. One whose heart has been "circumcised" by God's Spirit, rather than by obeying "the letter of His law," which God has now put in our mind, and written on our hearts because His Holy Spirit lives in us. Therefore, a true Jew is one whose heart is made right, which is evidenced by a "transformed" life because of the *sanctification* process of the Holy Spirit achieved by our total submission and obedience to God's Voice and His Word.

3. One who seeks praise from God, rather than from men.

Who is Israel? Discovering our True Identity in Jesus Christ and Why it Matters! The Foundation

Therefore, like the apostle Paul says to us in Second Corinthians 11:22, *"Are they HEBREWS? So am I. Are they ISRAELITES? So am I. Are they the SEED of ABRAHAM? So am I."* (NKJV) (emphasis added).

Hence, this also applies to those of us who are true disciples of Jesus Christ who is our Jewish Messiah.

As such, doesn't that make us a Jew, *spiritually* speaking, in God's sight, especially since the meaning of a true Jew from God's perspective, has already been defined by the apostle Paul in Romans 2:28–29?

Moreover, when we "receive" salvation by accepting Jesus Christ as our Lord and Savior, we are adopted into His family. Therefore, it doesn't matter who our *physical* parents are, or from what bloodline we descended from, *spiritually* speaking because it is only the blood of Jesus that changes everything!

Thus, both the Jews from the House of Judah and those of us who were formerly Gentiles, who have now been grafted into the commonwealth of Israel by our faith in Jesus Christ, are from the House of Israel (Jacob/Joseph/Ephraim). As such, God's people are referred to as the Israelites, the children of Israel, the elect, the Saints, and the body of Christ, *spiritually* speaking, based on the following Scriptures:

> *"There is neither JEW nor GREEK* [Gentile]*, there is neither SLAVE nor FREE, there is neither MALE nor FEMALE; for YOU ARE ALL ONE in CHRIST JESUS.*

And if YOU ARE CHRIST'S, then you are ABRAHAM'S SEED, and HEIRS ACCORDING to the PROMISE. " (Gal. 3:28–29, NKJV) (emphasis added).

"For you did not receive the spirit of bondage again to fear, but you received the SPIRIT of ADOPTION by whom we cry out, 'Abba, Father.'" (Rom. 8:15, NKJV) (emphasis added).

"Blessed be the God and Father of our Lord Jesus Christ, who has BLESSED us with every spiritual blessing in the HEAVENLY places in Christ, just as He chose us in Him before the FOUNDATION of the WORLD, that we should be HOLY and without BLAME before Him in LOVE, having **PREDESTINED** (7) (8) [**G4309:** *proorizo: to limit in advance, that is, (figuratively) predetermine:* ordain; **G3724:** *horizo: to mark* out or *bound;* appoint, decree, declare and specify] *us to ADOPTION as SONS by Jesus Christ to Himself, according to the good pleasure of His will, to the praise of the glory of His grace, by which He made us accepted in the Beloved."* (Eph. 1:3–6, NKJV) (emphasis added).

Take note that based on Ephesians 1:3–6, we are specifically told by the apostle Paul the following: Our God and Father of our Lord Jesus Christ, has *already* blessed us with *every* spiritual blessing in the *heavenly* places in Christ. This does not say He will bless us. It says He has *already* blessed us, meaning it has already been done. However, the only way these blessings will manifest in the *physical* earthly realm is by us walking according to the Spirit, rather than our flesh, by abiding in Christ.

Also, notice we are specifically told God chose us in Him *before* the foundation of the world that we should be *holy* and without *blame* before Him in love because He has "predestined" us to be adopted as sons by Jesus Christ Himself. In other words, God knew the end from the beginning and knew before He formed us in our mother's womb if we would accept Him, or reject Him, based on "our" own free will.

Furthermore, based on Galatians 3:28–29, all true disciples of Jesus Christ are from the "seed" of Abraham and "heirs" according to the promise of "the Spirit" that is based on the *everlasting* covenant God made with Abraham—the "Father of Many Nations."

It is so critical for God's people to know what the *Abrahamic* Covenant is, and "what" God promised to Abraham because this *everlasting* covenant is still in effect today. Therefore, this covenant applies to New Covenant believers.

In addition, because of what is currently transpiring concerning the nation of Israel, and the Jewish people, it is critical for believers in Jesus Christ to know the reasons "why" this *everlasting* covenant is "relevant" to New Covenant believers.

And, it is for this very reason, in Book 2, I will cover in detail what the *Abrahamic* Covenant is, and "how" and in "what" ways, it is still "applicable" and "relevant" to New Covenant believers.

If we continue to falsely believe Israel only pertains to the Jews from the House of Judah, and everything written at the front of the Bible does not pertain to New Covenant believers, then we will continue to remain a house divided against itself!

And, if this is the case, we will <u>not</u> stand in the days ahead based on what Jesus says to us in Matthew 12:25. He says to us, His disciples, *"Every KINGDOM divided against itself is brought to DESOLATION, and every CITY or HOUSE divided against itself will not STAND."* (NKJV) (emphasis added).

Therefore, since Jesus Christ is the Holy One of Israel, and we, as His disciples, are Israel too, then when we do <u>not</u> stand with the Jewish people, and the *physical* nation of Israel, without which we would have no New Covenant to stand on, we are "rejecting" and "rebelling" against God Almighty Himself! And, this is one of the many reasons why God's people are indeed perishing from a lack of knowledge based on the whole counsel of His Word.

Moreover, God's people cannot fully comprehend how we, the body of Christ, are from Abraham's "seed" and "heirs" according to the *everlasting* covenant *Yehôváh* established with Abraham, without understanding "what" the promises of this *everlasting* covenant are. This covenant which *Yehôváh* swore by Himself to protect, uphold, and defend until the heavens and *this* earth passes away.

Many believers in the body of Christ are *unknowingly* breaking covenant with *Yehôváh*, our heavenly Father, based on the apostate teachings many are embracing as truth. The main reason why this is the case is because of our ignorance based on the whole counsel of His Word, and because we do not understand our "Hebraic" roots in Christianity. And, when we break "covenant" with God, we will come out from under His umbrella of providence, protection, and provision for our lives, and we will reap His curses rather than His blessings.

Therefore, let's continue our journey to discover our true identity in Jesus Christ by first substantiating Israel, *spiritually* speaking, is *Yehôvah*, the God of Abraham, Isaac, and Jacob (Israel) and His only *begotten* Son, Jesus Christ, which I shall cover in the next chapter.

CHAPTER 6

YEHOVAH, THE GOD OF ABRAHAM, ISAAC, AND JACOB (ISRAEL) AND HIS ONLY BEGOTTEN SON—JESUS CHRIST, IS THE HOLY ONE OF ISRAEL

As I have said before, but it bears repeating, for everything God does, there is a dual fulfillment of Scripture. First, there is a meaning, *spiritually* speaking, which God has decreed in the heavenly realm. However, for there to be a manifestation, *physically* speaking, which takes place in the earthly realm, God's people must prophetically decree things which are not as though they are, intercede, and believe what we pray for, which *should* be in alignment with His Word, shall come to pass.

Therefore, for God's will to be established in the earth, He uses people to be His change agents, even those who do not acknowledge, or know Him, for there are no "ifs" in God's "eternal" plan.

God has declared in the heavenly realm the end from the beginning, and one thing you can be sure of is this: God will do whatever He has said that He will do!

This truth is substantiated in Isaiah 46:10, which exclaims, *"DECLARING the END from the BEGINNING, And from ANCIENT TIMES things that are not YET DONE, Saying, 'My COUNSEL shall STAND, And I will DO all My PLEASURE...'"* (NKJV) (emphasis added).

Who is Israel? Discovering our True Identity in Jesus Christ and Why it Matters! The Foundation

Now let's establish our heavenly Father, *Yehôvâh,* and His Son, Jesus Christ, is the Holy One of Israel. This is based on *some* of the thirty-eight Scriptures found in the Word of God conveying this truth. They are as follows:

> *"For our shield belongs to the LORD, And our KING to the HOLY ONE of ISRAEL."* (Psalm 89:18, NKJV) (emphasis added).

> *"But when he sees his children, The work of My hands, in his midst, They will hallow My name, And hallow the HOLY ONE of JACOB, And FEAR the GOD of ISRAEL."* (Isa. 29:23, NKJV) (emphasis added).

> *"For thus says the LORD GOD, the HOLY ONE of ISRAEL: 'In returning and rest you shall be saved; In quietness and confidence shall be your strength.' But you would not..."* (Isa. 30:15, NKJV) (emphasis added).

> *"For I am the LORD your GOD, The HOLY ONE of ISRAEL, your SAVIOR..."* (Isa. 43:3, NKJV) (emphasis added).

> *"As for our REDEEMER, the LORD of HOSTS is His NAME, The HOLY ONE of ISRAEL."* (Isa. 47:4, NKJV) (emphasis added).

168

"Thus says the LORD, your REDEEMER, The HOLY ONE of ISRAEL: 'I am the LORD your GOD, Who teaches you to profit, Who leads you by the way you should go.'" (Isa. 48:17, NKJV) (emphasis added).

"Thus says the LORD, The REDEEMER of ISRAEL, their HOLY ONE, To Him whom man despises, To Him whom the nation abhors, To the Servant of rulers: 'Kings shall see and arise, Princes also shall worship, Because of the LORD who is faithful, The HOLY ONE of ISRAEL; And He has CHOSEN you.'" (Isa. 49:7, NKJV) (emphasis added).

"For your MAKER is your HUSBAND, The LORD of HOSTS is His NAME; And your REDEEMER is the HOLY ONE of ISRAEL; He is called the GOD of the WHOLE EARTH." (Isa. 54:5, NKJV) (emphasis added).

"Surely you shall call a nation you do not know, And nations who do not know you shall run to you, Because of the LORD your GOD, And the HOLY ONE of ISRAEL; For He has glorified you." (Isa. 55:5, NKJV) (emphasis added).

"So I will make My HOLY NAME known in the midst of My people ISRAEL, and I will not let them profane My HOLY NAME anymore. Then the nations shall know that I am the LORD, the HOLY ONE in ISRAEL." (Ezek. 39:7, NKJV) (emphasis added).

In the next chapter, I will convey why *the Word* is God's only *begotten* Son of His love—the *firstborn* over all creation, and the *firstborn* of all God's sons and daughters as well. We cannot fully understand our true identity in Christ, without first understanding "who" the one and *only* true God is.

CHAPTER 7

THE WORD IS THE FIRSTBORN OVER ALL CREATION

The Word, whom our heavenly Father, *Yehôvah,* sent to the earth as the Son of Man in a body of flesh and blood in the Person of Jesus Christ, is indeed the *firstborn* over all creation. He was with God in the beginning and is God. For by Him all things were created that are in heaven, and that are on earth, visible and invisible, whether thrones, or dominions, or principalities, or powers. All things were created through Him, and for Him.

Long *before* the children of Israel, God's Hebrew people, crossed over the Jordan to take possession of the Promised Land, God promised the *physical* land of Canaan to Abraham and his descendants, when God established the *everlasting* covenant with him based on Genesis 15:17–21.

And, this is why God was referring to His people Israel when *Yehôvah* told Moses to say to Pharaoh in Exodus 4:22, *"...Thus says the LORD: 'Israel is My SON, My FIRSTBORN.'"* (NKJV) (emphasis added).

Moreover, this Scripture has a dual meaning and fulfillment.

Physically, speaking it is referring to the land, the first *physical* vineyard on the earth for God's chosen people, the children of Israel, they would take possession of as their inheritance. Yet His people would finally take possession of this land, only after they wandered in the wilderness for forty years for this reason: So God could "humble" and "test" them to know what was in their heart and to see if they would "keep" and "obey" His commandments.

The other meaning of Exodus 4:22, which states, *"...Thus says the LORD: 'Israel is My SON, My FIRSTBORN...'"* is referring to Jesus Christ, *Yehovah's* only *begotten* Son, who was and is *the Word,* who became flesh as the Son of Man in the Person of Jesus Christ.

Yet long before Jesus Christ would come to the earth in a body comprised of flesh and blood as the Son of Man in the Person of Jesus Christ, He *eternally* existed as *the Word* who was and is the *firstborn* over all creation.

The Word existed at the beginning with God, and was and is God, as substantiated in John 1:1–3 below, where we are specifically told that all things were made through Him.

> *"In the beginning was the **WORD**^{(1) (2)} [G3056: **logos**:* something said, or spoken (including the thought); utterance **G3004: lego**: (verb) to "lay forth," or to set discourse; call, speak, utter], *and the **WORD**^{(1) (2)} was with God, and the **WORD**^{(1) (2)} was God. He was in the beginning with God. All things were made through Him, and without Him nothing was made that was made."* (John 1:1–3, NKJV) (emphasis added).

Furthermore, it may come as a shock to some of you to realize that our heavenly Father, *Yehovah,* (qualified, selected, and chose) *the*

Word to "rule" and "reign" and ascend to the throne as royalty for counsel long before *the Word* came to the earth as the Son of Man in the Person of Jesus Christ.

This is based on Isaiah 43:15. Now let's closely examine what the prophet Isaiah reveals to us in the following Scripture:

> "*I am the Lord, your Holy One, the* **CREATOR** (3) [H1254: *bârâ*: to *create*; qualify, to select, or to choose] *of* **ISRAEL** (4) [H3478: *Yisrâ'êl*. he *will rule* as *God*, *Jisrael*, a symbolical name of Jacob; also (typically) of his posterity (descendants)], *your* **KING** (5) (6) [H4428: *melek*: a royal king; H4427: *mâlak*: to *rule* and *reign*; inceptively to *ascend the throne*; induct into royalty; hence to take counsel]. *" (Isa. 43:15, NKJV) (emphasis added).

Do not dismiss the significance based on the Hebrew meaning of the word "king" we now know *the Word* came down to meet with Abram as Melchizedek, *king of Salem*, which is based on Genesis 14:18.

In addition, do not dismiss the significance of what *Yehôvah* is saying in Isaiah 43:15. He is saying that He (qualified, selected, and chose) *the Word* as our King *before* He created anything else.

As such, my dear sisters and brothers in Christ, I ask the following question: "Who is our *King of kings and Lord of lords?*" The answer is Jesus Christ.

GOD (QUALIFIED, SELECTED, AND CHOSE) THE WORD BEFORE THE FOUNDATION OF THE WORLD

Now let's continue to examine God's Word, so we fully understand that God (qualified, selected, and chose) *the Word,* who became the Son of Man in the flesh in the Person of Jesus Christ, *before* the foundation of the world.

Yes, you heard me correctly. God (qualified, selected, and chose) *the Word* in the heavenly realm to "redeem" mankind *before* the foundation of the world was created, or man was "formed" from the primal dust of the earth based on Proverbs 8:22–31, which says the following:

"The **LORD** [7] [H3068: *Yhovah:* (the) *self-Existent* or Eternal; *Jehovah,* Jewish national name of God] **POSSESSED** [8] [H7069: *qânâh:* create; by extension to procure; especially by purchase in order to buy, own, or redeem] *ME at the beginning of His* **WAY** [9] [10] [H1870: *derek:* a *road* (as *trodden*); figuratively a *course* of life, or *mode* of action; according to a eastward highway, pathway, or custom; H1869: *dârak:* to *tread,* by implication "how" to walk], *Before His WORKS of OLD. I have been* **ESTABLISHED** [11] [H5258: *nâsak:* to *pour* out, especially as a libation which is a drink that is poured out; *anoint* as king] *from* **EVERLASTING** [12] [H5769: *'ôlâm:* perpetual, at any time, (beginning of the) world (+ without end); eternity], *From the beginning, BEFORE there*

174

was *EVER* an *EARTH.*" (Prov. 8:22–23, NKJV) (emphasis added).

"*WHEN* there were *NO* depths I was BROUGHT FORTH, *WHEN* there were *NO* fountains abounding with water. *BEFORE* the mountains were settled, *BEFORE* the hills, I was BROUGHT FORTH; While AS YET He had *NOT MADE* the EARTH or the FIELDS, or the PRIMAL DUST of the WORLD. WHEN He PREPARED the HEAVENS, I WAS THERE, *WHEN* He drew a circle on the face of the deep, *WHEN* He established the clouds above, *WHEN* He strengthened the fountains of the deep, *WHEN* He assigned to the sea its limit, So that the waters would not transgress His command, WHEN He MARKED OUT the FOUNDATIONS of the EARTH, THEN I was BESIDE Him as a MASTER CRAFTSMAN; And I was DAILY His DELIGHT, rejoicing always BEFORE Him, REJOICING in His INHABITED WORLD, And my DELIGHT was with the SONS of MEN.*" (Prov. 8:24–31, NKJV) (emphasis added).*

Before we proceed on our journey to understand who *the Word* is, we must stop a moment and reflect on the significance of what we were just told in Proverbs 8:24–31. This Scripture says *the Word* was daily our heavenly Father's delight rejoicing always before Him, rejoicing in His "inhabited" world, and His delight was with the "sons of men" when He marked out the foundations of the earth, which did not exist yet.

This passage of Scripture in context talks about the fact *the Word* was brought forth *before* our heavenly Father, *Yehovah,* and *E'lohim,* God, our Creator, had created the earth, including the fields, or the primal dust of the world. So how could the "sons of men" exist, when the primal dust of the world was not created yet? Especially since the first man Adam and all subsequent human beings would be "formed" by God, our Creator, from the primal dust of the world.

Again, how could *the Word* be rejoicing in His "inhabited" world, and His delight was with the "sons of men," *before* the earth, including the primal dust of the world, was even created yet?

GOD "CREATED" AN ETERNAL SOUL FOR EVERY MALE AND FEMALE BEFORE THE FOUNDATION OF THE WORLD

Our heavenly Father, *Yehovah,* and *E'lohim,* God, our Creator, "created" an eternal soul (spirit man) for *every* male and female who would ever be "conceived" in their mother's womb throughout the *synergy of the ages* at the foundation of the world. This would be long *before* He would "form" our inward parts and "cover" us in our mother's womb at His "preordained" time and for His "preordained" purpose. I will substantiate this truth according to God's Word in Chapter 11 of this book.

Now let's refocus our attention on the subject matter at hand. Understanding *who Yehovah,* our heavenly Father is, in relation to understanding *who* exactly *the Word* is, God sent to the earth as the

Son of Man in a body of flesh and blood in the Person of Jesus Christ, is so mind-boggling because of our limited understanding. Search this matter out for yourselves by reading Matthew Henry's commentary on Proverbs 8:22–31, which is available in the *Blue Letter Bible*. [13]

In addition, we are clearly told by the apostle John in John 1:18, the following: *"NO ONE has SEEN God at ANY TIME. The only begotten Son, who is in the BOSOM of the FATHER, He has DECLARED Him."* (NKJV) (emphasis added).

Based on John 1:18, the apostle John tells us our heavenly Father's *only begotten* Son is in the "bosom" of His Father, and NO ONE has *ever* seen God the Father at any time! And, based on the definition of the word "bosom" as defined by *Easton's Bible Dictionary*, the word "bosom" is concerning having a perfect knowledge of and the closest intimacy with God the Father, based on John 1:18. [14]

THE WORD IS THE FIRSTBORN OVER ALL CREATION

Now let's focus our attention on the fact *the Word* is the *firstborn* over all creation, which includes everything our heavenly Father, *Yehovah,* and *E'lōhim*, God, our Creator, would ever create in the heavens, on the earth, and under the earth, including us, His sons and daughters. *E'lōhim*, God, our Creator, created all things in and through *the Word* as substantiated in Proverbs 8:22–31 and John 1:1–3.

In addition, many will proclaim this passage of Scripture in Proverbs 8:22–31, is talking about the "Excellence of Wisdom" and you would be correct. The apostle Paul confirms this fact in First Corinthians 1:18 below:

> [*Christ the POWER and WISDOM of God*] *"For the MESSAGE of the CROSS is foolishness to those who are perishing, but to us who are being SAVED it is the POWER of GOD."* (1 Cor. 1:18, NKJV) (emphasis added).

Also, *the Word* who became the Son of Man in the Person of Jesus Christ in the flesh is referred to as the "Power and Wisdom of the Elect One" based on the Book of Enoch. [15]

Therefore, please allow me the privilege to digress on a rabbit's trail before we continue to learn more about *the Word,* who in the beginning was with God, and is God, and all things were made through Him, and without Him, nothing was made that was made.

What I am about to convey may not seem relevant to what we are currently addressing. However, it is. Furthermore, it will set the stage for what I will be teaching about in the very next chapter, and in Chapters 67 and 68 of Book 3.

THE BOOK OF ENOCH

Concerning the Book of Enoch, while the Book of Enoch is not in the Bible, the Holy Spirit led me to read it so I could understand what will happen at the end of *this* age as in the *days of Noah.* So, before you presume I am putting too much stock in anything other than the Bible, this is simply not true. The Bible is the *eternal* Word of God, and we are to stand on the unadulterated, uncompromised whole counsel of God's Word.

Yet at the same time, do we realize that a particular "religious" community decided what books would be canonized as "authoritative" Scripture? As such, we all need to get rid of our "religious" mindsets and "religious" spirits and be led by the Holy Spirit who will guide us into all truth, especially God's truth.

So, my question to you the reader is this: Why was the Book of Jasher not included as "authoritative" Scripture? Especially since the Book of Jasher is referenced in the Bible in Joshua 10:13, and Second Samuel 1:18, which specifically says, "…*indeed it is written in the Book of Jasher…*"

Does this mean the Book of Jasher is not the inspired Word of God just because it was not chosen to be canonized as "authoritative" Scripture by a particular "religious" community, even though we are told in God's Word there is a Book of Jasher?

Concerning the Book of Enoch, I found it to be a very interesting read, and it elaborated on some things the Bible alludes to but does not go in-depth on. For instance, the Book of Enoch talks in-depth about the angels who did not keep their proper domain and are in Sheol (Hades). They are reserved in chains as they wait for Judgment Day when the final judgment of God will take place before they are actually thrown into the *lake of fire.* This is

179

substantiated in the Bible in Jude 6:6, which says, *"And the angels who did not KEEP their proper DOMAIN, but left their own ABODE, He has RESERVED in everlasting CHAINS under darkness for the JUDGMENT of the great DAY..."* (NKJV) (emphasis added).

One of the reasons why the angels who did not keep their proper domain, but left their own abode, are "reserved" for judgment until Judgment Day commences, is because disciples of Jesus Christ who are resurrected in the *first* resurrection will be judging the angels.

This is based on what the apostle Paul says in First Corinthians 6:3 when he asks, *"Do you not know that we shall JUDGE angels? How much more, things that pertain to this life?"* (NKJV) (emphasis added).

The other reasons why the angels are "reserved" for judgment, I will cover in Chapter 68 of Book 3. For now, let's finish our discussion on Enoch.

Enoch is referenced in the Bible, and he was born in the seventh generation from Adam. In addition, because he walked closely with *Yehôvâh*, he was "translated" to heaven without ever dying a *physical* death, as some of us will be when the rapture takes place.

When the last trump is sounded, we will all be changed in the *twinkling of an eye* as we are "caught up" to meet Jesus in the air. However, the "rapture" only pertains to those few believers who are still alive and remain (survive) the tribulation period, that will take place on the earth to test all those who dwell on the earth, just before Jesus Christ appears the second time. I will cover this fact in-depth in Book 3 of this series.

According to God's Word, Enoch was "caught up" (raptured) to heaven without ever dying a *physical* death based on what the apostle Paul tells us in Hebrews 11:5, which specifically says, *"By FAITH Enoch was **TRANSLATED** [(16)] [(17)] [G3346: metatithemi: to transfer, or transport, or to change sides by carrying over, or to be removed] that he should not SEE [(18)] [(19)] [G1492: eidō: to know; perceive; understand] DEATH; and was not FOUND, because God had **TRANSLATED** [(16)] [(17)] him: for before his **TRANSLATION** [(16)] [(17)] he had this TESTIMONY, that he PLEASED God."* (KJV) (emphasis added).

Moreover, this *may* be one of the reasons why Enoch and Elijah will be God's two witnesses, based on Revelation Chapter 11, who will be prophesying in Jerusalem during the tribulation period because they did not experience a *physical* death. For we are specifically told in Hebrews 9:27, *"And as it is appointed for men to DIE once, but after this the JUDGMENT..."* (NKJV) (emphasis added).

However, read all of Hebrews 9:23–27 in "context" and this is specifically talking about the greatness of Christ's sacrifice and is referring to Jesus Christ only dying once as the Son of Man. Then He will come again for judgment.

Nevertheless, according to the Word of God, Enoch and Elijah never died a *physical* death, but the two witnesses who will be prophesying in Jerusalem during the tribulation period will die a *physical* death. Then they will be resurrected after three and a half days before they ascend back up into heaven in a cloud.

However, I believe the two final witnesses could be Moses and Elijah because they appeared on the *Mount of Transfiguration* with Jesus and His disciples as detailed in Matthew 17:1–5. They will also reappear sometime after six thousand years, just before the seventh millennium begins as well because Matthew Chapter 17 starts off by saying that after six days Jesus took His disciples up on a high mountain, and He was transfigured before them.

Mankind has been "ruling" and "reigning" with Jesus Christ on the earth for over six thousand years as I write this, and we are fast approaching the seventh millennium where we will once again *literally* tabernacle with God during the "marriage supper of the Lamb" that shall commence during the final Feast of Tabernacles held on planet earth.

In addition, *one day* with the Lord is as *one thousand years* based on Second Peter 3:8. It is also based on *one day* for each day of the creation week, where we have been working on the earth to establish God's kingdom on the earth as it is in heaven, for the past six thousand years. And it will be during the final Feast of Tabernacles ever held on planet earth; we will finally enter our final Sabbath day of rest in the *kingdom of heaven.*

Peter asked Jesus in Matthew 17:1–5, if He wanted him to build three tabernacles for Jesus, Moses, and Elijah because the "transfiguration" happened during the Feast of Tabernacles which is our heavenly Father's seventh holy convocation based on Leviticus Chapter 23. It shall come to pass that our "transfiguration" shall take place during this *same* holy convocation that is God's "appointed" time when we shall all be "transfigured" (changed) in the *twinkling of an eye*. Matthew 17:1–5 says the following:

> "*Now after SIX DAYS Jesus took Peter, James, and John his brother, led them up on a high mountain by themselves; and He was **TRANSFIGURED** [20] [21] [G3339: **metamorphoō**: to transform; G3445: **morphoō**: to fashion, or to form] before them. His FACE shone like the SUN, and His CLOTHES became as WHITE as the LIGHT. And behold, Moses and Elijah APPEARED to them, talking with Him. Then Peter answered and said to Jesus, 'Lord, it is good for us to be here; if You wish, let us make here three **TABERNACLES** [22] [G4633: **skēnē**: a tent, or cloth hut; used for habitation (sukkah) a temporary hut]: one for You, one for Moses, and one for Elijah.' While he was still speaking, behold, a bright CLOUD overshadowed them; and suddenly a VOICE came OUT of the CLOUD, saying, 'This is My beloved Son, in whom I am well pleased. Hear Him!' "* (Matt. 17:1–5, NKJV) (emphasis added).

Look at the Greek meaning of the word "transfigured" for it means "to be changed." Our bodies are our "tents," and our "tents" are a *temporary* dwelling place for our soul (spirit man) and God's Holy Spirit to dwell in while we are still living on the earth.

This is what will happen to us when we receive our glorified bodies. We will be "transfigured" (changed) in the *twinkling of an eye* at the sound of the last trump! And, instead of us hearing our heavenly Father say to Jesus as He did in Matthew 17:5, *"...This is My beloved Son, in whom I am well pleased. Hear Him!"* (NKJV)

We will hear Him say to us based on Matthew 25:21, *"...Well done, good and faithful servant; you were faithful over a few things, I will make you ruler over many things. Enter into the joy of your lord."* (NKJV) Hallelujah!

Another reason why I believe the two final witnesses could be Moses and Elijah is for the following reason: Since we are called to worship our heavenly Father, *Yehovah,* in Spirit and in truth, I believe one of these two witnesses could be Moses who brought us God's truth—His Law. The law was given during the very first Feast of Weeks (*Shavuot* or *Pentecost*), which was held at the base of Mount Sinai after God delivered the children of Israel out of their bondage in Egypt by His grace. Again, this is based on one of the promises He gave to Abraham when God established His *everlasting* covenant with him and his descendants.

Since we are specifically told according to Malachi 4:5, which says, *"Behold, I will send you Elijah the prophet Before the COMING of the great and dreadful DAY of the LORD..."* (NKJV) (emphasis added), one of the two witnesses will definitely be Elijah. The prophet Elijah represents the outpouring of the Holy Spirit during the Feast of Weeks (*Shavuot* or *Pentecost*) as depicted in the Book of Acts.

In summary, concerning the relevance of the Book of Enoch and what we can expect to take place in these final days, if you have

184

never read the Book of Enoch, then I highly recommend you do, for it will reveal many things the Bible does not elaborate on.

THIS IS ETERNAL LIFE: THAT WE MAY "KNOW" BOTH OUR HEAVENLY FATHER AND OUR LORD AND SAVIOR JESUS CHRIST WHOM HE SENT

Now let's continue to understand more fully why it is critical we know "who" *the Word* is in relationship to *Yehovah*, His and our heavenly Father. Based on John 17:1–5, it says that "knowing" our heavenly Father, *Yehovah*, the *only* true God, and His only *begotten* Son—*the Word* whom He sent to the earth as the Son of Man in a body of flesh and blood in the Person of Jesus Christ, is eternal life! This truth is substantiated in John 17:1–5, which says the following:

> *"Jesus spoke these words, lifted up His eyes to heaven, and said: 'Father, the hour has come. Glorify Your Son, that Your Son also may glorify You, as You have given Him authority over all flesh, that He should give eternal life to as many as You have given Him. And THIS is ETERNAL LIFE, that they may* **KNOW** (23) *[G1097: ginōskō: to learn to know (absolutely) to understand, perceive and have knowledge of (who God is experientially, not just intellectually)] You, the only true GOD, and JESUS CHRIST whom You have sent. I have glorified You on the earth. I have finished the work which You have given Me to do. And now, O Father, glorify Me together with Yourself, with the*

185

glory which I had with You before the world was.'" (John 17:1–5, NKJV) (emphasis added).

Again, we can "say" we believe in our heavenly Father, and our Lord and Savior Jesus Christ, all we want. Yet even the demons believe and tremble at this knowledge! However, do we really "know" the God of the Bible based on experiencing "who" He is because we have learned to absolutely understand the many different facets and emotions of "who" He is in a real tangible way by "walking" with Him, "talking" to Him, and "obeying" Him?

In other words, we can know about God intellectually based on what His Word says about Him. Yet without us cultivating a personal, intimate relationship with Him, we will never understand, perceive, or experience for ourselves who He truly is!

Your pastor, priest, or rabbi will *never* be able to allow you to "know" and "experience" on a personal, intimate basis, the God of the Bible. All they can do is point you, or lead you, to the God of the Bible, which every spiritual leader should do. For God is your source for everything you will ever need or desire.

Moreover, there are many people who do not mind using the generic name of "God" because their definition of "who" God is to them is based on what they have been taught to believe. All the different religions can readily accept the nebulous term of God. Everyone has a God they believe in—even atheists. There are all kinds of false gods people worship—money, power, sex, drugs, work, and so forth.

However, mentioning and referring to Jesus Christ is an entirely different matter for this reason: Believing in Jesus Christ distinguishes the *only* gate that leads to "walking" a very "narrow" path according to a very "narrow" way that results in eternal life.

The majority of people walk on the wide, easy path that most follow. However, for those who do, it will result in them reaping God's curses while they are still living on the earth, and eternal damnation when they die unless they repent.

Earlier in this chapter, in Proverbs 8:22–23, I defined the Hebrew meaning of what the phrase "the way" means which is as follows: A *trodden* road, course of life, mode of action along an eastward highway, pathway, or custom, which is defined by God as we follow in *only* His footsteps. This is the *only* way we will "walk" in His authority and power in order to trample on serpents and scorpions and crush the head of the serpent with every step we take!

In other words, "the way" describes "how" we are to walk our course of life every minute, every hour, and every day of the week everywhere we go! Following *the Word,* who is the Way, the Truth, and the Life, is a "lifestyle" and a lifelong journey based on a very "narrow" path, that we must follow if we hope to finish the race which is set before us, as we walk in the footsteps of Jesus Christ and follow *only* Him.

Yet we have made our faith "walk" all about following men and women who are dealing with issues just like we all are and in need a Savior too! Tragically, for the most part, we are only Christians when we attend church, yet when we go into the secular world, which is our mission field, we have the tendency to conform to what

187

is "socially" acceptable and be just like the lost are so we will be accepted and liked by them. We are more concerned about earning the approval of men rather than God!

In addition, there are many Christians who say it is not "politically correct" to talk about God in social settings because it will offend other people. Really?!

In fact, during this last election cycle, I heard *some* Christians say they have a problem with leaders, especially in the political sector of our society, who talk about God all the time in a setting that is outside the four walls of a building we call "the" Church.

I must ask these same people who are "professed" Christians, how we can truly love God with all our heart, soul, mind, and strength, and not want to talk about Him?

Equally important, how can we serve the One who has captivated our heart and transformed our lives by the power of His love, and us not want to "exalt" Him rather than ourselves? In addition, how can we not want to point people who are lost and have no hope of this world, to the *only* One who can offer them the hope of salvation, deliverance, and healing for the whole man—mind, body, and soul?

Listen to what the apostle Paul says to us in Philippians 2:5–11, about Jesus Christ who, being in the *form* of God, did not consider it robbery to be equal with God, but He *made* Himself of NO reputation. Therefore, God has highly "exalted" Jesus and has given Him the name that is *above* every name, of those in heaven, on the earth, and those under the earth. This is substantiated in Philippians 2:5–11, which says the following:

> *"Let this MIND be in YOU which was also in Christ Jesus, who, being in the FORM of God, did not consider it robbery to be EQUAL with God, but made Himself of NO REPUTATION, taking the FORM of a BONDSERVANT, and coming in the LIKENESS of MEN. And being found in APPEARANCE as a MAN, He HUMBLED Himself and became OBEDIENT to the POINT of DEATH, even the DEATH of the CROSS. Therefore God also has HIGHLY exalted Him [Jesus Christ] and given Him the NAME which is ABOVE every NAME, that at the NAME of Jesus every KNEE should BOW, of those in HEAVEN, and of those ON EARTH, and of those UNDER the EARTH, and that every TONGUE should CONFESS that Jesus Christ is LORD, to the GLORY of God the FATHER."* (Phil. 2:5–11, NKJV) (emphasis added).

Therefore, answer the following questions based on Philippians 2:5–11:

❖ How could *Yehoṿah*, God, our Creator, "exalt" Jesus *above* every name if they are the *same* Person in the Godhead?

❖ How could Jesus not think it to be robbery to be "equal" with God, yet He made Himself of NO reputation when He was willing to take the form of a bondservant and come to the earth in the likeness of men?

The answer is: They are one in Spirit, as we are one in the Spirit with God the Father, and His only *begotten* Son, *the Word,* who became the Son of Man in the flesh in the Person of Jesus Christ.

In addition, do not dismiss the significance that the very last thing the apostle Paul says to us in Philippians 2:5–11, is that *every* tongue should confess Jesus Christ is Lord to the glory of whom? The answer is: To the glory of God the Father.

When Jesus says to us, in Matthew 22:37, *"...You shall love the LORD your God with all your heart, with all your soul, and with all your mind."* (NKJV) Who is Jesus referring to? Is Jesus referring to Himself?

The answer to this question is not easy to understand for many people in the body of Christ, and for this reason, in the next chapter, I will cover in detail this truth: God the Father, God the Son, and God the Holy Spirit are the *same* God, for there is *only* one true God. They are three distinct Persons, or Powers, in the Godhead, and they choose to manifest themselves to us in different ways.

THE "PLURALITY" OF GOD IN THE GODHEAD

Thus, when Jesus stated in Matthew 22:37, we are to love the Lord our God, with all our heart, all our soul, and all our mind, He was referring to *Yehôvah*, His heavenly Father, who (qualified, selected, and chose) Him, *the Word,* as the *firstborn* over all creation based on Colossians 1:15, which says the following:

> *"He* [*the Word*] *is the IMAGE of the INVISIBLE GOD* [24] [G2316: *theos:* a *deity;* the supreme *Divinity,* or *Magistrate*], *the FIRSTBORN* [25] [26] [G4416: *prototokos:* firstborn G4413: *protos:* foremost (in time, place, order, or importance): beginning, before, best] *over all CREATION."* (Col. 1:15, NKJV) (emphasis added).

Therefore, *Yehovah,* our heavenly Father, as *'Elohiym,* God, our Creator, (qualified, selected, and chose) *the Word,* in His "invisible" image and likeness, which is Spirit, *before* they created our "invisible" eternal soul (spirit man) based on Genesis 1:26, which says the following:

> *"Then God said, 'Let us make MAN in our IMAGE, according to our LIKENESS...'"* (Gen. 1:26, NKJV) (emphasis added).

Based on Genesis 1:26, who is the "us" and "our" that *'Elohiym,* God, our Creator, is referring to when He says, *"Let us make MAN in our IMAGE, in our LIKENESS..."*?

The "us" and "our" that *'Elohiym,* God, our Creator, is referring to in Genesis 1:26, is the Holy Spirit, and the Son of His love—*the Word,* who is the *firstborn* over all creation.

Especially since God "spoke" forth His *Word* to "create" all creation in the heavenly realm *before* it ever manifested in the *physical*

191

earthly realm, based on the Scriptures listed below and on the following pages. There is *only* one supreme God, yet based on First John 5:7, the apostle John talks about the "plurality" of God in the Godhead as three distinct Persons: God the Father, God the Son (the "logos" Word), and God, the Holy Spirit.

> *"In the beginning **GOD*** [(27)] [H430: *'Ĕlōhîym*: is Plural of H433; *gods* in the ordinary sense as far as deity; but specifically used (in the plural thus, especially with the article) of the *supreme* God] ***CREATED*** [(28)] [H1254: *bârâ*: to *create*; to qualify, to select, or to choose] *the HEAVENS and the EARTH. The earth was without form, and void; and darkness was on the face of the deep. And the **SPIRIT*** [(29)] [H7307: *rûach*: *wind*; by resemblance *breath*, that is, a sensible (or even violent) exhalation] *of **GOD*** [(27)] *was hovering over the face of the waters. Then God said, 'Let there be **LIGHT*** [(30)] [(31)] [H215 & H216: *'ôr*: illumination, or to *be* (causatively *make*) *luminous*; *lightning*, *set on fire*, shine, or be *glorious*]*; and there was **LIGHT**.'"* [(30)] [(31)] (Gen. 1:1–3, NKJV) (emphasis added).

> *"For there are **THREE** that BEAR WITNESS in HEAVEN: the **FATHER*** [(32)] [G3962: *patēr*: a "father": parent], *the **WORD*** [(33)] [(34)] [G3056: *logos*: something said, or spoken (including the thought); utterance G3004: *legō*: (verb) to "lay forth," or to set discourse; call, speak, utter], *and the **HOLY*** [(35)] [G40: *hagios*: *sacred* (physically *pure*, morally *blameless*, or *religious*, ceremonially *consecrated*)] ***SPIRIT*** [(36)]

[**G4151:** *Pneuma*: the third person of the triune God, the Holy Spirit, coequal, coeternal with the Father and the Son; the rational spirit by which human beings feel, think and decide, the life-giving spirit; the influence which fills and governs the soul of anyone, the source of power; the breath of nostrils, or mouth—the breath of life; the Spirit of Truth]*; and these THREE are ONE."* (1 John 5:7, NKJV) (emphasis added).

*"In the beginning was the **WORD**** (33) (34)** [**G3056:** *logos*: something said, or spoken (including the thought); utterance **G3004:** *legō*: (verb) to "lay forth," or to set discourse; call, speak, utter], *and the **WORD**** (33) (34)** *was with* **GOD** *(27)* [**H430:** *'Elohiym*: is plural of H433; *gods* in the ordinary sense as far as deity; but specifically used (in the plural thus, especially with the article) of the *supreme* God]*, and the **WORD**** (33)** *(34)* *was* **GOD**. *(27)* *He was in the BEGINNING with* **GOD**. *(27)* *All THINGS were MADE through Him, and WITHOUT Him NOTHING was MADE that was MADE. In Him was **LIFE**** (37)** [**G2222:** *zoē*: the state of one who is possessed of vitality, or is animated; every living soul], *and the **LIFE**** (37)** *was the **LIGHT**** (38)** [**G5457:** *phōs*, or *phaō*: (to *shine* or make *manifest*); *luminousness; fire*] *of MEN. And the **LIGHT**** (38)** *shines in the darkness, and the darkness did not comprehend it."* (John 1:1–5, NKJV) (emphasis added).

193

"Jesus said to them, 'Most assuredly, I say to you, before Abraham was, I AM.'" (John 8:58, NKJV) (emphasis added).

"Father, I desire that they also whom You gave Me may be with Me where I am, that they may behold My GLORY (39) [G1391: *doxa*: dignity, honour, praise, and worship] *which You have given Me; for you LOVED Me BEFORE the FOUNDATION of the WORLD."* (John 17:24, NKJV) (emphasis added).

Therefore, based on the Scriptures listed on this page and the previous pages, there should be no doubt that *the Word* existed in glory *before* the world began.

This is based on what Jesus says to us in John 17:5 when He says, *"And now, O Father, GLORIFY Me together with Yourself, with the GLORY which I HAD with You BEFORE the WORLD was."* (NKJV) (emphasis added).

Moreover, *Yehováh* is *'Elóhiym*—God, our Creator, and our heavenly Father, who "formed" our bodies out of the dust from the ground which was taken from the earth.

This is based on Genesis 2:7, which says the following:

"And the LORD God formed MAN of the DUST of the GROUND, and BREATHED into his NOSTRILS the BREATH of LIFE; and MAN became a LIVING BEING." (Gen. 2:7, NKJV) (emphasis added).

Donna M. Rogers

WHAT IS AN ETERNAL "SPIRIT" AND "SOUL"?

Before we progress to understand our true identity as God's sons and daughters, let's define what an *eternal* "spirit" and "soul" is.

When Jesus tells us in Matthew 22:37, to love the Lord our God, with all our heart, with all our soul, and all our mind, why does Jesus specifically say heart, soul, and mind? He uses all three components that every human being possesses. Have you ever pondered this?

Our soul is comprised of the following four components, which all affect one another and are intricately linked to each other:

1. Our "mind" is our faculty of understanding. [40]

2. Our "thoughts" which is also our "soul" is comprised of our emotions, feelings, desires, affections, and aversions.

3. Our "heart" is the center and seat of our *spiritual* life and intelligence in the innermost part of our body. [41]

4. Our "soul" is also referred to as the *breath of life*, which without, we cannot be a living breathing being.[42]

Therefore, when we make the transition from being sojourners on the earth and return to being *eternal* "spirits" with a "soul" that God, our Creator, (qualified, selected, and chose) *before* the foundation of the world, our body comprised of bones and flesh returns to the earth from where it came.

195

Whereas, the "breath" of the *Spirit of Life* that we received from God, our Creator, which gives life to all flesh (even animals), returns immediately to God who gave it in the first place at the time of our *physical* death, which I will substantiate in the next chapter.

Now let's take a close look at Psalm 139:13–16. Also, worth mentioning, after you get done reading this Scripture, you will realize why abortion is such an abomination to the Lord! Psalm 139:13–16, says the following:

> *"For thou hast* **POSSESSED** [^(43)] [H7069: *qânâh*: created; by extension to procure, especially by purchase, or redeem] *my* **REINS** [^(44)] [H3629: *kilyâh*: a kidney (as an essential organ); figuratively the mind as the interior self] *: thou hast* **COVERED** [^(45)] [H5526: *sâkak*: fenced in, hedged in, joined together, protected and defended] *me in my MOTHER'S WOMB. I will praise thee; for I am FEARFULLY and WONDERFULLY MADE: MARVELLOUS are thy WORKS; and that my* **SOUL** [^(46)] [H5315: *nephesh*: which is the inner being of a man; our mind, which is our faculty of understanding; our thoughts which influence our emotions, feelings, desires, affections, and aversions; our heart which is the centre and seat of our spiritual life and intelligence in the innermost part of our body; and, our breath of life (spirit), which without, we cannot be a living, breathing, human being with the life force in our blood] *knoweth right well. My* **SUBSTANCE** [^(47)] [H6108: *ôtsem*: power; hence body] *was not hid from thee,*

196

when I was made in **SECRET** [48] [H5643: *sêther*: covering, shelter, hiding place, protection], *and curiously* **WROUGHT** [49] [H7551: *raqam*: embroider by implication to fabricate, or to knit] *in the* **LOWEST PARTS** [50] [H8482: *tachtîy*: the depths of a pit, the womb] *of the EARTH* [our bodies are made from the dust of the earth]. *Thine eyes did SEE my SUBSTANCE, yet being* **UNPERFECT** [51] [H1564: *golem*: embryo, fetus]*; and in thy BOOK all my MEMBERS* were *WRITTEN, which in CONTINUANCE were* **FASHIONED** [52] [53] [H3335: *yâtsar*: to mould into a form; especially as a *potter*; predetermined, or preordained, to be formed, or created, as a result of human activity; or divine activity of creation]*, when as YET there was NONE of them."* (Psalm 139:13–16, KJV) (emphasis added).

Wow! The first thing to take notice of based on Psalm 139:13–16, is we are told all of our "members" were written in God's book, which in "continuance" were fashioned (predetermined or preordained) when, as yet, there was none of them! This is talking about the fact there is no such thing as an "unplanned" pregnancy from God's perspective. It is also referring to our names being written in the Lamb's Book of Life *before* the foundation of the world. I will cover this subject more in-depth in Book 2.

The word "continuance" as used in Psalm 139:13–16, according to *Strong's Hebrew Lexicon* #H3117, is the Hebrew word "yôm" (pronounced "yome"), and means: Essentially "perpetually" in the process of time with regards to "life" or an "age."

The definition of "perpetually" means continuing, or enduring forever, for eternity.

The second thing we must take notice of based on Psalm 139:13–16, and ask ourselves is this profound question: How could we be woven in the depths of the earth and God saw our fetus before He would knit (embroider) us together in our mother's womb *before* one of our days on the earth ever came to be?

First, God foreknew the end from the beginning and He "predestined" everything in the heavens, on the earth, and under the earth, for His purposes and glory to prevail. This is substantiated in Revelation 1:8, which says, *"I am ALPHA and OMEGA, the BEGINNING and the ENDING, saith the Lord, which IS, and which WAS, and which IS to COME, the Almighty."* (KJV) (emphasis added).

We must always remember God views everything from an "eternal" perspective which has no beginning and has no end.

Therefore, God operates outside of time as we know it and from God's perspective time is "perpetual" in that it has no beginning and it has no end.

Moreover, based on the Hebrew meaning of the word "possessed" as used in Psalm 139:13–16, do not dismiss this significant truth: Just like *the Word* was (qualified, selected, and chosen) by extension of God Almighty Himself to procure by purchase our very soul, so it is with the soul of *every* human being whom our heavenly Father (qualified, selected, and chose) *before* one of our days on the earth ever came to be! Again, I will cover this in detail in Chapter 11 of this book.

For *every* human being is created in God's image and in God's likeness, and we have His Spirit, which is the *breath of life* (the life-force in our blood—for the life of the flesh is in the blood based on Leviticus 17:11), regardless of whether we acknowledge, or accept, Jesus Christ as our Lord and Savior.

As such, it is for this very reason, we can only be "reborn," or "born again," *spiritually* speaking, by placing our faith and trust in the One who created us in the first place, while we are still living on the earth, and while our *eternal* "soul" is still housed in these earthly vessels we call our bodies, which were "formed" out of the earth.

It is too late to be "reborn," or "born again," *spiritually* speaking, once we die a *physical* death.

Furthermore, from the very beginning of time, God foreknew who would accept, or reject, His only *begotten* Son—*the Word,* whom He sent to the earth as the Son of Man in the flesh in the Person of Jesus Christ, because all the days ordained for us were written in His book *before* one of them ever came to be.

In other words, God (qualified, selected, and chose) us to be "purchased" or "redeemed" by *the Word, before* the first human being ever sinned, and before *the Word* became flesh as the Son of Man in the Person of Jesus Christ. Therefore, *before* the foundation of the world, God came up with the *only* plan of "redemption" for the forgiveness of our sins so all mankind *might* be saved.

THE "PREEMINENCE" OF CHRIST

Now let's refocus our attention on the fact *the Word* was the *firstborn* over all creation.

The apostle Paul talks about the "preeminence" of Christ in Colossians 1:9–17, where he specifically says *the Word,* who became Jesus Christ in the flesh, is in the image of the "invisible" God, the *firstborn* over all creation. According to *Strong's Greek Lexicon* #G4409, the word "preeminence" is the Greek word "proteuo" (pronounced "prote-yoo'-o"), which means: To be first (in rank or influence). Colossians 1:9–17, says the following:

> *"For this reason we also, since the day we heard it, do not cease to pray for you, and to ask that you may be filled with the knowledge of His will in all wisdom and spiritual understanding; that you may walk worthy of the Lord, fully pleasing Him, being fruitful in every good work and increasing in the knowledge of God; strengthened with all might, according to His glorious power, for all patience and longsuffering with joy; giving thanks to the Father who has qualified us to be partakers of the inheritance of the saints in the light. He has DELIVERED us from the POWER of DARKNESS and CONVEYED us INTO the KINGDOM of the SON of His LOVE, in whom we have REDEMPTION through His BLOOD, the FORGIVENESS of SINS."* (Col. 1:9–14, NKJV) (emphasis added).

"He [the Word] is the image of the INVISIBLE God, the FIRSTBORN OVER all CREATION. For by Him all THINGS were CREATED that are in HEAVEN and that are on EARTH, visible and invisible, whether thrones or dominions or principalities or powers. All THINGS were CREATED through Him and for Him. And He is BEFORE all THINGS, and in Him all THINGS consist." (Col. 1:15–17, NKJV) (emphasis added).

Yes, indeed! The *Word* who came to the earth in the flesh as the Son of Man in the Person of Jesus Christ was and is God's *only* plan of "redemption" for all mankind *before* the foundation of the world.

It was at this time when God shared His dream with *the Word,* and the Holy Spirit, to have a family of sons and daughters on the earth, and in the heavens, for God's purposes and glory to prevail.

The *Creator of the Universe* wanted more than anything else to have a family created in His image and in His likeness, that would "walk" with Him, "talk" with Him, "listen" to Him, "worship" Him, and "obey" Him.

Because of us cultivating a personal, intimate relationship with *Yehovah*, our heavenly Father, and His Son, Jesus Christ, who was and is *the Word* made flesh, we would allow God, our Creator, to transform us and use us in order for Him to manifest His dreams and creativity in and through us, so that His will on the earth would be accomplished as it is in heaven.

Again, this is how we have eternal life now while we are still on the earth. It is by us "knowing" on a personal, intimate basis, our heavenly Father, *Yehôvah,* the *only* true God, and His Son, Jesus Christ, whom He sent.

In fact, Jesus modeled for us all what our purpose for being on the earth is in John 17:1–5, which He stated just *before* He made His ascension, back up into heaven. John 17:1–5, says the following:

> *"Jesus spoke these words, lifted up His eyes to heaven, and said: 'Father, the hour has come. Glorify Your Son, that Your Son also may glorify You, as You have given Him authority over all flesh, that He should give eternal life to as many as You have given Him. And THIS is ETERNAL LIFE, that THEY may KNOW You, the ONLY true God, and Jesus Christ whom You have sent. I have GLORIFIED You on the EARTH. I have FINISHED the WORK which you have GIVEN Me to DO. And now, O Father, GLORIFY Me together with Yourself, with the glory WHICH I HAD WITH YOU BEFORE the WORLD was.'"* (John 17:1–5, NKJV) (emphasis added).

There are two "key" things we should take notice of based on John 17:1–5. They are as follows:

The first "key" thing to take notice of is what Jesus said at the end of this Scripture which is this: Jesus specifically requested of His Father to glorify Him together with Himself with the glory He had with

Him *before* the world was, *because* He glorified His heavenly Father while He lived on the earth, and He finished the work which He had given Him to do.

In other words, Jesus fulfilled His "eternal" destiny for the very purpose which His heavenly Father (qualified, selected, and chose) Him to "do" *before* one of His days on this earth ever came to be that God "preordained" *before* the foundation of the world. Therefore, Jesus completed His assignment, and He glorified His heavenly Father while He was on His earthly mission.

So, it shall be with us, His disciples, *if* we follow in the footsteps of Jesus, and we fulfill our "eternal" destiny for the very purpose our heavenly Father (qualified, selected, and chose) us to "do" *before* one of our days on this earth ever came to be.

It is for this very reason, Jesus says to us in Matthew 7:21, *"Not everyone who says to Me, 'Lord, Lord,' shall ENTER the KINGDOM of HEAVEN, but he who does the WILL of My FATHER in heaven."* (NKJV) (emphasis added).

The second "key" thing to take notice of based on John 17:1–5, is this critical fact: It is one thing to know the Word of God; however, the most important thing we must seek to do is to "know" on a personal, intimate basis, our heavenly Father, *Yehováh*, and His Son, Jesus Christ, whom He sent, because this is "eternal" life!

In fact, according to John 5:37–40, Jesus tells us *Yehováh,* our heavenly Father, sent His Word to abide in us, yet we *think* we have eternal life by searching the Scriptures which testify of Him—*the*

Word. However, most are <u>not</u> willing to come to *the Word* so they may have life.

Then Jesus says of those who are <u>not</u> willing to come to Him the following: We have not heard His Father's Voice, or seen His form at *any* time, because we do <u>not</u> believe the Father has sent Him, *the Word,* who manifested Himself in the flesh, as the Son of Man in the Person of Jesus Christ. John 5:37–40, says the following:

> *"And the Father Himself, who sent Me, has testified of Me. You have <u>neither</u> HEARD His VOICE at <u>any</u> TIME, <u>nor</u> SEEN His FORM. But you DO <u>not</u> HAVE His WORD abiding <u>in</u> you, because whom He sent, Him you DO <u>not</u> BELIEVE. You search the Scriptures, for in them you THINK you have ETERNAL LIFE; and these are they which TESTIFY of Me. But you are not willing to COME to ME that you may have LIFE."*
> (John 5:37–40, NKJV) (emphasis added).

Unfortunately, due to their "spiritual" blindness this is the current state of many of God's Jewish people from the House of Judah who "religiously" study and hold fast to the Torah, yet they do not realize they have eternal life by "receiving" and "knowing" Jesus Christ as their Lord and Savior whom *Yehôvah* sent.

Therefore, we must intercede for our Jewish sisters and brothers and ask the Lord to remove their "spiritual" blindness, which He is already doing as the *fullness of the Gentiles* comes to its zenith. Yet at the same time, there are many in the body of Christ who have received Jesus Christ as their Lord and Savior and have countless

Bible studies but refuse to spend quality time with Him and experience His manifest presence on a continuous basis.

How can we claim to really know anyone if we hardly spend quality time with them?

Any relationship requires quality time spent together in order to grow deeper. And, this is especially true concerning our relationship with God.

Therefore, we must seek to "experience" eternal life now by really knowing Jesus and our heavenly Father in a real tangible way. We must nurture the most important relationship we will ever have while we are still living on the earth, so we can actually "live" the abundant life Jesus died to give us. However, this will require us to foster a personal, intimate relationship with the Holy Spirit.

ANOTHER HELPER—THE HOLY SPIRIT

Let's refocus our attention on the fact our heavenly Father, *Yehôvah,* who is Spirit and an all-consuming fire, sent the Son of His love—*the Word,* who is in the "bosom" of the Father Himself, to the earth in the flesh as the Son of Man in the Person of Jesus Christ.

As such, when the Son of Man, Jesus Christ, was crucified and resurrected from the grave three days and three nights later, and then He ascended back up into heaven from whence He came, *the Word,* who became flesh, was once again glorified together with His heavenly Father, with the glory which He had with Him *before* the world was.

Then it would come to pass our heavenly Father, *Yehovah* would send us another helper—God the Holy Spirit, the third Person of the Godhead, who is the glorified presence of God the Father, and God the Son. The Holy Spirit abides in the hearts of those who believe in God the Father, and His only *begotten* Son, Jesus Christ.

In addition, the Holy Spirit will teach us all things, and bring to our remembrance the things Jesus said to us according to His *eternal* Word as well.

As such, this is how our heavenly Father's greatest dream of all would be accomplished. His sons and daughters would have His grace and power for us to live our lives while we are still on the earth to please God, our Creator, as we fulfill our God-given destiny He "created" us for *before* the foundation of the world.

OUR HEAVENLY FATHER'S GREATEST DREAM OF ALL

Yehovah's greatest dream of all is that His sons and daughters would love Him, God their Creator, and Redeemer, with all their heart, soul, mind, and strength, once they remembered *who* they truly are—*eternal* "spiritual beings" created in His image and in His likeness *before* the foundation of the world. And, once they "believed" and "received" the Son of His love—*the Word*, who became the Son of Man in the Person of Jesus Christ, then they would, in turn, love each other because they "received" and "experienced" the *everlasting* love of their heavenly Father first.

Then *after* His sons and daughters chose to reciprocate His love for them while they still lived on the earth, when the purpose He created them for was finished, then like Jesus, they would once again be glorified with their heavenly Father, with the glory which they had before the world was, as they enter the *kingdom of heaven.*

This will occur when God resurrects the dead in Christ during the *first* resurrection, which will include those few who are still alive and remain (survive) the tribulation, which shall happen at the second appearing of Jesus Christ.

It will be at this time we shall be "caught up" in the clouds to meet the Lord in the air, which will take place only *after* the dead in Christ are resurrected *first,* based on First Thessalonians 4:15–18.

In addition, it will be at the return of Jesus Christ when we are "reborn," or "born again," *physically* speaking, because flesh and blood cannot enter the *kingdom of heaven.* I will cover this truth in-depth in Chapter 67 of Book 3.

However, our "spirit man" is "reborn," or "born again," *spiritually* speaking, the moment we receive Jesus Christ as our Lord and Savior.

Again, more than anything else, God desired a family in heaven and on the earth He could love. And, in return of His great love for us,

His created; we would love Him with all our mind, heart, soul and strength and love one another.

FAMILY IS VERY IMPORTANT TO GOD, AND HE DESIRES GODLY OFFSPRING WHICH IS A "REMNANT" OF THE SPIRIT

The family is so important to God, the word "family" is mentioned 138 times in His Word, and this is why God lists the genealogies of families throughout the Bible.

Furthermore, God established His very first covenant, which is the "Covenant of Marriage" between one man and one woman joining as one flesh in order to produce Godly offspring that would be "raised up" in the admonition of the Lord. And, as a result, they would serve and worship God, their Creator, and their Redeemer, while they still lived on the earth.

God wanted Godly offspring who would be a remnant of His Spirit based on Malachi 2:15, which states, *"But did He not make them one, HAVING a REMNANT of the SPIRIT? And WHY one? HE SEEKS GODLY OFFSPRING. Therefore take HEED to YOUR SPIRIT, And let none deal treacherously with the wife of his youth."* (NKJV) (emphasis added).

This is one of the primary reasons why Satan seeks to destroy fetuses in their mother's womb through abortion. So, he can destroy God's dream of having a family of sons and daughters who live on the earth that will serve God, their Creator, in the *kingdom of light*. It is for this very reason, Satan's ploy is to steal through deception, lies, and tragedies the true identity of God's sons and daughters, so they will serve him in the *kingdom of darkness*. Thus, they will sell their souls for the things of this world which the god of this world will offer them.

The primary reason Satan has been successful in orchestrating the greatest "identity" theft of God's sons and daughter's true identity in Christ, is for this reason· Many of God's people have left their first love, Jesus Christ, and they are not driven by eternity. Rather, their focus has become all about acquiring the prestige received from men, and the things of this world, which shall shortly pass away. Thus, many will lose their "souls," their "birthright," and their "inheritance," as God's "covenant" sons and daughters, *if* they do not repent and return to God before it is too late for all eternity!

If Satan cannot destroy God's sons and daughters *before* they are born, then he seeks to steal, kill, and destroy God's family from the moment they are born, so we will not live the "abundant" life Jesus died to give us while we are still living on the earth.

This is based on John 10:10, in which Jesus said to us, *"The thief [Satan] does not COME except to STEAL, and to KILL, and to DESTROY. I [Jesus] have come that they may have LIFE, and that they may have it more ABUNDANTLY."* (NKJV) (emphasis added).

Moreover, Satan knows if he can destroy the family, which is "the" foundational mountain of the seven mountains, or pillars, in our society, he will rule a nation.

Who is Israel? Discovering our True Identity in Jesus Christ and Why it Matters! The Foundation

Listen to the words of the apostle Paul in Ephesians 3:14–19, concerning God's dream of having a family in heaven and on the earth. It was for this very reason; God so loved the world, He was willing to sacrifice His only *begotten* Son, *the Word,* who became flesh as the Son of Man in the Person of Jesus Christ. Ephesians 3:14–19, says the following:

> *"For this reason I bow my knees to the FATHER of our Lord Jesus Christ, from whom the WHOLE FAMILY in HEAVEN and EARTH is NAMED, that He would grant you, according to the riches of His glory, to be strengthened with might through His Spirit in the inner man, that Christ may DWELL in YOUR HEARTS through FAITH; that you, being rooted and grounded in LOVE, may be able to comprehend with all the saints what is the width and length and depth and height—to KNOW the LOVE of Christ which passes knowledge; that you may be filled with ALL the FULLNESS of GOD."* (Eph. 3:14–19, NKJV) (emphasis added).

The apostle Paul clearly states to us in Ephesians 3:14–19, "...*the FATHER of our Lord Jesus Christ, from whom the whole FAMILY in HEAVEN and EARTH is NAMED...*" (emphasis added), is realizing His dream to have a family in the heavens and on the earth.

It was for this very reason, all human beings who would ever be "conceived" when a man and a woman joined as one flesh, which is supposed to be within the confines of the "Covenant of Marriage," began to be realized on the sixth day of creation only *after* God created a habitat for us to enjoy and rule over.

Have you ever stopped to think about the magnitude of God's love for us is so great, He has entrusted and enabled us with the ability to bring forth a living human being with an "eternal" spirit, soul, and body made of flesh and blood?

When God said in the beginning, *"Let us make MAN in our IMAGE, according to our LIKENESS,,,"* this is what God had in mind for His sons and daughters as well.

And, it is for this very reason, God has given His sons and daughters the creative ability to bring forth a "new" life when an embryo is formed from the "seed" (sperm) of a man, and a woman's "seed" (egg), joining as one in a woman's body.

Therefore, as the result of a man and a woman joining their flesh as one, God has given us the opportunity to be able to procreate a baby who is also made in the image and likeness of God the Father, God the Son of His love—*the Word*, and God the Holy Spirit.

God commanded us to be "fruitful" and "multiply" within the confines of His "Covenant of Marriage" which He defined as being between a man (husband) and a woman (wife)—it was all about God's dream of having a family on the earth who would love Him, and serve Him, once we "remembered" we are His children.

Do we have any idea what a gift it is to be blessed with children from our heavenly Father? Listen to what His Word says to us in Psalm 127:3, which proclaims, *"Behold, CHILDREN are a HERITAGE* from the Lord, *The FRUIT of the WOMB is a REWARD.*" (NKJV) (emphasis added)

How is it possible that Satan has convinced the majority of people having a child is a curse and an inconvenience, especially when an "unplanned" pregnancy occurs?

It may be an "unplanned" pregnancy from our perspective, however, when a pregnancy does result, it is God's will that specific child that He preordained *before* the foundation of the world, enters the *physical* earthly realm at His "appointed" time He predestined, so they may accomplish His purpose and destiny for their lives.

Equally important, that particular child will impact countless individuals they come into contact with during their lifetime. When individuals choose to kill a child through abortion, that child would have been someone's husband or wife, brother or sister, mother or father, or friend, if they had been allowed to live.

Again, reread Psalm 139:13–16, where we are specifically told all of our "members" were written in God's book, which in "continuance" were fashioned (predetermined or preordained) when, as yet, there was none of them!

God predetermined and preordained every "eternal" soul that was created in His image and in His likeness, would enter the earthly realm as an embryo/fetus/baby in their mother's womb, which always begins in "seed" form. Look at the stateliest tree in your yard. Was it always a big, magnificent tree, with massive branches covered with large amounts of foliage to provide shade and oxygen to sustain life? No, it started out as a sapling, which started from a "seed."

The same is true of a human being who begins life as a "seed" that develops into an embryo/fetus/baby who grows within the confines and protection of their mother's womb.

When an embryo/fetus/baby is being "formed" within their mother's womb, the embryo/fetus/baby has the following attributes:

1. A fetus has an "eternal" spirit.

2. A fetus has a soul which has feelings and emotions.

3. A fetus has a heart that beats.

4. A fetus has a mind that thinks.

5. A fetus has lungs to receive the essential oxygen that is passed through their mother's umbilical cord as the mother breathes for their child.

6. A fetus is given food (nutrients) with the aid of its mother's umbilical cord.

7. A fetus has bones, flesh, and blood.

Then once the baby is born, it begins to grow and matures exponentially—first as a child; then as a young adult; then as an

213

adult; then as a middle-aged adult; then as an elderly adult, if we are blessed with a long life as sojourners on the earth.

It is *Yehovah,* our heavenly Father, and the Son of His love—*the Word,* and the Holy Spirit, who gives every fetus (baby) in their mother's womb their "eternal" soul, which they created in their image and in their likeness *before* the foundation of the world. This is how God *foreknew* us *before* one of our days on the earth ever came to be.

Again, God "created" an "eternal" soul for *every* male and female who would ever be "conceived" at the foundation of the world. This was long *before* He would "form" us in our mother's womb at His preordained time and for His preordained purpose. I will substantiate this truth according to God's Word in Chapter 11 of this book.

However, the very first "eternal" soul came from God Himself—*the Word,* who is the Son of His love, long before the Son of Man in the Person of Jesus Christ was manifested on the earth in a body of flesh and blood. Do we realize God has a soul?

This is substantiated in Leviticus 26:11, which says, *"I will set My TABERNACLE* (54) [H4908: *mishkân:* residence, dwelling place] *among you, and My SOUL* (46) [H5315: *nephesh:* breath; mind; mortality] *shall not abhor you."* (NKJV) (emphasis added).

God has a soul, for God specifically says "My soul" in Leviticus 26:11. In addition, we are specifically told God Himself will place His dwelling place and take up residence amongst us whom He has created.

In closing, our heavenly Father has placed it upon my heart His people do not understand "who" the God we profess to serve really is. As such, before we can understand our true identity as God's sons and daughters, we must first seek to fully understand "who" our heavenly Father, and our Lord and Savior Jesus Christ is, based on the whole counsel of His *eternal* Word.

Therefore, in the next chapter, I will substantiate this truth: God the Father, God the Son, and God the Holy Spirit, are the same God, yet they are three distinct Persons, or Powers, in the Godhead.

CHAPTER 8

GOD THE FATHER, GOD THE SON, AND GOD THE HOLY SPIRIT ARE THE SAME GOD, YET THEY ARE THREE DISTINCT PERSONS IN THE GODHEAD

N ow that you know the truth that *Yehôvah* (qualified, selected, and chose) *the Word* as the *firstborn* over all creation, you may be saying to yourself, "Well, wait a minute, the *Word*, which is Jesus Christ who became flesh as the Son of Man and God are one—they are the *same* God based on what the Trinity doctrine says."

Yes, they are the same God, yet they are a "separate" and "distinct" Person or Power in the Godhead.

Moreover, the word "Trinity" is not found in the Bible, but the word "Godhead" is based on Romans 1:20 and Colossians 2:8–10, which says the following:

> *"For since the creation of the world His invisible ATTRIBUTES are clearly seen, being understood by the things that are made, even His eternal POWER and **GODHEAD** [1] [2] [3] [G2305: **theiotēs**: divinity; G2304: **theios**: godlike; G2316: **theos**: of uncertain affinity; a deity, especially the supreme Divinity; a Magistrate; judge], so that they are without excuse..."* (Rom. 1:20, NKJV) (emphasis added).

> *"Beware lest anyone cheat you through PHILOSOPHY and EMPTY DECEIT, according to the TRADITION of MEN, according to the BASIC PRINCIPLES of the WORLD, and not according to Christ. 'For in Him DWELLS all the FULLNESS of the **GODHEAD** [3] [4] [G2316: theos: of uncertain affinity; a deity, especially the supreme Divinity; figuratively a magistrate; judge; G2320: theotēs: divinity (abstractly)] bodily; and you are COMPLETE in Him, who is the HEAD of all PRINCIPALITY and POWER.'"* (Col. 2:8–10, NKJV) (emphasis added).

According to the King James Version of the *New Testament Greek Lexicon*, [5] the word "Theos" can mean the following:

1. A god, or goddess, a general name of deities, or divinities.

2. The Godhead (Trinity).

    a. God the Father, the first Person of the Trinity.

    b. Christ, the second Person of the Trinity.

    c. Holy Spirit, the third Person of the Trinity.

3. Spoken of the *only* one and true God:

    a. This refers to the things of God, such as His counsels, interests, things due to Him.

4. Whatever can, in any respect, be likened unto God, or resemble Him, in any way:

a. God's representative or Vice-regent.

1. Of magistrates and judges.

In addition, the Greek word "theos" can mean "God" or "gods," or "deity" or "deities," which are beings that have (or have attributed to them) the *essential* nature of a God.

The apostle Paul specifically states in Romans 1:20, *"For since the creation of the world His invisible ATTRIBUTES are CLEARLY SEEN, being understood by the things that are made, even His ETERNAL POWER and GODHEAD..."* (NKJV) (emphasis added).

Therefore, when Jesus' disciples, who are human beings that were created in His image and His likeness, "walk" according to the Spirit, rather than the flesh, do we not also "walk" according to the *essence* of God's nature? As such, we will exhibit the "fruit" of His Spirit, which is love, joy, peace, forbearance, kindness, goodness, faithfulness, gentleness, and self-control.

Furthermore, God the Father, and God the Son are "one" in the Spirit. This is based on John 10:30, which says, *"I and My Father are ONE."* (NKJV) (emphasis added).

They are each a distinct Person in the Godhead that has the same "invisible" attributes (nature).

As Jesus' disciples, we are also separate individuals with a distinct purpose who have the same "invisible" attributes as well, when we "walk" according to the Spirit, rather than our flesh. We then become "one" with them in the Spirit as we abide in God's manifest presence.   Everyone collectively comprises the body of Christ despite our unique purpose, and we become "one" body of believers, *spiritually* speaking, under the headship of Christ.

In addition, God the Father, God the Son, and God the Holy Spirit are "one" in the Spirit as they are all "one" and the same God in this regard: They are all supernatural beings, and they are holy, divine, and sacred. For this is the definition of a deity. As such, they have the natural attributes and exhibit the external characteristics of "the fruit of the Spirit."

Philippians 2:5–8 substantiates this truth.   As you read this passage of Scripture, keep in mind this is how we, as His disciples, are to become as we follow in the footsteps of Jesus according to the leading of the Holy Spirit. We too are being "fashioned," or "made," into the image and likeness of Christ as we humble ourselves, and become obedient to our heavenly Father. This will be based on how much we "choose" to crucify our flesh, and "submit" our will to God's will. Philippians 2:5–8, says the following:

> *"Let this mind be in you, which was also in Christ Jesus: Who, being in the* **FORM** ⁽⁶⁾ ⁽⁷⁾ [G3444: **morphē**: (through the idea of *adjustment* of parts); *shape*; figuratively *nature;* G3313: **meros**: (to *get* as a *section*, or *allotment*); a *division*, or *share*] *of God, thought it not ROBBERY to be EQUAL with God: But made Himself of no* **REPUTATION** ⁽⁸⁾ [G2758: **kenoō**: to *make empty*, that is, (figuratively) to *abase*, *neutralize*, *falsify;* make (of none effect, of no reputation, void), be in vain], *and took UPON Him*
> 220

the **FORM** [(6)] [(7)] of a SERVANT, and was **MADE** [(9)] [G1096: *ginomai*: *cause to be* ("gen"-erate), that is, (reflexively) to become (*come into being*); to be ordained to be] *in the LIKENESS of MEN: And being found in* **FASHION** [(10)] [G4976: *schēma*: a *figure* (as a *mode*, or *circumstance*), that is, (by implication) *external* condition] *as a MAN, He* **HUMBLED** [(11)] [G5013: *tapeinoō*: to *depress*, figuratively to *humiliate* (in condition, or heart); abase, bring low] *Himself, and became* **OBEDIENT** [(12)] [(13)] [G5255: *hupēkoos*: *attentively listening*, that is, (by implication) *submissive*; G5219: *hupakouō*: to *heed*, or *conform*, to a command, or authority; obey] *unto DEATH, even the DEATH of the CROSS.*" (Phil. 2:5–8, KJV) (emphasis added).

Therefore, Jesus emptied Himself, so He would not neutralize, falsify, or make of no reputation—the One who had sent Him. He did this so His earthly mission would not be in vain. In other words, He accomplished His mission because Jesus "chose" to humble Himself, and He "chose" to become obedient to the will of His Father, even unto death.

Are we willing to follow in Jesus' footsteps and drink from His cup of suffering (*lot* or *fate*) as we humble ourselves and become obedient to do the will of our heavenly Father for His name's sake even unto death? We cannot do this in our own strength. We must receive God's power and anointing from the Holy Spirit. This is why *after* Jesus was resurrected from the grave, and Mary Magdalene saw the "risen" Lord, Jesus commissioned His apostles and they "received" the Holy Spirit. This is based on John 20:21–23, which says the following:

> *"So Jesus said to them again, 'Peace to you! As the Father has sent Me, I also send you.' And when He had said this, HE BREATHED ON THEM, and said to them, 'RECEIVE the HOLY SPIRIT. If you forgive the sins of any, they are forgiven them; if you retain the sins of any, they are retained.'"* (John 20:21–23, NKJV) (emphasis added).

Therefore, Jesus' apostles "received" the Holy Spirit from God Himself, before they would receive the *baptismal of the Holy Spirit* with *fire* when the day of Pentecost had fully come. This is substantiated in the Book of Acts, Chapter 2.

Now let's refocus our attention on *the Word* who is God's only *begotten* Son, the *firstborn* over all creation. Our heavenly Father sent *the Word* to the earth in the flesh as the Son of Man in the Person of Jesus Christ. This is based on First John 5:6, which says, *"This is He* [the Word] *who CAME* [to the earth through the virgin birth] *by water and blood—Jesus Christ; not only by water, but by water and blood. And it is the SPIRIT who BEARS WITNESS, because the SPIRIT is TRUTH."* (NKJV) (emphasis added).

In addition, there are many Scriptures which testify God the Father, and God the Son, are two distinct Persons in the Godhead, yet they are the same God. And the third Person of the Godhead is the Holy Spirit, which is the *Spirit of God*—God the Father, and God the

Son, whose Spirit is the One who bears witness of this truth because He is the *Spirit of Truth!*

And, this is why Jesus tells us in Matthew 28:19, when we go and make disciples of all the nations, we are to baptize them in the name of the Father, the Son, and the Holy Spirit.

They are one in undivided "essence" and "Glory," which belong to all three, for we have God the Father, who is called the "Father of Glory" in Ephesians 1:17. We have *the Word,* who became the Son of Man in the Person of Jesus Christ, who is the brightness of His Father's Glory. He is the express image of His person we refer to as the "Son of His Glory" based on Hebrews 1:2–5. We also have the Holy Spirit, who is called the "Spirit of Glory" based on First Peter 4:14.

THE "PLURALITY" OF ELOHIYM IN THE GODHEAD

God the Father, God the Son, and God the Holy Spirit, are the same God, for together they depict the "plurality" of the triune "nature" or "essence" of *'Elohiym* in the Godhead.

Furthermore, God the Father, God the Son, and God the Holy Spirit, all work together and "rule" and "reign" in perfect harmony with one another. For there is no competition in the Godhead; there is only unity in their "oneness" despite the "plurality" of *'Elohiym* in the Godhead.

Speaking of the "plurality" of God, more specifically concerning *'Elohiym,* when we witness to our Jewish sisters and brothers, they will quote this one verse to substantiate God doesn't have a Son. This is based on Deuteronomy 6:4, which says, *"Hear, O Israel: The LORD our* **GOD** [(14)](#) [(15)](#) [**H430:** *'Elŏhîym:* is the Plural of H433; gods in the ordinary sense; but specifically used (in the plural thus, it is referring to the supreme God; **H433:** *'elôahh:* a *deity*, or the *deity*], *the LORD is* **ONE** [(16)](#) [**H259:** *'echâd: one*, (as an ordinal which is of, or relating to, someone, or a thing, concerning their, or its, position in a series) *first:* alike, altogether, together]*!"* (NKJV) (emphasis added).

Therefore, based on the Hebrew meaning of the word "God" in Deuteronomy 6:4, it is referring to "'Elŏhîym," which in this case, is plural in its usage. This is describing the "plurality" of God—the "triune" God; God the Father, God the Son, and God the Holy Spirit. They are "the" deity in the Godhead; the Supreme God who is also a magistrate (Judge).

They are all united as "one" God despite their different manifestations of the three unique Persons and Powers in the Godhead.

I once heard the following analogy, which was used to describe this "triune" nature of God, I believe will help us to better understand God's "triune" existence or the "plurality" of God as *'Elŏhîym.*

In this analogy, water was used as an example. Water can take on different manifestations depending upon what one chooses to do with it. Water in its original form is a colorless, transparent, odorless, and tasteless liquid that forms the seas, lakes, and rivers from the rain we receive and is the basis of the fluids of living organisms. However, if we freeze water, it becomes ice, or frozen water, which is then transformed into a brittle, transparent crystalline solid. If we boil water, it becomes steam, or vapor, into which water is converted when heated, forming a white mist of minuscule water droplets in the air.

In all these three different examples, water never stops being water just because it can be "transformed" for different uses and will manifest a new "form" in various ways. It is still water.

This is the closest analogy I can think of to describe the very essence of the "triune" God, or the "plurality" of God, in the Godhead. They are all the *same* God, yet they are three different Persons and Powers in the Godhead, who choose to manifest themselves to us in various ways.

In fact, this is one of the reasons why Jesus had to go back to His Father's house, which is in heaven where there are many mansions. Jesus tells us the reason "why" He had to go back to His Father's house which is this: He could prepare a place for us so when He comes again, He will receive us to Himself, so where He currently is (in heaven), there we may also be.

Jesus says to us in John 14:16, *"And I will pray the Father, and He will give you ANOTHER HELPER, that He may ABIDE with you forever..."* (NKJV) (emphasis added).

In John 14:1–6, Jesus tells us He is the Way, the Truth, and the Life, and no one comes to the Father except through Him.

Then immediately in John 14:7–11, Jesus reveals *who* the Father is.

225

In John 14:12–14, Jesus talks about this fact: He who believes in Him will also do the works He did, and even greater works than these, because He is going to His Father. As such, whatever we ask for in His Name, He will do, so His Father may be glorified in Him, the Son.

All this leads up to Jesus revealing the *Spirit of Truth*—the Holy Spirit, who is "the" other Helper that will dwell with us and be in us based on John 14:16.

Then in John 14:19–24, Jesus talks about the "indwelling" of the Father, and the Son, for those who have and keep His commandments because we love Him.

Therefore, God the Father, God the Son, and God the Holy Spirit are all "one" in unity, and they are all "deity" in respect to their divine status, quality, or nature, even though they are three distinct Persons in the Godhead.

In all three different manifestations of the Godhead, they are all referred to as "Lord" as well based on the following Scriptures where God the Father, is Lord; God the Son is Lord, and God the Holy Spirit is Lord.

> *"At that time Jesus answered and said, 'I thank You, FATHER, LORD of HEAVEN and EARTH, that You have hidden these things from the wise and prudent and have revealed them to babes.'"* (Matt. 11:25, NKJV) (emphasis added).

> *"God is faithful, by whom you were called into the*

226

fellowship of His Son, JESUS CHRIST our LORD." (1 Cor. 1:9, NKJV) (emphasis added).

"Now the LORD is the SPIRIT; and where the SPIRIT of the LORD is, there is liberty." (2 Cor. 3:17, NKJV) (emphasis added).

In all three of these Scriptures, the word "Lord," according to *Strong's Greek Lexicon* #G2962, is the Greek word "kurios" (pronounced "koo'-ree-os"), which means: Referring to *supremacy*: *supreme* in authority, that is, (as noun) *controller*; by implication *Mr.* (as a respectful title); God, Lord, Master, Sir.

WHEN WE PRAY TO GOD THE FATHER, WE ARE ALSO PRAYING TO GOD THE SON, AND TO GOD THE HOLY SPIRIT

As we pray or talk to God the Father, we are praying and talking to all three Persons of the Godhead at once because they are "one" in plurality. However, each Person in the Godhead chooses to manifest themselves to us in different ways.

Therefore, if we pray to God the Father, we are also praying to God the Son, and God the Holy Spirit, because we cannot know, hear, or see God the Father, except through God the Son. In addition, we cannot know, see, or hear God the Son, unless the Holy Spirit reveals God the Son to us.

We pray to God the Father, through the name of God the Son, Jesus Christ. Yet it is the Holy Spirit who enables us to hear, know, see, and receive what we have petitioned our heavenly Father for through prayer.

A BIBLICAL ANALOGY WHICH DEPICTS THE PLURALITY OF THE "NATURE" OR "ESSENCE" OF GOD AS "ONE" IN UNITY

One example I can think of that talks about the plurality of the "nature" or "essence" of God as "one" in unity, but "plurality," is as follows: God's Word tells us in Matthew 19:5, *"For this reason a man shall leave his father and mother and be joined to his wife, and the TWO shall become ONE flesh?"* (NKJV) (emphasis added).

Well, even though a husband and a wife become "one" flesh when they are joined "spiritually," "mentally," and "physically," this does not mean they are no longer two different "distinct" persons. Rather, the two "distinct" persons becoming "one" flesh, means they become "one" in spirit, mind, soul, and body. As such, what the husband does and says will affect the wife, and vice versa, because in the "Covenant of Marriage" they become one.

Now let's take a closer look at what the apostle Paul tells us in Colossians 1:9–16, which says the following:

> *"For this reason we also, since the day we heard it, do not cease to pray for you, and to ask that you may be filled with the knowledge of His will in all wisdom and spiritual understanding; that you may walk worthy of the Lord, fully pleasing Him, being fruitful in every*

good work and increasing in the knowledge of God; strengthened with all might, according to His glorious power, for all patience and longsuffering with joy; giving thanks to the Father who has qualified us to be partakers of the inheritance of the saints in the light. He has DELIVERED us from the POWER of DARKNESS and CONVEYED us into the KINGDOM of the SON of His LOVE, in whom we have REDEMPTION through His BLOOD, the FORGIVENESS of SINS." (Col. 1:9–14, NKJV) (emphasis added).

"He [*the Word (logos)* in Aramaic is '*Memra,*' which means the Word of God by which the universe was created and is the mind of God as revealed in creation] [17] *is the IMAGE of the INVISIBLE God, the firstborn OVER all* **CREATION** [18] [G2937: *ktisis:* original *formation* (properly the act; by implication the thing, literally, or figuratively); building, creation, creature, ordinance]. *For by Him all THINGS were* **CREATED** [19] [G2936: *ktizō:* (through the idea of the *proprietorship* of the manufacturer); to *fabricate,* that is, *found* (*form* originally); create, Creator] *that are in heaven and that are on earth, visible and invisible, whether thrones or dominions or principalities or powers. All THINGS were CREATED through Him and for Him."* (Col. 1:15–16, NKJV) (emphasis added).

In Colossians 1:9–14, the apostle Paul tells us to give thanks to

Yehôvah, our heavenly Father, who has qualified us to be partakers of the inheritance of the saints in the *kingdom of light.* He has conveyed us into the "kingdom" of the Son of His love, who is *Yehôvah's* only *begotten* Son—*the Word,* who became the Son of Man in the Person of Jesus Christ. He did this so that through His blood, we have redemption for the forgiveness of our sins.

Then we are told *the Word* is the image of the "invisible" God, and He is the *firstborn* over all creation. This is referring to the *Memra*—*the Word,* who is the "invisible" Spirit of *Yehôvah,* who is in the "bosom" of God the Father.

HOW THE WORD BECAME FLESH

The *Word,* who later became the Son of Man in the Person of Jesus Christ in the flesh, is referred to as God's only *begotten* Son. He was conceived as "flesh" and "blood" when the Holy Spirit overshadowed Mary, a virgin, who was highly favored by God.

Since *Yehôvah* knows the end from the beginning, He foreknew *before* the first Adam ever sinned this truth: The only way to settle man's inability to live in perfect obedience to His law, was for Him to come to the earth in the form of "flesh" and "blood" and redeem mankind, and the world, by sacrificing the Son of His love—*the Word,* who became flesh.

It is for this very reason, why God the Father, chose to incarnate Himself as *the Word,* the second Person of the Godhead—the Son of His love. He would send *the Word* to the earth as the Son of Man who would be conceived by a virgin through a miraculous conception which was orchestrated by the Holy Spirit. In other words, there was *no* fornication (sex) involved.

At this time it is worth mentioning this fact: Muslims who practice the Islam faith say Jesus cannot be, and is not, the Son of God because this would mean Mary had sex to conceive Him. Those that practice the Islam faith, do believe Jesus is Mary's son, but they *deny* Jesus is the Son of God, or He is God Himself.

This amazing story of how *the Word* became flesh so God could *physically* tabernacle (dwell) on the earth amongst His people in a body of flesh and blood, is revealed in Luke 1:26–33, which says the following:

> *"Now in the sixth month the angel Gabriel was sent by God to a city of Galilee named Nazareth, to a virgin betrothed to a man whose name was Joseph, of the HOUSE of DAVID* [a descendant of King David]. *The virgin's name was Mary. And having come in, the angel said to her, 'Rejoice, highly favored one, the LORD is with you; blessed are you among women!'"* (Luke 1:26–28, NKJV) (emphasis added).

> *"But when she saw him, she was troubled at his saying, and considered what manner of greeting this was. Then the angel said to her, 'Do not be afraid, Mary, for you have found favor with God. And behold, you will CONCEIVE in your WOMB and bring forth a Son, and shall call His name JESUS.* [20] [21] [22] [23] [24] [25]

231

(26) (27) *He will be great, and will be called the SON of the **HIGHEST*** (28) **[G5310: *hupsistos*: highest, that is, (masculine singular) the *Supreme* (God), or (neuter plural) the *heavens*]***; *and the Lord God will give Him the THRONE of His father David. And He will REIGN over the HOUSE of JACOB forever, and of His KINGDOM there will be NO END.'"* (Luke 1:29–33, NKJV) (emphasis added).

In this series of books, I interchangeably use Jesus' Hebrew name *Yehoshûa', Yeshûa,* or *Yâhshua,* which refers to our Lord and Savior Jesus Christ. I conveyed various transliterations of His name based on Luke 1:29–33, along with the corresponding Greek meanings of His name, at the time the angel Gabriel appeared to Mary and specifically told her what to name her Child.

THE PROPER NAME OF GOD

Based on the meaning of the name of Jesus in Hebrew, which is *Yehoshûa', Yeshûa,* or *Yâhshua,* this name actually means "the Lord (Yahweh) is salvation."

Furthermore, I predominately refer to our heavenly Father by the name of *Yehovâh,* (Yahweh [YHWH]), or *Elohîym.* The truth is God has many different names that are used to describe different aspects of His many-faceted characteristics, which are pronounced or spelled differently, based on what language a person may speak. In addition, there are many different translations of His Name depending upon what version of the Bible a person may be using. All I know is one day, when I was in imminent danger and invoked the power and authority I have in the name of Jesus Christ, the English version of His name since I speak English, it stopped a Rottweiler dead in its tracks from attacking me!

Therefore, for God's people to argue, or discard someone's teachings based on what name they use for Jesus, or our heavenly Father, should not be condoned. After all, isn't Jesus Christ the name by which most of us became saved in the first place?

As such, it is a process to come into alignment with the uncompromised, unadulterated, whole counsel of God's Word. We need time to "unlearn" many of the things we have been taught in a church, or in our culture.

In addition, God understands we have been led astray, and He is gracious and merciful and will meet us right where we are until His Holy Spirit unveils His truth to us. Once we know His truth, and we are willing to "receive" His truth, then we will be held accountable and no longer have an excuse for being in error.

At the same time, in John 5:43–44, Jesus says to us, *"I have come in My FATHER'S NAME, and you do not RECEIVE Me; if ANOTHER comes in his OWN name, HIM you will RECEIVE. How can you believe, who receive HONOR from one another, and do not SEEK the HONOR that COMES from the ONLY GOD?"* (NKJV) (emphasis added).

The "key" thing I want us to focus our attention on at this time, which is based on John 5:43–44, is this: Jesus specifically tells us He has come in His Father's Name. As such, what is our heavenly Father's Name? It is *Yehováh* (Yahweh [YHWH]).

Therefore, if Jesus Christ came in His Father's Name, then *Yehováh's* only *begotten* Son would be called *Yehóshûa'*, *Yêshûa,* or *Yáhshua,* rather than Jesus, because there are no "J's" in the Hebrew language. Yet we have been taught to call Him by the name of Jesus based on what our early church fathers have taught us, and based on the name used in our Bibles, which were translated by men.

Furthermore, God tells us in Zephaniah 3:9, He will restore to the "people" a *pure* language so they all may call on the name of the Lord to serve Him with one accord. This *pure* language God is indeed restoring in all the nations is the Hebrew language. It has been said to be the holy language with which God's law was written, and God communicates with His angels.

We are told in Philippians 2:9–11, our heavenly Father, *Yehováh,* has highly "exalted" His only *begotten* Son, and given Him the "name" which is *above* every "name" of those in heaven, of those on the earth, and of those under the earth, and at the "name" of His Son *every* tongue shall profess, and *every* knee shall bow. As such, I believe it is important for the body of Christ to use His correct name.

Jesus' correct "name" would be *Yehóshûa'*, *Yêshûa,* or *Yáhshua.* Therefore, once the Holy Spirit unveils and confirms what His correct Hebrew name is, then the body of Christ must use His correct Hebrew name so we can call upon the name of the Lord to serve Him with one accord.

Now let's refocus our attention on the remaining passages of Scripture found in the Book of Luke of "how" *the Word* became flesh so God could *physically* tabernacle (dwell) on the earth amongst His people in a body of flesh and blood.

In Luke 1:34–35, we are told without question Jesus is the Son of God, and His Father is the Most High, who is the Supreme God. We are also told "how" Jesus, the Son of God—the Holy One, was conceived, which happened because of the Holy Spirit overshadowing Mary, who was highly favored by God. Mary conceived the Son of God when the Holy Spirit came upon Mary, and the POWER of the Highest, Supreme God, overshadowed her! Luke 1:34–35, says the following:

> *"Then Mary said to the angel, 'How can this be, since I do not* **KNOW** [29] [G1097: *ginōskō*: the Jewish idiom for sexual intercourse between a man and a woman] *a man?' And the angel answered and said to her, 'The* **HOLY** [30] [G40: *hagios*: sacred (physically pure, morally *blameless*, or *religious*, ceremonially *consecrated*)] **SPIRIT** [31] [G4151: *Pneuma*: the third person of the triune God, the Holy Spirit, coequal, coeternal with the Father and the Son; the rational spirit by which human beings feel, thinks and decides, the life-giving spirit; the influence which fills and governs the soul of anyone, the source of power; the breath of nostrils, or mouth—the breath of life; the *Spirit of Truth*] *will COME UPON you, and the* **POWER** [32] [G1411: *dunamis*: strength, power, ability

for performing miracles] *of the* **HIGHEST** (28) [G5310: *hupsistos*: *highest*, that is, (masculine singular) the *Supreme* (God), or (neuter plural) the *heavens*] will **OVERSHADOW** (33) [G1982: *episkiazō*: to *cast a shade upon*, that is, (by analogy) to *envelop in a haze of brilliancy*; to *invest* with preternatural influence] *you; therefore, also, that HOLY ONE who is to be BORN will be CALLED the* **SON** (34) [G5207: *uihos*: a '*son*' immediate, remote, or figurative kinship; child] *of* **GOD** (3) [G2316: *theos*: *the deity* of the Godhead: 1) God the Father, the first person in the Godhead; 2) Christ, the second person in the Godhead; 3) the Holy Spirit, the third person in the Godhead; the only true God].' " (Luke 1:34–35, NKJV) (emphasis added).

This next statement may ruffle the feathers of practicing Catholics; nevertheless, God's truth must prevail. The virgin girl named Mary was born through the "seed" of a man just as all earthly children come from the "seed" (sperm) of their earthly fathers. Therefore, Mary inherited the sinful *nature* because of Adam's transgression just like the rest of us.

However, once the "dunamis" POWER of God cleansed Mary and redeemed her *when* the POWER of the *Highest*—Supreme God, overshadowed her by His Holy Spirit, it was then her body was indeed "sanctified" and "purified." Then she could miraculously conceive the Son of God in her womb because she "believed" what the Lord had told her through the angel Gabriel. And shortly, I will substantiate what I am saying based on God's Word. Many people worship Mary, Jesus' mother, and believe she was born without sin. Mary, like the rest of us, needed a Savior. This is substantiated in God's Word based on the very first thing Mary said in response to what Elizabeth said to her when she visited the house of Zacharias and Elizabeth. Zacharias and Elizabeth were her relatives who were also the father and mother of John the Baptist. This truth is substantiated in Luke 1:39–49. For now, let's look at Luke 1:39–45 below:

> *"Now Mary arose in those days and went into the hill country with haste, to a city of Judah, and entered the house of Zacharias and greeted Elizabeth. And it happened, when Elizabeth HEARD the GREETING of Mary, that the BABE LEAPED in her WOMB; and Elizabeth was filled with the Holy Spirit. Then she* [Elizabeth] *spoke out with a loud voice and said, 'Blessed are you among women, and blessed is the FRUIT of your WOMB! But why is this granted to me, that the MOTHER of my LORD should come to me? For indeed, as soon as the voice of your greeting sounded in my ears, the BABE LEAPED in my WOMB for JOY. Blessed is she who BELIEVED, for there will be a FULFILLMENT of those THINGS which were told her from the Lord.'"* (Luke 1:39–45, NKJV) (emphasis added).

Before we continue, we need to take notice of three things that are quite apparent based on Luke 1:39–45, before we examine what Mary said. First, take note of the fact when John the Baptist was a fetus in his mother's womb, he leaped for joy when his mother Elizabeth heard Mary's greeting.

Therefore, this means a fetus has an "eternal" soul with emotions and responds to things happening in their environment and what their mother is feeling.

Second, Elizabeth was "filled" with the Holy Spirit *before* Mary's baby was born, when Elizabeth said, *"For there will be a FULFILLMENT of THOSE THINGS which were told to her* [Mary] *from the Lord."*

In the Old Testament, there were times *Yehovah* chose to "fill" certain individuals with the Holy Spirit for His purposes to prevail long before Jesus Christ would be born, crucified, resurrected, and ascend back up into heaven.

As such, the only way Elizabeth could have known about Mary's encounter with the angel Gabriel, and Mary would be the mother of her Lord, is by Elizabeth receiving a revelation from the Holy Spirit. Because the Scriptures do not say, Mary had shared this encounter she had with the angel Gabriel, and what the angel spoke to her with Elizabeth.

Third, Elizabeth tells us *why* there would be a fulfillment of those things, which the Lord had told Mary through the angel Gabriel. It was because Mary "believed" what the Lord had spoken!

Now let's see what Mary's response to Elizabeth's revelation is in

Luke 1:46–49, which says the following:

> *"And Mary said: 'My SOUL MAGNIFIES the Lord, And my SPIRIT has rejoiced in God my SAVIOR. For He has regarded the LOWLY STATE of His MAIDSERVANT; For behold, henceforth all generations will call me blessed. For He who is mighty has done great THINGS for me, And HOLY is His NAME.'"* (Luke 1:46–49, NKJV) (emphasis added).

Based on what Mary said in Luke 1:46–49, why would Mary say *her* spirit rejoiced in God, *her* Savior if she didn't need a Savior just like the rest of us? She also said *her* soul "magnified" the Lord. Then she says that God has regarded the "lowly" state of *her*, His maidservant.

As such, in Mary's own words, she was not perfect and sinless. She needed a Savior just like the rest of us, even though Mary was highly favored and blessed by God. And, it was for this reason, God chose Mary to be His vessel to give birth to His Son.

Mary, like the rest of us, needed a Savior! Therefore, we are not to worship or hope to get our prayers answered through Mary, Jesus' mother. Especially since Jesus says to us in John 14:6, *"I am the WAY, the TRUTH, and the LIFE. No ONE comes to the FATHER EXCEPT through Me."* (NKJV) (emphasis added).

Therefore, God's plan of redemption He had *before* the foundation of the world would come to pass because of the "seed" of *the Word* being placed in Mary's womb when the Holy Spirit overshadowed her. As such, Jesus Christ was not born with the sinful nature, because He was not born by the "seed" of man which came from an *earthly* father. It is for this very reason, when we receive Jesus Christ as our Lord and Savior, we like Mary who "believed," are cleansed by His perfect blood that came from God the Father.

In addition, Jesus remained without sin, even though He was tempted with various trials and tribulations like we all are.

In fact, He "learned" obedience to God, His heavenly Father, by the things which He suffered while He was on the earth.

This is substantiated in Hebrews 5:8, which says, *"...though He was a Son, YET He learned OBEDIENCE by the THINGS which He SUFFERED."* (NKJV) (emphasis added).

So, it is with us, for our heavenly Father will not expect us to do what He first was not willing to do Himself!

Hence, for Jesus Christ to be without sin, when He took all of *our* sins upon Himself on the cross at Calvary, this means He had never sinned in the first place for He was "the" perfect "Passover Lamb" without spot or blemish from the foundation of the world.

The fact that Jesus took all of *our* sins upon Himself on the cross at Calvary is substantiated in Isaiah 53:6.

This Scripture says, *"All we like sheep have gone astray; We have turned, every one, to his own way; And the LORD has LAID on Him the INIQUITY of US ALL."* (NKJV) (emphasis added).

240

Therefore, when Jesus Christ was conceived, He did not inherit the sinful nature of the first Adam for this reason: He was conceived by the POWER of His heavenly Father when the Holy Spirit overshadowed Mary.

THE "WORD" IS THE ONLY "BEGOTTEN" SON OF GOD'S LOVE

It is critical we fully understand *the Word* was conceived by a miraculous conception *when* the Holy Spirit overshadowed Mary.

And, it is for this very reason, He is the only "begotten" Son of God's love—*the Word,* who existed with God, and was and is God *before* the world began. This was long before He would become the Son of Man in the Person of Jesus Christ.

Therefore, since *the Word* is the only *begotten* Son, who is in the "bosom" of the Father, who is the image of the "invisible" God who is Spirit and He is the *firstborn* over all creation based on Colossians 1:15, then *the Word* came from God, and is God. He was with God in the beginning based on John 1:1.

This is substantiated in Isaiah 43:10–11, where we are specifically told the following: Before God, there was no God "formed," nor shall there be any God after Him. Then the Lord says, besides Him, there is no Savior. This means *the Word,* and God the Father, are "one" and the "same" God. Isaiah 43:10–11, says the following:

> *"'You are My witnesses,' says the LORD, 'And My servant whom I have chosen, That you may KNOW*

and BELIEVE Me, And understand that I am He. BEFORE Me there was NO God FORMED, Nor shall there be AFTER Me. I, even I, am the LORD, And BESIDES Me there is NO SAVIOR.'" (Isa. 43:10–11, NKJV) (emphasis added).

The word "formed" as used in Isaiah 43:10–11, is the Hebrew word "yâtsar" (pronounced "yaw-tsar'"), which means: To mold into a form, such as *squeezing* into a shape for a predetermined purpose by a potter, which in this case is God.

In addition, *the Word* is in God's "image" and in His "likeness" just like we are.

The word "image" is the Hebrew word "tselem" (pronounced "tseh'-lem"), and means: A *phantom*, that is, (figuratively) an *illusion,* or *resemblance* of someone, or something.

Whereas, the word "likeness" is the Hebrew word "dᶜmûth" (pronounced "dem-ooth'"), which means: A *resemblance;* concretely a model, shape, or *like-*fashion in a similar manner.

Moreover, we know based on God's Word, God has all the *physical* attributes we do, especially since *Yehôvâh* manifested Himself through *the Word* in the *physical* earthly realm as the Son of Man.

As such, since we were created in His image and His likeness, God has a face, a mouth, ears, hair, a mind, a soul, and a body made up of flesh and blood with legs, arms, feet, and hands as we do.

YEHOVAH AND *THE WORD* ARE "ONE" AND THE "SAME" GOD YET TWO DISTINCT PERSONS (POWERS) IN THE GODHEAD.

When we submit ourselves to their Holy Spirit, we abide in them— both our heavenly Father and His Son whom He sent. Also, everything in God's Word that refers to *Yehôvah* in the Old Testament also refers to *Yêshûa'* (Jesus) in the New Testament, for the following reasons:

❖ In the Old Testament, *Yehôvah* is *Yêshûa'* concealed.
❖ In the New Testament, *Yêshûa'* is *Yehôvah* revealed.

God always uses the testimony of two or three witnesses to establish a matter; therefore, I will too.

EXAMPLE 1:

In Daniel 7:9, our heavenly Father, *Yehôvah,* is being revealed, yet in Revelation 1:13–15, "the Lamb" who was slain before the foundation of the world, Jesus Christ, is being revealed.

Yet their description is the same. Also, notice in Daniel 7:9, there is more than one throne.

Daniel 7:9 and Revelation 1:13–15, says the following:

> *"I watched till thrones* [plural] *were put in place, And the ANCIENT of DAYS was seated; His garment was white as snow, And the HAIR of His HEAD was like PURE WOOL. His THRONE was a FIERY FLAME, Its*

243

wheels a burning fire... " (Dan. 7:9, NKJV) (emphasis added).

"...and in the midst of the seven lampstands One like the SON of MAN, clothed with a garment down to the feet and girded about the chest with a golden band. His HEAD and HAIR were WHITE like WOOL, as WHITE as SNOW, and His EYES like a FLAME of FIRE; His FEET were like fine BRASS, as if refined in a FURNACE, and His VOICE as the SOUND of many WATERS..." (Rev. 1:13–15, NKJV) (emphasis added).

EXAMPLE 2:

In Psalm 24:7–10, the word "LORD" in all capital letters is referring to *Yehôvâh,* our heavenly Father, and God, our Creator. He (qualified, selected, and chose) *the Word,* who is the *firstborn* over all creation, for all things were created in and through *the Word* who became the Son of Man in the flesh in the Person of Jesus Christ. This is substantiated in Psalm 24:7–10, which says the following:

*"Lift up your heads, O you gates! And be lifted up, you everlasting doors! And the **KING** (35) (36) [**H4428**: melek: a royal king; **H4427**: mâlak: to rule and reign; inceptively to ascend the throne; induct into royalty; hence to take counsel] of GLORY shall come in. Who is this **KING** (35) (36) of GLORY? The **LORD** (22) [**H3068**: Y'hôvâh: (the) self-Existent, or eternal; Jehovah, Jewish national name of God] strong and mighty, The*

244

***LORD** (22) mighty in battle. Lift up your heads, O you gates! Lift up, you everlasting doors! And the **KING** (35) (36) of GLORY shall come in. Who is this **KING** (35) (36) of GLORY? The **LORD** (22) of **HOSTS** (37) [H6635:* tsâbâ': a mass of persons (or figurative things), especially regularly organized for company, worship, service, war, or hardship at an appointed time]*, He is the **KING** (35) (36) of GLORY. Selah."* (Psalm 24:7–10, NKJV) (emphasis added).

Therefore, the *King of Glory* specifically refers to *the Word,* who appeared to Abraham as Melchizedek, the *king of Salem,* who brought out "bread" and "wine" because He was and still is the High Priest of God the *Most High.* And, He appeared to Abraham before He *literally* became our Great High Priest under the *order of Melchizedek.*

In First Corinthians 2:7–8 below, the *Lord of Glory* is Jesus Christ because He is the One who was crucified. He is also the One Enoch refers to as the "Wisdom of God" in the Book of Enoch.

*"But we speak the WISDOM of **GOD** (3) [G2316:* theos: a deity; the supreme *Divinity,* or *Magistrate]* in a mystery, the hidden WISDOM which **GOD** (3) ORDAINED before the AGES for our GLORY, which NONE of the RULERS of this AGE knew; for had they KNOWN, they would NOT have CRUCIFIED the **LORD** (38) [G2962:* kurios: supreme *in authority, that is, (as noun)* controller, *by implication Mr. (as a respectful title): God, Lord, Master, Sir] of GLORY."* (1 Cor. 2:7–8, NKJV) (emphasis added).

245

EXAMPLE 3:

The last example I will use to substantiate the truth, *Yehôvah* and Jesus Christ are "one" and the "same" God, is in Psalm 97:9, which talks about *Yehôvah*. Psalm 97:9, says the following:

> *"For You, **LORD*** (22) [H3068: *Yhôvah:* (the) *self-Existent,* or eternal; *Jehovah,* Jewish national name of God], are **MOST HIGH** (39) [H5945: *'Elyôn:* an *elevation,* that is, (adjectively) *lofty* (comparatively); as title, the *Supreme;* (Most, on) high (-er, -est), upper (-most)] ABOVE all the EARTH; You are EXALTED far ABOVE all GODS."* (Psalm 97:9, NKJV) (emphasis added).

Whereas, John 3:31–36, talks about those who have "received" the Son's testimony which has certified God the Father, is the one and *only* true God. John 3:31–36, says the following:

> *"He who COMES from ABOVE is above ALL; he who is of the earth is earthly and speaks of the earth. He who COMES from HEAVEN is above ALL. And what He has SEEN and HEARD, that He TESTIFIES; and NO ONE RECEIVES His TESTIMONY. He who has RECEIVED His [Jesus'] TESTIMONY has CERTIFIED that **GOD** (3) [G2316: *theos:* a *deity;* the supreme Divinity, or Magistrate] is TRUE. For He whom **GOD** (3) has sent SPEAKS the WORDS of **GOD**, (3) for **GOD** (3) DOES NOT GIVE the SPIRIT by MEASURE. The Father LOVES the **SON** (34) [G5207: *uihos:* a 'son'*

immediate, remote, or figurative, kinship; child], *and
has GIVEN all THINGS into His HAND. He who
BELIEVES in the* **SON** (34) *has everlasting LIFE; and
he who DOES* not *BELIEVE the* **SON** (34) *shall* not
SEE LIFE, but the WRATH of **GOD** (3) *ABIDES on
him.*" (John 3:31–36, NKJV) (emphasis added).

In addition, based on John 3:31–36, we are specifically told this
indisputable truth: Those who believe in the Son has *everlasting
life*, yet, he who does not believe the Son shall not see life because
the *wrath of God* still abides on him.

Why must mankind believe in God's Son in order to be saved?
Because our heavenly Father, *Yehovah*, loves His only *begotten* Son,
the Word, who from the very beginning, was in the "bosom" of the
Father.

Therefore, the Son of His love, *the Word,* was willing to come to the
earth in order to die for the sins of God's sons and daughters who
were created in His image and in His likeness before the foundation
of the world.

Those who would "believe" in the Father's beloved Son, and
"receive" the testimony of the Son.

The "testimony" of God the Son, has certified, God the Father is the
one and *only* true God.

Thus, our heavenly Father, *Yehovah,* has given all things into His
Son's hand! In other words, whatever belongs to *Yehovah,* our
heavenly Father, belongs to His Son, Jesus Christ, who receives the

inheritance of His Father's nature and everything that belongs to Him as well.

After all, what parent doesn't give their beloved children everything they have because they love them with an *everlasting* love, especially since they are an extension of themselves?

Indeed, *the Word* who became flesh is *Yehôvah* Himself in Spirit and in truth.

THE WORD WAS SENT TO THE EARTH TO "TESTIFY" AND TO "BEAR WITNESS" TO HIS HEAVENLY FATHER'S TRUTH

Our heavenly Father, *Yehôvah,* sent *the Word* to the earth to "testify" and to "bear witness" to His truth. In fact, Jesus specifically tells us in John 7:16, His doctrine (instructions) is not from Him, but comes from His heavenly Father who sent Him.

Therefore, at this time I need to briefly address the fact we are called to worship our heavenly Father, *Yehôvah,* and our Lord and Savior Jesus Christ, in Spirit according to His truth, as God's sons and daughters.

As such, because *Yehôvah* and Jesus Christ are "one" and the "same" God, the same is true for all of God's commandments as well, including those found in the Torah. For Jesus says to us in Matthew 28:20, *"...teaching them to OBSERVE all THINGS that I have*

COMMANDED *you...*" (NKJV) (emphasis added), as we "disciple" all the nations and carry out the *Great Commission.*

In addition, Jesus tells us in John 13:34–35, *"A NEW COMMANDMENT I give to you, that you LOVE one another; as I have loved you, that you also LOVE ONE ANOTHER. By this ALL will KNOW that you are My DISCIPLES, if you have LOVE for ONE ANOTHER."* (NKJV) (emphasis added).

Jesus is adding this "new" commandment to all His other commandments He has already given us in the Torah written by His servant Moses.

In fact, Jesus says to us in John 5:45–47, *"Do not THINK that I shall ACCUSE you to the FATHER; there is ONE who ACCUSES you— MOSES, in whom you trust. For if you BELIEVED MOSES, you would BELIEVE ME; for he wrote about Me. But if you DO NOT BELIEVE his [Moses'] WRITINGS, how will you BELIEVE My WORDS?"* (NKJV) (emphasis added).

Concerning Moses' writings which are our heavenly Father's instructions for all His people, Jesus was and is the living Torah— the Word of God who became flesh.

Therefore, who do you think the commandments in the Torah came from in the first place?

They came from both, *Yehôvâh,* our heavenly Father, and *the Word,* whom our heavenly Father sent to the earth as the Son of Man in the Person of Jesus Christ, who is "one" and the "same" God in Spirit and in truth!

As such, Jesus would not violate His own law that He established in the first place.

If we do not believe Jesus and His early disciples kept the commandments found in the Torah, such as the *seventh*-day Sabbath, and the rest of our heavenly Father's holy convocations—which, by the way, are all *everlasting* ordinances—then we have been led astray and are deceived.

Hence, one of the many purposes of this series of books is to lead God's people back to the *gospel of the kingdom* that was once delivered to the saints, so we do not perish for all eternity *if* we do not repent, and make a course correction now. The early disciples not only preached and taught from the Torah—but they also obeyed our heavenly Father's commandments, especially based on the fact the New Testament was not written yet.

THE "CONCEALED ONE" AND THE "ELECT" HAD EXISTED IN THE PRESENCE OF THE *LORD OF SPIRITS BEFORE* THE WORLD WAS CREATED

Enoch says the "invisible" Word (*Memra*), who was in the "bosom" of *Yehovah* Himself, "preexisted" *before* He was manifested in the flesh on the earth as the Son of Man in the Person of Jesus Christ. Enoch refers to the "Concealed One" in Chapter 48 of the Book of Enoch. [(40)]

Therefore, as you read the excerpt which I have taken from the

Book of Enoch, do not dismiss the significance Enoch says "the elect" existed in the presence of the *Lord of Spirits* (plural) *before* the world was created.

Chapter 48 [1]

1. In that place, I beheld a fountain of righteousness, which never failed, encircled by many springs of wisdom. Of these all the thirsty drank, and were filled with wisdom, having their habitation with the righteous, the elect, and the holy.

2. In that hour was this Son of man invoked before the Lord of spirits, and his name in the presence of the Ancient of days.

3. Before the sun and the signs were created, before the stars of heaven were formed, his name was invoked in the presence of the Lord of spirits. A support shall he be for the righteous and the holy to lean upon, without falling; and he shall be the light of nations.

4. He shall be the hope of those whose hearts are troubled. All, who dwell on earth, shall fall down and worship before him; shall bless and glorify him, and sing praises to the name of the Lord of spirits.

5. Therefore the ELECT and the CONCEALED ONE existed in His presence before the world was created, and forever.

6. In his presence he existed, and has revealed to the saints and to the righteous the wisdom of the Lord of spirits; for he has preserved the lot of the righteous, because they have hated and rejected this world of iniquity, and have detested all its works and ways, in the name of the Lord of spirits.

7. For in his name shall they be preserved; and his will shall be their life. In those days shall the kings of the earth and the mighty men, who have gained the world by their achievements, become humble in countenance.

8. For in the day of their anxiety and trouble their souls shall not be saved; and they shall be in subjection to those whom I have chosen.

9. I will cast them like hay into the fire, and like lead into the water. Thus shall they burn in the presence of the righteous, and sink in the presence of the holy; nor shall a tenth part of them be found.

10. But in the day of their trouble, the world shall obtain tranquility.

11. In his presence shall they fall, and not be raised up again; nor shall there be any one to take them out of his hands, and to lift them up: for they have denied the Lord of spirits, and his Messiah. The name of the

Lord of spirits shall be blessed." (emphasis added).
[end of excerpt]

My dear sisters and brothers in Christ, God knew us *before* one of our days on the earth ever came to be and *before* He knit us together in our mother's womb.

We have been sent to the earth like Jesus was to "do" the will of our heavenly Father for His "eternal" purposes and glory to prevail, and for us to fulfill the destiny He created us for *before* one of our days on this earth ever came to be!

I will cover this fact in greater detail in Chapter 11 of this book when I convey why we must understand our true identity and purpose as God's sons and daughters in Christ.

In closing, if you still do not believe everything I have presented in this chapter, which is based on the whole counsel of God's Word, concerning whether *Yehôvah,* and *the Word* (Jesus Christ), are two distinct Persons (Powers) in the Godhead, even though they are "one" and the "same" God in Spirit and in truth, then ponder the following questions. Then come up with your own answers as you seek the Holy Spirit who will guide you into all truth.

1. How is it possible that *Yehôvah* (qualified, selected, and chose) *the Word* as the *firstborn* over all creation, if they are "one" and the "same" Person in the Godhead?

2. If God the Father, and God the Son, are "one" and the "same" Person in the Godhead...

    a. Who exactly was Jesus praying to when He was on the earth? Was He praying to Himself?

    b. Why did Jesus continually refer to His Father in everything He did or said? Again, God's Word says in John 1:18, *"No one has SEEN God at any TIME. The ONLY BEGOTTEN SON, who is in the BOSOM of the FATHER, He has DECLARED Him."* (NKJV) (emphasis added).

    c. Whose "voice" was heard from heaven? This is based on Matthew 3:17, which says, *"And suddenly a VOICE came from HEAVEN, saying, 'This is My beloved Son, in whom I am well pleased.'"* After all, Jesus was on the earth, and this "voice" came from heaven.

    d. Who resurrected Jesus Christ from the grave after He was crucified?

3. How can Jesus be seated at the right hand of God the Father, in heaven in the throne room of God, if they are "one" and the "same" Person in the Godhead?

4. How could God the Father, highly "exalt" Jesus above *every* name including His own, if they are "one" and the "same" Person in the Godhead? The definition of the word "exalt" means to "raise up" to a higher rank, or a position of greater power.

This is based on Philippians 2:9–11, which says, *"Therefore God also has highly EXALTED Him* [Jesus Christ] *and given Him the NAME which is ABOVE every NAME, that at the NAME of JESUS every knee should bow, of those in heaven, and of those on earth, and of those under the earth, and that every tongue should confess that Jesus Christ is Lord, to the GLORY of GOD the FATHER."* (NKJV) (emphasis added).

In addition, why would God the Father, have desired to "exalt" the name of Jesus above *every* name so that He (God the Father) could get the glory? In other words, if they are "one" and the "same" Person or Power in the Godhead, then there would be *no* need for God the Father, to do this, because He would automatically get the glory.

5.   How could *only* God the Father, know the "day" and the "hour" of Jesus' second coming if they are "one" and the "same" Person in the Godhead? This is based on Mark 13:32, which says, *"But of that DAY and HOUR no one KNOWS, not even the ANGELS in heaven, nor the SON, but only the FATHER."* (NKJV) (emphasis added).

6.   In Matthew 19:16–17, Jesus answers the rich young ruler's question, which is as follows: *"Good Teacher, what GOOD THING shall I DO that I may have ETERNAL LIFE?"* (NKJV) (emphasis added).

Jesus told him that His heavenly Father, *Yehôvah,* is the *only* One who is good when Jesus said, *"Why do you CALL me GOOD? No ONE is GOOD but ONE, that is, GOD. But if* *you want to **ENTER** into **LIFE**, **KEEP** the COMMANDMENTS."* (NKJV) (emphasis added).

Therefore, as I said before, but it bears repeating, we must keep both our heavenly Father's commandments found in the Old Testament, and the commandments of Jesus found in the New Testament based on Matthew 19:17, which specifically says, *"...But if you want to **ENTER** into **LIFE**, **KEEP** the COMMANDMENTS."* (NKJV) (emphasis added).

Again, when Jesus said this during His earthly ministry, the New Testament was not written yet. Therefore, we must have a personal, intimate relationship with our heavenly Father, *Yehôvah,* and our Lord and Savior Jesus Christ. And, we must keep *their* commandments to enter the *kingdom of heaven.* This is based on what Jesus says to us in Matthew 7:21, which says, *"Not **EVERYONE** who says to Me, 'Lord, Lord,' shall **ENTER** the **KINGDOM** of **HEAVEN**, but **HE** who **DOES** the **WILL** of My **FATHER** in **HEAVEN**.'"* (NKJV) (emphasis added).

The truth of the matter is many Christians only seek to understand what Jesus or the apostle Paul says to us in the New Testament.

Yet the majority of believers in the body of Christ are totally "dismissing" and "invalidating" our heavenly Father's commandments in the Old Testament written in the Torah by His servant Moses. And for those who do so, they are making a "fatal" error because they are "one" and the "same" God who does not change, although they are two distinct Persons or Powers in the Godhead.

Our heavenly Father's instructions are written to all the children of Israel throughout the *synergy of the ages*. These instructions are found in the Torah which was written by God's servant Moses, and they are reiterated by Jesus Himself.

God's instructions for all His people are the terms and conditions of us "walking" in a "Covenant of Marriage" with our heavenly Father *after* we become saved by grace through faith in Jesus Christ. As a matter of fact, in Book 3, I will substantiate in detail what I am proclaiming is true based on the whole counsel of God's unadulterated, uncompromised Word.

7. In Matthew 12:46–50, Jesus says that whoever does the will of His Father in heaven are His brothers, sisters, and mother. If our heavenly Father, *Yehôvah,* and Jesus Christ are "one" and the "same" God and Person or Power in the Godhead, then how can we be God's sons and daughters, and at the same time, be Jesus' sisters, brothers, and even His mother, because we do the will of our heavenly Father, *Yehôvah?* Matthew 12:46–50, says the following:

> *"While He was still talking to the multitudes, behold, His mother and brothers stood outside, seeking to speak with Him. Then one*

> *said to Him, 'Look, Your mother and Your brothers are standing outside, seeking to speak with You.' But He answered and said to the one who told Him, 'Who is My mother and who are My brothers?' And He stretched out His hand toward His disciples and said, 'Here are My mother and My brothers! For WHOEVER DOES the WILL of My FATHER in heaven is My brother and sister and mother.'"* (Matt. 12:46–50, NKJV) (emphasis added).

8. And last, but certainly not least, to have "eternal" life while we are still alive and living on planet earth, then we must "know" on a personal, intimate basis, *both* our heavenly Father, *Yehovah,* and His only *begotten* Son, Jesus Christ. This is based on John 17:3, which says the following:

> *"And THIS is ETERNAL LIFE, that they may KNOW You, the ONLY TRUE GOD, and JESUS CHRIST whom You have SENT."* (John 17:3, NKJV) (emphasis added).

Again, "knowing" on a personal, intimate basis the one and *only* true God and His Son, Jesus Christ, whom He sent is eternal life. As such, God does not want our religion—He wants our hearts!

Therefore, if you do not know how to cultivate a personal, intimate relationship with our heavenly Father, and His Son, Jesus Christ, whom He sent, or what this looks like, I wrote a teaching titled, *It Is Not About Religion! It is all About an Intimate Personal Relationship with Jesus Christ!*

This teaching can be accessed under the tab on my website titled, "Accept Jesus Now." [41]

And, if you have not yet made the most important decision you will ever make in your entire lifetime by receiving Jesus Christ as your personal Lord and Savior, now *is* the time to do so.

Now is the day of your salvation for we are not promised tomorrow. It is too late to be "reborn" again, *spiritually* speaking, after you die a *physical* death. This decision to "receive" Jesus Christ as your Lord and Savior *must* be made while you are still alive and living on planet earth.

In the next chapter, I will answer the thought-provoking question which is this: "Since God (qualified, selected, and chose) *the Word* in the image of Him, the "invisible" God, to be the *firstborn* over all creation, then where did God the Father come from?"

Who is Israel? Discovering our True Identity in Jesus Christ and Why it Matters! The Foundation

CHAPTER 9

WHERE DID GOD THE FATHER COME FROM?

S ince God (qualified, selected, and chose) *the Word* in the image of Him, the "invisible" God, to be the *firstborn* over all creation, then where did God the Father come from? The answer is: God has *always* existed.

Furthermore, in the last chapter, I covered in-depth the fact *the Word* is from the "bosom" of God the Father, and God (qualified, selected, and chose) *the Word* who is in the image of the "invisible" God, to be the *firstborn* over all creation.

As such, in the following Scriptures, I have defined the different references to "God," "Lord," "King," "Almighty," "Savior," "Redeemer," and "Lord of Hosts," with their corresponding Hebrew or Greek definitions. This substantiates God the Father, and God the Son, are "one" and the "same" God beyond a shadow of a doubt.

> *"'I am ALPHA and OMEGA, the BEGINNING and the ENDING,' saith the* **LORD** *(1)* [G2962: *kurios*: *supreme* in authority, that is, (as noun) *controller*; by implication *Mr.* (as a respectful title); God, Lord, Master, Sir], *which IS, and which WAS, and which IS to COME, the* **ALMIGHTY** *(2)* [G3841: *pantokratōr*: the all-ruling, that is, *God* (as absolute and universal *sovereign*): *omnipotent*: having unlimited power; able to do anything]. "*(Rev. 1:8, KJV) (emphasis added).

261

"'You are My witnesses,' says the **_LORD_** [3] [H3068: **_Y'hôvâh_**: (the) *self-Existent,* or eternal; *Jehovah,* Jewish national name of God], *'And My servant whom I have chosen, That you may KNOW and BELIEVE Me, And understand that I am He. BEFORE Me there was NO GOD* [4] [H410: **_'El_**: *strength*; as adjective *mighty*; especially the *Almighty* (but used also of any *deity*)] *FORMED* [5] [H3335: **_yâtsar_**: (through the *squeezing* into shape); to *mould* into a form; especially as a *potter*; figuratively to *determine* (that is, form a resolution); X earthen, fashion, form, frame, make (-r), potter, purpose], *Nor shall there be after Me. I, even I, am the **_LORD_*** [3] [H3068: **_Y'hôvâh_**], *And BESIDES Me there is no SAVIOR* [6] [H3467: **_yâsha_**: to *be open, wide,* or *free,* that is, (by implication) to *be safe*; causatively to *free,* or *succor*; avenging, defend, deliver (-er), help, preserve, rescue, be safe, bring (having) salvation, save (-iour), get victory]."* (Isa. 43:10–11, NKJV) (emphasis added).

*"Thus says the **_LORD_*** [3] [H3068: **_Y'hôvâh_**], *the **_KING_*** [7] [8] [H4428: **_melek_**: a royal king; H4427: **_mâlak_**: to *rule* and *reign*; inceptively to *ascend the throne*; induct into royalty; hence to take counsel] *of ISRAEL, And His **_REDEEMER_*** [9] [H1350: **_gâ'al_**: to *redeem* that is, to *be the next of kin* (and as such to *buy back* a relative's property, *marry* his widow, etc.) avenger, deliver, (kinsfolk (-man), purchase, ransom, revenger], *the **_LORD_*** [3] *of **_HOSTS_*** [10] [H6635:

tsâbâ': a *mass* of persons (or figurative things), especially regularly organized for company, worship, service, war, or hardship, at an appointed time]:*'I am the FIRST and I am the LAST; Besides Me there is no GOD* [11] [H430: *'Elôhîym*: is Plural of H433; *gods* in the ordinary sense as far as deity; but specifically used (in the plural thus, especially with the article) of the supreme *God*].'" (Isa. 44:6, NKJV) (emphasis added).

"Now to the KING [12] [13] [G935: *basileus*: foundation of power; a *sovereign;* G939: *basis*: *bainō* (to *walk*); a *pace* ("base"), that is, (by implication) the *foot*] *ETERNAL* [14] [G165: *aiōn*: an *age;* by extension *perpetuity* (also past); by implication the *world;* specifically (Jewish) a Messianic period (present or future); age, course, eternal, (for) ever (-more), (beginning of the, while the) world (began, without end); eternity], *IMMORTAL* [15] [G862: *aphthartos*: *undecaying* (in essence, or continuance); incorruptible, incorruption], *INVISIBLE* [16] [G517: *aoratos*: invisible thing], *to GOD* [17] [G2316: *theos*: a *deity;* the supreme *Divinity,* or *Magistrate*] who alone is wise, be honor and glory forever and ever. Amen."* (1 Tim. 1:17, NKJV) (emphasis added).

"I urge you in the sight of GOD [17] [G2316: *theos*] *who gives LIFE to all THINGS, and BEFORE Christ Jesus who witnessed the good confession before Pontius Pilate that you keep this COMMANDMENT without spot, blameless UNTIL our LORD* [1] [G2962:

kurios] *Jesus Christ's APPEARING, which He will manifest in His own time, He who is the blessed and only **POTENTATE*** [(18)] [G1413: *dunastēs*: Lord, master, or ruler, of *great* and *mighty* authority], *the **KING*** [(12)] [(13)] [G935: *basileus*: G939: *basis*] *of kings and our **LORD*** [(1)] [G2962: *kurios*] *of lords, WHO ALONE HAS **IMMORTALITY*** [(19)] [G110: *athanasia*: deathlessness], *dwelling in UNAPPROACHABLE LIGHT, whom no MAN HAS SEEN or CAN SEE, to whom be honor and everlasting power. Amen."* (1 Tim. 6:13–16, NKJV) (emphasis added).

*"I said, 'O my **GOD*** [(4)] [H410: *'El*], *Do not take me away in the midst of my days; Your years are throughout all GENERATIONS. Of old You laid the FOUNDATION of the EARTH, And the HEAVENS are the work of Your hands. They will PERISH, but YOU will ENDURE; Yes, they will all grow old like a garment; Like a cloak You will change them, And they will be changed. But YOU are the SAME, And YOUR YEARS will have NO END.'"* (Psalm 102:24–27, NKJV) (emphasis added).

Moreover, God is "omniscient" because He knows everything from the beginning to the end. God is "omnipotent" because He has unlimited power, and there is *nothing* He cannot do. God is "omnipresent" because God is Spirit; therefore, He is present everywhere and is not confined to "time" or "geographical" locations.

264

And last, but certainly not least, God is all-knowing. How is God all-knowing? It is because He gives *every* living being, both man and animal, His Spirit and His *breath of life* based on the following Scriptures:

"*The* **SPIRIT** [20] [H7307: *rûach*: *wind*, by resemblance *breath*, that is, a sensible (or even violent) exhalation] *of* **GOD** [4] [H410: *'êl*: *strength*; as adjective *mighty*, especially the *Almighty* (but used also of any *deity*)] *has MADE me, And the* **BREATH** [21] [H5397: *n'shâmâh*: a *puff*, that is, *wind*, angry, or vital *breath*, divine *inspiration*, *intellect*, or (concretely) an *animal*: blast, inspiration, soul and spirit] *of the ALMIGHTY gives me* **LIFE** [22] [H2421: *châyâh*: to *live*, whether literally, or figuratively; causatively to *revive*: - keep alive, give (promise) life, (let, suffer to) live, nourish up, preserve (alive), quicken, recover, repair, restore (to life), revive and to be made whole]." (Job 33:4, NKJV) (emphasis added).

"*Who gave Him charge over the earth? Or who appointed Him over the whole world? If He should set His heart on it, If He should GATHER to Himself His* **SPIRIT** [20] [H7307: *rûach*] *and His* **BREATH** [21] [H5397: *n'shâmâh*], *all FLESH would PERISH together, And MAN would RETURN to DUST.*" (Job 34:13–15, NKJV) (emphasis added).

We must also remember we are specifically told in Leviticus 17:13–14, "the blood" is the life of all flesh, and it is "the blood" that sustains life.

Moreover, Leviticus 17:11, says, *"For the LIFE of the FLESH is in the BLOOD, and I have given it to you upon the altar to make ATONEMENT for your SOULS; for it is the BLOOD that makes ATONEMENT for the SOUL."* (NKJV) (emphasis added).

As such, wherever we go, and no matter what we are doing, God is with us as substantiated in Psalm 139:1–7 below:

> *"O LORD, You have searched me and known me. You know my sitting down and my rising up; You understand my thought afar off. You comprehend my path and my lying down, And are ACQUAINTED with ALL MY WAYS. For there is not a word on my tongue, But behold, O LORD, You know it altogether. You have hedged me behind and before, And laid Your hand upon me. Such knowledge is too wonderful for me; It is high, I cannot attain it. WHERE CAN I GO FROM YOUR SPIRIT? Or WHERE CAN I FLEE FROM YOUR PRESENCE?"* (Psalm 139:1–7, NKJV) (emphasis added).

Therefore, we cannot "hide" our secret thoughts, intents, or motives from God.

This is substantiated by Jeremiah 23:23–24, which says, *"'Am I a God near at hand,' says the LORD, 'And not a God afar off? Can anyone*

HIDE *himself in SECRET places, so I shall not SEE him?' says the* LORD; *'DO I not FILL HEAVEN and EARTH?' says the* LORD." (NKJV) (emphasis added).

Moreover, God is in charge of everything *except* our free will to "choose" whom we will serve while we are still on the earth. As illustrated in the story of Jonah, when God wanted him to go to Nineveh, yet Jonah clearly did not want to, God has the perfect plan for our lives and will orchestrate things, events, or circumstances in our lives to persuade us to "see" and "do" things His way!

Furthermore, God has placed it on my heart many of His people do not really know Him. Because if we really knew the God, we profess to serve, we would have the *reverential* fear of God Almighty and act accordingly! Instead, too often we have made God in "our" image and in "our" likeness when He is the One who created us in His image and in His likeness.

Like Adam and Eve, too many have eaten from the "tree of the knowledge of good and evil" instead of the "tree of life," which is Jesus Christ. For it is God's Word that gives us life!

We do not fully "know" the God of the Bible because all we hear about is the loving, merciful God, which gives us a *false* sense of security and does not compel us to *work out* our *own* salvation with fear and trembling.

The apostle Paul says to us in Philippians 2:12–13, *"Therefore, my beloved, as you have always obeyed, not as in my presence only, but now much more in my absence, WORK OUT YOUR own SALVATION with FEAR and TREMBLING; for it is God who works in you both to will and to do for His good pleasure.*" (NKJV) (emphasis added).

As such, we *must* also know about the "severity" of God and His "righteous" requirements, which is the beginning of us having the *reverential* fear of the Lord many believers in the body of Christ obviously no longer have as illustrated by how we live our lives.

A critical truth God's people must understand is this: Everything that happens is because God allows it to happen for His Word to be fulfilled for His "eternal" purposes and glory to prevail.

Listen to what God says to us in Isaiah 45:7, as He proclaims, *"I form the LIGHT and create DARKNESS, I make PEACE and create CALAMITY; I, the Lord, DO all these THINGS."* (NKJV) (emphasis added).

Therefore, as clearly substantiated by the Word of God, God does create calamity at times to get us to repent and return to Him, so we will "do" what He has told us to do.

One biblical example of this being the case is based on Jonah 1:1–17, which tells the story of the calamity God orchestrated when Jonah refused to "do" what God had told him to do. God commanded Jonah to arise and go to Nineveh and cry out against their wickedness.

However, Jonah disobeyed fled to Joppa and got on a ship going to Tarshish so he could escape from the presence of the Lord. God responded to Jonah's disobedience with a storm at sea that ultimately resulted in Jonah being thrown off the ship.

Moreover, we are specifically told the Lord had prepared a great fish to swallow Jonah, where he would be in the belly of this great fish for three days and three nights. See Jonah 1:1–17. Long story short—Jonah repented and did what the Lord wanted him to do in the first place.

Furthermore, in Deuteronomy 32:39, God says to us, *"Now see that I, even I, am He, And there is no God besides Me; I KILL and I make ALIVE; I WOUND and I HEAL; Nor is there any who can DELIVER from My HAND."* (NKJV) (emphasis added).

As such, we like to blame our trials and tribulations on Satan, yet it is God who is allowing these trials and tribulations to happen to us for many different reasons. Do a word search in the Bible on the word "test" and you will discover there are 278 instances in the Word of God where God will test us for various reasons.

God must test us for this reason: Without being tested, we could not have a "testimony!" In addition, without us ever walking through the various trials and tribulations, how could we know God can deliver, heal, and save us in order to set us free? How would we know He is faithful if we never had the battle to savor the victory when we "overcome" our various trials and tribulations?

Granted sometimes our trials and tribulations we must walk through are a result of spiritual warfare and us making "poor" choices which are not in alignment with God's Word. However, Satan (a.k.a. the Devil) cannot do anything without God knowing about it and authorizing it, which is substantiated in Luke 22:31, when Jesus said to Peter, *"Simon, Simon! Indeed, Satan has ASKED for you, that he may SIFT you as wheat."* (NKJV) (emphasis added).

Therefore, Peter's faith was tested, but in the end, he made the right choice by repenting and returning to his first love—Jesus Christ. However, Jesus knew Peter would repent, and He made intercession for him to do so.

This is based on Luke 22:32, where Jesus said to him, *"But I have PRAYED for you, that your FAITH should not FAIL; and when you have RETURNED to ME, strengthen your brethren."* (NKJV) (emphasis added).

In addition, based on Colossians 1:16, the apostle Paul tells us God is the One who created all things in heaven, and on the earth, *visible,* and *invisible,* which includes thrones, dominions, principalities, and powers, including the *rulers of the darkness* of this age, and the *spiritual hosts of wickedness* in the *heavenly* places.

As such, because all things were created through Him and for Him, there are no "ifs" in God's "eternal" plan, and His "eternal" Word shall be fulfilled, so His "eternal" purposes shall prevail.

Therefore, all things, even "unclean" or "evil" spirits, are subjected to His "rule" and "reign!"

As a matter of fact, do we realize *some* of the spirits that "afflicts" men are sent from God? On the next page I have listed a couple of biblical examples which substantiate this fact:

The first biblical example is when God sent a "distressing" spirit to King Saul, which is based on First Samuel 16:14–15; 16:23; 18:10; and 19:9.

The second biblical example is when a "lying" spirit came forward and stood before the Lord, and it was granted that this "lying" spirit be put in the mouth of all the prophets of Ahab so he would go up to Ramoth Gilead and fall there. This is based on First Kings Chapter 22, which you should read in its entirety. However, note we are specifically told in First Kings 22:23 below, God has put a "lying" spirit in the mouths of Ahab's prophets.

> *"Therefore look! The LORD has PUT a LYING SPIRIT in the MOUTH of all these PROPHETS of yours, and the LORD has DECLARED DISASTER against you."* (1 Kings 22:23, NKJV) (emphasis added).

In addition, God is the "Lord of the Spirits" (plural) of all flesh, which is based on Numbers 16:22 and Numbers 27:16. Perform a word search in the Bible on the word "spirit" and "spirits" and study every Scripture on this subject as I have, and you will know what I am proclaiming is true.

Moreover, God can "harden" an individual's spirit and make their heart "obstinate" as well after He has given an individual the opportunity to "repent" to "choose" a different path, yet they refuse to do so. Following are two biblical examples substantiating this truth:

271

The first biblical example is found in Exodus 4:21 when God "hardened" Pharaoh's heart so he would not let His people go.

The second biblical example is in Deuteronomy 2:30, when in the case of Sihon, *king of Heshbon*, God "hardened" his spirit and made his heart "obstinate" so He might deliver him into the hands of his enemy.

This is why Proverbs 9:10 says, *"The FEAR of the LORD is the beginning of WISDOM, And the KNOWLEDGE of the HOLY ONE is UNDERSTANDING."* (NKJV) (emphasis added).

And, Psalm 111:10 proclaims, *"The FEAR of the LORD is the beginning of WISDOM; a GOOD UNDERSTANDING have all those who DO His COMMANDMENTS. His praise endures forever."* (NKJV) (emphasis added).

For the truth of the matter is this: If we are "disobedient" to God's Word, then God will allow us to reap the consequences of our actions. In fact, He will sometimes use "adverse" circumstances to get our attention, so we will repent and stop rebelling against Him and His Word, so we do not perish for all eternity.

In addition, as I will cover in detail in Chapter 53 of Book 3, due to a lack of knowledge based on the whole counsel of God's Word, sometimes we are the ones that "grant" or "give" our dominion and our authority in Christ over to Satan. This happens when we sin against God and His Word. When we "choose" to give Satan the "legal" right to wreak havoc in our lives because we "choose" to sin against God and His Word, we by our own accord, have transferred ourselves out of the *kingdom of light* into the *kingdom of darkness.*

As such, we will reap God's curses instead of His blessings because we have broken covenant with God. Hence, God's hands are "legally" tied based on His principles, laws, and decrees according to His *eternal* Word because we have exercised our free will when we "choose" to sin against Him and His Word!

The apostle Paul tells us in Second Corinthians 10:5–7, we must *cast down* arguments and *every* high thing that "exalts" itself against the *knowledge of God*, as we bring *every* thought into "captivity" to the *obedience of Christ.*

In other words, we are required to take action! Then the apostle Paul specifically says in Second Corinthians 10:6, God will be ready to punish all disobedience *when* our obedience is fulfilled.

In conclusion, the bottom line is this: God has always existed, and His *eternal* Word shall never pass away! Therefore, He will do what He has "decreed" and "declared" since the foundation of the world because *"it is written…"*

In the next chapter, we will continue our journey to answer the thought-provoking question: "When did God (qualify, select, and choose) *the Word* in the image of Him the "invisible" God, to be the *firstborn* over all creation?"

Who is Israel? Discovering our True Identity in Jesus Christ and Why it Matters! The Foundation

CHAPTER 10

WHEN DID GOD (QUALIFY, SELECT, AND CHOOSE) THE WORD IN HIS INVISIBLE IMAGE TO BE THE FIRSTBORN OVER ALL CREATION?

W e are told when God (qualified, selected, and chose) *the Word* in His "invisible" image, to be the *firstborn* over all of creation. This is in the very first passage of Scripture in Genesis 1:1–2. We are specifically told *the Word* was with God when the earth was without form, and void, and darkness was on the face of the deep. Genesis 1:1–2, says the following:

> *"In the BEGINNING GOD* (1) [H430: *'Elôhíym:* is Plural of H433; *gods* in the ordinary sense as far as deity; but specifically used (in the plural thus, especially with the article) of the supreme *God*] *CREATED* (2) [H1254: *bârâ:* to create; qualify, to select, or to choose] *the HEAVENS* [plural] *and the EARTH. The EARTH was without FORM, and VOID; and DARKNESS was on the FACE of the DEEP. And the SPIRIT* (3) [H7307: *rûach: wind;* by resemblance *breath,* that is, a sensible (or even violent) exhalation] *of GOD* (1) *was hovering over the FACE of the WATERS."* (Gen. 1:1–2, NKJV) (emphasis added).

Therefore, based on Genesis 1:1–2, we are told the following five things "existed" at the beginning of time:

1. *'Elōhīym* (plural): referring to the Gods in the Godhead, which is the supreme God, and they are all deity. The "plurality" of *'Elōhīym* is God the Father, God the Son, and God the Holy Spirit. Moreover, *the Word*—the Son of His love is "eternal" (meaning He has always existed), which is substantiated in John 1:1–3 below:

   > *"In the BEGINNING was the **WORD*** (4) (5) *[**G3056:** **logos:** something said, or spoken (including the thought); utterance **G3004:** **legō:** verb: to 'lay forth,' or to set discourse; call, speak, utter], and the **WORD*** (4) (5) *was with **GOD*** (6) *[**G2316:** **theos:** a deity; the supreme Divinity, or Magistrate], and the **WORD*** (4) (5) *was **GOD**.* (6) *He was in the BEGINNING with **GOD**.* (6) *All THINGS were MADE through Him, and without Him nothing was MADE that was MADE."* (John 1:1–3, NKJV) (emphasis added).

2. The *Spirit of God* (*Rūach:* the wind which is the breath of God) according to Genesis 1:2, which says, *"...And the SPIRIT of GOD was hovering over the face of the waters."* (NKJV) (emphasis added).

3. The earth according to Genesis 1:2, which says, *"The EARTH was without form, and void; and darkness was on the face of the deep."* (NKJV) (emphasis added).

4. Darkness according to Genesis 1:2, which says, *"The earth was without form, and void; and DARKNESS was on the face of the deep."* (NKJV) (emphasis added).

Moreover, "darkness" which is His "secret" place, according to Psalm 18:11 below, was prevalent in the beginning when the earth was *without* form and the heavens had *no* light based on Jeremiah 4:23 below:

> *"He made DARKNESS His SECRET PLACE; His canopy around Him was DARK WATERS And THICK CLOUDS of the SKIES."* (Psalm 18:11, NKJV) (emphasis added).

> *"I beheld the EARTH, and indeed it was without FORM, and VOID; And the HEAVENS, they had NO LIGHT."* (Jer. 4:23, NKJV) (emphasis added).

5. Water according to Genesis 1:2, which says, *"...And the Spirit of God was hovering over the face of the WATERS."* (NKJV) (emphasis added).

In fact, when we are specifically told in Genesis 1:2, the earth was without form and void and darkness was on the face of the deep, the word "deep" according to *Strong's Hebrew Lexicon* #H8415, is the Hebrew word "t⁰hôm" (pronounced "teh-home'"), and means: An *abyss* (as a *surging* mass of water), especially the *deep* (the *main* sea, or the subterranean *water supply*): deep (place), or depth.

Again, the apostle Paul tells us in Colossians 1:15–17, *the Word* is the *firstborn* over all creation, for by Him all things were "created" in the heavens (plural) and on the earth. In other words, Jesus is "the Word" of God, therefore, when God first "spoke" it was His "Living" Word that created everything. Therefore, *the Word* is the *firstborn* over all creation.

Moreover, all things were "created" by Him and for Him, and He is before all things, and in Him, all things consist.

Therefore, up until this time, God's Spirit was hovering over the face of the waters based on Genesis 1:2, which says, *"The EARTH was without FORM, and VOID; and DARKNESS was on the FACE of the DEEP. And the SPIRIT of GOD was HOVERING over the FACE of the WATERS."* (NKJV) (emphasis added).

As such, for *the Word* to be the *firstborn* over all creation, the very first thing *Elohîym,* God, our Creator, "spoke" into existence based on Genesis 1:3, was "light."

And, the "living" Word which was "spoken" by God, our Creator, was fulfilled by the Holy Spirit.

In addition, I believe this is when *Yehovah* (qualified, selected, and chose) *the Word* to be our King. This is substantiated in Isaiah 43:15, which says, *"I am the Lord your Holy One, the CREATOR of ISRAEL your KING."* (NKJV) (emphasis added).

The word "Creator" as used in Isaiah 43:15, according to *Strong's Hebrew Lexicon* #H1254, is the Hebrew word "bârâ" (pronounced

278

"baw-raw'"), which means: To *create*; (qualify) to select or choose.

Then it would come to pass at a specific "preordained" time in the *synergy of the ages,* our heavenly Father, *Yehôvaĥ,* would send *the Word* to the earth. *The Word* was sent to the earth as the Son of Man in the Person of Jesus Christ—His only *begotten* Son. His only *begotten* Son was conceived by God's Spirit who would be born through a virgin girl named Mary, "when" the Holy Spirit overshadowed her.

Yes, indeed! *Yehôvaĥ* (qualified, selected, and chose) *the Word* who was in His own "bosom" when *Elohîym,* God, our Creator, "spoke" through *the Word* and said, *"Let there be Light..."* which is substantiated in Genesis 1:3 below:

> *"Then **GOD** (1) [H430: 'Elohîym] **SAID** (7) [H559: 'âmar: to say; appoint; command; declare; demand; determine; speak; or utter], 'Let there be **LIGHT**' (8) (9) [H215 & H216: 'ôr: illumination, or to be (causatively make) luminous; lightning, set on fire, shine, or be glorious]; and there was **LIGHT**." (8) (9)* (Gen. 1:3, NKJV) (emphasis added).

The definition of the word "Word" as used in John 1:1–3, we already covered at the beginning of this chapter. It is the Greek word "logos" (pronounced "log'-os"), which means: Something that is said, or spoken, (including the thought), or utterance.

And, the Greek word "logos" is taken from the root of the Greek word "legō" (pronounced "leg'-o,"), which is a verb, meaning it is an *action* word. It means: To "lay forth" or to set discourse; call, speak, or utter. As such, *the Word* has basically the same meaning of the Hebrew word "said" which is used in Genesis 1:3, and is the Hebrew word "'âmar" (pronounced "aw-mar'"), which means: To say, appoint, command, declare, demand, determine, speak, or utter.

Hence, when *'Elôhíym* "spoke" forth His "logos" Word and said, *"Let there be Light"* this is when *the Word* was (qualified, selected, and chosen) to become "the" *Light of the World.*

Now let's hear from Jesus Himself who testifies to this truth according to His "eternal" Word based on the Scriptures below:

> *"Then Jesus spoke to them again, saying, 'I am the* **LIGHT** (10) [G5457: *phôs* or *phaô*: (to *shine* or make *manifest*); *luminousness; fire*] *of the WORLD. He who follows Me shall not WALK in DARKNESS, but have the* **LIGHT** (10) *of* **LIFE** (11) [G2222: *zôê*: the state of one who is possessed of vitality, or is animated; every living soul].'"* (John 8:12, NKJV) (emphasis added).

> *"I have COME as a* **LIGHT** (10) [G5457: *phôs* or *phaô*: (to *shine* or make *manifest*); *luminousness; fire*] *into the WORLD, that whoever BELIEVES in Me should not ABIDE in DARKNESS."* (John 12:46, NKJV) (emphasis added).

The apostle John tells us *the Word* is the source of all life, which is given to *every* man who will ever be born into the world. This is based on the following Scriptures:

> *"In Him was LIFE* [(11)] *[G2222: zōē], and the LIFE,* [(11)]
> *was the LIGHT* [(10)] *[G5457: phōs or phao] of MEN."*
> (John 1:4, NKJV) (emphasis added).

> *"That was the true LIGHT* [(10)] *[G5457: phōs or phao]*
> *which gives LIGHT* [(12)] *[G5461: phōtizō: to shed rays,*
> *that is, to shine, or (transitively) to brighten up*
> *(literally, or figuratively); make to see] to EVERY*
> *MAN COMING into the WORLD."* (John 1:9, NKJV)
> (emphasis added).

In other words, God's "light" is *the Word* and those who refuse to eat from His "tree of life" and produce the "fruit" thereof will experience *eternal* death.

After we are born, *physically* speaking, in a body of flesh and blood, we must be "reborn" again, *spiritually* speaking, after we "repent" and thus, "think" differently, which should be according to God's *eternal* Word.

This should happen *when* we come to the saving knowledge of "who" we really are in Christ, and to "whom" we truly belong to, which is based on the desires and *eternal* purposes of the very One who created us in the first place.

Therefore, *the Word,* who was and is the *firstborn* over all creation, has the "power" and "authority" to tell us, His created, in John 14:6, *"...I AM the WAY, the TRUTH, and the LIFE* [(11)] *[G2222: zōē]. NO*

ONE comes to the Father EXCEPT through ME." (NKJV) (emphasis added).

As such, everything that was ever created is given life and sustained by the Word of God. The very fact you woke up this morning and God blessed you with another day of life is because God is sustaining you by His "spoken" *eternal* Word!

Moreover, in John 9:5, Jesus says to us, His created, *"As long as I AM in the WORLD, I AM the **LIGHT** [(10)]* [G5457: *phōs* or *phao*] *of the WORLD."* (NKJV) (emphasis added).

Therefore, since God's Word is *eternal*, it shall never pass away, and *if* we "believe" in the Word of God, neither shall we.

WE ARE THE "LIGHT OF THE WORLD" BECAUSE GOD'S WORD, HIS LIFE, AND HIS LIGHT, ABIDES IN US, HIS REDEEMED

One of the reasons why we are left in the world *after* we "receive" Jesus Christ as our Lord and Savior is because we are the *Light of the World*. His "Word," His "Life," and His "Light" abides in us, His redeemed!

The Scriptures on the next two pages substantiates this truth: The Word is a "lamp" and a "light" unto our path. In addition, God's commandments are a "lamp," and His law is a "light" as well based on Proverbs 6:23. This fact plays an instrumental role in the *Parable of the Wise and Foolish Virgins* Jesus talks about in Matthew Chapter 25. If we want to keep our lamps continuously lit so that our love for *the Word* is never extinguished, then we need to heed the following Scriptures:

"Your **WORD** (13) [H1697: *dâbâr:* a *word;* by implication a *matter* (as *spoken* of) of *thing;* Oracle of God; decree; commandment; judgment; promise, provision, work] *is a* **LAMP** (14) [H5216: *nêrâh:* to *glisten;* a *lamp* (that is, the burner), or *light* (literally, or figuratively); candle] *to my feet And a* **LIGHT** (8) (9) [H215 & H216: *'ôr: illumination,* or to *be* (causatively *make*) *luminous; lightning, set on fire,* shine, or be *glorious*] *to my PATH."* (Psalm 119:105, NKJV) (emphasis added).

"For the **COMMANDMENT** (15) [H4687: *mitsvâh:* a *command,* whether human or divine (collectively the Law); (which was) commanded (-ment), law, ordinance, precept] *is a* **LAMP** (14) [H5216: *nêrâh:* to *glisten;* a *lamp* (that is, the burner), or *light* (literally or figuratively); candle]*, And the* **LAW** (16) [H8451: *tôrâh:* a *precept* or *statute,* especially the *Decalogue* or *Pentateuch:* direction or instruction based on the *Mosaic* or *Deuteronomic* Law] *a* **LIGHT** (8) (9) [H215 & H216: *'ôr: illumination* or to *be* (causatively *make*) *luminous; lightning, set on fire,* shine, or be *glorious*]*; REPROOFS of INSTRUCTION are the WAY of LIFE..."* (Prov. 6:23, NKJV) (emphasis added).

*"For with You is the FOUNTAIN of **LIFE*** [17] [18]
[H2416: *chay*: alive; H2421: *châyâh*: or to *live*, or to *revive; preserve*, quicken, recover, repair, restore, save, to be made whole]*; In Your **LIGHT*** [8] [9] [H215 & H216: *'ôr*: *illumination*, or to *be* (causatively *make*) *luminous; lightning, set on fire*, shine, or be *glorious*] *we SEE **LIGHT**."* [8] [9] (Psalm 36:9, NKJV) (emphasis added).

*"The entrance of Your **WORDS*** [13] [H1697: *dâbâr*: a *word*; by implication a *matter* (as *spoken* of) of *thing*; Oracle of God; decree; commandment; judgment; promise, provision, work] *gives **LIGHT*** [8] [9] [H215 & H216: *'ôr*: *illumination*, or to *be* (causatively *make*) *luminous; lightning, set on fire*, shine, or be *glorious*]..."* (Psalm 119:130, NKJV) (emphasis added).

Do not dismiss the significance the word "commandment" as used in Proverbs 6:23, is the Hebrew word "mitsvâh" (pronounced "mitsvaw'"), which means: The full volume of Moses, "collectively" the law. The law is detailed in the Torah in the Old Testament written by Moses. This includes God's *everlasting* ordinances as well.

As such, if we see an increase of darkness in the world, which we are, then it is obvious God's people are not "walking," "living," or "discipling" the nations according to His commandments (collectively the law), which is based on His *eternal* Word.

God's "eternal" Word is a "lamp" and a "light" to illuminate the *narrow* path we should traverse to be in a "covenant" relationship with the Creator of the heavens and the earth and everything in them.

Our heavenly Father, *Yehovah,* and our Lord and Savior Jesus Christ, really wants His people to understand His truth as proclaimed by the prophet Isaiah in Isaiah 51:4 and Isaiah 8:20.

TO THE "LAW" AND THE "TESTIMONY"! IF WE DO NOT SPEAK ACCORDING TO THIS WORD—THERE IS "NO" LIGHT IN US

First, we will take a look at Isaiah 51:4, which says the following:

> *"Listen to Me, My PEOPLE; And give EAR to Me, O My NATION: For LAW* [16] [H8451: *tôrâh*: a *precept* or *statute*, especially the *Decalogue* or *Pentateuch:* direction or instruction based on the *Mosaic* or *Deuteronomic* Law] *will PROCEED from Me, And I will make My JUSTICE* [19] [H4941: *mishpât*: verdict (favorable or unfavorable pronounced judicially, especially a *sentence* or formal decree of divine *law,* including a particular *right,* or *privilege* (statutory or customary), or even a *style:* based on a ceremony or custom, manner of law, ordinance, or sentence] *rest As a LIGHT* [8] [9] [H215 & H216: *'ôr*: *illumination* or to *be* (causatively *make*) *luminous; lightning, set on fire*, shine, or be *glorious*] *of the PEOPLES."* (Isa. 51:4, NKJV) (emphasis added).

Next, in Isaiah 8:20, which is based on Isaiah 8:11–22, this passage of Scripture is about us "fearing" the Lord and "heeding" His commandments. In Isaiah 8:20, we are told the following:

> *"To the **LAW*** [(16)] [H8451: *tôrâh*: a *precept* or *statute*, especially the *Decalogue* or *Pentateuch:* direction or instruction based on the *Mosaic* or *Deuteronomic* Law] *and to the **TESTIMONY*** [(20)] [H8584: *t'ûdâh*: *attestation*, that is, a *precept, usage*]! *If they DO NOT SPEAK according to this **WORD*** [(13)] [H1697: *dâbâr*: a *word*; by implication a *matter* (as *spoken* of) of *thing*; Oracle of God; decree; commandment; judgment; promise, provision, work], *it is BECAUSE there is no LIGHT in THEM."* (Isa. 8:20, NKJV) (emphasis added).

Do not dismiss the significance, in Isaiah 8:20, we are specifically told if we do not "speak" or have the "testimony" of God's law (the Torah), God's Word says it is because there is **no** light in us!

Why is this case? Because of our Lawgiver, whose Holy Spirit lives in us, is the living Torah!

In other words, Jesus did not abolish God's law. Rather, He came to fulfill (consummate, execute, ratify [confirm]) the law, and the prophets, with His precious blood. And, since His Holy Spirit lives in us, we should "be" the living Torah.

Therefore, true disciples of Jesus Christ should have the demonstrated "testimony" of our heavenly Father's instructions He has now put in our mind, and written on our hearts, under the New Covenant.

Hence, if we do not have the "testimony" of our heavenly Father's law, then we are not His covenant people even though we claim to be. This is why Jesus will say to many believers who practice "lawlessness" come Judgment Day, *"I never knew you; depart from Me, you who practice LAWLESSNESS!"* (Matthew 7:23).

In addition, we need to "listen" to and "heed" what God says to us in Psalm 19:7–11, about His *laws*, His *statutes*, His *commandments*, and His *judgments*, which *should* result in us having the *reverential* fear of the Lord. Psalm 19:7–11, says the following:

> "The **LAW** (16) **[H8451: *tôrâh*: a *precept* or *statute*, especially the *Decalogue* or *Pentateuch*: direction or instruction based on the *Mosaic* or *Deuteronomic* Law]** of the LORD is **PERFECT** (21) **[H8549: *tâmîym*: entire** (literally, figuratively or morally); also (as noun) integrity, truth; without blemish, complete, full, perfect, sincerely (-ity), sound, without spot, undefiled, upright (-ly), whole], **CONVERTING** (22) **[H7725: *shûb*: to *turn* back; *repent* by turning away]** the *SOUL;* The **TESTIMONY** (23) (24) (25) **[H5715: *'êdûth*: witness; H5707: *êd*: specifically a recorder, that is, Prince as a witness; H5749: *ûd*: duplicate or repeat;** by implication to *protest, testify;* admonish, charge, lift up, call to record, testify, give warning or to bear witness] of the LORD is SURE, making wise the simple; The **STATUTES** (26) **[H6490: *piqqûd*:**

287

appointed, that is, a *mandate* (of God; plural only, collectively for the Law); commandment, precept] *of the LORD are RIGHT, rejoicing the heart; The* **COMMANDMENT** (15) [**H4687: *mitsvâh*:** a *command, whether human or divine (collectively the Law); (which was) commanded (-ment), law, ordinance, precept]* of the LORD is PURE, enlightening the eyes; The **FEAR** (27) [**H3374: *yir'âh*:** morally *reverence*] of the LORD is CLEAN, enduring forever; The **JUDGMENTS** (28) [**H4941: *mishpâṭ*:** verdict (favorable or unfavorable pronounced judicially, especially a *sentence* or formal decree of divine *law*; including a particular *right*, or *privilege* (statutory or customary), or even a *style*: based on a ceremony or custom, manner of law, ordinance, or sentence] *of the LORD are TRUE and RIGHTEOUS altogether. More to be DESIRED are they than GOLD, Yea, than much fine gold; Sweeter also than honey and the honeycomb. Moreover BY THEM Your SERVANT is WARNED, And in KEEPING THEM there is GREAT REWARD."* (Psalm 19:7–11, NKJV) (emphasis added).

Do not dismiss the significance of the Hebrew meaning of the word "perfect" as used in Psalm 19:7–11. The word "perfect" is the Hebrew word "tâmîym" (pronounced "taw-meem'"), which means the following: Integrity, truth; without blemish, complete, full, perfect, sincerely (-ity), sound, without spot, and undefiled. We are specifically told in Psalm 19:7–11, the law of God is what makes us "perfect" and "complete" in Christ lacking nothing, and is what "converts" a person's soul!

IF WE DESIRE TO BE THE BRIDE OF CHRIST, WE MUST "WALK" ACCORDING TO OUR HEAVENLY FATHER'S INSTRUCTIONS WRITTEN IN THE TORAH, WHICH IS THE DOCTRINE OF CHRIST

God's law, which is detailed in the Torah written by God's servant Moses, are simply our heavenly Father's instructions for all His people to "walk" and "live" according to for this sole purpose: To bring us to maturity and completeness in our faith so we *may* become a bride who is without spot or blemish in Jesus Christ.

Therefore, if we desire to be the *bride of Christ* who is without spot or blemish because we are people of integrity because we "walk" according to God's truth, which is based on the sound doctrine of Christ, then we will not be defiled.

In addition, Jesus Christ was and is the *living* Torah, and His disciples should be too. And, as Proverbs 6:23, states very clearly to us, "reproofs" of instruction are "the way" of life for disciples of Jesus Christ.

As such, please understand I am not saying we must keep God's law to "become" saved.

However, once we "become" saved by our faith in Jesus Christ, we will keep God's laws, statutes, ordinances, and judgments, because we love Him and want to please the One we love and serve with all our heart, mind, soul, and strength.

From God's perspective, this is "how" we show Him we love Him. As a matter of fact, "listen" to and "heed" what God tells us in Proverbs 28:9, which says the following:

*"One who TURNS AWAY his EAR from **HEARING** [29] [H8085: shâmaʿ: to hear intelligently (often with implication of attention, obedience, etc.; consent, discern; obey; regard and understand] the **LAW** [16] [H8451: tôrâh: a precept or statute, especially the Decalogue or Pentateuch], Even his PRAYER is an **ABOMINATION** [30] [H8441: tôʿêbah: something disgusting (morally), that is, (as noun) an abhorrence; especially idolatry or (concretely) an idol]."* (Prov. 28:9, NKJV) (emphasis added).

For those of you who do not believe God has terms and conditions for keeping His covenant—Psalm 25:10, proclaims, *"All the ways of the LORD are loving and faithful toward those who KEEP the DEMANDS of his COVENANT."* (NIV) (emphasis added).

And, Psalm 25:14 says, *"The LORD CONFIDES in those who FEAR him; he MAKES his COVENANT KNOWN to THEM."* (NIV) (emphasis added).

Therefore, in Chapter 52 of Book 3, I will cover in detail why God's instructions, which were written by God's servant Moses in the Torah, are still applicable to New Covenant believers.

In addition, in Chapter 56 of Book 3, I will convey in-depth why "love" essentially fulfills the law, *if* we "walk" according to the Spirit, rather than our flesh. Otherwise, we will be judged according to the law come Judgment Day. This truth is based on the following two facts:

❖ God has now put His laws in our mind, and written them on our hearts, instead of on two tablets of stone, under the New Covenant.

❖ We have received God's "grace" through the Holy Spirit who lives in us which empowers us to "keep" God's commandments.

Do we realize God's "grace" gives us His "power" and His "strength" to "do" all things pertaining to this life, which includes "pursuing" godliness so we can be victorious in Christ? This is substantiated in the Scriptures below:

> *"And He said to me, 'My GRACE is sufficient for you, for My STRENGTH is made perfect in weakness.' Therefore most gladly I will rather boast in MY INFIRMITIES, that the POWER of CHRIST may REST UPON me."* (2 Cor. 12:9, NKJV) (emphasis added).

> *"GRACE and peace be multiplied to you in the knowledge of God and of Jesus our Lord, as His DIVINE POWER has given to us all things that pertain to life and godliness, through the knowledge of Him who called us by glory and virtue..."* (2 Peter 1:2–3, NKJV) (emphasis added).

Yet many believers are of the "opinion" God's "grace" is a license to sin and to live according to what we deem right in our own eyes, because we "become" saved by God's "grace" which is a free gift based on what Jesus did on the cross at Calvary.

However, the apostle Paul tells us in Hebrews 12:14–15, we are to "pursue" peace with all people and "holiness" without which, no one will see the Lord, and we will fall short of the grace of God.

Therefore, if we do not want to fall short of the grace of God, then we will "pursue" holiness by keeping His commandments because we have been given God's "grace" which is His "power" and His "strength" to do so.

In fact, God defines our "love" for Him in Second John 1:6, which says, *"THIS is LOVE, that we WALK according to His COMMANDMENTS. This is the COMMANDMENT, that as you have HEARD from the BEGINNING, you should WALK in it."* (NKJV) (emphasis added).

Hence, when Jesus says to us, His disciples, in John 14:15, *"If you LOVE me, KEEP My COMMANDMENTS..."* (NKJV) (emphasis added), Jesus was referring to our heavenly Father's instructions written in the Torah that we have heard from the beginning for this reason: The New Testament did not exist at the time of Jesus Christ's earthly ministry.

As such, if we believe Jesus did away with the law, then we are deceived because Jesus preached and walked according to the law that He "decreed" and "established" as *the Word* in the first place. This was long before He would be sent by our heavenly Father, *Yehôvah,* to fulfill (consummate, execute, and ratify [confirm]) the *first* Covenant with His precious blood when He became the "mediator" of the New Covenant.

Jesus did not "abolish" the law. Rather, He set us free from "the curse" we would have received for not keeping the *letter of the law.* I cover this truth in-depth in Chapter 47 of Book 3.

In other words, *the Word* was sent to the earth by our heavenly Father, *Yehôvah,* as the Son of Man in the Person of Jesus Christ for this reason: To "confirm" (which is the Hebrew word "gabar" which literally means "he shall make strong") the *first* covenant God established with all the children of Israel through His servant Moses.

Again, this is especially true since God has now put His laws in our mind, and written them on our heart, instead of on two tablets of stone, under the New Covenant.

WE MUST ALLOW GOD'S WORD TO DEFINE "WHO" WE ARE IN CHRIST

We must look to the whole counsel of God's Word to define "who" we are in Jesus Christ as God's children, rather than seeking to find our "identity" of "who" we are from the enemy and the world.

It is only then will we discover not only "who" we truly are, but we will also discover to "whom" we belong. God's sons and daughters "walk" and "live" according to His Way, His Truth, and His Life. This is based on His "eternal" Word which shall *never* pass away!

Who is Israel? Discovering our True Identity in Jesus Christ and Why it Matters! The Foundation

Many believers in the body of Christ "profess" to have the testimony of Jesus Christ, but we need to answer the following questions honestly:

❖ Are we "walking" worthy of the Lord, fully pleasing Him because we "obey" Him?

❖ Are we being "fruitful" in every good work and increasing in the knowledge of God as we mature in our faith?

For we will only have *true* fellowship with one another, and the blood of Jesus will cleanse us from all our sins only *if* we "walk" in the "light" as He is in the light.

This is based on First John 1:7, which says, *"But if we WALK in the **LIGHT** (10) [G5457: phōs or phaō: (to shine or make manifest); luminousness; fire] as He is in the **LIGHT**, (10) we have FELLOWSHIP with ONE ANOTHER, and the BLOOD of JESUS CHRIST His Son CLEANSES us from all SIN."* (NKJV) (emphasis added).

Now I am going to allow the Word of God to speak His truth of "who" we are in Christ, as His sons and daughters, based on the following Scriptures:

> *"I have heard of you, that the SPIRIT of GOD is in you, and that **LIGHT** (10) [G5457: phōs or phaō: (to shine or make manifest); luminousness; fire] and UNDERSTANDING and excellent WISDOM are FOUND in you."* (Dan. 5:14, NKJV) (emph. added).

294

*"I, the **LORD** [31] [H3068: Yehôvăh: self-Existent, or eternal; Jehovah], have called You in RIGHTEOUSNESS, And will hold Your hand; I will KEEP You and GIVE You as a COVENANT to the people, As a **LIGHT** [8] [9] [H215 & H216: 'ôr: illumination, or to be (causatively make) luminous; lightning, set on fire, shine, or be glorious] to the Gentiles [pagan, heathen people who are out of covenant with God]... "* (Isa. 42:6, NKJV) (emphasis added).

*"The people who sat in DARKNESS have SEEN a great **LIGHT** [10] [G5457: phŏs or phaŏ: (to shine or make manifest); luminousness; fire], And upon those who sat in the REGION and SHADOW of DEATH **LIGHT** [10] has DAWNED."* (Matt. 4:16, NKJV) (emphasis added).

*"You are the **LIGHT** [10] [G5457: phŏs or phaŏ: (to shine or make manifest); luminousness; fire] of the WORLD. A city that is set on a hill cannot be hidden."* (Matt. 5:14, NKJV) (emphasis added).

*"Let YOUR **LIGHT** [10] [G5457: phŏs or phaŏ: (to shine or make manifest); luminousness; fire] so shine before MEN, that they may see YOUR good WORKS and GLORIFY YOUR FATHER in heaven."* (Matt. 5:16, NKJV) (emphasis added).

*"For so the **LORD** [32] [G2962: kurios: supreme in authority as in God, or Master] has COMMANDED*

us: 'I have SET [established] *you as a **LIGHT*** [(10)] *[G5457: **phōs** or **phaō***: *(to shine* or make *manifest); luminousness; fire] to the Gentiles,* [heathen, pagan people, or nations, that are out of covenant with God] *That you should be for SALVATION to the ends of the earth.'"* (Acts 13:47, NKJV) (emphasis added).

*"For it is the **GOD*** [(6)] *[G2316: **theos**: a deity;* the supreme *Divinity,* or *Magistrate] who COMMANDED **LIGHT*** [(10)] *[G5457: **phōs** or **phaō***: *(to shine*. or make *manifest); luminousness; fire] to SHINE OUT of DARKNESS, who has SHONE in our HEARTS to give the **LIGHT*** [(33)] *[G5462: **phōtismos**: illumination] of the KNOWLEDGE of the GLORY of **GOD*** [(6)] *in the FACE of JESUS CHRIST."* (2 Cor. 4:6, NKJV) (emphasis added).

*"For YOU were once DARKNESS, but now YOU are **LIGHT*** [(10)] *[G5457: **phōs** or **phaō***: *(to shine* or make *manifest); luminousness; fire] in the **LORD*** [(32)] *[G2962: **kurios**: supreme* in authority as in God, or Master]. *WALK as CHILDREN of **LIGHT**."* [(10)] (Eph. 5:8, NKJV) (emphasis added).

*"Do all THINGS without COMPLAINING and DISPUTING, that YOU may become BLAMELESS and HARMLESS, CHILDREN of **GOD*** [(6)] *[G2316: **theos**: a deity;* especially *the* Supreme *Divinity,* or *Magistrate] without FAULT in the MIDST of a CROOKED and PERVERSE GENERATION, among*

Donna M. Rogers

*whom YOU shine as **LIGHTS*** [34] [G5458: ***phōstēr:*** an *illuminator*] *in the WORLD, HOLDING FAST the WORD of **LIFE*** [11] [G2222: ***zōē:*** the state of one who is possessed of vitality, or is animated; every living soul], *so that I may REJOICE in the DAY of CHRIST that I have not RUN in VAIN or LABORED in VAIN."* (Phil. 2:14–16, NKJV) (emphasis added).

*"For this reason we also, since the day we heard it, do not cease to pray for you, and to ask that you may be FILLED with the KNOWLEDGE of His WILL in all WISDOM and SPIRITUAL UNDERSTANDING; that you may WALK WORTHY of the **LORD*** [32] [G2962: ***kurios:*** *supreme* in authority as in God, or Master], *fully PLEASING Him, being FRUITFUL in every GOOD WORK and INCREASING in the KNOWLEDGE of **GOD*** [6] [G2316: ***theos:*** a *deity; especially the* Supreme *Divinity, or Magistrate*]; *strengthened with all MIGHT, according to His GLORIOUS POWER, for all PATIENCE and LONGSUFFERING with JOY; giving thanks to the FATHER who has QUALIFIED US to be PARTAKERS of the INHERITANCE of the SAINTS in the **LIGHT*** [10] [G5457: ***phōs*** or ***phao:*** (to *shine* or make *manifest*); *luminousness; fire*]." (Col. 1:9–12, NKJV) (emphasis added).

*"YOU are all SONS of **LIGHT*** [10] [G5457: ***phōs*** or ***phao:*** (to *shine* or make *manifest*); *luminousness; fire*] *and SONS of the DAY. We are not of the NIGHT*

297

nor of DARKNESS." (1 Thess. 5:5, NKJV) (emphasis added).

*"Therefore do not be ASHAMED of the **TESTIMONY*** ⁽³⁵⁾ [G3142: ***marturion***: something *evidential*, that is, (generally) *evidence* given, or (specifically) the *Decalogue* (in the sacred Tabernacle); witness] *of our* **LORD** ⁽³²⁾ [G2962: ***kurios***: *supreme* in authority as in God, or Master], *nor of me His prisoner, but SHARE with me in the SUFFERINGS for the GOSPEL according to the POWER of **GOD*** ⁽⁶⁾ [G2316: ***theos***: a *deity;* especially *the* Supreme *Divinity,* or *Magistrate*], *who has SAVED us and CALLED us with a HOLY CALLING, not according to OUR WORKS, but according to HIS OWN PURPOSE and GRACE which was GIVEN to US in CHRIST JESUS before TIME began, but has now been REVEALED by the APPEARING of our SAVIOR JESUS CHRIST, who has abolished DEATH and brought **LIFE*** ⁽¹¹⁾ [G2222: ***zoē***: the state of one who is possessed of vitality, or is animated; every living soul] *and **IMMORTALITY*** ⁽³⁶⁾ [G861: ***aphtharsia***: *incorruptibility;* generally *unending existence;* (figuratively) genuineness and sincerity] *to **LIGHT*** ⁽¹²⁾ [G5461: ***phōtizō***: to *shed rays,* that is, to *shine,* or (transitively) to *brighten* up (literally, or figuratively); make to see] *through the GOSPEL, to which I was appointed a preacher, an apostle, and a teacher of the Gentiles."* (2 Tim. 1:8–11, NKJV) (emphasis added).

"Every good gift and every perfect gift is from above, and comes down from the FATHER of **LIGHTS** [10] *[G5457:* **phōs** *or* **phaō**: *(to* shine *or* make manifest*); luminousness; fire], with whom there is no variation or shadow of turning. Of His own WILL He BROUGHT US FORTH by the* **WORD** [4] [5] *[G3056:* **logos**: something said, or spoken, (including the thought); utterance *G3004:* **legō**: *verb: to* 'lay forth,' *or to set discourse; call, speak, utter], of TRUTH, that we might be a kind of* **FIRSTFRUITS** [37] [38] *[G536:* **aparchē**: *a* beginning *of sacrifice; G756:* **archomai**: *(through the implication of* precedence*); to* commence *(in order of time); rehearse from the beginning] of His* **CREATURES** [39] *[G2938:* **ktisma**: *an original* formation *(concretely), that is,* product *(created thing)]."* (James 1:17–18, NKJV) (emphasis added).

"But you are a CHOSEN generation, a ROYAL PRIESTHOOD, a HOLY NATION, His own SPECIAL PEOPLE, that you may PROCLAIM the praises of Him who CALLED you OUT of DARKNESS into HIS marvelous **LIGHT** [10] *[G5457:* **phōs** *or* **phaō**: *(to* shine *or* make manifest*);* luminousness; fire*]..."* (1 Peter 2:9, NKJV) (emphasis added).

"This is the message which we have heard from Him and declare to you, that **GOD** [6] *[G2316:* **theos**: *a* deity; *especially the* Supreme Divinity, *or* Magistrate*] is* **LIGHT** [10] *[G5457:* **phōs** *or* **phaō**: *(to* shine *or*

make *manifest*); *luminousness; fire*] *and in Him is NO DARKNESS at ALL."* (1 John 1:5, NKJV) (emphasis added).

"Again, a NEW commandment I write to you, which thing is TRUE in HIM and in YOU, because the darkness is passing away, and the TRUE **LIGHT** [(10)] [G5457: *phōs* or *phao*: (to *shine* or make *manifest*); *luminousness; fire*] *is already SHINING."* (1 John 2:8, NKJV) (emphasis added).

"He who SAYS he is in the **LIGHT** [(10)] [G5457: *phōs* or *phao*: (to *shine* or make *manifest*); *luminousness; fire*], *and HATES his BROTHER, is in DARKNESS until NOW."* (1 John 2:9, NKJV) (emphasis added).

"ARISE, SHINE; For YOUR **LIGHT** [(8)] [(9)] [H215 & H216: *'ôr*: *illumination*, or to *be* (causatively *make*) *luminous; lightning*, set on fire, shine, or be *glorious*] *has COME! And the GLORY of the* **LORD** [(31)] [H3068: *Yehôvâh*: *self-Existent*, or eternal; *Jehovah*] *is RISEN upon YOU. For behold, the DARKNESS shall COVER the EARTH, And DEEP DARKNESS the PEOPLE; But the* **LORD** [(31)] *will ARISE over YOU, And His GLORY will be seen UPON you. The Gentiles shall come to your* **LIGHT**, [(8)] [(9)] *And KINGS to the BRIGHTNESS of your RISING."* (Isa. 60:1–3, NKJV) (emphasis added).

Yes, indeed! The *Word* is the *Light of the World*, and so are we, His disciples, *if* we abide in Him and "keep" and "obey" His commandments. Do not dismiss the significance in Isaiah 60:1–3, Isaiah the prophet specifically says our light *has* come, and the glory of the Lord *has* already risen upon us! This was back in the Old Testament under the *first* Covenant.

For those of us who are of the "opinion" under the New Covenant we are *now* under the "dispensation" of God's grace that was not in effect under the *first* covenant, this is not true at all, and I can cite many biblical examples of this fact, and I will do so throughout this series of books.

However, based on 2 Timothy 1:8–11, we just read, I want you to focus your attention on what 2 Timothy 1:9, specifically says which is as follows: *"... who has saved us and called us with a holy calling, not according to our works, but according to His own purpose and GRACE which was GIVEN to US in CHRIST JESUS before TIME began..."*

Therefore, based on the Word of God we were given His "grace" before time began in Christ Jesus. As such, this false teaching on the "dispensation" of God's grace is erroneous, and it can, and it has led many believers to presume God's "grace" is a license for permissiveness and licentiousness. Licentiousness means the following:

❖ Lacking legal or moral restraints; especially: disregarding sexual restraints; *licentious* behavior; *licentious* revelers.

❖ Marked by disregard for strict rules of correctness.

❖ Unrestrained by law (God's law); or general morality; lawless; immoral.

❖ Going beyond customary, or proper bounds, or limits; disregarding rules (God's commandments).

This has led many believers to lack "legal" or "moral" restraints, especially relating to "sexual" restraints. Discarding or dismissing God's laws—His commandments, ordinances, statutes, and judgments, results in God's people practicing "lawlessness."

To which Jesus will say to those who practice "lawlessness" on Judgment Day, He never knew them. The reason why He will say He never knew those who practice "lawlessness" is for this reason: He will blot their name out of the Lamb's Book of Life. It will be as though they had never been born, or in this case, "reborn" again, *spiritually* speaking!

The unfortunate truth is this: Many of God's people do not truly want to hear God's truth because it would require them to change the way they are living. And, when you try to disciple God's people with His truth, which is based on His law (the Torah), they will say you are being "legalistic" and dismiss you as they call you a Pharisee.

Sadly, they do not understand you are trying to disciple them with "reproofs" of instruction, based on the whole counsel of God's Word, so they will not perish, because of their "lawlessness," come Judgment Day.

Now let's refocus our attention on God's plan of redemption before the foundation of the world. As I have clearly conveyed in this chapter and previous chapters, *the Word* who was sent to the earth as the Son of Man in the flesh in the Person of Jesus Christ, was God's *only* plan of "redemption" for all mankind *before* the foundation of the world.

Before God created the world, He shared His dream with *the Word,* and the Holy Spirit, to have a family of sons and daughters on the earth, and in the heavens (angels), for God's purposes and glory to prevail according to His predetermined plan.

Yet the *Creator of the Universe* wanted more than anything else to have a family created in His image and in His likeness, that would "love" Him, "worship" Him, "walk" with Him, "talk" with Him, "listen" to Him, and "obey" Him, because He first loved us with an *everlasting* love.

WE ARE SUPPOSED TO BE "RULING" AND "REIGNING" ON THE EARTH NOW AS WE CO-LABOR WITH GOD TO ESTABLISH HIS KINGDOM

As a result of us cultivating a personal, intimate relationship with *Yehovah,* our heavenly Father, and His only *begotten* Son, Jesus Christ, we would allow God, our Creator, to use us in order for God to manifest His dreams and creativity in and through us, His created. As we co-labor with our *King of kings and Lord of lords*, it will result in His "eternal" will being accomplished on the earth as it is in heaven.

Who is Israel? Discovering our True Identity in Jesus Christ and Why it Matters! The Foundation

When God created us in His image and in His likeness, He commanded us in Genesis 1:26–28, to be "fruitful" and "multiply" as we filled the earth with a godly remnant of His Spirit.

He also commanded us to "subdue" (bring into bondage, force, keep under, bring into subjection), and take "dominion" (prevail against, reign and rule to take) over the fish of the sea, over the birds of the air, and over *every* living thing that moves on the earth for this reason: For His glory and *eternal* purposes to prevail, in and through us, His created.

Therefore, God's people are *supposed* to be "ruling" and "reigning" on the earth with Jesus Christ *now* by abiding in Him through the Holy Spirit, because without Him, we can do nothing!

Moreover, we are admonished by Jesus in Matthew 6:33, to *first* seek the "kingdom" of God and His "righteousness" above all else, and then He says, *"...and all these things shall be added to you."* (NKJV) (emphasis added).

Do you know why we must *first* seek the "kingdom" of God and His "righteousness?" It is because this is the *only* way we will find out what God's purpose is for creating us. He has a unique assignment and destiny for *every* person He ever "formed" in their mother's womb He "predestined" us for *before* one of our days on the earth ever came to be.

It is only by us seeking God's face and heart will we understand what His good, perfect, and pleasing will is for us while we are still living on the earth so we can fulfill our God-given destiny.

Then like Jesus, after we are done with our earthly assignment, and we have died a *physical* death, we will then be glorified like Jesus was at the *first* resurrection of the dead in Christ.

Only *after* the *first* resurrection takes place, is "when" we will *enter* the *kingdom of heaven,* and hear the seven most important words ever spoken by Jesus based on Matthew 25:21, which is this: *"Well done my good and faithful servant!"* (NKJV)

Yet Jesus is not finished with this statement. He immediately qualifies this "conditional" statement of "what" makes us a good and faithful servant when He says to us, "… *you were FAITHFUL over a few THINGS, I will make you RULER over many THINGS. Enter into the joy of your lord."* (NKJV) (emphasis added).

So, the significance of this statement made by Jesus is this: If we do not "rule" and "reign" with Him on the earth as it is in heaven over a *few* things *now* by *first* seeking the "kingdom" of God and His "righteousness" above all else, then you can rest assured He will not make you a *ruler* over many things later after *this* earth passes away and you pass away!

Unfortunately, for the most part, the body of Christ has totally missed one of our main "kingdom" mandates from our heavenly Father, which is this: We are to establish His *kingdom,* His *righteousness,* His *justice,* and His *judgments,* which are based on His *laws,* His *ordinances,* His *statutes,* His *precepts,* and His *principles,* which are based on His "eternal" Word.

305

Who is Israel? Discovering our True Identity in Jesus Christ and Why it Matters! The Foundation

God's Ekklēsia is to "establish" and "execute" His government on the earth as it is in heaven. This is the *gospel of the kingdom*!

We have not been taught (discipled) we are to "rule" and "reign" with Jesus on the earth now in order to establish His "kingdom" "rule" and "reign" on the earth as it is in heaven.

This is why the body of Christ, for the most part, is no longer the "salt" and "light" in our society, and the world, we are called to be.

Now let's refocus our attention on the "preeminence" of Christ. Again, the definition of the word "preeminence" is the Greek word "prōteuō" which means: To be first (in rank or influence). The apostle Paul talks about the *preeminence of Christ* in Colossians 1:9–17.

If we now know *the Word* was the first "eternal" soul which was (qualified, selected, and chosen) from God's own Spirit *before* the foundation of the world as the *firstborn* over all creation, then this would mean *the Word* would be the *firstborn* of other "eternal" souls.

In fact, the apostle Paul substantiates this truth when he says to us in Romans 8:29, *"For whom He FOREKNEW, He also PREDESTINED to be CONFORMED to the IMAGE of His SON, that He might be the FIRSTBORN among MANY BRETHREN."* (NKJV) (emphasis added).

Yes, indeed! Just like Jesus, our heavenly Father "predestined" each of us to come to the earth in a body of flesh and blood at an

306

"appointed" time and generation in the *synergy of the ages,* for a specific purpose in order for God's "eternal" purposes and glory to prevail, in and through us, His sons and daughters.

As such, now that you know "who" the God we serve is, in the next chapter, we will discover when God created an "eternal" soul (spirit man), for *every* male and female who would ever be conceived that would be brought forth at an "appointed" time and generation in the *synergy of the ages.*

Our "eternal" soul (spirit man) was made in the "invisible" image and likeness of God *before* the foundation of the world.

Who is Israel? Discovering our True Identity in Jesus Christ and Why it Matters! The Foundation

CHAPTER 11

UNDERSTANDING OUR TRUE IDENTITY IN CHRIST AND OUR PURPOSE AS GOD'S SONS AND DAUGHTERS

The Lord has placed it on my heart that His people do not really *know* who we are in Christ, and *what* our purpose for being left on the earth is all about. As such, if the whole purpose of accepting Jesus Christ as our Lord and Savior is to escape the fiery furnace of *eternal* damnation, then the moment we accepted Jesus Christ as our Lord and Savior, He would take us off the earth. Yet He doesn't because this is our "testing" ground, which will determine "how" and "where" we will live for all eternity!

Rather, God has placed us on the earth and left us here for a "cause greater than ourselves" for the following seven reasons:

1. To bring God glory in all the earth by "loving" Him, "worshiping" Him, "praising" Him, "serving" Him, and "walking" with Him as we "obey" Him with all our mind, heart, soul, and strength.

2. To "rule" and "reign" with Jesus Christ as *we* establish God's *Kingdom* and His *Righteousness* on the earth as it is in heaven. We do this by invoking both "prayer" and "action" as we use the weapons of our warfare, which is God's Word that we must stand on, decree, and speak forth in the earthly *physical* realm. And, as we do our part, then God will act in

the *spiritual* realm when our obedience to His *eternal* Word is fulfilled. *Spiritually* speaking, we have *already* been "raised up" with Christ Jesus, and we are sitting together with Him in the *heavenly* places based on Ephesians 2:4–7 below:

> *"But God, who is rich in mercy, because of His great love with which He loved us, even when we were dead in trespasses, MADE US ALIVE TOGETHER WITH CHRIST (by grace you have been saved), and RAISED US UP TOGETHER, and MADE US SIT TOGETHER in the HEAVENLY PLACES in CHRIST JESUS, that in the ages to come He might show the exceeding riches of His grace in His kindness toward us in Christ Jesus."* (Eph. 2:4–7, NKJV) (emphasis added).

In addition, Jesus has already given us, His disciples, the "keys" of the *kingdom of heaven* we are to use while we are still living on the earth based on Matthew 16:19 below:

> *"And I will GIVE you the KEYS of the KINGDOM of HEAVEN, and WHATEVER you BIND on EARTH will be bound in HEAVEN, and WHATEVER you LOOSE on EARTH will be loosed in HEAVEN."* (Matt. 16:19, NKJV) (emphasis added).

Furthermore, *when* God created us in His image and His likeness, He commanded us to be "fruitful" and "multiply" so we will fulfill His dream to have a family on the earth for His *eternal* purposes and glory to be fulfilled according to the good pleasure of His will.

This is based on Ephesians 1:3–6 below. This Scripture talks about our redemption in Christ. Notice the apostle Paul says God and the Father of our Lord Jesus Christ, has *already* blessed us with *every* "spiritual" blessing in the *heavenly* places in Christ. Moreover, we are specifically told He *chose* us in Him *before* the foundation of the world.

> *"Blessed be the God and Father of our Lord Jesus Christ, who has BLESSED us with every SPIRITUAL BLESSING in the heavenly PLACES in Christ, just as He CHOSE US in Him before the FOUNDATION of the WORLD, that we should be HOLY and WITHOUT BLAME before Him in LOVE, having PREDESTINED us to ADOPTION as SONS by JESUS CHRIST to HIMSELF, according to the GOOD PLEASURE of His WILL, to the praise of the GLORY of HIS GRACE, by which He made us ACCEPTED in the BELOVED."* (Eph. 1:3–6, NKJV) (emphasis added).

In addition, God has commanded us to take "dominion" and "subdue" *every* living thing that moves on the earth based on

311

Genesis 1:26–28. The word "dominion" as used in this passage of Scripture means to rule, have dominion, dominate, and tread down.

Whereas, the word "subdue" as used in this passage of Scripture means to subject, force, keep under and make subservient. The word "subservient" essentially means to prepare (or disciple) believers in the body of Christ to obey God's Word without question, so they will learn to become submissive, deferential, compliant, dutiful, and obedient to God.

In addition, God's Ekklēsia (the body of Christ or "the" Church) is *supposed* to be the head and not the tail! Yet God's people have failed miserably in our main mandate of *why* He left us on the earth because we have not been taught this fundamental truth.

3. Moreover, we have been called to be the "salt" and "light" to a lost and dying world. As a matter of fact, God has established an *everlasting* "Covenant of Salt" with His people. See Leviticus 2:13; Numbers 18:19; Second Chronicles 13:5; Matthew 5:13–16; Mark 9:49–50; Luke 14:34; and Colossians 4:6.

I already covered in detail in the last chapter how we are called to illuminate His light because Jesus Christ is "the" *Light of the World,* and so are we. As such, we are called to "dispel" (drive away, get rid of, or eliminate) the *darkness.*

312

We do this as we share the "good news" of the *gospel of the kingdom* with those who are lost in darkness because they cannot see the truth, and thus, they are ensnared by the ploys of the enemy and being used by Satan.

Whereas, Jesus' disciples are likened unto "salt" regarding its "cleansing" and "preserving" attributes for we are called to prevent further decay in our world. Moreover, another application of us using "salt" is based on Colossians 4:6. In this Scripture, the apostle Paul admonishes us to let our speech always be with grace and seasoned with salt so we may know how we are to answer each person who may come to us searching for answers to their questions and for help.

4.   To make a difference in the lives of others and "show" them the love of Christ.

Again, in Chapter 56 of Book 3, I will convey why "love" is *essentially* the fulfillment of the law, and the prophets, *when* we "walk" according to God's commandments based on the whole counsel of His Word. Otherwise, we will be judged according to the law. And, if we do not love one another as Jesus has commanded us to do based on John 13:34, when He gave us a "new" commandment that we love one another as He has loved us, then we will be judged according to the law.

In fact, we will be judged by Jesus based on John 5:22, which proclaims, *"For the Father JUDGES no one, but has committed all JUDGMENT to the Son...* " (NKJV) (emphasis added).

Therefore, we would be very *wise* and should pay close attention to what Jesus tells us based on the whole counsel of His Word, rather than what our spiritual leaders tell us from their pulpits.

5.   To remember *who* we truly are—*spiritual* "eternal" beings that reside in these earthly vessels we call our bodies—and to help others remember who they truly are too as we carry out the *Great Commission.* For we are all God's children created in His image and in His likeness *before* the foundation of the world.

Hence, the whole purpose of us carrying out the *Great Commission* is to help bring God's lost sheep back into a "covenant" relationship with our heavenly Father, and God, our Creator. This is made possible only by the blood of Jesus Christ, His only *begotten* Son of His love—*the Word,* whom He sent.

6.   To fulfill our destiny according to the good pleasure of His will, He created us for *before* one of our days on the earth ever came to be.

7.   To "do" *only* the "will" of our heavenly Father for His glory and purposes to prevail. Again, Jesus says to us in Matthew 7:21, *"Not everyone who says to me, 'Lord, Lord,' shall*

314

ENTER the kingdom of heaven, but ONLY the one who <u>does</u> the WILL of My FATHER who is in HEAVEN." (NKJV) (emphasis added).

❖ If we do not read, study, and meditate on the whole counsel of God's Word for ourselves, how will we know if we are fulfilling God's will for our life?

❖ How will we renew our mind and our heart so we can be transformed by the power of the Holy Spirit living inside of us?

❖ How will we obey God's Word, *if* we do not know what it says?

❖ With the great apostasy coming out of many pulpits in the churches during these last days, are we really going to rely on where our soul will spend eternity based on what someone else tells us?

❖ Or, will we investigate the whole counsel of God's Word for ourselves to know what it really says?

Please listen. Your spiritual leader cannot do these things for you! Come Judgment Day, *every* man will stand *alone* before God, and He will hold *only* you accountable based on what is written in the books (plural) that will be opened on *that* fateful day.

315

If we have lived our lives for the One we "profess" to love with all our mind, heart, soul, and strength, then when we are finished with our "earthly" assignment, we will be "caught up" in glory just like Jesus was *after* the *first* resurrection of the dead in Christ takes place. And, we will hear Jesus say to us, *"Well done, good and faithful servant; you were faithful over a few things, I will make you ruler over many things. Enter into the joy of your lord."*

Now let's continue our journey to understand *who* we truly are as God's sons and daughters in Christ.

Just like *Yehôvah,* our heavenly Father did with all creation, they (God the Father, God the Son, and God the Holy Spirit), "created" an *eternal* soul (spirit man) for *every* human being that would ever be conceived *before* the foundation of the world. This is based on Genesis 1:26–28, which says the following:

*"Then God said, 'Let US **MAKE** [(1)]* [H6213: *'âsâh:* to *do* or *make,* in the broadest sense and widest application; accomplish, advance, appoint, become, bear, bestow, bring forth, bruise, be busy, to use] *MAN in OUR **IMAGE** [(2)]* [H6754: *tselem: to shade;* a *phantom,* that is, (figuratively) *illusion, resemblance;* hence a *representative figure], according to OUR **LIKENESS** [(3)]* [H1823: *d'mûth:* resemblance; concretely *model, shape;* adverbially *like;* fashion, like (-ness, as), manner, similitude]*; let them have **DOMINION** [(4)] [(5)]* [H7287: *râdâh:* to *tread* down, that is, *subjugate;* specifically to *crumble* off; (come to,

make to) have dominion, prevail against, reign, (bear, make to) rule, (-r, over), take], *take over the fish of the sea, over the birds of the air, and over the cattle, over all the earth and over every creeping thing that creeps on the earth.' So God* **CREATED** [6] [H1254: **bârâ':** to *create;* (qualified), *select, feed* (as formative processes); choose, create (creator)] *MAN in His OWN* **IMAGE;** [2] *in the* **IMAGE** [2] *of God He* **CREATED** [6] *him; MALE and FEMALE He* **CREATED** [6] *THEM. Then God blessed THEM, and God said to THEM, 'Be fruitful and multiply; FILL the EARTH and* **SUBDUE** [7] [8] [H3533: **kâbash:** to *tread* down; hence negatively to *disregard;* positively to *conquer, subjugate, violate;* bring into bondage, force, keep under, subdue, bring into subjection] *it; have* **DOMINION,** [4] [5] *takeover the fish of the sea, over the birds of the air, and over every LIVING THING that moves on the earth.'"* (Gen. 1:26–28, NKJV) (emphasis added).

The Holy Spirit gave me the revelation God "created" an *eternal* soul (spirit man) for *every* human being that would ever be conceived *before* the foundation of the world. I received this revelation when I kept questioning the Lord and asking Him why, in Genesis Chapter 1, He gives the account of making both "male" and "female" in His image and in His likeness.

However, it is not until Genesis 2:7, we learn about Adam, the first human being God ever "formed," rather than "created," from the dust of the earth.

317

Notice in Genesis 1:26–28, the word "created" is used three times rather than the word "formed," as when God "formed" man from the dust of the earth. This is based on Genesis 2:7, which says, *"And the Lord God **FORMED*** (9) [H3335: *yâtsar: squeezing* into shape; to *mould* into a form; especially as a *potter;* figuratively to *determine* (that is, form a resolution); X earthen, fashion, form, frame, make (-r), potter, purpose] *MAN of the DUST of the GROUND, and BREATHED into his NOSTRILS the BREATH of LIFE; and MAN became a LIVING being. "* (NKJV) (emphasis added).

ELOHIYM CREATED AN "ETERNAL" SOUL (SPIRIT MAN) FOR EVERY MALE AND FEMALE BEFORE THE FOUNDATION OF THE WORLD

Now I will substantiate the accuracy of the revelation I received from the Holy Spirit.

This revelation is concerning the fact our heavenly Father through *the Word* and the Holy Spirit "created" an *eternal* soul (spirit man) for *every* human being who would ever be conceived *before* the foundation of the world.

In addition, our eternal soul (spirit man) resided in heaven before our heavenly Father would send us to the earth to dwell in a body of flesh and blood, at an "appointed" time, to be part of an "appointed" generation, in the *synergy of the ages.*

Do you remember in Chapter 8 of this book, I included an excerpt

318

from the Book of Enoch which specifically said: "the elect" existed in the presence of the *Lord of Spirits* (plural) before the world was created?

As such, like *the Word*, we were sent to the earth for us to fulfill our destiny of why our heavenly Father created us in the first place for His *eternal* purposes to prevail, in and through us, His sons and daughters.

God confirmed this revelation according to His Word based on Genesis 2:1, which says, *"Thus the heavens and the earth, and all the HOST of THEM, were finished."* (NKJV) (emphasis added).

When it says all the "host of them" were finished, this is the fulfillment of Genesis 1:27, which says, *"So God created MAN in His own image; in the image of God He created him; MALE and FEMALE He created THEM."* (NKJV) (emphasis added).

Notice in Genesis 1:27, it specifically says God created "him" (singular), and then it says He created "them" (plural)—male and female.

As I have said before, but it bears repeating, before the *physical* manifestation of what God does in the *spiritual* realm occurs on the earth, God will "decree" and "establish" it in the *heavenly* realm first.

Furthermore, we are told God "created" man in His own "image" and "likeness." As such, when God "created" them—both male and female in His own "image," this is referring to His "invisible" Spirit.

319

For the apostle Paul tells us in Colossians 1:15, *the Word,* who is the *firstborn* over all creation, is the "image" of the "invisible" God.

Therefore, based on Genesis 2:1, we are specifically told the heavens, the earth, and all the "host of them" were finished. This is referring to when God "created" in the *heavenly* realm the "spirit man" for *every* human being, both male and female, who would ever to be conceived in their mother's womb which He would send to the earth at an "appointed" time throughout the *synergy of the ages.*

According to *Strong's Hebrew Lexicon* #H6635, the word "host" as used in Genesis 2:1, is the Hebrew word "tsâbâ'" (pronounced "tsaw-baw'"), which means: A *mass* of persons (or figurative things), especially regularly organized for company, worship, service, war, or hardship at an "appointed" time. Therefore, the phrase a "mass of persons" is not just referring to the *first* man Adam, God "formed" from the dust of the earth.

So let's take a look at this entire passage of Scripture, which will substantiate what I am saying. This is based on Genesis 2:1–7, which says the following:

> "Thus the HEAVENS and the EARTH, and all the
> HOST (10) [H6635: *tsâbâ'*: a *mass* of persons (or
> figurative things), especially regularly organized for
> company, worship, service, war, or hardship at an
> appointed time] of THEM [the word "them" refers to
> the "hosts" of both heaven and earth], were finished.
> And on the SEVENTH DAY God ENDED His WORK

which He had DONE, and He **RESTED** (11) [H7673: **shâbath**: to *repose*, that is, *desist* from exertion; to rest and to celebrate—to keep the Sabbath] *on the SEVENTH DAY from all His WORK which He had DONE. Then God* **BLESSED** (12) [H1288: **bârak**: to *kneel, praise, or thank*; by implication to *bless* God (as an act of adoration), and (vice-versa) man (as a benefit)] *the SEVENTH DAY and* **SANCTIFIED** (13) [H6942: **qâdash**: to be or to keep holy by consecrating or dedicating oneself to be ceremonially or morally clean by purifying or sanctifying oneself] *it* [the seventh day], *because in it* [the seventh day] *He* **RESTED** (11) *from all His WORK which God had CREATED and MADE."* (Gen. 2:1–3, NKJV) (emphasis added).

"This is the **HISTORY** (14) [H8435: **tôldâh**: (note: *history* is synonymous with the word *generations* as used in the KJV; (plural only) *descent*, that is, *family*; (figuratively) *history*; birth, generations] *of the HEAVENS and the EARTH when THEY* [the heavens and the earth and the "*mass* of persons" based on the word "host" in Genesis 2:1] *were* **CREATED** (6) [H1254: **bârâ'**: to *create*; (qualified), *select, feed* (as formative processes); choose, create (creator)], *in the DAY that the LORD God MADE the EARTH and the HEAVENS, BEFORE any PLANT of the FIELD was in the EARTH and BEFORE any HERB of the FIELD had GROWN. For the LORD God had not caused it to rain on the earth, and THERE WAS NO MAN to*

*TILL the GROUND; but a mist went up from the earth and watered the whole face of the ground. And the LORD God **FORMED*** [(9)]* [**H3335: yâtsar***: squeezing into shape; to *mould* into a form; especially as a *potter*; figuratively to *determine* (that is, form a resolution); X earthen, fashion, form, frame, make (-r), potter, purpose] MAN of the DUST of the GROUND, and BREATHED into HIS NOSTRILS the BREATH of LIFE; and MAN BECAME a LIVING **BEING*** [(15)] [(16)]* [**H5315: nephesh***: a breathing creature of a living being (with the life in the blood); the seat of emotions and passions or activity of the will; the inner being of a man; soul, mind, emotion].* " (Gen. 2:4–7, NKJV) (emphasis added).

WHY GOD "CREATED" A "MASS OF PERSONS" BEFORE THE FOUNDATION OF THE WORLD

When God "created" the heavens and the earth through *the Word,* and by His Holy Spirit, He also "created" a "mass of persons" (plural), based on the Hebrew meaning of the word "host" as used in Genesis 2:1, for the following five reasons:

1. To enjoy the pleasure of His company as His family.

2. To worship Him.

3. To serve Him.

322

4. To be His soldiers (warriors) in a time of war, or to engage in spiritual warfare for His Kingdom to prevail on the earth, as it is in heaven.

5. To endure hardships for His name's sake, and for His glory to prevail, so He can display His power to save, heal, and deliver His people.

You may be thinking to yourself this "mass of persons" referred to as "hosts" in Genesis 2:1, is talking about the angels, rather than the *eternal* soul (spirit man) of every male and female, who would ever be conceived.

However, it is referring to all of God's family that would reside in the heavens (the angels), and that would be sent to the earth—our eternal (spirit man) at an "appointed" time.

In fact, Jesus substantiates this truth in Matthew 22:30, when He says in the "resurrection" we will neither marry, or be given in marriage because we will be like "the angels" of God in heaven.

He states this truth because this is what we were like at the beginning of time when God "created" the eternal soul (spirit man) of every male and female who would ever be conceived, *before* one of our days on this earth ever came to be!

Therefore, based on Genesis 1:26–28, this is when God the Father, and God the Son of His love—*the Word,* and God the Holy Spirit, made our *eternal* soul (spirit man) in their "image" (of the "invisible" God—His Spirit), and in their "likeness" which includes

His DNA, His creativity, and His inspiration to dream, in and through us, His created.

This is substantiated in Job 32:8, which says, *"But there is a SPIRIT in MAN: and the INSPIRATION of the ALMIGHTY giveth THEM UNDERSTANDING."* (KJV) (emphasis added).

GOD'S PEOPLE ARE TO "RULE" AND "REIGN" ON THE EARTH NOW

From the very beginning of time, God gave our *eternal* soul (spirit man), the commandment to "rule" and "reign" on the earth, and bring *every* living thing that moves on the earth under "subjection" to us, as we are "speaking" and "doing" our heavenly Father's will.

However, the occultists have had this revelation as well. Therefore, they "speak" and "act" according to the inspiration of the demonic realm to bring chaos, death, and destruction into the earthly realm.

Yet believers in Jesus Christ, who have the true authority to "rule" and "reign" on the earth, sit by and hold our peace, and thereby we "allow" the enemy to "rule" and "reign," and creation is bound by this "illegitimate" authority!

God's Word says we are *supposed* to be the head, and not the tail! Jesus substantiates this truth in Luke 10:19, when He says to us, *"Behold, I give you the AUTHORITY to TRAMPLE on serpents and scorpions, and OVER all the POWER of the ENEMY, and nothing shall by any means hurt you."* (NKJV) (emphasis added).

Equally important, this is why Jesus tells us "how" we are to pray in Matthew 6:9–10, which says, *"In this manner, therefore, pray: Our Father in heaven, Hallowed be Your NAME* [note: we are to hallow God the Father's name].*YOUR KINGDOM come. YOUR WILL be done on EARTH as it is in HEAVEN."* (NKJV) (emphasis added).

Therefore, the *only* way God's kingdom and His will shall be "done" on the earth as it is in heaven, is by His people who live on the earth praying to our heavenly Father in the name of Jesus Christ. Then we must "do" the will of our heavenly Father based on His Voice we hear through the Holy Spirit, which should be in alignment based on the whole counsel of His *eternal* Word. Like Nehemiah, we are God's change agents on the earth, and the majority of the time, God uses His people to answer the prayers of the saints.

This has been mankind's purpose for being on the earth for the last six thousand years as the final hours of man's "rule" and "reign" on the earth is quickly coming to a close. It will be then, during the *seventh* millennium, which represents the *seventh* day of the creation week (seven thousand years based on Second Peter 3:8), God's "faithful" remnant will enter our final Sabbath day of rest.

Yes, indeed! Once our work throughout the *synergy of the ages* of our existence on planet earth is finished, it will be then His "faithful" remnant will enter into our final Sabbath day of rest in the *kingdom of heaven.*

Until this time we will remain on planet earth for this reason: We are to "do" the will of our heavenly Father so that God's *glory* and *eternal* purposes He "preordained" us for *before* the foundation of the world will be totally fulfilled.

325

When everything has been accomplished according to God's good, perfect, and pleasing will, then God's "faithful" remnant will rest from all of our labor during the seventh millennium in the *kingdom of heaven* for one thousand years. This is based on Second Peter 3:8, which says, *"But, beloved, do not forget this one thing, that with the Lord one DAY is as a thousand YEARS, and a thousand YEARS as one DAY."* (NKJV) (emphasis added).

Until all things that have been spoken by the mouth of God's holy prophets throughout the *synergy of the ages* has been totally fulfilled, then God has given mankind the mandate to "rule" and to "reign" on the earth. This is substantiated in Psalm 115:16, which says, *"The HEAVEN, even the HEAVENS, are the LORD'S; But the EARTH He has GIVEN to the CHILDREN of MEN."* (NKJV) (emphasis added).

WE ARE GOD'S "EKKLĒSIA," AND OUR "MAIN" MANDATE IS TO ESTABLISH GOD'S GOVERNMENT ON THE EARTH

Unfortunately, one of the primary reasons why God's Ekklēsia, which is the body of Christ, has failed miserably in establishing God's government on the earth as it is in heaven, is due to our ignorance based on the whole counsel of His Word. A lot of this error has been based on the definition of the word "Church" as used in our Bible.

According to *Strong's Greek Lexicon* #G1577, the word "Church" is the Greek word "Ekklēsia" (pronounced "ek-klay-see'-ah"), which means: The "assembly" of the Israelites when they were in the wilderness. It also refers to the whole body of Christians who are scattered throughout the earth.

More specifically, the Ekklēsia refers to the governing council of elders who convene at the public place of the council, and observe their own religious rights as they sit at the gates of the city in order to "rule" and "reign." They govern at the gates of the city for this reason: For their voice to be heard as they disciple, the nation, or nations, based on God's righteous requirements found in His Word.

In other words, this council "deliberates" and "rules" according to the regulations prescribed based on the whole counsel of God's Word, for the sake of the body of Christ, and is also for the purpose of discipling the nations.

According to the *NAS New Testament Greek Lexicon,* the word "Ekklēsia" means the following: [17]

1. A gathering of citizens called out from their homes into some public place, an assembly.

2. An assembly of the people convened at the public place of the council for deliberating.

3. An assembly of believers which is referring to the Israelites.

4. Any gathering, or throng of men, assembled by chance, tumultuously in a Christian sense.

327

5. An assembly of Christians gathered for worship in a religious meeting.

6. A company of Christians, or of those who, hoping for eternal salvation through Jesus Christ, observe their own religious rites, hold their own religious meetings, and manage their own affairs, according to regulations prescribed for the body for order's sake.

7. Those who anywhere, in a city, or village constitute such a company, and they are united into one body.

8. The whole body of Christians scattered throughout the earth.

9. The assembly of faithful Christians already dead and received into heaven.

There is *only* one body of Christ, under the headship of Jesus Christ who is "the" prophet Moses told the children of Israel the Lord would "raise up" based on Stephen's account of how Israel rebelled against God in Acts 7:37–39.

Moreover, Stephen, who was a Jew, would have been familiar with the word "Ekklēsia" instead of the word "Church" which refers to the children of Israel in the Old Testament based on the *Tanakh,* in the *Septuagint,* which was the Greek version of the Old Testament in the first century. Therefore, the word "Ekklēsia" is synonymous with the word "Church" which refers to the "called out" people of

God—who are the children of Israel. This is substantiated in Acts 7:37–39, which says the following:

> *"This is that Moses who said to the CHILDREN of ISRAEL, 'The LORD your God will raise up for you a Prophet like me from YOUR BRETHREN. Him you shall HEAR.' 'This is he who was in the* **CONGREGATION** [18] [G1577: *ekklēsia:* a *calling out, that is, (concretely) a popular meeting, especially a religious congregation* (Jewish *synagogue*, or Christian community of members on earth or saints in heaven or both); Assembly, Church] *in the WILDERNESS with the ANGEL who SPOKE to him on MOUNT SINAI, and with our fathers, the one who received the LIVING ORACLES to give to us, whom our fathers would not OBEY, but REJECTED..."* (Acts 7:37–39, NKJV) (emphasis added).

Moreover, we are taught the primary reason for accepting Jesus Christ as our Lord and Savior is, so our souls will not perish in the *lake of fire* when we die. However, if this was truly the case and the *only* reason for us becoming saved, then the moment we *became* saved, God would have taken us off the earth!

Therefore, one of the reasons why we are left on the earth and commanded to carry out the *Great Commission* is to help save, heal, and set free those who are experiencing hell while they are still living on the earth, because they are held captive by the enemy! They are *spiritually* blinded as to their true identity as God's sons and daughters who were created in His image, and in His likeness, *before* the foundation of the world.

329

Also, Jesus tells us the "why" behind us carrying out the *Great
Commission* to disciple all the nations. This is based on Luke 4:18–
19, which says the following:

> *"The SPIRIT of the LORD is UPON Me, Because He
> has ANOINTED Me To PREACH the GOSPEL to the
> POOR; He has SENT Me to HEAL the
> BROKENHEARTED, To PROCLAIM LIBERTY to the
> CAPTIVES And RECOVERY of SIGHT to the BLIND,
> To set at LIBERTY those who are OPPRESSED; To
> PROCLAIM the ACCEPTABLE YEAR of the LORD."*
> (Luke 4:18–19, NKJV) (emphasis added).

This is the job description and God-given mandate of *every* "born
again" blood-bought disciple of Jesus Christ no matter what our
vocation happens to be.

Furthermore, Jesus Christ died for the salvation of the whole man—
body, soul, and spirit—while we are still living on earth. Thus, we
already have eternal life by "knowing" both our heavenly Father and
the Son of His love—*the Word,* who became the Son of Man in the
Person of Jesus Christ in the flesh. This is accomplished by us
cultivating a personal, intimate relationship with them, and obeying
their commandments.

As far as us "ruling" and "reigning" on the earth with Jesus Christ is
concerned, this has been one of our main mandates as God's
Ekklēsia during the past six thousand years since God created the
first man Adam. Unfortunately, because we have not been properly
discipled, the body of Christ has missed one of our main "kingdom"

mandates of why we have been left on the earth which is for this reason: To establish the *kingdom of God* on the earth as it is in heaven as God's people "execute" His government using His power and authority we have *already* been given to disciple the nations.

In addition, many people in the body of Christ are taught and believe when Jesus comes back the second time; we will be *immediately* "ruling" and "reigning" with Him on *this* earth for a thousand years.

This belief is in error for the following three reasons:

1. We have been "ruling" and "reigning" as His Ekklēsia during the past 6,000 years since God gave this mandate to the first Adam. And, this is one of the reasons that—the last Adam— Jesus Christ, came to the earth the first time. He came to set up His Kingdom "rule" and "reign" on the earth which would be accomplished through His disciples who abide in Him.

2. When Jesus Christ returns the second time, *this* earth will be *entirely* "depopulated" and fully "consumed" (annihilated) at the brightness of His second coming. In Chapter 68 of Book 3, I will convey this truth based on the whole counsel of God's Word.

3. After the one thousand years is over when all things are made new in the New Beginning, which is based on Revelation 21. It will be then that the *wife of Christ* will descend out of the *kingdom of heaven* and we will come

back to the "new" earth. Then we will *literally* "rule" and "reign" with Christ on the "new" earth.

As such, we will not be "ruling" and "reigning" with Jesus Christ on *this* earth *immediately* upon His second coming like we have been taught to believe.

JESUS CHRIST CAME TO THE EARTH THE FIRST TIME TO "SEEK" AND TO "SAVE" THAT "WHICH" WAS LOST

One of the many reasons "why" *the Word* came to the earth as the Son of Man in the Person of Jesus Christ the first time, was to *seek* and to *save* that *which* was lost. This is based on Luke 19:10, which proclaims, *"...for the Son of Man has come to SEEK and to **SAVE*** [19] [G4982: *sōzō*: to save, deliver; heal, preserve or protect to make whole] *that WHICH was **LOST*** [20] [G622: *apollumi*: to *destroy* fully (reflexively to *perish*, or *lose*), literally or figuratively; destroy, die, lose, mar, perish]. *"* (NKJV) (emphasis added).

What were some of the things *which* were lost due to the first Adam's transgression? Our authority and power to "subdue" and take "dominion" which God gave us and blessed us with to "rule" and "reign" on the earth with Him. Look at the definition of "dominion" again. It means to "rule" and "reign" as God's Ekklēsia on the earth.

In other words, Jesus Christ came the first time to restore His government on the earth as it is in heaven, which was lost when the

332

first Adam transferred the government of God on the earth to the *god of this age,* who is Satan. This happened as a result of Adam's transgression against God. Up until this time, the first Adam was given God's "authority" and "power" as His ambassador to "subdue" and have "dominion" over every living thing that moves on the earth.

This is one of the reasons why when Jesus Christ came to the earth the first time, He did not preach the gospel concerning Himself publicly, that He would die, and then be resurrected from the grave, even though He shared this with His disciples in private.

Rather, Jesus Christ came to the earth the first time to preach the *gospel of the kingdom* He came to re-establish on the earth, which was lost *when* the first Adam gave his "authority" and "power" God his Creator, gave him over to Satan.

Again, Jesus Christ came to the earth the first time to re-establish His government on the earth as it is in heaven, even though it was not in the manner His disciples had hoped for which would have resulted in revolting against their Roman oppressors. It is for this very reason, from *that* time forward, Jesus began to preach and say according to Matthew 4:17, *"...REPENT, for the KINGDOM of HEAVEN is at HAND."* (NKJV) (emphasis added).

Over two thousand years ago, when Jesus Christ began His Galilean ministry after John the Baptist was put in prison, Jesus specifically said the "time is fulfilled," and the *kingdom of God* is at hand.

Jesus did not say the time *will be* fulfilled, and the *kingdom of God* will come sometime in the future when He comes back the second time to set up His Kingdom on the earth. Jesus Christ has already set up His Kingdom on the earth.

Yet most people in the body of Christ do not realize this truth: One of the main reasons why Jesus Christ came to the earth the first time was to *seek* and to *save* that "which" was lost by the first Adam's transgression when death entered the world.

This is substantiated by what Jesus says to us specifically in Mark 1:15. Jesus said over two thousand years ago, *before* He went to the cross at Calvary, the "set" or "proper" season (time) for His "kingdom" which is His "rule" and "reign," *has* drawn nigh.

Moreover, the very first thing Jesus said when He shared the "good news" of the *gospel of the kingdom* (a.k.a. the Great Commission), was for people to "repent!" He proclaimed repentance was necessary so we would "think" differently, and feel "moral" compunction. Thus, we would demonstrate our faith by entrusting our spiritual well-being to Him (Christ—the Anointed One). This is based on Mark 1:15, which says the following:

> "The **TIME** (21) [G2540: *kairos*: of uncertain affinity; an *occasion*, that is, *set* or *proper* time; synonymous with the word *seasons*] is **FULFILLED** (22) (23) [G4137: *pleroo*: to make replete or satisfy, execute (an office) by consummating, executing, and ratifying (confirm) a period or to accomplish a task to make complete and render perfect so that God's will and promises as made know in the law will be obeyed as it should], and the **KINGDOM** (24) [G932: *basileia*: Kingdom rule

334

and reign of royalty in a realm (literally or figuratively)] *of GOD is at HAND* (25) [G1448: *eggizo*: to make *near*, that is, (reflexively) *approach; to draw nigh*]. *REPENT* (26) [G3340: *metanoeo*: to *think differently* or *afterwards*, that is, *reconsider* (morally to feel compunction)], *and BELIEVE* (27) [G4100: *pisteuo*: to *have faith* (in, upon, or with respect to, a person or thing), that is, *credit*; by implication to *entrust* (especially one's spiritual well-being to Christ)] *in the GOSPEL* (28) (29) [G2098: *euaggelion*: a *good message*; G2097: *euaggelizo*: to *announce good news* ("evangelize") especially the gospel; declare, show, bring good tidings and to preach]. *"* (Mark 1:15, NKJV) (emphasis added).

Yes, indeed! Well over two thousand years ago, Jesus was announcing the "good news" and preaching the *gospel of the kingdom* [G932: *basileia*: kingdom "rule" and "reign" of royalty in a realm on the earth as it is in heaven].

This is why Jesus made the announcement the *kingdom of heaven* is "at hand" over two thousand years ago! Because the meaning of the phrase "at hand" means to draw, or come near to, or to approach God, in order to "rule" and "reign" in Him and with Him. In addition, this is why Jesus said to us in Matthew 16:19; He has *already* given us the "keys" of the *kingdom of heaven.*

Based on what the apostle Paul tells us in Hebrews 12:22, the *kingdom of heaven* is located on *Mount Zion* in the *city of the living God* in the *heavenly* Jerusalem which is located somewhere in the universe. Therefore, the *kingdom of heaven, physically* speaking, is the region above the clouds, which is the seat of order of all things *eternal* and consummately perfect where God dwells with other heavenly beings—the angels.

So, for what purpose did Jesus preach the *gospel of the kingdom* over two thousand years ago, and said to us then, based on Matthew 4:17, the *kingdom of heaven* is at hand?

Jesus was prophetically "declaring" and "decreeing," while we were still dead in our transgressions, one of the reasons *why* He had come to the earth to die for us is for this reason: That He, Jesus Christ, would *seek* and *save* that "which" was lost when the first Adam brought sin into the world.

In fact, the apostle Paul says to us in Romans 5:17–19, that by one man's offense that death "reigned" through him, the first Adam. But *now,* for those who have received the abundance of "grace" and the gift of "righteousness" in Christ, "reign" in life *through* Jesus Christ. Romans 5:17–19, says the following:

> *"For if by the ONE MAN'S OFFENSE* [Adam's transgression] *DEATH REIGNED* (30) [G936: *basileuō*: to *rule* (literally or figuratively): king, reign] *through the ONE, much more those who receive ABUNDANCE of GRACE and of the GIFT of RIGHTEOUSNESS will REIGN* (30) *in LIFE through the One, JESUS CHRIST."* (Rom. 5:17, NKJV) (emphasis added).

336

"Therefore, as through ONE MAN'S OFFENSE [Adam's transgression] *JUDGMENT came to all MEN, resulting in* **CONDEMNATION** [31] [32] [G2631: **katakrima**: an *adverse sentence;* G2632: **katakrino**: to *judge against,* that is, *sentence:* condemn, damn], *even so through one MAN'S* **RIGHTEOUS** [33] [G1345: **dikaioma**: an *equitable deed;* by implication a *statute* or *decision;* judgment, justification, ordinance] *ACT the FREE GIFT came to all MEN, resulting in* **JUSTIFICATION** [34] [G1347: **dikaiosis**: *acquittal* (for Christ's sake)] *of* **LIFE** [35] [G2222: **zoe**: the state of one who is possessed of vitality or is animated; every living soul]. *For as by ONE MAN'S DISOBEDIENCE many were MADE SINNERS, so also by ONE MAN'S OBEDIENCE many will be MADE* **RIGHTEOUS** [36] [G1342: **dikaios**: *equitable* (in character or act); by implication *innocent, holy* (absolutely or relatively); just]. *"* (Rom. 5:18–19, NKJV) (emphasis added).

As substantiated in Romans 5:18–19, this is why the apostle Paul says to us in Romans 8:1, the following: *"There is therefore NOW NO* **CONDEMNATION** [37] [38] [G2631: **katakrima**: an *adverse sentence* (the verdict); G2632: **katakrino**: to *judge against,* that is, *sentence;* condemn, damn] *to those who are in CHRIST JESUS, who DO NOT WALK according to the FLESH, but according to the SPIRIT."* (NKJV) (emphasis added).

This statement made by the apostle Paul is "conditional, " and it is based on whether we "walk" according to the flesh, or according to the Spirit. It is not a license to sin! Many believers in the body of Christ are of the "opinion" Jesus took care of everything on the cross for us. Therefore, there is no longer a need for us to *work out* our *own* salvation with *fear* and with *trembling*. This "mindset" is contrary to God's Word based on Philippians 2:12 and many other Scriptures.

Then the apostle Paul continues to explain to us in Romans 5:20–21, based on what Jesus Christ did for us, grace would abound much more where sin abounded so grace might "reign" through "righteousness" to eternal life through Jesus Christ our Lord. This is substantiated in Romans 5:20–21, which says the following:

> *"Moreover the LAW ENTERED that the OFFENSE might ABOUND. But where SIN ABOUNDED, GRACE ABOUNDED MUCH MORE, so that as SIN*
> *REIGNED* [(30)] **[G936: *basileuō*: to *rule* (literally or figuratively); King, reign]** *in DEATH, even so GRACE might REIGN* [(30)] *through RIGHTEOUSNESS to ETERNAL LIFE* [(35)] **[G2222: *zōē*: the state of one who is possessed of vitality or is animated; every living soul]** *through JESUS CHRIST our LORD."* (Rom. 5:20–21, NKJV) (emphasis added).

The apostle Paul is not giving us the green light to sin more because God's grace abounds more due to what Jesus Christ did on the cross at Calvary based on Romans 5:20–21. In fact, the apostle Paul addresses this in Romans 6:1–4, when he says in Christ we have "died" to sin and are no longer to live in sin! Romans 6:1–4, says the following:

Donna M. Rogers

*"What shall we say then? SHALL WE CONTINUE IN SIN that GRACE may ABOUND? CERTAINLY NOT! How shall we who DIED to SIN LIVE ANY LONGER IN IT? Or DO YOU NOT KNOW that as MANY OF US as were BAPTIZED into CHRIST JESUS were BAPTIZED into His DEATH? Therefore WE were BURIED with Him through BAPTISM into DEATH, that just as CHRIST was RAISED from the DEAD by the GLORY of the FATHER, even so WE also should WALK in NEWNESS of **LIFE*** [35] [G2222: *zōē*: the state of one who is possessed of vitality or is animated; every living soul]*."* (Rom. 6:1–4, NKJV) (emphasis added).

Therefore, as a result of Jesus Christ's death, resurrection, and ascension back into heaven, it would shortly come to pass, the *kingdom of heaven* would reside "in" us, *spiritually* speaking, through His Holy Spirit. This is why Jesus Christ preached, *"Repent, for the KINGDOM of HEAVEN is at HAND."* (NKJV) (emphasis added).

For those who would repent (change their way of thinking) after they heard and "believed" the *gospel of the kingdom* Jesus Christ and His early disciples preached, then the *kingdom of heaven* was indeed at hand!

The *kingdom of heaven* was at hand as Jesus Christ's disciples "learned" to dwell in God's manifest presence through His Holy Spirit, God liberally poured out on all who believed in the *gospel of the kingdom* after Jesus Christ's death, resurrection, and ascension

339

into heaven. As such, we are *now* "raised up" together with Christ and are sitting together with Him in the *heavenly* places based on what the apostle Paul tells us in Ephesians 2:4–6 below:

> *"But God, who is RICH in MERCY, because of His GREAT LOVE with which He loved us, even WHEN we were DEAD in TRESPASSES,* [Our heavenly Father—*Yehovah*] *MADE us ALIVE TOGETHER with CHRIST (by grace you have been saved), and RAISED us UP TOGETHER, and made us SIT TOGETHER in the HEAVENLY PLACES in CHRIST JESUS..."* (Eph. 2:4–6, NKJV) (emphasis added).

Therefore, *true* disciples of Jesus Christ "rule" and "reign" on the earth with Him *now* as it is in heaven, which only takes place *when* we "walk" according to the Spirit because we have "learned" to crucify our flesh and have died to our sins!

On those few occasions when we realize we have sinned, then we are to follow what we are told to do in First John 1:9. This Scripture says the following: *"If* [this makes this statement conditional] *we CONFESS our SINS, He is FAITHFUL and just to FORGIVE us OUR SINS and to CLEANSE US from all UNRIGHTEOUSNESS."* (NKJV) (emphasis added).

We must always stay humble and be willing to repent when we have sinned. We must confess our sins to God who is faithful to forgive us and cleanse us from all unrighteousness. Then, as a result, we will allow God to establish His will in and through us, as we abide in Christ Jesus and He abides in us through His Holy Spirit who dwells in our hearts. However, this means we must "submit" to His will rather than our own, and "obey" God based on what the Holy Spirit leads us to "say" and "do," just like Jesus did during His earthly ministry.

This is what it *truly* means to be "born again," *spiritually* speaking, and this is *why* Jesus told Nicodemus in the Book of John beginning in Chapter 3, concerning "what" it takes for one to be "born again" in order to see the *kingdom of God.*

Jesus told Nicodemus that unless one is born of *water* and the *Spirit,* he cannot *enter* the *kingdom of God,* because that which is born of the flesh is flesh, and that which is born of the Spirit is spirit.

There is much more to this statement which was made by Jesus than is readily apparent. As such, in Chapter 67 of Book 3, I will convey what it *truly* means to be "reborn," or "born again," *physically* speaking.

In Chapter 68 of Book 3, I will convey what happens to our body, soul, and spirit when we are no longer sojourners on this earth. It will be then, that we will make our final transition from life on the earth to spending eternity with God in the heavenly realm. We will remain in heaven until the "new" heavens, and the "new" earth is created. Then we will descend from heaven as the *wife of Christ,* back down to the "new" earth to start a New Beginning.

Until the New Beginning happens on the "new" earth, we will return to being just like the angels of God in heaven (see Matthew 22:30).

Who is Israel? Discovering our True Identity in Jesus Christ and Why it Matters! The Foundation

Our soul (spirit man) will once again dwell with God in the *heavenly* realm after the *first* resurrection of the dead in Christ takes place. It will be then; we will receive our "glorified" bodies.

After we receive our glorified bodies, then we will be glorified together with our heavenly Father once again, just like we were *before* one of our days on this earth ever came to be.

Like, Jesus who talks about this truth in John 17:4–5, we will be glorified together with our heavenly Father, with the glory which we had with Him before the world was.

Hence, as Jesus' disciples, we must also "glorify" our heavenly Father while we live on the earth, and we must finish the work He has given us to do. We must fulfill our destiny of why our heavenly Father created us in the first place in order to enter the *kingdom of heaven* based on what Jesus says to us in Matthew 7:21.

Therefore, if you have not been living in order to "do" the will of your heavenly Father, as long as you are still breathing, it is not too late to repent and make a course correction now, before it is too late for all eternity.

We *must* stop being caught up in the things of this world which shall shortly pass away. Instead, we must be driven by eternity, so we will be found "faithful" as we seek first to "establish" His *kingdom* and His *righteousness* on the earth as it is in heaven, which will be evidenced by us bearing "fruit" which is worthy of repentance.

In the next chapter, we will discover why *the Word,* who was and is in the image of the "invisible" God, *chose* to take the form of a "bondservant" and come to the earth as the Son of Man in the Person of Jesus Christ.

Who is Israel? Discovering our True Identity in Jesus Christ and Why it Matters! The Foundation

CHAPTER 12

WHY DID THE WORD WHO WAS IN THE IMAGE OF THE INVISIBLE GOD CHOOSE TO TAKE THE FORM OF A BONDSERVANT AND COME TO THE EARTH IN THE LIKENESS OF MEN?

The *Word* who was created in the "invisible" image of His heavenly Father, *Yehôvãh,* who is Spirit, had to have an earthly vessel (body) God could use to manifest Himself in when He came to the earth to be born as the Son of Man with a body of flesh and blood.

This had to happen before *Yehôvãh's* Son of His love—*the Word,* who became the Son of Man in the flesh in the Person of Jesus Christ, could die for the forgiveness of our sins by shedding His precious blood. This was the *only* way God could remarry His wife—Israel, and her treacherous sister Judah, to whom He had issued a *certificate of divorce,* because of her "spiritual" harlotry based on Jeremiah 3:8 below:

> *"Then I saw that for all the causes for which backsliding ISRAEL had committed adultery, I HAD PUT HER AWAY and GIVEN her a CERTIFICATE of DIVORCE; yet her treacherous sister JUDAH did not FEAR, but went and PLAYED the HARLOT also."* (Jer. 3:8, NKJV) (emphasis added).

345

Also, worth mentioning is this fact: Notice in Jeremiah 3:8, God is distinctly identifying Israel and Judah as being two separate "houses" and two separate "kingdoms."

As such, if we are of the "opinion" Israel refers to only the Jews from the House of Judah, then why is God speaking of both Israel and her sister Judah? Therefore, when Jeremiah talks about backsliding Israel, he is referring to the ten tribes of Israel that comprised the *northern* kingdom of the nation of Israel after King Solomon's death that was scattered all over the world into the Gentile nations.

Whereas, the word "Judah" as used by Jeremiah in this passage of Scripture, is the Hebrew word "Yᵉhûdâh" (pronounced "yeh-hoo-daw'"), which refers to the tribe that descended from the first of its territory. Also, it is specifically referring to the Jews from the House of Judah, who are descendants of Jacob's son, Judah.

In Isaiah 54:5 below, Isaiah proclaims this truth: We are "betrothed" to *Yehovah,* our heavenly Father, who is our Maker, and our Redeemer—our Lord and Savior Jesus Christ, who is the Holy One of Israel. This means we must be faithful to *only* Him because He is our husband who has paid a very high price for His bride with His life, even though the "consummation" of the wedding hasn't taken place yet.

> *"For YOUR MAKER is your HUSBAND, The LORD of HOSTS is His NAME; And your REDEEMER is the HOLY ONE of ISRAEL; He is called the GOD of the whole EARTH."* (Isa. 54:5, NKJV) (emphasis added).

346

Therefore, we became "betrothed" to *Yehôvah,* our heavenly Father, when we accepted His only *begotten* Son, Jesus Christ, whom He sent to the earth as the Son of Man in the Person of Jesus Christ, who is our Lord and Savior.

Do you remember that moment in time He first captivated your heart with His *everlasting* love for you, when you realized you needed a Savior in your life? It was at that moment, many of us promised to love our beloved Savior, Redeemer, Father, and Friend, with all our mind, heart, soul, and strength for all eternity, and He became our first love. In addition, isn't this essentially what we promise our spouses when we exchange wedding vows with them before God? We vow to love them, and be faithful to *only* them, for better or worse, until death do we part, correct?

Furthermore, you are probably wondering what this has to do with our heavenly Father, *Yehôvah,* requiring Jesus Christ to die for us, His bride. As such, I will address this subject in the next section.

GOD COULD <u>NOT</u> BREAK HIS OWN LAW CONCERNING DIVORCE

We need to understand God could not break His own law written in Deuteronomy 24:1–4, which is God's law concerning divorce. Deuteronomy 24:1–4, says the following:

> *"When a MAN TAKES a WIFE and MARRIES her, and it HAPPENS that SHE finds NO FAVOR in HIS EYES because HE has FOUND some UNCLEANNESS*

> *in HER, and he WRITES her a CERTIFICATE of
> DIVORCE, puts it in HER HAND, and SENDS HER
> OUT OF HIS HOUSE, when she has departed from
> his house, and goes and becomes another man's wife,
> if the latter husband detests her and writes her a
> certificate of divorce, puts it in her hand, and sends
> her out of his house, or if the latter husband dies who
> took her as his wife, then HER FORMER HUSBAND
> who DIVORCED HER must NOT TAKE HER BACK
> to be HIS WIFE after SHE has been DEFILED; for
> that is an ABOMINATION before the LORD, and you
> shall not bring SIN on the LAND which the LORD
> your God is GIVING you as an INHERITANCE."*
> (Deut. 24:1–4, NKJV) (emphasis added).

Deuteronomy 24:1–4, specifically says the following: When a man finds some "uncleanness" with his wife, writes her a *certificate of divorce,* puts it in her hand, and sends her out of his house, under no circumstances is her *former* husband who divorced her permitted to take her back as his wife after she has been "defiled" by other men. For this is an abomination to the Lord, and this sin will "defile" the whole land, God has given us as an inheritance because we are His sons and daughters who are in a covenant relationship with Him.

This Scripture has a *literal* application of sexual adultery, which is one of the two biblical grounds for a man and a woman breaking a marriage covenant. However, in regards to our betrothal to God, He is talking about "spiritual" adultery committed by His people who are running after false idols and false gods. This includes His people who practice and embrace the pagan "customs," "traditions," and "rituals" of heathen nations.

GOD'S "COVENANT OF MARRIAGE" HE ESTABLISHED WITH ALL TWELVE TRIBES OF ISRAEL THROUGHOUT THE SYNERGY OF THE AGES

God established a "Covenant of Marriage" with the children of Israel who were gathered at the base of Mount Sinai, after they experienced God's "grace" and "mercy" when He led them out of Egypt, from their bondage and slavery, at the hands of Pharaoh, who knew not Joseph. This was based on one of the promises God gave to Abraham, because of the *everlasting* covenant He established with him and his descendants. I cover this fact in Chapter 20 of Book 2.

After God's servant Moses had led the children of Israel out of Egypt, God established His written instructions in the Torah, detailing the terms and conditions of being in a "Covenant of Marriage" with Him. This was given to all the children of Israel when God issued His Levitical laws and the Ten Commandments, through His servant Moses during the very first Feast of Weeks (*Shavuot* or *Pentecost*), which was held long ago at the base of Mount Sinai.

Until the time of Jesus appearing in the flesh came to pass, *this* covenant was "confirmed" (ratified) only *temporarily* by the blood of animals, which could only cover the sins of the people. Only by the blood of Jesus could mankind obtain *eternal* redemption as

349

Who is Israel? Discovering our True Identity in Jesus Christ and Why it Matters! The Foundation

Jesus Christ, our Great High Priest, entered the Most Holy Place once and for all, having obtained *eternal* redemption for our sins based on Hebrews 9:12–15, which says the following:

> *"Not with the blood of goats and calves, but with His OWN BLOOD He ENTERED the most HOLY PLACE ONCE for ALL, having OBTAINED ETERNAL REDEMPTION. For if the blood of bulls and goats and the ashes of a heifer, sprinkling the unclean, SANCTIFIES for the PURIFYING of the FLESH, how much more shall the BLOOD of CHRIST, who through the ETERNAL SPIRIT offered HIMSELF without SPOT to God, CLEANSE your CONSCIENCE from DEAD WORKS to SERVE the LIVING GOD? And FOR THIS REASON He is the MEDIATOR of the NEW COVENANT, by MEANS of DEATH, for the REDEMPTION of the TRANSGRESSIONS under the FIRST COVENANT, that THOSE WHO ARE CALLED may RECEIVE the PROMISE of the ETERNAL INHERITANCE."* (Heb. 9:12–15, NKJV) (emphasis added).

Notice based on Hebrews 9:12–15, Jesus Christ did not abolish the *first* covenant. Rather, He offered Himself, through the "eternal Spirit," without spot or blemish, to cleanse our conscience from dead works so we can serve the living God.

Moreover, only by the blood of Jesus Christ, has He "redeemed" *once* and for all, the transgressions committed by God's people

350

under the *first* covenant, by obtaining *eternal* redemption for our sins, as He entered the Most Holy Place as our Great High Priest.

Thus, it is for *this* very reason, Jesus Christ is the "mediator" of the New Covenant where God has now put His laws in our mind, and written them on our hearts, rather than on two tablets of stone.

In fact, it is so critical for God's people to understand this indisputable truth; I will cover in detail in Chapters 40–46 of Book 3, "what" the New Covenant is. I will also convey "what" the primary differences are under the *first* covenant (Old Covenant), with regards to the New Covenant. The *first* covenant (Old Covenant) is not "obsolete" like many in the body of Christ "erroneously" believe it is.

SOME OF GOD'S TERMS AND CONDITIONS OF HIS "COVENANT OF MARRIAGE" FOR ALL HIS PEOPLE

In Exodus 19:3–6, we are told about *some* of the terms and conditions of us being in a "Covenant of Marriage" with our heavenly Father, *Yehovah,* based on the *first* covenant, which was "ratified" (confirmed) by Jesus Christ's precious blood. Exodus 19:3–6, says the following:

> *"And Moses WENT UP to God, and the LORD called*
> *to him from the mountain, saying, 'Thus you shall say*
> *to the HOUSE of JACOB, and tell the CHILDREN of*
> *ISRAEL: 'You have seen what I did to the Egyptians,*
> *and how I bore you on eagles' wings and brought you*

> *to Myself. Now therefore, if* [this makes this promise conditional] *you will indeed OBEY My VOICE and KEEP My COVENANT, then you shall be a SPECIAL TREASURE to Me ABOVE all PEOPLE; for all the EARTH is Mine. And you shall be to Me a KINGDOM of PRIESTS and a HOLY NATION.' These are the words which you shall speak to the CHILDREN of ISRAEL.'"* (Exod. 19:3–6, NKJV) (emphasis added).

One of the reasons why our heavenly Father, *Yehôvah,* sent His only *begotten* Son the first time, was to "restore" and "reconcile" us back into "walking" in a "Marriage Covenant" with our heavenly Father. This could only be achieved by Him dying for us so our sins could be forgiven by the blood of "the" perfect "Passover Lamb"—Jesus Christ, who never sinned.

In Exodus 19:3–6, we are told that this promise from God is to all the children of Israel. The children of Israel are called to be a kingdom of priests and a holy nation. Yet this promise from God to the children of Israel is "conditional." This "conditional" promise is based on whether we will "obey" His Voice and "keep" His covenant after we receive Jesus Christ as our Lord and Savior. Jesus Christ having been perfected, He became the author of eternal salvation to all who "obey" Him. This fact is substantiated in Hebrews 5:9.

God's terms and conditions of being in a "Marriage Covenant" with Him, as told to the children of Israel long ago as detailed in Exodus 19:3–6, applies to New Covenant believers. The children of Israel in *this* generation, along with all the children of Israel throughout the *synergy of the ages,* are called a *chosen* generation, a *royal*

352

priesthood, and a *holy* nation. We are God's special people, so that we may proclaim the praises of Him who has called us out of darkness into His marvelous light. This is substantiated in First Peter 2:9, which is in the New Testament.

In Exodus 19:3–6, when Moses went up to God on the mountain and was told to proclaim what the Lord had said to the children of Israel when he came back down, this is the first time the trumpet of God (shofar) was sounded. In this case, the shofar was used to gather the assembly, so God's people could receive His law, which are the terms and conditions of His "Marriage Covenant" between Abraham's God, and all the children of Israel forevermore.

This is one of the reasons why we are commanded to keep and commemorate the Feast of Trumpets on a yearly basis as a "memorial" which is commemorated with the blowing of trumpets. This is based on Leviticus 23:23–24, which proclaims, *"Then the LORD spoke to Moses, saying, 'Speak to the CHILDREN of ISRAEL, saying: 'In the SEVENTH month, on the FIRST day of the MONTH, you shall have a SABBATH-REST, a MEMORIAL of BLOWING of TRUMPETS, a HOLY CONVOCATION.' "* (NKJV) (emphasis added).

We are commanded to keep and commemorate the Feast of Trumpets as a "memorial," because it is our wedding anniversary as the nation of Israel, *spiritually* speaking. Each year when we keep and commemorate the Feast of Trumpets, we are "reconfirming" or "renewing" our wedding vows we made with our heavenly Father as a *holy* nation, and a *royal* priesthood, which was made for all the children of Israel, who comprise the nation of Israel, *spiritually* speaking. You will understand the full significance of this fact when

353

Who is Israel? Discovering our True Identity in Jesus Christ and Why it Matters! The Foundation

I will cover in Chapter 16 of this book, the "customs" of the *ancient* Jewish wedding ceremony.

This pivotal and awesome scene of when God's people received His law, which details *some* of the terms and conditions of the "Marriage Covenant" between God, and all the children of Israel, is described in Exodus 19:16–20, which says the following:

> *"Then it came to PASS on the THIRD DAY, in the MORNING, that there were THUNDERINGS and LIGHTNINGS, and a THICK CLOUD on the MOUNTAIN; and the SOUND of the TRUMPET was VERY LOUD, so that all the PEOPLE who were in the CAMP TREMBLED. And MOSES brought the PEOPLE OUT of the CAMP to MEET with GOD, and THEY STOOD at the FOOT of the MOUNTAIN. Now MOUNT SINAI was COMPLETELY in SMOKE, because the LORD DESCENDED UPON IT in FIRE. Its SMOKE ASCENDED like the SMOKE of a FURNACE, and the WHOLE MOUNTAIN QUAKED GREATLY. And when the BLAST of the TRUMPET SOUNDED LONG and became LOUDER and LOUDER, MOSES SPOKE, and GOD ANSWERED HIM by VOICE. Then the LORD came DOWN UPON MOUNT SINAI, on the TOP of the MOUNTAIN. And the LORD CALLED MOSES to the TOP of the MOUNTAIN, and MOSES WENT UP."*
> (Exod. 19:16–20, NKJV) (emphasis added).

This scene depicted in Exodus 19:16–20, occurred during the very first Feast of Weeks (*Shavuot* or *Pentecost*) when the Lord descended upon Mount Sinai in the fire. The children of Israel did not want to hear God's Voice for themselves—for they could not stand in His manifest presence as Moses had learned to do. This is one of the reasons why Moses became the "mediator" between God and His people under the *first* covenant.

AS IT WAS IN THE BEGINNING, SO IT SHALL BE IN THE END

The front of the Bible reveals to us concerning what will happen at the end of days—perhaps even more than the Book of Daniel, or the Book of Revelation does.

Accordingly, this scene described in Exodus 19:16–20, depicts what will happen on the *great* and very *terrible* "Day of the Lord" in which the prophet Joel asks, *"Who can endure it?"*

We would like to believe we are ready for the Lord's return. However, as detailed in Exodus 20:18–21, the people of God were *terribly* afraid of God's presence as they witnessed the thunder, the lightning, the mountain smoking, as they heard the very loud sound of the trumpet blasts when God came down upon Mount Sinai.

As such, the children of Israel trembled and were afraid. We are explicitly told in Exodus 20:21, the people stood afar off, while *only* Moses drew near the thick darkness where God was, because Moses had learned to stand in God's manifest presence, and thus, he was not afraid. Moses knew His God for he had already begun his relationship with the revelation of God's fiery presence in the burning bush. In addition, Moses had seen His God swallow the "gods" of Egypt, where the people only heard the stories. Now, as they beheld God in all His awesome power and majesty, they drew back in terror, leaving Moses to act as a go-between as he had already been doing with Pharaoh. They didn't realize they too could approach this God, and today we must come to the same realization, we do not need a "go-between" to distance ourselves from our heavenly Father.

When we set up certain individuals as being "holier" than we are, we inadvertently begin setting up layers of separation between our heavenly Father and us. Jesus tore the veil that separated God's people from the Holy of Holies, and He is the *only* way we may approach our heavenly Father without condemnation. Therefore, we have nothing to fear.

Rather than choosing to hide when we sin, or we *realize* our inadequacies as Adam and Eve did, we can choose to come boldly before Him, because of Jesus' boundless sufficiency, more than makes up for our deep inadequacies. We can position ourselves in a place of knowing our heavenly Father and being known by Him.

Again, this awesome scene, which is depicted in Exodus 19:16–20, is a prophetic shadow picture of what Jesus Christ will do later when He returns the *second* time on the "Day of the Lord" when we meet Him in the clouds.

The "Day of the Lord" is when Jesus Christ who is the "ark" of the

New Covenant will once again "confirm" all of God's *everlasting* covenants (plural). This will occur when the "temple of God" will be opened in heaven, and the "ark" of His covenant will be seen in His temple, and there will be lightning, noises, thunderings, an earthquake, and great hail based on Revelation 11:19.

This will be the total fulfillment of Daniel 9:27 below:

> *"Then He* [the Messiah Jesus Christ] *shall **CONFIRM*** [1] [H1396: *gâbar*: to be strong; by implication to prevail, confirm, strengthen] *a **COVENANT*** [2] [H1285: *b'rîyth*: (in the sense of *cutting* (like H1254); a *compact* (made by passing between *pieces* of flesh)] *with many for ONE WEEK; But in the MIDDLE OF THE WEEK He* [the Messiah died in the middle of the week on Wednesday, not on Friday; and this is talking about the first coming of Jesus Christ based on the seventy weeks of Daniel] *shall bring an END to SACRIFICE and OFFERING..."* (Dan. 9:27, NKJV) (emphasis added).

When Daniel 9:27, states, *"But in the middle of the week..."* concerning when our Messiah brought an end to sacrifice and offering—Daniel states this because Jesus Christ was "the" final sacrifice for all time forevermore for the forgiveness of our sins. Thus, the phrase "the middle of the week" has a dual meaning which is as follows:

First, our Messiah did not die on a Friday, especially on Good Friday. Rather, He died on a Wednesday, in the middle of the week, on that particular Passover over two thousand years ago. I will substantiate this fact in-depth in Book 3.

Second, what was spoken by the prophet Daniel in Daniel 9:27, like so many of the prophecies spoken by the mouth of the "Prophets of Old" throughout the *synergy of the ages,* this particular prophecy is a dual fulfillment prophecy. What this means is that it will have a total fulfillment in the future, even though part of the prophecy was fulfilled in the past.

As such, this prophecy will have a total fulfillment at the end of the *synergy of the ages,* and it reveals the "time frame" of when Jesus Christ our Messiah came to the earth the first time. This same prophecy reveals when Jesus will return the second time as well. I will cover this indisputable truth in-depth in Chapter 18 of this book.

In addition, when the prophet Daniel says in Daniel 9:27, that He shall "confirm" (strengthen) a "covenant," this means a covenant already exists. And indeed, it does! Because *this* covenant Jesus Christ will "confirm" once again at the end of the *synergy of the ages,* is referring to the *everlasting* covenant God established with Abraham and his descendants.

Jesus will "confirm" this *everlasting* covenant with many, when He descends from heaven in a cloud, at the sound of the last trumpet. His appearing will be evident to all who dwell on the earth. There will be lightning, fire, and a *great* earthquake, of such a magnitude and intensity, which has not occurred since men were on the earth. This is based on Revelation 16:18.

It will be at this time, His "faithful" remnant—those few men (or women) who are still alive and remain (survive) on planet earth, after the tribulation of those days, will then be "caught up" to meet Him in the air. The "catching away" (rapture) will occur *only* after the dead in Christ are raised in the *first* resurrection.

Unfortunately, the body of Christ has been led astray to believe the "He" in Daniel 9:27, is the Antichrist. I will cover this truth and so much more in Chapter 67 of Book 3.

Now let's refocus our attention on this "Covenant of Marriage" God established through His servant Moses with all the children of Israel.

WITH "ONE" VOICE, THE CHILDREN OF ISRAEL UNANIMOUSLY "CONSENTED" TO AND "AFFIRMED" THE "COVENANT OF MARRIAGE" BETWEEN *YEHOVAH* AND ALL HIS PEOPLE FOREVERMORE

Long ago the children of Israel, from all twelve tribes of Israel, received our heavenly Father's instructions as detailed in the Torah. His instructions are the terms and conditions of "walking" in a "Marriage Covenant" with our heavenly Father, *Yehovah*, who is the God of Abraham, Isaac, and Jacob (Israel), and is the Holy One of Israel.

This *first* covenant was *initially* "confirmed" with the blood of animals, and would later be "confirmed" (ratified) with Jesus' blood.

In addition, this *first* covenant was "consented" to and "affirmed" by all the children of Israel, and "mediated" by God's servant Moses, the "mediator" between God and His people under the *first* covenant, as established in the Old Testament.

However, this *first* covenant God established with the children of Israel was the result of the *everlasting* covenant God established with Abraham and his descendants.

Again, this *first* covenant was "consented" to and "affirmed" by all the children of Israel according to Exodus 24:1–3.

In fact, we are told in Exodus 24:3, when Moses came and told the people all the "words of the Lord," and all the "judgments," all the people answered with "one" voice and said: "All the words which the Lord has said we will do." This is what we proclaim when we take our marriage vows, and we say, "I do."

So, if you want to know what all the "words of the Lord" were, including all His "judgments" the children of Israel agreed to with "one" voice. Then read the Book of Exodus beginning in Chapter 20:1–17, which begins with the Ten Commandments and goes all the way through Exodus 23:1–33. This details *some* of the terms and conditions of this *first* covenant God established with all the children of Israel which are still valid to *this* very day.

Also, all twelve tribes of the children of Israel, not just the Jews from the tribe of Judah, were standing at the base of Mount Sinai on that particular day long ago. And, with "one" voice, they unanimously "consented" to and "affirmed" this "Covenant of Marriage" between our heavenly Father, and all His people forevermore.

Furthermore, this *first* covenant is also for those who were not *physically* there on *that* particular day as well, which I will cover in Chapter 16 of this book, and in Chapter 52 of Book 3.

What this means is this: The *first* covenant which *Yehôvah* established with all the children of Israel long ago is still in effect for New Covenant believers.

Again, God established a New Covenant with the Jews from the House of Judah, and those of us who were formerly Gentiles from the House of Israel (Jacob/Joseph/Ephraim).

Those of us from the House of Israel have now been grafted into the commonwealth of Israel by our faith in Jesus Christ, who is the Holy One of Israel.

This truth leads me to the next point concerning "which" God we are truly worshiping based on this fact: God only has one "law" and one "custom" for all His people. God does not have one set of instructions for the Jews from the House of Judah and another set of instructions for those of us who are from the House of Israel.

WHICH GOD ARE WE ACTUALLY WORSHIPING?

Unfortunately, because of our lack of knowledge of who we truly are in Christ, and our lack of knowledge concerning all of God's *everlasting* covenants we do not understand our "Hebraic" roots in

Christianity. As such, many of God's people who are from the House of Israel are doing the very same thing the children of Israel did so long ago when they decided to worship the "golden calf," instead of the one and only true God, who is the Holy One of Israel. This story is detailed in the Book of Exodus beginning in Chapter 32.

When the people saw that Moses was delayed in coming back down from the mountain after he met with God, these very same people who had just made a vow to be faithful to *Yehôvâh*—by "obeying" His Voice, and "keeping" His covenant—turned back to "worshiping" their false gods. These false gods are the ones they had learned about while they were in Egypt (the world). Thus, the children of Israel went right back to practicing the pagan rituals thereof.

Therefore, the children of Israel began to worship the "golden calf" despite their miraculous encounter with *Yehôvâh*, their God, and Creator, who had just delivered them from Egypt and their bondage by His "mercy" and His "grace." They still yearned for the things they had while in Egypt, and wanted to practice the pagan "customs," "traditions," and "rituals" they had spent most their life embracing.

In other words, God had taken His people out of the world they had known so they would no longer "practice" or "walk" according to the pagan, heathen "customs," "traditions," and "rituals" thereof!

Egypt, which represents the things and practices of the world system, still had a "stronghold" in their mind, and in their hearts.

362

Yehôvah delivered them from their bondage and slavery by extending to them His "grace" and "mercy," yet they held onto these pagan, heathen "customs," "traditions," and "rituals" which was and still is an abomination to the Lord.

As such, I will cover in-depth in Book 3, some of these pagan, heathen "customs," "traditions," and "rituals" we have inherited from our early church fathers, which are based on the "traditions," "customs," and "doctrines" of men. In other words, God did not establish them, nor did He tell us to "observe" or "commemorate" them. To the contrary!

In fact, God has told us according to His eternal Word, which does not change, based on Leviticus 18:30, that His people are to keep *only* His ordinances. Some of these ordinances are His appointed "customs" which are His seven holy convocations He commands us to keep in Leviticus 23. He commands us to not practice any of these abominable "customs" for this reason: So we do not defile ourselves by them because He is the Lord our God.

God has explicitly told us according to His eternal Word; we are not to celebrate these "customs" and "traditions" of men, many of which are rooted in the occult. Yet as our ancestors did long ago when they worshiped the "golden calf" instead of *Yehôvah,* the one and *only* true God, many believers in the body of Christ are still embracing these abominable "customs" we learned about from the world, and we have been deceived into bringing them in the Church.

Now let's discover what *Yehôvah's* reaction was concerning the children of Israel "worshiping" the "golden calf" instead of Him, their Savior. Because the children of Israel wanted to "worship" the "golden calf," instead of *Yehôvâh,* the one and, *only* true God, He wanted to wipe them all out, just like He did in the *days of Noah,* and begin a new nation through Moses.

However, Moses interceded on behalf of the people, and he reminded God of the *everlasting* covenant He established with Abraham.

Moses said to *Yehôvâh* in Exodus 32:13, *"REMEMBER Abraham, Isaac, and Israel* [Jacob], *Your servants, to whom YOU SWORE BY YOUR OWN SELF, and said to them, 'I will multiply your descendants as the stars of heaven; and all this land that I have spoken of I give to your descendants, and they shall inherit it forever.'"* (NKJV) (emphasis added).

We are told in Exodus 32:14, because of the intercession of Moses, *Yehôvâh* once again chose "mercy" over judgment. Nevertheless, about three thousand men of the people fell (died) that day.

In addition, God said whoever sinned against Him, He would blot them out of His book (the Lamb's Book of Life), on the day when He visits for punishment (the Day of the Lord). It will be then He will visit and render His "eternal" punishment upon them for their sin against Him.

Yet God was still merciful when He chose to render only "select" judgment that day for this reason: God remembered His *everlasting* covenant with Abraham, Isaac, and Jacob, and the "covenant" promises thereof.

FROM THE VERY BEGINNING, GOD EXTENDED HIS "MERCY" AND "GRACE" TO HIS PEOPLE

For those who believe that because we are under the New Covenant, we are now under the dispensation of His "mercy" and "grace," this doctrine is not consistent with the whole counsel of God's Word.

We are told in Malachi 3:6, which says, *"For I am the Lord, I do not CHANGE..."* (NKJV) (emphasis added). And, Hebrews 13:8 says, *"Jesus Christ is the SAME yesterday, today, and forever."* (NKJV) (emphasis added).

Therefore, from the very beginning, God extended His "mercy" and "grace" to the children of Israel *despite* their "spiritual" harlotry and disobedience! And, He continues to do so to *this* very day, for this reason: He remembers the *everlasting* covenant He established with Abraham, His friend.

Based on Moses interceding on behalf of the children of Israel that day, God spared *some* of them and established the Day of Atonement for the sins of the nation, *after* the death of Aaron's two sons when they offered *profane* fire before the Lord. This is based on Leviticus 16:1–3, which says the following:

> *"Now the Lord spoke to Moses after the DEATH of the TWO SONS of AARON, when THEY OFFERED PROFANE FIRE before the Lord, and DIED; and the Lord said to Moses: 'Tell AARON YOUR BROTHER NOT to COME at just ANY TIME into the HOLY PLACE inside the VEIL, before the MERCY SEAT which is on the ARK, lest he DIE; for I will APPEAR in*

> *the CLOUD above the MERCY SEAT. Thus Aaron shall come into the Holy Place: with the blood of a young bull as a sin offering, and of a ram as a burnt offering.'"* (Lev. 16:1–3, NKJV) (emphasis added).

Furthermore, despite the children of Israel's marriage vow to *Yehôvah* to "obey" His Voice, and "keep" His covenant, they could not. This is based on the written testimony of the Old Testament substantiating time and time again they fell short of the terms and conditions of the "Marriage Covenant" *Yehôvah* established with all the children of Israel at the base of Mount Sinai.

And, it is for this very reason, God sent His only *begotten* Son, Jesus Christ, to die for His beloved bride who continually defiled herself, because of her inability to keep the letter of His law.

THE ONLY WAY GOD COULD "LEGALLY" REMARRY HIS BRIDE AFTER ISSUING HER A CERTIFICATE OF DIVORCE, WAS TO DIE FOR HER

Based on the "spiritual" harlotry from His people from both the House of Judah, and the House of Israel (Jacob/Joseph/Ephraim), the only way God could "legally" remarry His bride after issuing her a *certificate of divorce* due to her "spiritual" adultery (harlotry), which "defiled" her, was to die for her.

This is based on Romans 7:2, which says the following:

"For the WOMAN [who represents the body of Christ who is Israel] *who has a HUSBAND* [God] *is BOUND by the LAW to HER HUSBAND as long as HE LIVES. But if the HUSBAND* [Jesus] *DIES, she is RELEASED from the LAW of her HUSBAND."* (Rom. 7:2, NKJV) (emphasis added).

Therefore, this is one of the reasons why Jesus Christ had to die on the cross at Calvary, so that His wife who had committed "spiritual" adultery against God, who was her husband, could be released from the law of her husband.

Yet Jesus did not "abolish" the law, He established in the first place! As such, one of the reasons why Jesus Christ died was to set us free from being under the *letter of the law,* which said a husband could not remarry His wife who had "defiled" herself, because of committing adultery.

Because God loves His children with an *everlasting* love, He was willing to give up His own life for His bride who had "defiled" herself, because of her "spiritual" harlotry and fornication!

Our heavenly Father, *Yehovah,* sent us His only *begotten* Son, Jesus Christ, who was willing to die for us based on the "bride price" our heavenly Father required of Him, which cost Him His very life.

Hence, our bridegroom, and our "Kinsman Redeemer," purchased us with His precious blood because Jesus was willing to die for us all on the cross at Calvary. *Yehovah* was willing to sacrifice His only *begotten* Son of His love, so we could be saved, healed, and delivered from reaping "spiritual" death, for "the wages of sin is death!" If His great sacrifice does not make you want to cry, and fall to your knees with gratitude and thanksgiving, to our Lord and Savior Jesus Christ, then I do not know what will.

Most of you reading this are parents. Can you imagine the pain and the anguish, our heavenly Father must have felt, as He willingly allowed His precious Son of His love, to bear the incredible agony of the cross, that He was required to suffer for us all? It must have been unbearable for our heavenly Father to hear His beloved Son cry out in desperation, and say, *"Eli, Eli, lama sabachthani?" that is, "My God, My God, why have You FORSAKEN Me?"* (Matthew 27:46, NKJV) (emphasis added).

Yet God did not allow His emotions, and His tremendous suffering, to thwart Him from fulfilling His mission for the following reason: He believed with all His heart, soul, mind, and strength, His sons and daughters, whom He created in His own image, and in His own likeness, before the foundation of the world, was worth dying for so they would not perish for all eternity! As proclaimed in John 15:13, *"Greater love has no one than this, than to lay down one's life for his friends."* (NKJV) (emphasis added).

WITH JESUS' DEATH, HE HAS RELEASED US FROM THE LAW OF OUR HUSBAND

If we were still under the *letter of the law,* rather than the *Spirit of His Grace,* then God could not have "legally" brought us back into a "Marriage Covenant" with Him, because of our "spiritual" harlotry, for Romans 6:23 says, *"For the WAGES of SIN is DEATH, but the gift of God is ETERNAL LIFE in Christ Jesus our Lord."* (NKJV) (emphasis added).

With His death, Jesus Christ has released us from the law of our husband, which would have "legally" prohibited our Lawgiver from taking us back as His wife once we became defiled.

In other words, Jesus Christ did away with "the curse" we would reap by not following the *letter of the law*.

Therefore, our heavenly Father, *Yehovah,* and His only *begotten* Son, Jesus Christ, desires and deserves our total obedience, because He wants us to love Him, and others, as He loves us. As such, God wants our hearts, and not our religion!

All praise and honor must be given to *Yehovah*, our heavenly Father, and our Redeemer, Jesus Christ.

God loves us so much He was willing to die for us, His bride, so we could once again be in a "Covenant of Marriage" with God, our Creator, and inherit the covenant promises thereof.

What an incredible God we serve! The Supreme God of the Universe and everything in it was willing to die for the very people He created in the first place.

More than anything else, God, our Creator, desired a family on the earth and in the heavens who would love Him for who He is because He first loved us, His created, with an *everlasting* love despite our obstinate behavior.

369

JESUS DIED FOR US IN ORDER TO "EXECUTE" THE WILL OF THE "TESTATOR" (*YEHOVAH*, OUR HEAVENLY FATHER), WHICH COULD ONLY BE IN FORCE AFTER THE "TESTATOR" IS DEAD

Another reason why *the Word,* who became the Son of Man in the flesh in the Person of Jesus Christ, *willingly* chose to die for us, and shed His precious blood at Calvary, was to "execute" the will of the "testator" (*Yehovah*, God the Father), which could only be in force *after* the "testator" is dead.

Otherwise, the "Testament" has no POWER at all while the "testator" lives. God's only *begotten* Son, *the Word,* who became the Son of Man in the flesh in the Person of Jesus Christ, had to die so we would receive "power" from the "testator" who is God Almighty Himself!

And, because Jesus Christ, God's only *begotten* Son, died for us, and was resurrected from the grave, God's people are given His "power" and "grace" through the Holy Spirit, which empowers us to "obey" His Voice and "keep" His covenant established in the Torah under *first* covenant in the Old Testament. This *is* the "testament" of God the Father, established through His servant Moses under the *first* covenant. This is substantiated in Hebrews 9:16–22, which says the following:

> *"For where there is a* ***TESTAMENT*** *(3)* [G1242: *diathēkē:* a *disposition,* that is, (specifically) a *contract* (especially a devisory *will*); covenant; (the *first* covenant established in the Old Testament—

which is the testament of God the Father and is His marriage contract with His bride], *there must also of NECESSITY be the DEATH of the TESTATOR* [(4)] [G1303: *diatithemai:* to *put apart,* that is, (figuratively) *dispose* (by assignment, compact or bequest); appoint, make, testator; to dispose of by will, make a testament or to make a covenant, enter into a covenant, with one]. *For a TESTAMENT* [(3)] *is in FORCE* [(5)] [G949: *bebaios:* (through the idea of *basality*); *stable* (literally or figuratively); firm, of force, steadfast, sure] *after MEN are DEAD, since it has NO POWER AT ALL While the TESTATOR* [(4)] *LIVES. Therefore not even the first COVENANT was DEDICATED without BLOOD. For when Moses had SPOKEN every PRECEPT to all the PEOPLE according to the LAW, he took the BLOOD of calves and goats, with water, scarlet wool, and hyssop, and SPRINKLED both the BOOK ITSELF and all the PEOPLE, saying, 'This is the BLOOD of the COVENANT* [(3)] [G1242: *diatheke:* a disposition or contract (especially a *devisory* will or testament)] *which God has COMMANDED you.' Then likewise he SPRINKLED with BLOOD both the TABERNACLE and all the VESSELS of the MINISTRY. And ACCORDING to the LAW almost all THINGS are PURIFIED with BLOOD, and WITHOUT SHEDDING of BLOOD there is NO REMISSION."* (Heb. 9:16–22, NKJV) (emphasis added).

Who is Israel? Discovering our True Identity in Jesus Christ and Why it Matters! The Foundation

The apostle Paul continues to talk about the greatness of Christ's sacrifice for all the children of Israel in Hebrews 9:23–28, which says the following:

> "Therefore it was necessary that the COPIES of the THINGS in the HEAVENS should be PURIFIED with these, but the HEAVENLY THINGS THEMSELVES with BETTER SACRIFICES than these. For Christ has not ENTERED the HOLY PLACES made with hands, which are copies of the true, but into HEAVEN itself, NOW to APPEAR in the PRESENCE of GOD for us; not that He should offer Himself often, as the high priest enters the Most Holy Place every year with blood of another—He then would have had to suffer often since the foundation of the world; but NOW, ONCE at the END of the AGES, He has APPEARED to PUT AWAY SIN by the SACRIFICE of HIMSELF. And as it is APPOINTED for MEN to DIE ONCE, but after this THE JUDGMENT, so CHRIST was OFFERED once to BEAR the SINS of MANY. **To those who eagerly wait for Him** He will APPEAR a SECOND TIME, APART from SIN, for SALVATION."
> (Heb. 9:23–28, NKJV) (emphasis added).

Based on Hebrews 9:23–28, do not dismiss this fact: Jesus Christ died at the "end of the age" over two thousand years ago *when* He appeared the first time to "put away" sin by sacrificing Himself on the cross at Calvary.

Therefore, the first time Jesus appeared was to bear the sins of

372

many, which is "the" "good news" we are to share with the lost!

Yet the "good news" gets better because we are specifically told Jesus Christ will "appear" a second time for the *eternal* salvation for those who have been crucified with Christ. He will come for His bride— His "faithful" remnant—those who have "put away" their sins as they pick up their cross daily, and follow in the footsteps of their Master. He has given them His power and His grace to "obey" His Voice and "keep" His covenant. Hallelujah, and thank you, Jesus!

In summary, one of the main reasons why our heavenly Father chose to send His only *begotten* Son, Jesus Christ, to the earth the first time was for this *righteous* cause: Jesus had to die for His wife whom *Yehôváh* had issued a *certificate of divorce*, because of her spiritual harlotry, and her unfaithfulness to "obey" His Voice and "keep" His covenant.

As such, the Word who became the Son of Man in the flesh in the Person of Jesus Christ was sent to the earth to become "the" mediator of the New Covenant. He shed His precious blood to "confirm" [H1396: gabar: to be strong; by implication to prevail, confirm, strengthen] the *first* covenant our heavenly Father, *Yehôváh*, made with all twelve tribes of the children of Israel at the base of Mount Sinai. Again, this *first* covenant was a result of the *everlasting* covenant God established with Abraham and his descendants.

Hence, this *first* covenant is a "Marriage Covenant" with His bride— His Ekklēsia (the Church)—which includes both the Jews from the House of Judah and those of us who were formerly Gentiles from the House of Israel (Jacob/Joseph/Ephraim). Again, those of us who are from the House of Israel have now been grafted into the commonwealth of Israel by our faith in our Jewish Messiah.

God loves us so much, the *Creator of the Universe* and everything in it, was willing to die for His wife who broke her marriage vows (covenant) with her husband whom she had vowed to love with all her mind, heart, soul, and strength.

Therefore, if God's people, once they have come to the saving knowledge of the truth, *intentionally* sin, and do not "obey" God's Voice, and "keep" His covenant, there is **no** sacrifice for sins left. This is based on Hebrews 6:4–6; 10:26–27; and 10:28–29; which I will cover in-depth in Chapter 42 of Book 3.

Again, Jesus Christ came the first time to "put away" sin by the sacrifice of Himself on the cross at Calvary. As such, God did not give us His "grace" and "mercy" as a license to sin which is evidenced by so many people in the body of Christ living just like the world does, because many have lost the *reverential* fear of God Almighty!

Unfortunately, many believers in the body of Christ do not believe we must *work out* our *own* salvation with fear and trembling, and finish the race which is set before us because we are no longer driven by eternity.

Furthermore, contrary to what most teach and believe, Jesus Christ will only "appear" a second time to bring salvation to those who have died to their sins. Those who will "obey" His Voice and "keep" His *everlasting* covenants (plural), which God has established with mankind throughout the *synergy of the ages*, which were all "ratified" (confirmed) by the precious blood of Jesus Christ.

In the next chapter, I will convey "how" what was spoken by the Lord through the prophet Hosea came to fruition. This is based on Hosea 11:1, which says, *"When ISRAEL was a CHILD, I LOVED HIM, And OUT of EGYPT I called My SON."* (NKJV) (emphasis added).

Who is Israel? Discovering our True Identity in Jesus Christ and Why it Matters! The Foundation

CHAPTER 13

HOW AND WHEN DID *YEHOVAH* CALL ISRAEL (JESUS) OUT OF EGYPT WHEN HE WAS A CHILD?

ccording to Matthew 2:2, over two thousand years ago, *after* Jesus was born in Bethlehem, in the land of Judah, in the days of Herod, the king, wise men came from the East to Jerusalem saying, *"Where is He who has been born King of the Jews? For we have seen His star in the East and have come to worship Him."* (NKJV)

When King Herod heard this, he was troubled, and all of Jerusalem with him. Therefore, King Herod gathered all the chief priests, and scribes of the people together, and inquired of them, where the Christ was to be born.

So, they said to him in Matthew 2:5–6, *"...In Bethlehem of Judea, for thus it is written by the prophet: 'But you, Bethlehem, in the land of Judah, Are not the least among the rulers of Judah; For out of you shall come a RULER Who will SHEPHERD My people ISRAEL.'"* (NKJV) (emphasis added).

This Scripture in Matthew 2:5–6, has a dual fulfillment, or meaning. Before Jesus was born in Bethlehem, King David was God's anointed and appointed king, who did indeed shepherd God's people in Israel, even though initially, David was king over the *tribe of Judah,* and he ruled from Hebron. However, after seven years, the other Israelite tribes chose him to be their king as well.

Jesus would later be born in Judea, from the *tribe of Judah,* and be referred to as the "Son of David." He would become the One who would fulfill the *everlasting* covenant God established with King David, called the *Davidic* Covenant.

Because of this *everlasting* covenant, God promised King David in Second Samuel 7:12–16, the following:

1.   When his days are fulfilled, and he has died, God would set up his "seed" after him, who would come from his body, and establish his kingdom.

2.   This was fulfilled by David's son, Solomon, who would build a house for the Lord (Solomon's Temple). The Lord would establish the throne of his kingdom forever, even though Solomon committed "iniquity" against the Lord. Solomon became "unfaithful" to the Lord, because he followed the pagan customs of foreign nations, and worshiped their false gods due to the influence of his many wives who led him astray. God gave Solomon mercy because of His promise to his father, King David.

This is based on Second Samuel 7:14–15, which says, *"I will be his Father, and he shall be My son. If he commits iniquity, I will chasten him with the rod of men and with the blows of the sons of men. But My MERCY shall not DEPART from him, as I took it from Saul, whom I removed from before you."* (NKJV) (emphasis added).

3.   God told King David his house, his kingdom, and his throne would be established *forever* as long as the sun, the moon, and the stars give their light.

As such, it would come to pass this would be the total fulfillment of Joseph's dream based on Genesis 37:9. Again, Joseph is a prophetic shadow picture of Jesus Christ. Therefore, when the sun, the moon, and the stars no longer give their light, every knee shall bow, and every tongue shall confess to the *King of kings and the Lord of lords* when Jesus Christ returns.

Listen to what God says to us in Psalm 89:35–37 below. *Yehôvah* is saying He has sworn by His *holiness* and will not lie to David for this reason: David's "seed" shall endure forever, and his throne before *Yehôvah* shall be established *forever,* as the sun and like the moon, His faithful witnesses in the sky. This is based on the *everlasting* covenant He established with King David.

> *"Once I have sworn by My HOLINESS; I will not lie to David: His SEED shall ENDURE forever, And his THRONE as the SUN before Me; It shall be ESTABLISHED forever like the MOON, Even like the faithful WITNESS in the SKY."* (Psalm 89:35–37, NKJV) (emphasis added).

This promise was *partially* fulfilled by Jesus Christ when He came to the earth the first time based on Isaiah 9:6–7 and Jeremiah 23:5–6, which says the following:

> *"For unto us a Child is born, Unto us a Son is given; And the GOVERNMENT will be upon His*

SHOULDER. And His name will be called Wonderful, Counselor, Mighty God, Everlasting Father, Prince of Peace. Of the increase of His GOVERNMENT and PEACE There will be NO END, Upon the THRONE of DAVID and over His KINGDOM, To ORDER IT and ESTABLISH IT with JUDGMENT and JUSTICE From THAT TIME FORWARD, even FOREVER. The ZEAL of the LORD of HOSTS will PERFORM THIS." (Isa. 9:6–7, NKJV) (emphasis added).

"'Behold, the days are coming,' says the LORD, 'That I WILL RAISE to David a BRANCH of RIGHTEOUSNESS; a KING shall REIGN and PROSPER, And execute JUDGMENT and RIGHTEOUSNESS in the EARTH. In His days Judah will be SAVED, And Israel will DWELL SAFELY; Now this is His name by which He will be called: THE LORD OUR RIGHTEOUSNESS.'" (Jer. 23:5–6, NKJV) (emphasis added).

God promised King David the following: If the "ordinances" of heaven remained—the sun to govern the day, and the moon and the stars to rule the night, then King David would have a "seed" upon his throne. This is based on Jeremiah 33:19–26, which details God's covenant He established with nature for both "the day" and "the night." Jeremiah 33:19–26, says the following:

"And the word of the LORD came to Jeremiah, saying, 'Thus says the LORD: 'If you can break My COVENANT with the DAY and My COVENANT with

380

the NIGHT, so that there will *NOT* be *DAY* and
NIGHT in *THEIR SEASON, THEN* My *COVENANT*
may also be BROKEN with David My servant, so that
he shall *NOT* have a *SON* to *REIGN* on *HIS*
THRONE, and with the *LEVITES*, the *PRIESTS*, My
MINISTERS. As the host of heaven cannot be
numbered, *nor* the sand of the sea measured, so will I
MULTIPLY the *DESCENDANTS* of *DAVID* My
servant and the *LEVITES* who *MINISTER* to Me.'"
(Jer. 33.19–22, NKJV) (emphasis added).

"Moreover the word of the LORD came to Jeremiah,
saying, 'Have you not considered what these people
have spoken, saying, 'The *two* **FAMILIES** [1] [H4940:
mishpâchâh: a *family*, that is, circle of relatives; by
extension a *tribe* or *people;* the two houses (the Jews
from the House of Judah and those of us who were
formerly Gentiles from the House of Israel
(Jacob/Joseph/Ephraim) who were grafted into the
commonwealth of Israel] which the LORD has
CHOSEN, He has also CAST THEM OFF'? Thus they
have DESPISED My PEOPLE, as if they should *NO*
MORE be a **NATION** [2] [H1471: *gôy*: a foreign
nation; hence a Gentile, heathen, nation, people]
before *THEM*.'" (Jer. 33:23–24 NKJV) (emphasis
added).

"Thus says the LORD: 'If My COVENANT is *NOT* with
DAY and *NIGHT*, and if I have *NOT APPOINTED*
the **ORDINANCES** [3] [H2708: *chûqqâh*: appointed,

custom, manner or statute] *of HEAVEN and EARTH, then I will CAST AWAY the DESCENDANTS of JACOB and DAVID My SERVANT, so that I will not TAKE any of his DESCENDANTS to be RULERS OVER the DESCENDANTS of ABRAHAM, ISAAC, and JACOB. For I will cause their CAPTIVES to RETURN, and will have MERCY on THEM.'"* (Jer. 33:25–26, NKJV) (emphasis added).

Therefore, the *everlasting* covenant *Yehôvâh* established with King David is still in effect for this reason: *Yehôvâh* has given His only *begotten* Son, Jesus Christ, the throne of His father, David. He will "rule" and "reign" over the House of Jacob forevermore, and of His kingdom, there will be no end. This is based on Luke 1:32–33 below:

> *"He will be great, and will be called the SON of the HIGHEST; and the Lord God will give Him the THRONE of His FATHER DAVID. And He will REIGN OVER the HOUSE of JACOB forever, and of His KINGDOM there will be NO END."* (Luke 1:32–33, NKJV) (emphasis added).

In addition, just before Jesus Christ returns, many end-time Scriptures proclaim the following: The sun, the moon, and the stars will no longer give their light because the fulfillment of all things will come to pass at the second coming of Jesus Christ.

This is substantiated in Jeremiah 31:35–36, which says the following:

*"Thus says the LORD, Who gives the SUN for a light by day, The **ORDINANCES** (3) [H2708: chûqqâh: appointed, custom, manner or statute] of the MOON and the STARS for a light by night, Who disturbs the sea, And its waves roar (The LORD of hosts is His name): 'If those **ORDINANCES** (3) DEPART From before Me, says the LORD, THEN the SEED of ISRAEL shall also CEASE from being a **NATION** (2) [H1471: gôy: a foreign nation; hence a Gentile, heathen, nation, people] before Me FOREVER.'"* (Jer. 31:35–36, NKJV) (emphasis added).

Therefore, my dear sisters and brothers in Christ, "Who is the "seed" of Israel?" The "seed" of Israel are all disciples of Jesus Christ since Jesus Christ is Israel. He is the "root" (vine) of Israel—the "tree of life" and we are the branches.

Moreover, another prophecy, which was foretold by the prophet Micah, did indeed come to pass concerning the coming of Jesus Christ, our Jewish Messiah. This is based on Micah 5:2, which says the following:

*"But you, **BETHLEHEM** (4) [H1035: bêyth lechem: house of bread; a place in Palestine] **EPHRATHAH** (5) [H672: 'ephrâth: fruitfulness; Ephrath, another name for Bethlehem; once used in Psalm 132:6 perhaps for Ephraim], Though you are little among the THOUSANDS of JUDAH, Yet OUT of you shall COME FORTH to Me The One to be RULER in ISRAEL, Whose GOINGS FORTH are FROM of OLD,*

From EVERLASTING." (Micah 5:2, NKJV) (emphasis added).

This would indeed fulfill that which was spoken of by the prophet Hosea based on Hosea 11:1 below:

> *"When* **ISRAEL** [6] [**H3478:** *Yisrá'él:* he will rule as God; a symbolical name of Jacob; also (typically) of his posterity; God prevails] *was a CHILD, I loved him, And out of Egypt I called My* **SON** [7] [**H1121:** *bén:* a son (as a *builder* of the family name); including grandson, subject, nation, quality or condition, etc.; anointed one, appointed to, branch, *firstborn*, mighty; whelp, worthy]. *"* (Hos. 11:1, NKJV) (emphasis added).

Again, Jesus is God's only *begotten* Son, whom He called out of Egypt when he was a small Child, who is also the anointed One, the *firstborn* over all creation, and He is worthy.

Long before *Yehovâh* gave the children of Israel the terms and conditions of keeping His covenant, and He chose Moses to be the "mediator" of that covenant, He brought the children of Israel out of Egypt based on the *everlasting* covenant He established with Abraham and his descendants.

Based on Haggai 2:4–5, when *Yehovâh* brought the children of Israel out of Egypt, He did so because of His promise to Abraham. This was long before *Yehovâh* would send His only *begotten* Son, Jesus Christ for this purpose: To fulfill (consummate, execute, and ratify [confirm]) the *first* covenant with the children of Israel—all twelve tribes of Israel, at the base of Mount Sinai *after* they came out of Egypt. Also, notice *Yehôvâh* is telling Zerubbabel, and Joshua, that His Spirit remains among them. This is substantiated in Haggai 2:4–5 below:

> *"'Yet now be strong, Zerubbabel,' says the* LORD; *'and be strong, Joshua, son of Jehozadak, the high priest; and be strong, all you people of the land,' says the* LORD, *'and work; for I am with you,' says the* LORD *of hosts. 'According to the* **WORD** (8) [H1697: *dâbâr*: a word; by implication, a matter (as spoken of) or thing; the oracle of God] *that I* **COVENANTED** (9) [H3772: *kârath*: specifically to *covenant* (that is, make an alliance or bargain, originally by cutting flesh and passing between the pieces): confederate, covenant, make a league (covenant)] *with you WHEN you came OUT of EGYPT, so My* **SPIRIT** (10) [H7307: *rûach*: *wind*; by resemblance *breath*, that is, a sensible (or even violent) exhalation] *REMAINS AMONG YOU; do not fear!"* (Hag. 2:4–5, NKJV) (emphasis added).

So, whose Spirit is *Yehôvâh* referring to other than the Holy Spirit? He is referring to *the Word* before He was manifested as the Son of Man in a body of flesh and blood in the Person of Jesus Christ. It was *Yehôvâh,* who led the children of Israel by a *cloud* during the day, and a *pillar of fire* at night. This is based on Exodus 13:21, which says the following:

> *"And the* **LORD** (11) [H3068: *Yehôvâh*: *self-Existent,* or eternal; *Jehovah*] *went before THEM* [the children of

Israel] *by DAY in a PILLAR of CLOUD to LEAD THE WAY, and by NIGHT in a PILLAR of FIRE to give them* **LIGHT** [(12)] [(13)] **[H215 & H216: *'ôr: illumination, or to be* (causatively *make*) *luminous; lightning, set on fire*, shine, or be *glorious*]**, *so as to go by day and night."* (Exod. 13:21, NKJV) (emphasis added).

Therefore, as I have stated before, but it bears repeating, everything *Yehôvah* accomplishes for His will to prevail on the earth as it is in heaven, He does first in the *spiritual* realm. As such, *spiritually* speaking, *the Word* who is the "invisible" image of God, is the One who led the children of Israel out of Egypt into the wilderness while they were still in their infancy as a nation.

After *the Word* was *literally* manifested in a body of flesh and blood on the earth as the Son of Man in the Person of Jesus Christ, *Yehôvah* would call His Son, Jesus (Israel), out of Egypt once again as a small Child when the danger from King Herod had passed. This is based on Matthew 2:19–20 below:

> *"Now when HEROD was DEAD, behold, an ANGEL of the LORD appeared in a DREAM to Joseph in Egypt, saying, 'Arise, take the young Child and His mother, and GO to the LAND of ISRAEL, for those who SOUGHT the young Child's LIFE are DEAD.'"* (Matt. 2:19–20, NKJV) (emphasis added).

Indeed, this would fulfill the word spoken by the Lord through the prophet Hosea. This is based on Hosea 11:1, which states, *"When* **ISRAEL** [(6)] **[H3478: *Yisrä'él*]** *was a CHILD, I loved him, And OUT* *of EGYPT I called My **SON*** [7] [H1121: *bén*].*" (NKJV) (emphasis added).

Therefore, like Abraham, Isaac, and Joseph who is Jacob's son, Jesus also went to the *literal* nation of Egypt as a young Child. This occurred when his earthly father Joseph had a dream. In this dream, the Angel of the Lord appeared, telling him to take Jesus and Mary to Egypt to escape King Herod, who was killing all the young children in his quest to destroy Jesus when He was a young Child. Therefore, at the beginning of time, the nation of Egypt was a *place of refuge* for God's people to flee to in order to escape harm or to seek refuge during times of famine.

This escape to Egypt by Joseph, Mary, and Jesus when He was a young Child, happened immediately after the wise men had come to Joseph and Mary's "house" to worship Jesus as a young Child (he was not a baby in a manger). This is based on Matthew 2:9–11, which says the following:

> *"When they heard the king* [Herod], *they departed; and behold, the STAR which they had seen in the East went before them, till it came and STOOD over WHERE the YOUNG CHILD was. When they saw the STAR, they rejoiced with exceedingly great joy. And when they had come into the HOUSE, they saw the YOUNG CHILD with Mary His mother, and fell down and WORSHIPED Him. And when they had OPENED their TREASURES, they presented GIFTS to Him: gold, frankincense, and myrrh."* (Matt. 2:9–11, NKJV) (emphasis added).

Therefore, as you can clearly see, based on Matthew 2:9–11, the manger story where three wise men came to visit Jesus as a babe laying in a manger is not true at all, or biblical. This is one of many examples of how we have compromised the Word of God to perpetuate our "traditions" based on the doctrines of men.

Now let's refocus our attention on the significance of the gifts the wise men had given to Jesus as a young Child. For the wise men gave Joseph and Mary enough gold and valuable commodities in their day, to not only travel to Egypt but also remain there until the danger to Jesus as a young Child had passed with the death of King Herod.

Their departure to Egypt is substantiated in Matthew 2:13, which says, *"Now WHEN they had DEPARTED, behold, an angel of the Lord APPEARED to Joseph in a DREAM, saying, 'Arise, take the YOUNG CHILD and HIS MOTHER, FLEE to EGYPT, and STAY THERE until I bring you WORD; for Herod will seek the YOUNG CHILD to DESTROY Him.'"* (NKJV) (emphasis added).

Then in Matthew 2:14–15, we are told the following: Joseph, Jesus' earthly father who was married to Mary, was obedient to do what the Angel of the Lord told him to do so Jesus would be safe. Also, that which was spoken of by the Lord through the prophet Hosea would be fulfilled as well. Matthew 2:14–15, says the following:

> *"When he [Joseph] arose, he took the YOUNG CHILD [Jesus] and HIS MOTHER [Mary] by NIGHT and DEPARTED for EGYPT, and was there until the DEATH of HEROD, that it might be FULFILLED*

which was SPOKEN by the LORD through the PROPHET, saying, 'OUT of EGYPT I called My SON.'" (Mat. 2:14–15, NKJV) (emphasis added).

This act of obedience by Joseph would indeed fulfill that which was spoken by the prophet Hosea. This is based on Hosea 11:1, which states, *"When **ISRAEL** [6] [H3478: Yisra'el] was a CHILD, I loved him, And OUT of EGYPT I called My **SON** [7] [H1121: bên]."* (NKJV) (emphasis added).

Therefore, when Jesus was taken as a young Child into Egypt by his earthly father Joseph, and His mother Mary, He was no older than two years old.

We know this because shortly after His escape to Egypt, King Herod ordered all male children who were in Bethlehem, and in all its districts, two years old and younger, were to be put to death. This is based on Matthew 2:16–18, says the following:

"Then Herod, when he saw that he was DECEIVED by the WISE MEN, was exceedingly ANGRY; and he sent forth and put to DEATH all the MALE CHILDREN who were in Bethlehem and in all its districts, from TWO YEARS OLD and UNDER, according to the TIME which he had DETERMINED from the WISE MEN. Then was FULFILLED what was SPOKEN by JEREMIAH the PROPHET, saying: 'A voice was heard in Ramah, Lamentation, weeping, and great mourning, Rachel weeping for her children, Refusing to be comforted, Because they are no more.'" (Matt. 2:16–18, NKJV) (emphasis added).

389

Also, notice, based on Matthew 2:16–18, this horrific act ordered by King Herod of putting to death all the male children in Bethlehem, and all its districts who were two years old and under, also fulfilled that which was spoken by the prophet Jeremiah in Jeremiah 31:15.

This substantiates this truth: God will allow and use what the enemy does for evil, even incomprehensible atrocities like this, to fulfill His *eternal* purposes, so Scripture will be fulfilled based on what He reveals in advance to His servants, the prophets. Moreover, everything the *true* prophets of God prophesy about in advance shall come to pass because God will "do" or "allow" what they "say" to "confirm" and "fulfill" His Word for His *eternal* purposes and glory to prevail.

In conclusion, God did indeed call His only *begotten* Son—Israel— who is Jesus, out of Egypt when He was a small Child. This is substantiated in Hosea 11:1 which states, *"When ISRAEL* [6] *[H3478: Yisrāʾēl] was a CHILD, I loved him, And OUT of EGYPT I called My SON* [7] *[H1121: bēn]."* (NKJV) (emphasis added).

Therefore, Jesus Christ is Israel, and so are we, His disciples. Israel, *spiritually* speaking, includes both the Jews from the House of Judah and those of us who were *formerly* Gentiles from the House of Israel (Jacob/Joseph/Ephraim). Again, those of us from the House of Israel have now been grafted into the commonwealth of Israel by our faith in our Jewish Messiah, Jesus Christ, who is the Holy One of Israel.

In addition, our heavenly Father, *Yehôvah,* is the God of Abraham, Isaac, and Jacob (Israel). As such, "Israel" is also a symbolic name of the patriarch Jacob and of his posterity—all twelve tribes of Israel who are the children of Israel.

As such, long before *the Word,* who became Jesus Christ in the flesh, was manifested on the earth in a body of flesh and blood, and born to a virgin girl named Mary, God also called the children of Israel out of Egypt. This is because of one of the promises He made to Abraham, which was based on the *everlasting* covenant God established with Abraham and his descendants, Christendom refers to as the *Abrahamic* Covenant.

In the next chapter, I will convey the truth, according to God's Word, God's throne became the "pledge" or "security" deposit for the promises He gave to Abraham when He established the *everlasting* covenant with Abraham—the "Father of Many Nations."

Who is Israel? Discovering our True Identity in Jesus Christ and Why it Matters! The Foundation

CHAPTER 14

GOD'S THRONE IS THE "PLEDGE" OR "SECURITY" DEPOSIT FOR THE "COVENANT" PROMISES HE GAVE TO ABRAHAM

A braham "believed" and "obeyed" God, and thus, God established an *everlasting* covenant with Abraham, *Yehôvâh* swore by Himself, because He could swear no higher than Himself, to protect, defend, and uphold forever!

Before we continue, I will briefly describe what a "covenant" is. The word "covenant" is referenced 315 times in the Bible. It is a written contract (compact), that is sealed (ratified) in blood, and the agreement is all-inclusive—meaning everything that belongs to one party belongs to the other party as well. Therefore, all covenants are an "agreement," "oath," "pledge," or "promise" that is "legally" binding between two or more parties.

According to *Strong's Hebrew Lexicon* #H1285, the word for "covenant" is the Hebrew word "bĕriyth" (pronounced "ber-eeth'"). It is from *Strong's Hebrew Lexicon* #H1262, which means: In the sense of cutting a compact (which is made by passing between pieces of flesh); confederacy, confederate, covenant, or league.

In the New Testament, the King James Version does not use the word "covenant" with respect to the New Covenant. Instead, the KJV uses the word "testament." According to *Strong's Greek Lexicon* #G1242, the word "testament" is the Greek word "diathēkē" (pronounced "dee-ath-ay'-kay,"), which means: A disposition,

393

(specifically) a contract (especially) a devisory will, covenant or testament.

Therefore, the definition of a covenant God establishes with His people is a solemn, binding, "legal" agreement, or promise, sealed with blood between two or more parties. Moreover, God's covenants (plural) have either "blessings" associated with keeping His covenant, or "curses" associated with breaking it. God is faithful, and He always honors keeping His end of His covenants, even though His people do not.

As I will convey later in this chapter, *Yehôvah* pledged His throne as the security deposit for keeping His end of this *everlasting* covenant He established with Abraham and his descendants.

Thus, the only stipulation of this *everlasting* covenant God required of Abraham is this: Abraham had to believe in God by placing his faith and trust in Him, which was evidenced by his total obedience to His Voice.

In addition, this *everlasting* covenant God established with Abraham was long *before* Jesus would come to the earth in a body of flesh and blood in the Person of Jesus Christ, and become "the" perfect "Passover Lamb" without spot or blemish.

As a matter of fact, in Galatians 3:5–9, the apostle Paul is talking about how we become saved. However, he says something quite profound in Galatians 3:8. He proclaims the gospel was preached to Abraham "beforehand," saying, *"In you* [Abraham] *all the nations shall be blessed."* (NKJV)

Did you catch the significance of this? Before *the Word* was manifested in a body of flesh and blood as the Son of Man in the Person of Jesus Christ, the gospel was preached to Abraham who believed! Therefore, God accounted Abraham's faith in Him for *righteousness* as substantiated in Galatians 3:5–9 below:

> "Therefore He who supplies the Spirit to you and works miracles among you, does He do it by the WORKS of the LAW, or by the HEARING of FAITH? Just as Abraham 'BELIEVED God, and it was ACCOUNTED to him for RIGHTEOUSNESS.' Therefore know that only THOSE WHO are of FAITH are SONS of ABRAHAM. And the Scripture, foreseeing that God would JUSTIFY the GENTILES by FAITH, preached the GOSPEL to Abraham beforehand, saying, 'In you [Abraham] all the NATIONS shall be BLESSED.' So then those who are of FAITH are BLESSED with BELIEVING Abraham."
> (Gal. 3:5–9, NKJV) (emphasis added).

In addition, the apostle Paul tells us in Romans 4:9, Abraham was "justified" *before* undergoing circumcision, which was the "sign" of this *everlasting* covenant God established with Abraham, because of his faith, which God accounted to him for *righteousness*. This is substantiated in Romans 4:9, which says the following:

> "Does this blessedness then come upon the circumcised only, or upon the uncircumcised also? For we say that FAITH was accounted to Abraham for

RIGHTEOUSNESS." (Rom. 4:9, NKJV) (emphasis added).

Based on the promises God gave to Abraham, because He established this *everlasting* covenant with him and his descendants, *Yehôvah* promised Abraham the following: He would give all the children of Israel, both the Jews from the House of Judah, and those of us who were formerly Gentiles from the House of Israel (Jacob/Joseph/Ephraim), an opportunity to "walk" in a covenant relationship with Him.

In addition, one of the promises *Yehôvah* gave to Abraham is this: God would "multiply" Abraham's descendants as the *stars of heaven,* and as the *sand which is on the seashore,* and we would "possess" the gate of our enemies. It would come to pass that from Abraham's *spiritual* "seed," all the nations of the earth shall be blessed.

As such, *Yehôvah* would eventually fulfill this promise to Abraham, the "Father of Many Nations," through Jesus Christ. This is substantiated in Hebrews 6:13–20, which says the following:

> *"For when God made a PROMISE to Abraham, because He could SWEAR BY no ONE greater, He SWORE by Himself, saying, 'Surely blessing I will bless you, and multiplying I will multiply you.' And so, after he [Abraham] had PATIENTLY ENDURED, he obtained the PROMISE. For men indeed swear by the greater, and an oath for confirmation is for them an*

end of all dispute. Thus GOD, DETERMINING to SHOW MORE ABUNDANTLY to the HEIRS of PROMISE the IMMUTABILITY of His COUNSEL, CONFIRMED it by an OATH, that by TWO IMMUTABLE THINGS, in which it is IMPOSSIBLE for GOD to LIE, we might have STRONG CONSOLATION, who have FLED for REFUGE to LAY HOLD of the HOPE set before us. This HOPE we have as an ANCHOR of the SOUL, both SURE and STEADFAST, and which ENTERS the PRESENCE behind the VEIL, where the FORERUNNER has ENTERED for us, even JESUS, having become High Priest FOREVER according to the ORDER of MELCHIZEDEK." (Heb. 6:13–20, NKJV) (emphasis added).

Again, *Yehôvah* would fulfill this promise to Abraham through His only *begotten* Son, Jesus Christ, who is the Holy One of Israel. It is for this very reason, Jesus Christ's genealogy says in Matthew 1:1, *"The Book of the Genealogy of Jesus Christ, the Son of David, the Son of Abraham..."* (NKJV)

In addition, Psalm 105:8–12, proclaims this truth: *Yehôvah* remembers His covenant forever by *the Word*, which He commanded for a *thousand* generations. This is the "covenant" He made with Abraham, the "oath" He swore to Isaac, and He "confirmed" it to Jacob for an *everlasting* statute for all Israel. This is substantiated in Psalm 105:8–12, which says the following:

"He [*Yehôvah*, our heavenly Father, and God, our Creator—the God of Abraham, Isaac, and Jacob

397

Who is Israel? Discovering our True Identity in Jesus Christ and Why it Matters! The Foundation

(Israel)] *REMEMBERS His COVENANT FOREVER, The WORD which He COMMANDED, for a THOUSAND GENERATIONS, The COVENANT which He [Yehôvâh] made with Abraham, And His OATH to Isaac, And CONFIRMED it to Jacob for a STATUTE, To Israel as an EVERLASTING COVENANT, Saying, 'To you I will give the LAND of CANAAN As the ALLOTMENT of your INHERITANCE,' When they were few in number, Indeed very few, and strangers in it.* "(Psalm 105:8–12, NKJV) (emphasis added).

This *same* covenant is an *everlasting* covenant for all the children of Israel. Moreover, this is the *same* covenant Jesus Christ fulfilled (consummated, executed, and ratified [confirmed]) with His precious blood, when He became the "mediator" of the New Covenant. Therefore, this *everlasting* covenant is still in effect to *this* very day and applies to New Covenant believers.

In addition, *Yehôvâh* established His terms and conditions of "walking" in a "Marriage Covenant" with Him through Moses. He was the "mediator" of the *first* covenant, *Yehôvâh* established with all the children of Israel at the base of Mount Sinai, which was the result of this *everlasting* covenant God established with Abraham.

Thus, *Yehôvâh* "saved" the children of Israel—the Hebrew people, *before* He gave them His requirements for keeping His covenant with Him, just as we are saved by His grace *before* we come to the saving knowledge of His requirements found in His Word.

398

Therefore, it is by our faith in God's only *begotten* Son, Jesus Christ; we become saved. It is not by us keeping the *letter of the law.* Rather, it is by us placing our faith and trust in the One who gave us the law in the first place.

Our "faith" in Jesus will be evidenced by our "obedience" to His laws (commandments). This fact is substantiated by Jesus Himself in John 8:51. He says to us, *"Most assuredly, I say to you, if anyone KEEPS My WORD he shall NEVER see DEATH."* (NKJV) (emphasis added).

Thus, *Yehôvah* issued His *laws*, His *statutes*, His *decrees*, His *ordinances*, and His *judgments*, which are the terms and conditions of being in a "Marriage Covenant" with Him, for all the children of Israel throughout the *synergy of the ages.*

In other words, all of God's people are to "keep" His *laws*, His *statutes*, His *decrees*, His *ordinances*, and His *judgments*, which are detailed in the first five books of the Bible referred to as the Book of the Covenant (the Torah).

Again, Moses was the "mediator" of this covenant which would be confirmed (ratified) with the children of Israel as detailed in Exodus 24:1–8.

Moses used the blood of animals that he sprinkled on the altar of the Tabernacle, and he also sprinkled the blood on the people and said, *"This is the BLOOD of the COVENANT which the LORD has made with you ACCORDING to all these WORDS."* (NKJV) (emphasis added).

399

Who is Israel? Discovering our True Identity in Jesus Christ and Why it Matters! The Foundation

If the children of Israel lived according to the terms and conditions of *Yehovah's* "Marriage Covenant," they would be His children, and He would be their God. Moreover, *Yehovah*, in the Book of Deuteronomy, which is the Book of the Law, tells us in advance the "blessings" we will reap for keeping His covenant. Also, *Yehovah* tells us in advance the "curses" we will reap for breaking His covenant.

In addition, Jesus Christ fulfilled (consummated, executed, and ratified [confirmed]) the *first* Covenant *Yehovah* first established through His servant Moses with His blood as He hung on the cross at Calvary. Therefore, Jesus became the "mediator" of the New Covenant through His death, resurrection, and ascension into heaven as our Great High Priest.

Yehovah's laws, which are the terms and conditions of keeping His covenant He first established through Moses, He has now put His laws, which Jesus did not abolish, in our mind, and written them on the tablets of our hearts, rather than on two tablets of stone under the New Covenant.

Thus, Jesus did not abolish the law, on the cross at Calvary.

Therefore, when Jesus "confirmed" the *first* covenant *Yehovah* established through His servant Moses for all the children of Israel, He did so to strengthen it, not to abolish it.

Again, the Hebrew word for "confirmed" is "gabar" which literally means: "He shall make strong."

Also, under the New Covenant, *Yehôvah's* people would receive the promise of His Holy Spirit living in "our" temple—our body—who would give us God's grace and power to live according to God's *laws*. His laws are according to His *commandments*, His *statutes*, His *decrees*, His *ordinances*, and His *judgments* so we *may* inherit all the covenant promises found in His Word.

It is also by faith we receive the *baptismal of the Holy Spirit* with *fire*, which is God's "dunamis" power that is accompanied by signs, wonders, and miracles to enable us to establish His will on the earth as it is in heaven. All these things are *freely* given to all of God's children by faith in His Son, Jesus Christ, because of His death, resurrection, and ascension into heaven.

Therefore, the New Covenant is the ultimate fulfillment of the *everlasting* covenant *Yehôvah* established with Abraham based on his faith and obedience alone!

Again, God views all the covenants He has established as "one" *everlasting* covenant for all His people and for all time. Therefore, even though there are multiple covenants (plural), *Yehôvah* has established throughout the *synergy of the ages* of mankind's existence, collectively, they are interwoven with one another so together; they fulfill *Yehôvah's eternal* plan of "redemption," "reconciliation," and "restoration" of all creation, which is far greater than each covenant by itself could ever achieve.

This *everlasting* covenant God established with Abraham and his descendants, is so important to *Yehôvah,* He pledged His throne as a security deposit. He swore by Himself, that until *this* earth, and the heavens pass away, He will uphold, protect, and defend this

401

everlasting covenant He established with Abraham—the "Father of Many Nations," and his descendants. This covenant is in effect for a *thousand* generations for those who "love" Him, and "keep" His commandments.

In addition, as is the case with all true disciples of Jesus Christ, all God required of Abraham was his "faith" and his "obedience."

Therefore, this *everlasting* covenant God established with Abraham was not based on the "collective" behavior of the children of Israel, nor, is our salvation based on the "collective" behavior of the body of Christ.

God established the *Abrahamic* Covenant based on Abraham's faith, trust, and obedience to Him period. God credited Abraham's faith in Him, as *righteousness.* So, it is with us!

Moreover, God made many promises to bless Abraham's "physical" and "spiritual" descendants, which also includes the land of the *physical* nation of Israel, a *literal* nation on the earth located in the Middle East. It also includes many blessings concerning the "spiritual" nation of Israel, the body of Christ, which is comprised of both Jews and Gentiles who have placed their faith in Jesus Christ.

God is faithful and will honor what He told Abraham for the sake of His Holy Name, and this is substantiated in Ezekiel 36:22, which says the following:

> *"Therefore say to the HOUSE of ISRAEL, 'Thus says the Lord GOD: 'I do not DO this for YOUR SAKE, O*

HOUSE of ISRAEL, BUT for My HOLY NAME'S
SAKE, which you have PROFANED among the
NATIONS wherever you WENT.'" (Ezek. 36:22,
NKJV) (emphasis added).

Take the time to read and study all of Ezekiel Chapter 36, to fully
understand what God means when He says to us, *"I do not DO this
for YOUR SAKE, O HOUSE of ISRAEL..."* (NKJV) (emphasis
added).

Yehovah is speaking to those of us who were formerly Gentiles from
the House of Israel (Jacob/Joseph/Ephraim), whom He scattered
all over the world, because we broke covenant with Him, and we
never returned to the land He promised to Abraham like the Jews
from the House of Judah did.

As such, we "profane" His Holy Name everywhere we go. This is
what it really means to not use the Lord's name in vain.

In other words, in the body of Christ, there are many wolves in
sheep's clothing who "profess" with their mouths, they are
Christians, and they love the Lord. Yet these *same* people speak
forth "perverse" things, and they are filled with pride and
arrogance, and as such, they practice "lawlessness," which is evil in
the sight of God.

Many so-called believers are "deceptively" using the name of Jesus
Christ in vain to advance their evil agenda because they truly serve
the *kingdom of darkness* by the things they "say" and by "the way"
they live their lives. Yes, indeed! Satan has infiltrated the body of
Christ, and based on Second Corinthians 11:14, he masquerades

himself as an *angel of light* to deceive those who do not "walk" in God's love, or, in God's light.

Moreover, God's Word defines what "evil" is based on Proverbs 8:13, which says, *"The FEAR of the LORD is to hate EVIL; PRIDE and ARROGANCE and the EVIL WAY And the PERVERSE MOUTH I HATE."* (NKJV) (emphasis added).

These are the same attributes Satan has used from the beginning of time, which caused his "eternal" separation from God.

Furthermore, God's Word says to us in Proverbs 16:18, *"PRIDE goes before DESTRUCTION And a HAUGHTY SPIRIT before a FALL."* (NKJV) (emphasis added).

This is exactly why *"...it will not be by MIGHT, nor by POWER, but by My Spirit,"* says the *Lord of Heaven's Armies,* America shall be saved as well!

What I have just stated, and what I am about to convey, may seem irrelevant to the subject at hand, but I can assure you it is not. So please be patient and stay with me, because shortly you will understand why I am specifically bringing up America at this point, even though God has an *eternal* "prophetic" destiny for all the nations which shall be fulfilled.

God shall save America for His *eternal* purposes and glory to be re-established in this nation for the sake of His Holy Name, even though many of His people bring dishonor to the Lord by "the way" we live our lives.

404

For now, let's refocus our attention on the *literal* nation of Israel, which was *Yehovah's* first *physical* vineyard, for His chosen people to be a light to the rest of the world, until they were scattered all over the world in AD 70 when both Jerusalem, and the temple were destroyed.

AMERICA WAS "RAISED UP" BY GOD BASED ON ONE OF THE PROMISES GOD GAVE TO ABRAHAM

God "raised up" America to fulfill one of the promises *Yehovah* gave to Abraham which is this: In his "seed" all the nations of the world would be blessed. This is indeed one of the reasons why America has "spiritual" ties to the nation of Israel.

Yes, indeed! America was "birthed" because of one of the promises God made with Abraham. God told Abraham, He would make him into a *great* nation. This is substantiated in Genesis 12:1–3, which says the following:

> *"Now the LORD had said to Abram: 'GET OUT of your COUNTRY, From your FAMILY And from your FATHER'S HOUSE, To a LAND that I will SHOW you. I will make you a great NATION; I will BLESS YOU And make YOUR NAME GREAT; And you shall be a BLESSING. I will BLESS those who BLESS YOU, And I will CURSE him who CURSES YOU; And in you [Abram] all the FAMILIES of the EARTH shall be BLESSED.'"* (Gen. 12:1–3, NKJV) (emphasis added).

Who is Israel? Discovering our True Identity in Jesus Christ and Why it Matters! The Foundation

From the very beginning, the Israelites were chosen to be God's *kingdom of priests* and a *holy* nation, before they entered the Promised Land. This is substantiated in Exodus 19:3–6, which says the following:

> "And Moses went up to God, and the LORD called to him from the mountain, saying, 'Thus you shall say to the HOUSE of JACOB, and tell the CHILDREN of ISRAEL: 'You have seen what I did to the Egyptians, and how I bore you on eagles' wings and brought you to Myself. Now therefore, if [the word "if" makes this promise conditional] you will indeed OBEY My VOICE and KEEP My COVENANT, then [based on the condition of whether or not we will "obey" His Voice and "keep" His covenant] you shall be a SPECIAL TREASURE to Me ABOVE all PEOPLE; for all the EARTH is Mine. And you shall be to Me a KINGDOM of PRIESTS and a holy NATION.' These are the WORDS which you shall SPEAK to the CHILDREN of ISRAEL.'" (Exod. 19:3–6, NKJV) (emphasis added).

However, as substantiated based on the historical written records in the Old Testament, we know despite the Israelites' intent to "do" and "obey" all the commandments God required, time and time again, they fell short of their end of the covenant, just like many believers are doing today.

Therefore, it would come to pass; God would send His only *begotten* Son, Jesus Christ, as their long-awaited Messiah. Although, tragically, *some* of the Jews rejected Him, and thus, the Gentiles were given an opportunity to be grafted into the commonwealth of Israel, only by the blood of Jesus Christ. This is substantiated in Ephesians 2:11–13.

Furthermore, Jesus told the Pharisees and the Sadducees, the *kingdom of God* would be taken from them, and given to another nation, due to their rejection of Him, and their unbelief. This is based on Matthew 21:43, which states, *"I tell you, the Kingdom of God will be TAKEN AWAY from you and GIVEN to a NATION that will PRODUCE the PROPER FRUIT."* (NLT) (emphasis added).

Thus, two new nations, both a "spiritual" and a "physical" nation, had to be birthed by God that would produce the "proper" fruit.

GOD "RAISED UP" A NEW "SPIRITUAL" NATION THAT WOULD PRODUCE THE "PROPER" FRUIT

First and foremost, a new "spiritual" nation was born. It is called the body of Christ, which includes both the Jews from the House of Judah, and those of us who were formerly Gentiles from the House of Israel (Jacob/Joseph/Ephraim), who were grafted into the commonwealth of Israel by our faith in God's only *begotten* Son, Jesus Christ.

This truth is substantiated by the apostle Paul in Galatians 3:28–29, when he states, *"There is neither JEW nor GREEK* [Gentile]*, there is neither SLAVE nor FREE, there is neither MALE nor FEMALE; for you are all ONE in CHRIST JESUS. And if you are CHRIST'S,* then you are ABRAHAM'S SEED, and HEIRS according to the PROMISE." (NKJV) (emphasis added).

This truth is once again proclaimed by the apostle Paul in Romans 3:21–26, which says the following:

> "But now apart from the LAW the RIGHTEOUSNESS of GOD has been made known, to which the LAW and the PROPHETS testify. This RIGHTEOUSNESS is GIVEN through FAITH in JESUS CHRIST to all WHO BELIEVE. There is no DIFFERENCE between JEW and GENTILE, for all have SINNED and FALL SHORT of the GLORY of GOD, and all are JUSTIFIED freely by His GRACE through the REDEMPTION that came by CHRIST JESUS. God presented CHRIST as a SACRIFICE of ATONEMENT, through the SHEDDING of his BLOOD—to be RECEIVED by FAITH. He did this to demonstrate His RIGHTEOUSNESS, because in his forbearance he had LEFT THE SINS COMMITTED beforehand UNPUNISHED— he did it to demonstrate His RIGHTEOUSNESS at the PRESENT TIME, so as to be JUST and the ONE WHO JUSTIFIES those who have FAITH in JESUS." (Rom. 3:21–26, NIV) (emphasis added).

Therefore, to reiterate the "spiritual" nation which was "raised up" by God that would produce the proper "fruit" is the body of Christ. We are a *royal* priesthood and a *holy* nation. This is proclaimed by First Peter 2:9, which states, *"But you are a CHOSEN*

GENERATION, a <u>ROYAL PRIESTHOOD</u>, a <u>HOLY NATION</u>, His own SPECIAL PEOPLE, that you may proclaim the praises of Him who called you out of darkness into His marvelous light." (NKJV) (emphasis added).

Furthermore, do not dismiss the significance, this is the same thing God told Moses at Mount Sinai to tell the children of Israel in Exodus 19:6, which proclaims, "'And you shall be to Me a KINGDOM of PRIESTS and a HOLY NATION.' These are the WORDS which you shall SPEAK to the CHILDREN of ISRAEL." (NKJV) (emphasis added).

Equally important, note the "conditions" God has established for His people to be in a "covenant" relationship with Him. This is based on Exodus 19:5, which states, "Now therefore, if [the word "if" makes this promise conditional] you will indeed OBEY My VOICE and KEEP My COVENANT, then [based on the condition of whether or not we will "obey" His Voice and "keep" His covenant] you shall be a SPECIAL TREASURE to Me ABOVE all PEOPLE; for all the EARTH is Mine." (NKJV) (emphasis added).

Therefore, contrary to what is taught, we are *only* God's "covenant" people *if* we "obey" God's Voice, and "keep" His covenant, by obeying His commandments *after* we "become" saved. These are the terms and conditions of the "Covenant of Marriage" we entered into after we "accepted" and "received" His only *begotten* Son, Jesus Christ, as our Lord and Savior, by our faith in Him.

Jesus substantiates this truth when He says to us in Luke 6:46, "But why do you CALL Me 'Lord, Lord,' and <u>NOT DO</u> the THINGS which I SAY?" (NKJV) (emphasis added).

Moreover, the body of Christ is the "spiritual" nation God "raised up" who would bear the proper "fruit" and would indeed fulfill one of the promises God made to Abraham.

This is based on Genesis 18:17–18, in which the Lord states, *"...Shall I hide from Abraham what I am doing, since Abraham will surely become a GREAT and POWERFUL NATION, and all NATIONS on EARTH will be BLESSED through HIM?"* (NIV) (emphasis added).

Still, a new "physical" nation had to be "raised up" by God that would bear the proper "fruit," until the prophecy spoken by the prophet Isaiah came to pass, which resulted in the nation of Israel being "reborn" on May 14, 1948. This is based on Isaiah 66:8 below:

> *"Who has heard such a thing? Who has seen such things? Shall the EARTH be made to give BIRTH in one day? Or shall a NATION be BORN at ONCE? For as soon as ZION was in LABOR, She gave BIRTH to her CHILDREN."* (Isa. 66:8, NKJV) (emphasis added).

Up until the time the nation of Israel was "reborn" in May 1948, the twelve tribes of Israel were scattered all over the world, when the temple and Jerusalem were destroyed at the hands of the Romans in AD 70.

Therefore, God needed to "raise up" a *literal* nation on the earth that would bear the "proper" fruit.

And, it is for this very reason, God "raised up" America.

GOD "RAISED UP" AMERICA TO BE A NEW "PHYSICAL" NATION THAT WOULD PRODUCE THE PROPER "FRUIT"

Have you ever noticed the USA in JerUSAlem?

Yes, indeed! America was birthed for God's purposes and glory from the very beginning to be His premier "physical" nation in the world that would produce the proper "fruit," until the *fullness of the Gentiles* is fulfilled.

Then God will once again turn His full attention back to the "physical" nation of Israel, which was "reborn" in 1948, and to the Jews from the House of Judah, who are still *spiritually* blinded by God until the *fullness of the Gentiles* comes to fruition.

Again, we are now entering the time of the *fullness of the Gentiles*, and the leading missionary organizations project from statistical data, the gospel will be presented to all 6,000 ethnic people groups from among the 238 nations by 2016–2017.

Therefore, this will fulfill one of God's primary mandates for the body of Christ. This is based on Matthew 24:14, which says the following:

> *"And this GOSPEL of the KINGDOM will be PREACHED in all the WORLD as a WITNESS to all the NATIONS, and then the END* [1] [G5056: *telos*: the termination, the limit at which a thing ceases to be (always of the end of some act or state, but not of the end of a period of time); the last in any succession

411

> or series that by which a thing is finished, its close,
> issued the end to which all things relate, the aim,
> eternal purpose] *will COME."* (Matt. 24:14, NKJV)
> (emphasis added).

The word "end" as used in Matthew 24:14, does not necessarily mean the end of the world. Rather, it could mean the end of one assignment, and the beginning of another, until all things are fulfilled in accordance with God's *eternal* Word.

As such, after the *gospel of the kingdom* is preached in the entire world as a witness unto all the nations, the Lord will then turn His full attention back to the *physical* nation of Israel, and His Jewish people, as it was in the beginning for this reason: They are loved on account of the patriarchs as indicated in Romans 11:28–32, which says the following:

> *"Concerning the **GOSPEL** (2)* [G2098: *euaggelion:* a good message, that is, the *gospel of the kingdom* and of salvation through Christ] *they are ENEMIES for YOUR SAKE, but concerning the **ELECTION** (3)* [G1589: *eklogē:* (divine) *selection* (abstractly or concretely); chosen, election] *they are BELOVED for the SAKE of the FATHERS* [Abraham, Isaac, and Jacob]. *For the GIFTS and the CALLING of GOD are IRREVOCABLE. For as YOU WERE ONCE DISOBEDIENT to GOD, yet HAVE NOW OBTAINED MERCY through THEIR DISOBEDIENCE, even so THESE also have NOW BEEN DISOBEDIENT, that THROUGH the MERCY*

SHOWN you THEY also may *OBTAIN MERCY*. For
GOD has COMMITTED them all to DISOBEDIENCE,
That He might have MERCY on ALL." (Rom. 11:28–
32, NKJV) (emphasis added).

WHY DID GOD BLESS AMERICA?

God did indeed bless America, and He made this nation His new
physical vineyard, until the re-establishment of the nation of Israel
in 1948. America was "unique" and "set apart" for God's glory and
purposes from the very beginning for the following reasons:

1. It was the first nation ever to be established because the
    people first loved God, and it has been God's *physical*
    vineyard (country) to carry out the *Great Commission* and to
    shine His "light" to the rest of the world. In other words,
    America did produce the proper "fruit" for a long time.

    As Ronald Reagan once emphasized, America *was* a shining
    city upon a hill, whose beacon of light guided freedom-
    loving people everywhere, as God's people in America were
    instrumental in carrying out the *Great Commission* to all the
    other nations of the world.

2. It was the only country in history to have been founded on
    Judeo-Christian beliefs because our founding fathers had
    one common denominator: Their devotion to God, our
    Creator. America was founded on Judeo-Christian values.
    Moreover, our ancestors established a covenant with God
    called the *Mayflower Compact*, which was the first governing

document of the Plymouth Colony. In this compact (covenant), they specifically stated their purpose for coming to America was for the glory of God, and to make advancements for the Christian faith, when they said, *"Having undertaken, for the Glory of God, and advancements of the Christian faith and honor of our King and Country, for the sole purpose of..."*[4]

3. We were instrumental in helping rc-establish the nation of Israel in 1948, and up until recently, we were Israel's greatest ally. However, because of the recent presidential election, the tide is now turning as we are witnessing President Trump, and his administration is publicly taking a decisive stand with our long-time friend and ally—the state of Israel. In addition, Trump is fostering a respectful relationship with the Prime Minister of Israel, Benjamin Netanyahu. As such the Trump administration is seeking to "restore" and "reconcile" our friendship and support for the nation of Israel, which was severely damaged and strained by the actions of the previous administration. Hallelujah and thank you, Jesus!

4. Moreover, America did indeed become the greatest and the most powerful nation ever to exist, because God did indeed bless America based on His promise to Abraham in Genesis 18:18. Again, God told Abraham, he would surely become a "great" and "powerful" nation, and all the nations of the earth would be blessed through him, "spiritually" and "physically" speaking.

414

Donna M. Rogers

THE FATE OF AMERICA HANGS IN THE BALANCE

Now fast forward to 2017, and America is on the verge of extinction, even though God extended His mercy with our recent presidential election due to His faithful remnant crying out to Him for His mercy and divine intervention.

We can rejoice that God's mercy triumphs over judgment, based on His faithful remnant tapping into the "root" of the covenant of mercy that God established with our forefathers in this nation, and the cries of His faithful remnant. However, do not think for one minute that God is "winking" at our iniquity in this nation and He approves of our "fruit" just because He chose to extend His mercy to us at this time.

Read the Book of Habakkuk. Then you will understand that even though God's judgment is delayed due to the prayers of His faithful remnant in this nation, and even though God's judgment may not come quickly, it shall come to pass at the "appointed" time, which speaks of the end and it will not prove false.

Back in 2004, when I wrote my first book for the Lord titled, *Shattered Dreams—Wake Up America Before It Is Too Late!,* the Holy Spirit prophetically showed me the demise of America, before there were many apparent "signs" anything was amiss.

He told me the "root" cause of everything we would be reaping in this nation is because His people have left our first love—Jesus Christ. Until this "root" cause is dealt with, we will continue our downward spiral.

In fact, because we have left our first love—Jesus Christ, as Jesus says

415

to us in Matthew 24:12, "lawlessness" will abound because the love of many for our Lord has grown cold. Therefore, we will not love one another as we have been commanded to do, and we will continue to rebel and forsake God, our Creator, by "practicing" evil, because we have left the "ancient" path that leads to life.

As such, for the most part, the body of Christ is not "obeying" God's Voice, or "keeping" His covenant, which is based on the whole counsel of His *everlasting* Word which shall never pass away. Hence, many who "profess" with their mouths, they are His—but their hearts are far from Him, are rejecting the very One they "profess" to serve!

Moreover, it is because we have been blessed by God with great wealth and abundance, we have become prideful and arrogant. In addition, we have lost the *reverential* fear of the Lord, who is the One that gives us the power to get wealth, so He may establish His covenant, which He swore to our fathers (Abraham, Isaac, and Jacob [Israel]), as it is to *this* very day. This is based on Deuteronomy 8:18.

In addition, it is quite apparent, most of God's people in America, no longer have the *reverential* fear of the Lord, which is evidenced by "the way" we live our lives. As such, this is the "root" cause of why we are losing our freedoms. For Second Corinthians 3:17, proclaims, *"Now the LORD is the SPIRIT; and WHERE the SPIRIT of the LORD is, there is LIBERTY."* (NKJV) (emphasis added).

Therefore, as we are witnessing now, for the most part, the *Spirit of the Lord* no longer resides in the vast majority of His people in this nation, because God's Holy Spirit will not dwell in temples that

416

have become "defiled" due to our sins and our transgressions.

As a matter of fact, based on what the apostles say to us in Acts 5:32, God has given the Holy Spirit to those who "obey" Him!

Moreover, God can and will take His presence from us based on Psalm 51:11, which says, *"Do not CAST me AWAY from YOUR PRESENCE, And do not take Your HOLY SPIRIT from me."* (NKJV) (emphasis added).

So obviously, based on this Scripture, God can cast us away from His presence, and He can take His Holy Spirit from us as well, because of our indifference when it comes to "grieving" the Holy Spirit.

Do we realize that even some of the television shows, or the types of movies Christians choose to watch, does, in fact, grieve the Holy Spirit?

In addition, the altars of the *unholy* priests, people who are held captive and being used by Satan, are flourishing throughout our land, and are more numerous, than the holy altars of God's *royal* priesthood in this nation.

In fact, this is evidenced by the state of the "spiritual," "ethical," and "moral" depravity we see in all sectors of the seven foundational mountains, or pillars, in our society.

This impacts, effects, and influences our culture, for better or worse, including the religious mountain.

However, God has a plan to restore this nation back to Him once again. But first He must "destroy" and "uproot" the foundations in this nation which have not been built on His government—His *justice*, His *righteousness*, and His *judgments*. He must "reform" many things to re-establish His kingdom "rule" and "reign" in our nation for His *eternal* purposes to prevail once again.

Yet it begins with the "transformation" of His people—in our "hearts" and in our "homes."

As such, He will shake everything that can be shaken! In addition, God will release His glory like never before. At the same time, He will also be releasing His *righteous* judgments. And, God's *righteous* judgments begin with His Church.

This is based on First Peter 4:17 which says, *"For the time has come for JUDGMENT to BEGIN at the HOUSE of GOD; and if it begins with us first, WHAT WILL BE THE END of those who DO not OBEY the GOSPEL of GOD?"* (NKJV) (emphasis added).

Do not dismiss the significance that we are specifically told in First Peter 4:17 that those who do not "obey" the gospel of God will be dealt with in the end—when Judgment Day commences.

Tragically, there are many believers in the body of Christ who do not "obey" the gospel and unless they repent—they shall perish for all eternity when God renders His final judgment on Judgment Day.

When God gets done re-structuring this nation and His church, all this will result in His people repenting, and returning to Him, with all our mind, heart, soul, and strength, so we do not perish for all eternity. Unfortunately, it sometimes takes great persecution and calamity, to compel people to turn from our wicked ways, which is

418

the fourth requirement of Second Chronicles 7:14. Many of God's people in America do not even realize we have broken "covenant" with God, due to our lack of knowledge concerning the whole counsel of His Word.

Hence, one of the purposes of this series of books is to properly disciple God's people in the body of Christ, so we can turn from our wicked ways, and return to God, so He will hear our prayers and heal our land.

GOD IS IN THE PROCESS OF USHERING IN MAJOR "REFORMATION" IN THE BODY OF CHRIST AND AMERICA

In the meanwhile, God is in the process of bringing major "reformation" to America, and to the body of Christ, which shall impact the entire world, and usher in "the" final Great Awakening, which shall precede the return of Jesus Christ.

As such, please allow me the privilege to speak briefly about this major "reformation." One of my mandates from God is to help facilitate, and usher in the "rebuilding" of the broken down "spiritual" wall which is prevalent in this nation, that will impact all the nations of the world. This will ultimately fulfill one of the promises God made to Abraham, because of the *everlasting* covenant He established with him and his descendants.

Our work as the body of Christ has just begun to bring the much needed "reformation" into both the church and this nation. In addition, we must continue to intercede without ceasing like never before. However, prayer alone is not enough! We must also take clear, decisive action as well! This will result in the body of Christ actually "doing" what Nehemiah and Ezra did. We must seek to "reconcile," "restore," and "rebuild" the broken down "spiritual" wall in our nation, which shall usher in the final Great Awakening to all the nations of the world.

Therefore, despite the recent victory which resulted in the changing of the guard in Washington D.C. with the miraculous election of Donald J. Trump who is the 45th President of the United States of America, our nation is still on the verge of forever being lost due to the broken down "spiritual" wall across America.

As such, concerning the broken down "spiritual" wall across our nation, God is looking for His Church to establish His government in this nation, not the other way around. In other words, do not think our government will rebuild the broken down "spiritual" wall in America!

As in the case of Nehemiah, God is beseeching the body of Christ to invoke both "prayer" and "action." We must bring "reformation" into the seven mountains in our society.

This will happen when His people become the "salt" and the "light" we are called to be in all sectors of our society as we properly "disciple" the nations.

The seven mountains, or pillars, in our society are as follows: Religion, Family, Government, Business, Education, Arts/Entertainment, and the Media mountains.

God already has His people strategically placed in each of these mountains, or pillars, in our society.

But we cannot properly "disciple" the nations, or effectively impact these foundational mountains, or pillars, in our society, until God's people are properly "discipled" first, based on the whole counsel of His uncompromised, unadulterated Word.

Again, this is one of the reasons for this series of books I have written for the body of Christ, and the high-level strategic plan I wrote for the Lord back in 2010, which can be accessed on my website under the tab titled, "God's Strategic Plan."

Because the truth is this: The majority of God's people in the body of Christ do not even realize God, who has reconciled us to Himself through Jesus Christ, has given each one of us, the "ministry of reconciliation" based on Second Corinthians 5:18.

In other words, every disciple of Jesus Christ has been given a ministry by God to bring "reconciliation" to people, places, and things such as the misguided ideologies which are so prevalent in our society that is based on the *kingdom of darkness,* instead of the *kingdom of light.*

Again, God's people are called to be the "salt" and the "light" in their sphere of influence which shall influence and impact a particular mountain, or pillar, in our society that God has *already* placed us in.

The mountain we will influence and impact for God's kingdom will be directly related to the talents and the spiritual gifts He has given us. These are to be used in our chosen vocation, to dispel the darkness and establish His kingdom in that particular mountain, or pillar, in our society.

TRUE REVIVAL BEGINS IN THE "HEARTS" AND "HOMES" OF GOD'S PEOPLE WHICH WILL BE EVIDENT WHEN WE BEAR "FRUIT" WORTHY OF REPENTANCE

The rebuilding of the broken down "spiritual" wall all across America will not become a reality until God's people rebuild the broken down "spiritual" walls in our own lives for this reason: True revival begins in the "hearts" and "homes" of God's people.

And, we will bear the proper "fruit" which is worthy of repentance, *when* God's people apply God's Word to "the way" we live our lives. This should be in alignment with the uncompromised, unadulterated whole counsel of God's Word, especially concerning our heavenly Father's instructions written in the Torah.

In fact, take the time to listen to this video with Lance Wallnau and Gordon Robertson that recently came out entitled, *Dismantling Political Correctness.* I have provided the link to this video in the appendix at the back of this book. [5]

When you listen to this video, pay particular attention to the end of this video when Lance and Gordon talk about what the body of Christ needs to pray for and "do" next, which goes right in line with what the Lord has placed upon my heart since 2010.

Lance Wallnau said in this video the following: The body of Christ must mobilize a grassroots "reformation" to see monumental change happen in America. This is what needs to happen next *if* the body of Christ wants to see great "reformation" come to this nation, which shall usher in the final Great Awakening worldwide.

In the meanwhile, I am proclaiming this truth: This next "reformation" must happen first in the Church with God's people. And, as Gordon Robertson said in this video, it begins with God's people not only being taught the Torah, we also need to apply God's instructions to "the way" we live our lives before we can properly disciple the nations.

Concerning what Gordon Robertson said about the Torah, we are told in Nehemiah 8:1–18, all the people were gathered together as one accord in the open square and Ezra, the scribe, read the Book of the Law of Moses, which the Lord had commanded Israel. Ezra did this so that the ears of all the people were attentive to the Book of the Law.

If you take the time to read Chapters 8 and 9 of the Book of Nehemiah, you will discover that Nehemiah partnered with Ezra. They led the city, not a church, in a city-wide worship service where they initiated a Bible study on the Law of Moses, in order to bring the people back to "walking" in a covenant relationship with the Lord. This is what brought about a national repentance in Nehemiah's day, which is what God is looking for to take place in all the nations, especially in America.

Again, based on Second Peter 3:9, God is not slack concerning His promise, and His will for our lives is that we will be longsuffering as He is toward us so that no one should perish, but all would come to repentance so they may be saved. God always gives His people the opportunity to repent, and to return to Him, even though we have broken covenant with Him.

In fact, we are told in the Book of Nehemiah, the people wept and repented when they were taught by Ezra the words of the Book of the Law.

Because they recognized the sin in their lives, acknowledged their guilt, and then they took steps to eradicate their sins as they came back into alignment with God's uncompromised Word.

This resulted in God's people bearing "fruit" worthy of repentance. Then they were in the proper condition to be "reconciled" and "restored" to walking in a covenant relationship with the Lord.

Therefore, just as Nehemiah partnered with Ezra, in Chapters 8 and 9 of the Book of Nehemiah, we desperately need the "reformers" and "forerunners" that God has "raised up" for a time such as this, to come forth.

Then they must initiate city-wide worship, and teach the Book of the Law to God's people.

When God's people realize how far we have drifted from God's *righteous* requirements, and how we have broken covenant with our heavenly Father, this revelation *should* result in national repentance, which must begin with His *holy* nation.

The "reformation" God is looking for will truly begin when God's people repent and return to Him, on an individual basis for this reason: True "reconciliation," "restoration," and "transformation" which shall lead to Revival begins in us, God's people!

UNFORTUNATELY, ONE CAN HARDLY TELL THE DIFFERENCE BETWEEN THE CHURCH AND THE WORLD ANY LONGER

We cannot change what the problem is without first acknowledging the fact we do have a problem. Sadly, the majority of God's people in the body of Christ truly believe there is nothing wrong with us at all. When the truth is: One can hardly tell anymore the difference between God's people, and the people who live in the world!

The body of Christ is called by God to be "set apart," and to live "holy," because the God we serve is Holy. In fact, God has called us out of the world instead of "conforming" to the world.

In other words, we cannot be living like the rest of the world does! Also, if we were *truly* establishing God's "kingdom," and His "righteousness" in our land, which begins in the "hearts" and "homes" of God's people, there is no way our nation would resemble Satan's lair, rather than One Nation Under God!

As such, God does have a major controversy with the body of Christ in this nation. And unfortunately, God must humble us greatly, so we will sincerely repent, and turn from our wicked ways, so He will hear our prayers from heaven, and heal our land.

I know beyond a shadow of a doubt God wants America back so she can finish her purpose of why He raised us up in the first place because countless souls are at stake for all eternity! Therefore, hear the Word of the Lord He has called me to proclaim: America shall "rise up" out of the ashes with a "new" cry of freedom in Christ Jesus!

GOD WANTS AMERICA TO RETURN TO HIM FOR MANY REASONS

The "good news" is this: God wants America to return to Him until He is done with this nation for the following reasons:

1. So we can finish our prophetic destiny of why He raised America up in the first place which is this: To further the *gospel of the kingdom* to all the nations of the world for the glory of God and to make advancements for the Christian faith.

2. For the honor of His name's sake. This is based on the covenant He established with our founding fathers when this nation was founded on Judeo-Christian values, and because of the *everlasting* covenant God established with Abraham, the "Father of Many Nations."

3. To delay the New World Order/One World Order/Revived Roman Empire/Islamic Caliphate (Antichrist Kingdom) from coming to their fullness *before* God's "appointed" time to fulfill end-time prophecy. America's sovereignty is the *only* thing keeping the New World Order/One World Order from being fully established.

4. And last, but certainly not least, so the majority of God's people in this nation will repent and arise to help bring in the end-time harvest of souls. However, first God will orchestrate circumstances that will bring us to our knees, as He strips away all our false idols, our pride, and our arrogance, by His refining fire! God has to remove the impurities from our lives that keep us captive and causes us not to submit our allegiance to only Him fully. Only then, will the vast majority of believers in the body of Christ, finally submit to His will and His Word so that God can orchestrate His purpose for His glory, in and through us, His people.

In addition, just like Daniel prayed so long ago in Daniel 9:3–5, and he stood in the gap for his nation, we too would be wise to make our prayers and supplications to God with fasting and sincere repentance for "breaking" His covenant.

For we are all guilty for departing from His precepts and His judgments due to our ignorance of what the whole counsel of His Word says, and not understanding our "Hebraic" roots in Christianity.

Daniel 9:3–5, says the following:

> *"Then I set my face toward the Lord God to make REQUEST by prayer and supplications, with fasting, sackcloth, and ashes* [sincere repentance which bears the proper "fruit" worthy of repentance]. *And I PRAYED to the LORD my God, and made CONFESSION, and said, 'O Lord, great and awesome God, who KEEPS His COVENANT and MERCY with*

> *those who LOVE HIM, and with those who KEEP His*
> *COMMANDMENTS,   we   have   SINNED   and*
> *committed INIQUITY, we have done WICKEDLY and*
> *REBELLED, even by departing from your PRECEPTS*
> *and   your   JUDGMENTS.'"*   (Dan.   9:3–5,   NKJV)
> (emphasis added).

Notice this verse in Daniel 9:3–5, specifically says, God "keeps" His covenant and mercy with those who "love" Him and "keep" His commandments.

We all have sinned, committed iniquity, done wickedly, and rebelled against Him because we have departed from His precepts and His *righteous* judgments.

GOD'S PURPOSE FOR "RAISING UP" AMERICA IS COMING TO ITS ZENITH AS THE FULLNESS OF THE GENTILES IS COMING TO FRUITION

God's purpose for "raising up" the United States of America in the first place as the premier nation (physical vineyard) to share the *gospel of the kingdom* to all the nations of the world is coming to its zenith because the *fullness of the Gentiles* is at hand.

It is for this very reason, why all the eyes of the world are being refocused on the *physical* nation of Israel, as it was in the beginning, in this hour. Make no mistake about it; we are "the" generation who witnessed the rebirth of the nation of Israel on May 14, 1948, which was the fulfillment of Isaiah 66:8.

Therefore, as we are witnessing now—the nation of Israel will once again become *Yehovah's physical* vineyard for the salvation of all Israel as God removes the "spiritual" blindness off of the Jews from the House of Judah. He is doing this because the *fullness of the Gentiles* is at hand!

GOD PLEDGED HIS THRONE TO KEEP THE *EVERLASTING* COVENANT HE ESTABLISHED WITH ABRAHAM AND HIS DESCENDANTS

The Lord really wants His people to understand this truth, which is based on Genesis 22:15–18. Listen to how serious God is concerning the *Abrahamic* Covenant He established with Abraham, which was one of the reasons for Israel becoming a nation again, *despite* all odds, on May 14, 1948. Genesis 22:15–18, proclaims the following:

> *"Then the Angel of the LORD called to Abraham a second time out of heaven, and said: 'By Myself I have SWORN,' says the LORD, 'BECAUSE you have done this THING, and have not WITHHELD your son, YOUR ONLY SON— BLESSING I will BLESS YOU, and MULTIPLYING I will MULTIPLY YOUR DESCENDANTS as the stars of the heaven and as the sand which is on the seashore; and YOUR DESCENDANTS shall POSSESS the GATE of their ENEMIES. In your SEED all the NATIONS of the EARTH shall be BLESSED, because you* [Abraham] *have OBEYED My VOICE.'"* (Gen. 22:15–18, NKJV) (emphasis added).

429

Do not dismiss the significance of what God was saying when He said, *"By myself have I sworn."* As such, God pledged His own throne to keep this *everlasting* covenant He established with Abraham and his descendants because Abraham "believed" God and "obeyed" His Voice.

ANYONE WHO BREAKS THE ABRAHAMIC COVENANT IS GOING AGAINST GOD ALMIGHTY HIMSELF!

If anyone breaks the *Abrahamic* covenant, they are rebelling against God Almighty Himself! As such, as Hebrews 10:31, and Deuteronomy 32:41, proclaims: It is a fearful thing to fall into the hands of the living God, because if He whets His glittering sword and His hand takes hold of judgment, then He will render vengeance to His enemies and repay those who hate Him.

We are specifically warned in Ezekiel 7:2–4, when the end has come, God will unleash His anger and judge everyone according to their ways. It will be at this time He will repay every man for their abominations *if* we do not repent, turn from our wicked ways, and do what is right in His sight while there is still time to make a course correction. Now let's closely examine what the Lord says to us in Ezekiel 7:2–4, which says the following:

> *"And you, son of man, thus says the Lord GOD to the LAND of ISRAEL: 'An END! The END has COME UPON the FOUR CORNERS of the LAND. Now the END has COME UPON you, And I will SEND My ANGER AGAINST YOU; I will JUDGE you*

ACCORDING to YOUR WAYS, And I will REPAY you for all YOUR ABOMINATIONS. My EYE will <u>NOT</u> SPARE you, Nor will I have PITY; But I will REPAY your WAYS, And your ABOMINATIONS will be in your MIDST; Then you shall KNOW that I am the LORD!'" (Ezek. 7:2–4, NKJV) (emphasis added).

Based on Ezekiel 7:2–4, while this is talking about the "physical" land of Israel it has a *spiritually* meaning which is this: Since our bodies are taken from the dust of the earth, this Scripture is also talking about disciples of Jesus Christ who are Israel because we serve the God of Abraham, Isaac, and Jacob who is the Holy One of Israel.

In fact, in the next chapter we will discover, *spiritually* speaking, Israel is Jesus Christ and His disciples. Whereas, *physically* speaking, Israel is the land God promised to give to Abraham and his descendants, as an inheritance based on the *everlasting* covenant God established with all Israel.

Chapter 15

"Spiritually" Speaking, Israel Is Jesus Christ and His Disciples, and "Physically" Speaking, Israel Is the Land God Promised to Give Abraham and His Descendants

A s I have already conveyed, Israel *spiritually* speaking, is Jesus Christ and His disciples. Now we will continue our journey to understand how, *spiritually* speaking, Israel is the body of Christ. Moreover, we will begin to look at Israel as the *physical* (literal) nation on the earth, which was birthed, because of one of the promises God gave to Abraham based on Genesis 12:4–9, and Genesis 15:18–21.

Israel is the *only* "physical" nation on the earth defined by the land God promised to Abraham and his descendants. And, Israel is the only "physical" nation in the entire world, God established as a *literal* nation on the earth, which would bring forth the *firstfruits* of His increase. This was based on the *Abrahamic* Covenant; God made a vow by Himself because He could swear by none greater than Himself, never to break this *everlasting* covenant.

Moreover, long before the "physical" nation of Israel was born, which was God's first physical vineyard to be a light to the rest of the world, God already had a plan to "raise up" a "spiritual" nation. He did this so the promises He gave to Abraham, because of the *everlasting* covenant *Yehôvâh* established with him, could be realized through his descendants, which would become "heirs" of God's covenant promises as well.

In the last chapter, I already conveyed this truth: Jesus during His earthly ministry, told the Pharisees and Sadducees, the *kingdom of God* would be taken from them, and given to another nation due to their rejection of Him and their unbelief. This is based on Matthew 21:43, which states, *"I tell you, the kingdom of God will be TAKEN AWAY from you and GIVEN to a NATION that will PRODUCE the proper FRUIT."* (NLT) (emphasis added).

Therefore, two new nations (both a "spiritual" and a "physical" nation) had to be birthed which would produce the "proper" fruit.

As I said before, but it bears repeating, with God, there are always two realms—a "spiritual" realm and a "physical" realm. As such, everything first happens in the "spiritual" (heavenly realm), before it is manifested in the "natural" (earthly) realm.

First and foremost, a new "spiritual" nation was born, and it is called His Ekklēsia, or more commonly referred to as the body of Christ, or the Church. Again, the body of Christ is comprised of Jews from the House of Judah, and those of us who were formerly Gentiles from the House of Israel (Jacob/Joseph/Ephraim), who have now been grafted into the commonwealth of Israel by our faith in Jesus Christ.

However, *spiritually* speaking, there is no distinction between Jew or

434

Gentile, slave or free, male or female. Again, this truth is substantiated by the apostle Paul in Galatians 3:28–29, when he states, *"There is neither JEW nor GREEK* [Gentile], *there is neither SLAVE nor FREE, there is neither MALE nor FEMALE; for you are all ONE in CHRIST JESUS. And if you are CHRIST'S, then you are ABRAHAM'S SEED, and HEIRS according to the PROMISE."* (NKJV) (emphasis added).

Let's take it a step further. In Christ, since we are all "one," we should not label ourselves as being Baptists, Lutherans, Evangelicals, Methodists, Messianic Jews, Pentecostals, and so forth. In addition, we should not have "black" churches, "Hispanic" churches, "white" churches, etc. For we are all "one" in Christ Jesus, and there is *only* "one" body of Christ.

As such, let me drive home this point with the following question to help place this in the proper perspective for all eternity. When we stand at the "judgment seat of Christ," do you think Jesus will ask us what church we attended, what denomination we belonged to, or what title we assigned to ourselves—whether we are an apostle, a prophet, and so forth? No!

Therefore, we need to get rid of these labels and mindsets that divide the body of Christ, especially since the return of Jesus Christ is fast approaching, and He is coming back for a bride who is fully mature, without spot or blemish, and lacking nothing in Him.

Again, we are all "one" in Christ, *spiritually* speaking, by our faith in Jesus Christ based on Romans 3:21–26. We are all "justified" by faith in Jesus Christ by God's grace through our redemption in

Christ, because of God's "righteousness," not ours! For we have all sinned and fallen short of the Glory of God based on Romans 3:21–26. So, we need to get over ourselves and realize the gifts we have are from Him because He expects us to use them for His glory to prevail rather than our own. Romans 3:21–26, says the following:

> *"But now the* **RIGHTEOUSNESS** [^(1)] [G1343: ***dikaiosune***: equity (of character or act: justification] *of GOD APART from the LAW is REVEALED, being WITNESSED by the LAW and the PROPHETS, even the RIGHTEOUSNESS of GOD, through* **FAITH** [^(2)] [G4102: ***pistis***: persuasion, that is, *credence*; moral *conviction* (of *religious* truth, or the truthfulness of God or a religious teacher), especially *reliance* upon Christ for salvation; having fidelity] *in JESUS CHRIST, to ALL and on ALL who* **BELIEVE** [^(3)] [G4100: ***pisteuo***: to *have faith* (in, upon, or with respect to, a person or thing), that is, credit; by implication to entrust (especially one's spiritual well-being to Christ)]. *For there is no difference; for ALL HAVE SINNED and FALL SHORT of the GLORY of GOD, being* **JUSTIFIED** [^(4)] [G1344: ***dikaioo***: to render, show or regard as just or innocent—righteous] *FREELY by His* **GRACE** [^(5)] [G5485: ***charis***: manner or act of the divine influence upon the heart and its reflection in the life of one by having graciousness, gratitude, favour, gift, grace, thanks, worthy, or pleasure] *through the* **REDEMPTION** [^(6)] [G629: ***apolutrosis***: the act of paying the ransom in

Donna M. Rogers

full for the riddance or deliverance of our sins] *that is in CHRIST JESUS, whom God SET FORTH as a* **PROPITIATION** [7] [G2435: *hilastērion*: expiatory (place or thing), that is an atoning victim, mercy seat] *by His BLOOD, through* **FAITH**, [2] *to demonstrate His RIGHTEOUSNESS, because in His forbearance God had PASSED OVER the SINS that were PREVIOUSLY COMMITTED, to demonstrate at the PRESENT TIME His RIGHTEOUSNESS, that He might be JUST and the JUSTIFIER of the ONE who has* **FAITH** [2] *in JESUS."* (Rom. 3:21–26, NKJV) (emphasis added).

Now let's refocus our attention on the "spiritual" nation God chose to "raise up" which would bear the "proper" fruit.

To reiterate, the "spiritual" nation God "raised up" is the body of Christ, and we are a *royal* priesthood and a *holy* nation. This is proclaimed by First Peter 2:9, which states, *"But you are a CHOSEN GENERATION, a ROYAL PRIESTHOOD, a HOLY NATION, His own SPECIAL PEOPLE, that you may proclaim the praises of Him who called you out of darkness into His marvelous light."* (NKJV) (emphasis added).

Again, do not dismiss the significance this is the same thing God told Moses at Mount Sinai to tell the children of Israel (all twelve tribes) in Exodus 19:6, when God said, *"'And you shall be to Me a KINGDOM of PRIESTS and a HOLY NATION.' These are the WORDS which you shall SPEAK to the CHILDREN of ISRAEL."* (NKJV) (emphasis added).

437

As such, this "spiritual" *holy* nation, which is also a *royal* priesthood, who is called by God to be a *kingdom of priests*, would fulfill the promise God made to Abraham in Genesis 18:17–18, in which the Lord stated, "*...Shall I hide from Abraham what I am doing, since Abraham will surely become a GREAT and POWERFUL nation, and all NATIONS on EARTH will be BLESSED through him?*" (NIV) (emphasis added).

God's Ekklēsia is called to be a *great* and *powerful* "nation," God will use to bless all the nations of the world as we carry out the *Great Commission,* and proclaim the "good news" of the *gospel of the kingdom* to the lost.

Again, this is the kingdom "mandate" for *every* disciple of Jesus Christ, no matter what our chosen vocation happens to be. We have been born for a time such as this to help bring in the end-time harvest of souls into the kingdom.

I pray to the *Lord of the Harvest,* He will send out laborers into His vineyard because the harvest truly is great, but the laborers are few. May His Church arise and establish His Kingdom in this "kairos" season for the "set time" to favor Zion has come. We must be about our heavenly Father's business as we seek the LORD while He may still be found, and we call upon Him while He is near for our redemption draws nigh!

In the next chapter, we will discover why Israel, *spiritually* speaking, is the body of Christ.

438

CHAPTER 16

"SPIRITUAL" ISRAEL IS COMPRISED OF JEWS FROM THE HOUSE OF JUDAH AND FORMER GENTILES FROM THE HOUSE OF ISRAEL (JACOB/JOSEPH/EPHRAIM)

O nce again, we will look at the nation of Israel from a "spiritual" perspective. Just as the *literal* nation of Israel was the *firstfruits* of God's increase concerning all the other nations of the world, it is also the *firstfruits* of God's increase concerning a "spiritual" nation God would "raise up" as well.

In Jeremiah 2:1–3, God is referring to the love of Israel's betrothal, when Israel is referred to *"...as holiness to the Lord, the firstfruits of His increase!"* It also says concerning those who were holy unto the Lord, that they went after Him in a land not *yet* sown, while they were still in the wilderness.

In other words, *before* the *physical* land which would define the *literal* nation of Israel would manifest in the world, there was a *spiritual* manifestation which took place first. Jeremiah 2:1–3, says the following:

> *"Moreover the word of the LORD came to me, saying,*
> *'Go and cry in the hearing of JERUSALEM,' saying,*
> *'Thus says the LORD: 'I REMEMBER YOU, The*
> *KINDNESS of your YOUTH, The LOVE of your*
> *BETROTHAL, When you WENT AFTER ME in the*

WILDERNESS, In a LAND not SOWN. Israel was HOLINESS to the LORD, the FIRSTFRUITS of His INCREASE. All that devour him will OFFEND; DISASTER will come UPON them,' says the LORD.'" (Jer. 2:1–3, NKJV) (emphasis added).

Therefore, this passage of Scripture in Jeremiah 2:1–3, is not only referring to the *physical* land which comprises the nation of Israel, which is geographically located in the Middle East. It is also referring to a group of people who comprise a "spiritual" nation that is referred to as Israel.

It is for this very reason, this Scripture in Jeremiah 2:1–3, is also referring to all disciples of Jesus Christ, those who have now been grafted into the commonwealth of Israel based on Ephesians 2:11–13.

Moreover, all *true* disciples of Jesus Christ are "spiritual" descendants of Abraham, the "Father of Many Nations," and "heirs" according to the promises God gave Abraham and his descendants when He established the *everlasting* covenant with him.

This includes all twelve tribes of Israel, from both the House of Judah and the House of Israel (Jacob/Joseph/Ephraim). In Jesus Christ, *spiritually* speaking, we became the One New Man when Jesus died on the cross at Calvary based on Ephesians 2:14–17.

Yet we remain a "house" divided, *physically* speaking, which I will cover in-depth in Chapter 63 of Book 3.

What God is saying to His people based on Jeremiah 2:1–3, is this: He remembers the love and kindness we had for Him when we first received Jesus Christ as our Lord and Savior, although we were still in the wilderness. However, since this time, many who call themselves by His name—Christians, have allowed our love for Him and others to grow cold, because we have left our first love—Jesus Christ!

When God first called us out of the world (the wilderness) to share in the "covenant" promises of inheriting the Promised Land of eternal life, we were so enamored by His kindness and love for us, we, in turn, loved Him back with all our heart, soul, mind, and strength.

It was during the courtship phase of our relationship with the One who captivated our heart; we would do anything to please the One who first loved us. Therefore, we pledged everything we were, in exchange for everything He was and could give us as our husband, as we took a solemn vow to spend the rest of our lives living for Him, and fostering a deeper intimacy with the *Lover of our Soul.*

We also vowed, no one else, or anything else, could compare to the love, hope, and promise we found in Him. Thus, we were deeply committed, and only had eyes for Him—our husband, our Savior, and the Redeemer of our soul!

We also pledged a vow of fidelity, pledging we would never be unfaithful to Him. In other words, we would not commit "spiritual" adultery, or fornication. As such, God had first place in our mind, and in our heart, therefore, we lived our life accordingly.

441

Who is Israel? Discovering our True Identity in Jesus Christ and Why it Matters! The Foundation

In this hour, God is saying to His people He remembers the love and kindness we had for Him in the beginning, and He is beckoning us to return to Him like we did when we first believed. Based on Isaiah 54:5 below, God is not only our Creator, our heavenly Father, and our husband. He is also our Redeemer, who is the Holy One of Israel. He is our all in all, and He is truly everything we could ever need or desire!

> *"For your Maker is your HUSBAND, The LORD of HOSTS is His NAME; And your Redeemer* [Jesus Christ] *is the HOLY ONE of ISRAEL; He is called the GOD of the whole EARTH."* (Isa. 54:5, NKJV).

As such, Jesus Christ is the "root" or "vine" of *spiritual* Israel. Therefore, His disciples are the *branches of righteousness*, which are grafted into "the" *Branch of Righteousness*—Jesus Christ, our King.

He is "executing" His *judgment* and His *righteousness* in the earth through us, His people, whom God promised King David He would "raise up" based on Jeremiah 23:5. We are the branches, and He is the vine. As such, we are grafted into the "root" of the Holy One of Israel—Jesus Christ, who is "the" "tree of life."

Also, notice based on Isaiah 54:5, the prophet is referring to Jesus Christ as our husband. This is before we have entered the *kingdom of heaven* where we will "consummate" our wedding during the "marriage supper of the Lamb," which shall be held during the final Feast of Tabernacles. Why does the prophet Isaiah say Jesus Christ is already our husband?

442

It is because of this fact: Jesus Christ, our Messiah, is Jewish. Therefore, we are *already* married to Him based on the "customs" of the *ancient* Jewish wedding ceremony. As such, we pledged our marriage vows to Him the moment we received Him as our Lord and Savior.

According to the "customs" of the *ancient* Jewish wedding ceremony, when a man and a woman became "betrothed" to one another, which we now refer to as an "engagement," they were considered husband and wife. This was based on a "covenant" agreement, which is a binding, legal, written contract, between the man and the woman.

In addition, according to Jewish law, when a man and a woman mutually promise to marry each other at some future time, they must remain faithful to each other by remaining pure (a virgin) until they consummate their wedding. This is the bedrock of the terms and conditions of the covenant they agreed to when the young man went to the father's house of the prospective bride and offered to pay the price for his bride, which is part of the "betrothal" contract.

Then, if the father approves of the marriage, the bride is called in, and they all drink a cup of wine together. By drinking the cup of wine, the bride promises to be faithful and be committed to the bridegroom, until he comes back for her. The bridegroom then goes to his father's house to build a chamber in his father's house.

At the "appointed" time, only after the bridegroom's father determines it is time for his son to go and get his bride, and bring her back to his house, will the "consummation" of the wedding take place.

If you haven't already connected the *spiritual* significance of what this means for the body of Christ, who is also referred to as the *bride of Christ*, then I shall spell it out for you.

When God first called us out of the world (the wilderness when we were still lost), it was because He loved us so much He was willing to pay an extremely high price for His bride, to bring her back into a "Marriage Covenant" with Him.

Therefore, *Yehovah*, our heavenly Father, who is the Father of the bride, required His only *begotten* Son—Jesus Christ, to be sacrificed. This act of His sacrificial love for His bride required Him to pay the ultimate price, which cost Him His very life. Hence, on the cross at Calvary, He shed His precious blood for us.

Jesus' blood is "the" cup (*lot* or *fate*) of the New Covenant we drank from, *symbolically* speaking when we received God's only *begotten* Son, Jesus Christ, as the Lord of our life. Jesus Christ is the *Savior of the World,* because of what He did on the cross.

Jesus Christ shed His blood for His bride because this was the "bride-price" the father of the bride required from His Son, to take her back into His house as His wife.

Because Jesus Christ shed His precious blood for His bride, this is the "sign" of the New Covenant. This is substantiated in Matthew

26:28, which says, *"For this is My BLOOD of the NEW COVENANT, which is SHED for many for the REMISSION of SINS."* (NKJV) (emphasis added).

As such, when we "received" Jesus Christ as both our Savior and the Lord of our life, we became the *bride of Christ, spiritually* speaking.

Again, Jesus' blood is the price Jesus was *willing* to pay for us to become His bride based on the "bride-price" His Father required.

Therefore, since our bridegroom paid a high cost for us, His bride, what this means is this: We are no longer single and available to anyone else—we were purchased (redeemed) by His blood. As such, we are no longer able to do only "what" we want, "when" we want, based on "what" we deem right in our own eyes!

This means we cannot continue to live independently for all the reasons substantiated in First Corinthians 6:19–20 below:

> *"Or do you not KNOW that YOUR BODY is the TEMPLE of the HOLY SPIRIT who is in you, whom you have from God, and you are not your own? For you were BOUGHT at a PRICE; therefore GLORIFY God in YOUR BODY and in YOUR SPIRIT, which are God's."* (1 Cor. 6:19–20, NKJV) (emphasis added).

Now let's continue to learn about the "betrothal" contract, which is a binding, legal, written contract, which is between the two parties who are to be husband and wife. God's part of the contract which He established with us under the New Covenant was fulfilled (consummated, executed, and ratified [confirmed]) with the blood of His only *begotten* Son, Jesus Christ, who was and is *the Word* made flesh.

Therefore, the terms and conditions of this binding "legal" agreement we entered into when we received Jesus Christ as our Lord and Savior, is based on the whole counsel of God's Word. Jesus tells us in John 14:15, *"If you LOVE me, keep My COMMANDMENTS."* (NKJV) (emphasis added).

Moreover, God always keeps His end of the covenant; however, the "betrothal" contract depends upon the actions of both parties involved.

Thus, *we* break covenant with God when we commit "spiritual" adultery or fornication. We do this by not remaining pure and holy (virgins), *when* we chase after the false gods of the world, have idols in our lives, or live according to the "customs," "traditions," and "doctrines" of men, instead of the commandments of God.

According to God's Word, which contains the terms and conditions for the "betrothal" contract, there are *only* two "biblical" reasons for ending a marriage which is as follows:

1. Adultery
2. Abandonment by an "unbeliever"

And, the same two reasons apply to us when we break our "Covenant of Marriage" with God.

As such, we are "adulterers" when we do not live according to God's commandments based on the whole counsel of His Word, including our heavenly Father's instructions found in the Torah. Also, *if* we are not "walking" in love, then we can "profess" with our lips all we want we are His, but in God's eyes, *we* have broken our "Covenant of Marriage" with Him.

And, unless we repent and return to our first love—Jesus Christ, then we have voided the "marriage" contract with our heavenly Father, which Jesus died to "restore" and "reconcile" us back to. Thus, we have no right to expect to inherit the "covenant" promises thereof.

When you learn about the significance of the *everlasting* covenant God established with Abraham and his descendants, you will know beyond a shadow of a doubt the reason why God told Abraham He would make him into a great nation, bless him, and make his name great. It was for this reason: Abraham had faith in God, which was evidenced by his obedience.

Above all else, Abraham obeyed *Yehôvah's* commandments and His Voice. Therefore, *Yehôvah* did indeed keep all the promises He made to Abraham based on the *everlasting* covenant God established with him. So much so, the genealogy of Jesus Christ begins with Abraham, rather than Adam, or Seth!

In addition, God told Abraham all the people on the earth would be blessed through him—the "Father of Many Nations," because of this fact: Abraham "walked" *faithfully* before God according to the terms and conditions spelled out by *Yehôvah* in Deuteronomy 28:1–2, which says the following:

447

> "Now it shall come to pass, if [the word "if" makes this promise conditional] you diligently OBEY the VOICE of the LORD your God, to OBSERVE carefully all His COMMANDMENTS which I COMMAND you TODAY, that the LORD your God will set you HIGH ABOVE all NATIONS of the EARTH. And all these BLESSINGS shall COME UPON YOU and OVERTAKE you, BECAUSE you OBEY the VOICE of the LORD YOUR GOD..." (Deut. 28:1–2, NKJV) (emphasis added).

Again, Abraham walked before God based on God's terms and conditions of "walking" in a covenant relationship with Him. This was *before* Moses gave the children of Israel the terms and conditions of "walking" in a covenant relationship with *Yehovah*, during the very first Feast of Weeks (*Shavuot* or *Pentecost*), which took place at the base of Mount Sinai. This pivotal event is detailed in Exodus Chapters 19 and 20—something you should take the time to read on your own.

Now let's compare Deuteronomy 28:1–2, with the words from the Lord for all the children of Israel based on Exodus 19:3–6, which says the following:

> "And Moses WENT UP to God, and the LORD called to him from the mountain, saying, 'Thus you shall say to the HOUSE of JACOB, and tell the CHILDREN of ISRAEL: 'You have seen what I did to the Egyptians, and how I bore you on eagles' wings and brought you to Myself. Now therefore, if [the word "if" makes this

promise conditional] *you will indeed OBEY My VOICE and KEEP My COVENANT, then* [based on the condition of whether or not we will "obey" His Voice and "keep" His covenant] *you shall be a SPECIAL TREASURE to Me ABOVE all PEOPLE; for all the EARTH is Mine.'"* (Exod. 19:3–6, NKJV) (emphasis added).

Now let's look at what the New Testament says about the body of Christ based on the terms and conditions of "walking" in a "covenant" relationship with *Yehôva̓h*, our heavenly Father, and His only *begotten* Son, Jesus Christ, who is our Lord and Savior, based on the following Scriptures:

*"GO therefore and make **DISCIPLES*** [1] [G3100: **mathēteuo̓**: *to become a pupil,* transitively to *disciple, that is, enrol as scholar; instruct, teach*] *of all the NATIONS, baptizing them in the NAME of the Father and of the Son and of the Holy Spirit, TEACHING THEM TO OBSERVE all THINGS THAT I HAVE COMMANDED YOU; and lo, I am with you always, even to the end of the age. Amen."* (Matt. 28:19–20, NKJV) (emphasis added).

"But you are a CHOSEN GENERATION, a ROYAL PRIESTHOOD, a HOLY NATION, His own SPECIAL PEOPLE, that you may proclaim the praises of Him who called you out of darkness into His marvelous light..." (1 Peter 2:9, NKJV) (emphasis added).

Who is Israel? Discovering our True Identity in Jesus Christ and Why it Matters! The Foundation

Notice in Matthew 28:19–20, Jesus is reiterating in the New Testament we are to make "disciples" of all the nations, and teach them to "observe" (guard, hold fast to, and keep) all, not some, of the things He has commanded us.

As such, since *Yehovah* and Jesus Christ are the same God, yet they are two distinct Persons in the Godhead, when Jesus tells us to "observe" all the things He has commanded us, He is also referring to our heavenly Father's instructions written in the Torah, for this reason: When Jesus gave us this commandment, the New Testament was not yet written.

Furthermore, Jesus commanded us to make "disciples" of all the nations. He did not say make "converts." The definition of a "disciple" is to enroll as a scholar, instruct, and teach new converts to the faith the whole counsel of God's Word, rather than try to "convert" people simply by saying a sinner's prayer. In fact, God's Word tells us in Psalm 19:7, it is the "law" of the Lord, which is perfect, and His "law" is what "converts" a person's soul!

Therefore, when we evangelize people and just have them say a sinner's prayer without properly "discipling" them based on the whole counsel of God's Word, and issuing an admonition to them to repent and stop sinning, it is a mockery to God because *this* practice is not biblical at all!

Then we wonder *why* the majority of believers in the body of Christ do not "live" or "walk" according to the whole counsel of God's Word?

When we are told in First Peter 2:9, that we are a *chosen* generation, a *royal* priesthood, and a *holy* nation—His own *special* people—so we may proclaim the praises of Him who has called us out of darkness into His marvelous light, we need to take notice of this fact: This passage of Scripture does not spell out the terms and conditions of "walking" in a covenant relationship with our heavenly Father at all! Why?

Jesus expects us to be a "disciple" (student) of the Torah once we become saved, which requires us to study the Old Testament. God's instructions are still applicable to New Covenant believers as they were in the day they were spoken, written, and decreed at the base of Mount Sinai long ago for all twelve tribes of Israel. This is based on the reasons stated in Deuteronomy 29:12–13, which says the following:

> *"... that YOU may ENTER into COVENANT with the LORD your God, and into His OATH, which the LORD YOUR God makes with you TODAY, that He may establish you TODAY as a PEOPLE for Himself, and that He may be God to you, just as He has SPOKEN to you, and just as He has SWORN to YOUR FATHERS, to ABRAHAM, ISAAC, and JACOB."* (Deut. 29:12–13, NKJV) (emphasis added).

Next, in Deuteronomy 29:14–15, pay attention to this fact: Moses specifically says regarding the covenant *Yehôvah* commanded him to make with all the children of Israel in the land of Moab, and he "renewed" it with the children of Israel in Horeb, this *same* covenant applies to those of us who were not there on *that*

451

particular day long ago. In addition, this *first* covenant was "renewed" and "ratified" (executed) with the blood of Jesus Christ, who became the "mediator" of the New Covenant where God has now put His laws in our mind and written them on our hearts, rather than on two tablets of stone. Deuteronomy 29:14–15, says the following:

> *"I make this COVENANT and this OATH, not WITH YOU ALONE, but with him who stands here with us today before the LORD our God, AS WELL AS WITH HIM WHO IS NOT HERE WITH US TODAY..."*
> (Deut. 29:14–15, NKJV) (emphasis added).

This means this "covenant" and this "oath" applies to all of *Yehôvâh's* children who came forth on the earth throughout the *synergy of the ages,* since the time *this* generation of Israelites stood in the land of Moab and Horeb so long ago. This "covenant" which God promised to Abraham and his descendants, is a result of the *everlasting* covenant God established with Abraham.

Moreover, this *same* "covenant" and "oath" was ratified by the precious blood of Jesus Christ who came to fulfill (consummate, execute, and ratify [confirm]) all the *everlasting* covenants (plural) *Yehôvâh* has established with mankind and creation throughout the *synergy of the ages.*

In the next chapter, we will discover why the nation of Israel is the first *physical* nation in the world established by God as the *firstfruits* of His increase, because of the *everlasting* covenant He made with Abraham and his descendants.

452

CHAPTER 17

THE NATION OF ISRAEL IS THE FIRST "PHYSICAL" NATION IN THE WORLD GOD ESTABLISHED AS THE FIRSTFRUITS OF HIS INCREASE

As I have said before, but it bears repeating, everything God chooses to do, His will is first established in the *spiritual* realm, before it shall manifest in the *physical* earthly realm. Therefore, there is a manifestation of His will, *spiritually* speaking, and *physically* speaking, also.

First, we will look at the *literal* nation of Israel, which was established by God in the *physical* earthly realm, God originally established for His chosen people—the Hebrew people.

As substantiated in Exodus Chapter 5, when God first sent Moses to tell Pharaoh, the *king of Egypt*, to let His people go so they may hold a "feast" to Him in the wilderness, the Lord first appeared to Moses in a *flame of fire* from the midst of a bush.

This is when God first revealed His identity to Moses as the God of his father—the God of Abraham, Isaac, and Jacob. This is based on Exodus 3:6, which says the following:

> *"Moreover He said, 'I am the God of your FATHER— the God of ABRAHAM, the God of ISAAC, and the God of JACOB* [Israel].*' And Moses HID his FACE,*

for he was AFRAID to LOOK upon God." (Exod. 3:6, NKJV) (emphasis added).

In Exodus 3:18, God specifically tells Moses He is *Yehôvah*, the God of the Hebrew people. Then God commands Moses to lead His Hebrew people out of their bondage from their enslavement to Pharaoh, the *king of Egypt. Yehôvah* commands Moses to take His Hebrew people into the wilderness where they would begin their exodus out of Egypt into the Promised Land—a land flowing with milk and honey. The land God promised to Abraham, because of the *everlasting* covenant *Yehôvah* established with him and his descendants. Exodus 3:18, says the following:

> *"Then they will heed YOUR VOICE; and you shall COME, YOU and the ELDERS of ISRAEL, to the KING of EGYPT; and YOU shall SAY to him, 'The LORD God of the HEBREWS has MET with US; and now, please, let us go THREE DAYS' JOURNEY into the WILDERNESS, that we may SACRIFICE to the LORD our God.'"* (Exod. 3:18, NKJV) (emphasis added).

Moreover, we must take notice of what God tells Moses to say to Pharaoh in Exodus 4:22–23. God specifically says in Exodus 4:22, *"...ISRAEL is My SON, My FIRSTBORN..."* (NKJV) (emphasis added).

As such, in Exodus 4:22–23, God is saying concerning His Hebrew people—the Israelites, the following: They are His *firstborn* son as it relates to a "nation" of people. In other words, Israel was the

454

"firstborn," or the "firstfruits," of all the other nations in the entire world, before the *literal* nation of Israel was born! This is substantiated in Exodus 4:22–23, which says the following:

> *"Then you shall SAY to Pharaoh, 'Thus says the LORD: 'ISRAEL is My SON, My FIRSTBORN. So I say to you, LET My SON GO that HE may SERVE Me. But if you REFUSE to LET HIM GO, indeed I will KILL your SON, your FIRSTBORN.'"* (Exod. 4:22–23, NKJV) (emphasis added).

However, as I have already conveyed, the ultimate fulfillment of this Scripture is referring to God's only *begotten* Son—Jesus Christ, who is the "root" of all Israel (the *root of David*). As such, both the Jews from the House of Judah and those of us who were formerly Gentiles from the House of Israel (Jacob/Joseph/Ephraim), are the branches of the "fig tree" nation of Israel.

The total fulfillment concerning the nation of people, who are called Israel, refers to those of us who place our faith and trust in Jesus Christ, who is our Maker—the Lord of Hosts. He is also our Husband, and our Redeemer, who is called the Holy One of Israel.

This is substantiated in Isaiah 54:5, which proclaims, *"For your MAKER is your HUSBAND, The LORD of HOSTS is His NAME; And your REDEEMER is the HOLY ONE of ISRAEL; He is called the GOD of the whole EARTH."* (NKJV) (emphasis added).

In addition, even though Moses was to tell Pharaoh they would be going on a three days' journey into the wilderness so they could sacrifice to the Lord, God had other plans. And, it would come to pass; He would orchestrate the greatest escape ever recorded in history. God did this for this reason: He "remembered" His *everlasting* covenant He established with Abraham, and God promised Abraham, He would set His Hebrew people free. Yet this great "escape" would commence after God *first* displayed His power, and His glory, to Pharaoh, the Egyptians, and His chosen people.

THE NUMBER 40 IN THE BIBLE IS RELATED TO "PREPARATION," "PROBATION," OR "TRIAL"

Based on the written biblical accounts of the Old Testament, we are told their exodus into the Promised Land should have been an eleven-day journey. However, due to their "unbelief" and "disobedience," it took forty years for the Hebrew people to cross over into the Promised Land under the leadership of Joshua after Moses died. This is based on the following Scriptures:

> *"It is ELEVEN DAYS' JOURNEY from Horeb by way of Mount Seir to Kadesh Barnea."* (Deut. 1:2, NKJV) (emphasis added).

> *"So the Lord's ANGER was aroused AGAINST Israel, and He made them WANDER in the WILDERNESS FORTY YEARS, until all the GENERATION that had DONE EVIL in the SIGHT of the LORD was GONE."* (Num. 32:13, NKJV) (emphasis added).

Therefore, the number forty, biblically speaking, is always related to "preparation," "probation," or "trial," and there are countless examples found throughout the Scriptures to substantiate this. However, to validate this truth, I will provide the following four examples:

1. Forty years referred to the time frame when God caused it to rain upon the earth, and He destroyed the *wicked* inhabitants off the face of the earth during the flood. This is based on Genesis 7:4, which says, *"For after seven more days I will cause it to rain on the earth FORTY DAYS and FORTY NIGHTS, and I will destroy from the face of the earth all living things that I have made."* (NKJV) (emphasis added).

2. Forty years referred to the time frame when the Israelites wandered for forty years in the wilderness. This is based on Deuteronomy 8:2, which says, *"And you shall REMEMBER that the LORD your God LED you all the WAY these FORTY YEARS in the WILDERNESS, to HUMBLE you and TEST you, to KNOW WHAT was in YOUR HEART, whether you would KEEP His COMMANDMENTS or NOT."* (NKJV) (emphasis added).

Why did God choose forty years for the Hebrew people to wander in the wilderness? We are told the answer to this question in Numbers 14:34, which says, *"According to the NUMBER of the DAYS in which you SPIED OUT the LAND, FORTY DAYS, for EACH DAY you shall BEAR YOUR GUILT ONE YEAR, namely FORTY YEARS, and you shall know My REJECTION."* (NKJV) (emphasis added).

3. Forty years referred to the time frame when Moses went up to the mountain to meet with God. It was then he received the tablets of stone—the Ten Commandments, God wrote with His own finger so Moses could teach the Hebrew people the terms and conditions of the "Covenant of Marriage," God first established through His servant Moses, which is referred to as the *Mosaic* Covenant. This is based on Exodus 24:18, which says, *"So Moses went into the MIDST of the CLOUD and WENT UP into the MOUNTAIN. And Moses was on the mountain FORTY DAYS and FORTY NIGHTS."* (NKJV) (emphasis added).

    Moses prophetically enacted what Jesus would do later when He was led into the wilderness by the Spirit. As such, Moses was required to fast during a period of forty days and forty nights as well. This is substantiated in Exodus 34:28, which proclaims, *"So he [Moses] was there with the Lord FORTY DAYS and FORTY NIGHTS; he [Moses] neither ATE BREAD nor DRANK WATER. And He [Yehovâh] WROTE on the TABLETS the WORDS of the COVENANT, the TEN COMMANDMENTS."* (NKJV) (emphasis added).

    This is the Book of the Covenant; all the Israelites would "affirm" in Exodus 24:1–8, which says the following:

    > *"Now He said to Moses, 'COME UP to the LORD, YOU and AARON, NADAB and ABIHU, and SEVENTY OF THE ELDERS OF ISRAEL, and WORSHIP from AFAR. And MOSES ALONE SHALL COME NEAR THE LORD,*

> *but THEY shall not COME NEAR; nor shall the PEOPLE GO UP with HIM.'"* (Exod. 24:1–2, NKJV) (emphasis added).

> *"So Moses came and told the PEOPLE all the WORDS of the LORD and all the JUDGMENTS. And all the PEOPLE ANSWERED WITH ONE VOICE and said, 'ALL THE WORDS WHICH THE LORD HAS SAID WE WILL DO.' And Moses WROTE all the WORDS of the LORD. And he rose early in the morning, and BUILT AN ALTAR at the foot of the mountain, and TWELVE PILLARS ACCORDING to the TWELVE TRIBES of ISRAEL. Then he sent young men of the children of Israel, who offered burnt offerings and sacrificed peace offerings of oxen to the LORD. And Moses took HALF the BLOOD and put it in basins, and HALF the BLOOD he sprinkled on the altar."* (Exod. 24:3–6, NKJV) (emphasis added).

Next in Exodus 24:7–8, we are told that Moses was the "mediator" of this covenant, and he used the blood from the sacrifice of animals to sprinkle on the people to "confirm" this covenant with God, and His people.

This was "the blood" of the *first* covenant; the LORD made with all the children of Israel according to all these words. Exodus 24:7–8, says the following:

> "Then he [Moses] took the BOOK of the
> COVENANT and READ in the HEARING of
> the PEOPLE. And they said, 'All that the
> LORD has said WE WILL DO, and be
> OBEDIENT.' And Moses TOOK the BLOOD,
> SPRINKLED IT on the PEOPLE, and said,
> 'This is the BLOOD of the COVENANT which
> the LORD has made with you ACCORDING to
> ALL these WORDS.'" (Exod. 24:7–8, NKJV)
> (emphasis added).

Later, this Book of the Covenant, with the Ten
Commandments at the heart of it, would be "reconfirmed"
and "ratified" with the blood of our "Passover Lamb." Jesus
Christ would become the "mediator" of the New Covenant,
where God would now put His laws in our mind, and write
them on our hearts, instead of on two tablets of stone.

Therefore, it would come to pass, Jesus would use His blood
to "confirm" (ratify) the Book of the Law—the Torah,
written by Moses to "strengthen" this *first* covenant.

Also, worth mentioning is this fact: In the Book of
Deuteronomy God details the "blessings" we will reap for
"walking" in a covenant relationship with Him, versus the
"curses" we will reap for "breaking" covenant with Him. We
need to realize we shall reap these "blessings," or "curses,"
while we are still living on the earth.

God gave the Book of the Law to all twelve tribes of the

children of Israel, which are His terms and conditions of "walking" in a "Marriage Covenant" with Him.

In addition, God gave this "covenant" through His servant Moses at the base of Mount Sinai during the very first enactment and observation of the Feast of Weeks (*Shavuot* or *Pentecost*).

This feast is our heavenly Father's *fourth* holy convocation out of seven, which is detailed in Leviticus Chapter 23. This holy convocation, like the rest, is an *everlasting* ordinance (statute) for all eternity.

This is "the" feast Moses and Aaron referred to when they told Pharaoh in Exodus Chapter 5, to let God's people go so they may hold a feast to Him in the wilderness. This is based on Exodus 5:1, which says, *"Afterward Moses and Aaron went in and told Pharaoh, ' Thus says the LORD God of Israel: 'Let My people go, that they may hold a FEAST to Me in the wilderness.'"* (NKJV) (emphasis added).

4.   Forty refers to the time frame Jesus fasted, and He was led by the Spirit into the wilderness when He was tempted by Satan.

This is based on Matthew 4:1–3, which says, *"Then Jesus was LED UP by the SPIRIT into the WILDERNESS to be TEMPTED by the DEVIL. And when He had fasted FORTY DAYS and FORTY NIGHTS, afterward He was hungry. Now when the TEMPTER came to Him, he said, 'If You are the Son of God, command that these stones become bread.'"* (NKJV) (emphasis added).

Who is Israel? Discovering our True Identity in Jesus Christ and Why it Matters! The Foundation

Based on Matthew 4:1–3, it is worth mentioning this fact: The "presence" of God does not keep Satan from testing us at all, which is based on the fact Jesus was the Son of God.

Rather, as Jesus demonstrated for us, we "overcome" our testing by the tempter (Satan), by "speaking" and "standing" on the Word of God as we submit to God first and foremost. This is substantiated in James 4:7, which says, *"Therefore SUBMIT to God. RESIST the DEVIL and he will FLEE from you."* (NKJV) (emphasis added).

As I have substantiated based on God's Word the number forty, biblically speaking, is always related to "preparation," "probation," or "trial."

It is for this reason, based on Deuteronomy 31:2–4, we are specifically told it was Joshua, not Moses, who led the Hebrew people (referred to as the Israelites), into the Promised Land. This was after they spent forty long years being tried and prepared by God before they crossed over the Jordan River to finally take possession of the Promised Land.

Remember, the word "Hebrew" in Aramaic is the word "'ibrîy," which comes from the root word "abar," meaning to "Cross Over," or, it means to "Pass Over," *spiritually,* and *behaviorally,* speaking. Deuteronomy 31:2–4, says the following:

> *"And he* [Moses] *said to them: 'I am one hundred and twenty years old today* [it was Moses' 120th birthday]. *I can NO LONGER GO OUT and COME*

462

*IN. Also the L*ORD* has said to me, 'YOU shall not CROSS OVER this Jordan.' The L*ORD* your God Himself CROSSES OVER before you; He* [God Himself] *will DESTROY these NATIONS from before you, and you shall DISPOSSESS them. JOSHUA* [1] [2] [3] [H3091: *Y*ʻhoṡhûa̅: *Jehovah-saved;* H3068: *Y*ḣovaḣ: the self-Existent or Eternal Jehovah; H3467: *Yásha*: to *be open, wide* or *free,* that is, (by implication) to *be safe*; causatively to *free* or *succor;* bring salvation, save (savior), get victory] *himself CROSSES OVER before you, just as the L*ORD* has said. And the L*ORD* will do to them as He did to Sihon and Og, the kings of the Amorites and their land, when He destroyed them.'"* (Deut. 31:2–4, NKJV) (emphasis added).

Yahshua is a common alternative form of the Hebrew name "Yʻhoṡhûa," which is synonymous with the name Joshua.

This name corresponds to the Greek spelling "Iesous," which comes from the English spelling of the name Jesus.

Furthermore, the Hebrew spelling of *Yahshua* (יֹשׁוּע) appears in some of the later books of the Hebrew Bible, and Joshua, the son of Nun, is referred to as Joshua, the High Priest. [4]

Therefore, long before *the Word* was manifested on the earth in a body of flesh and blood as the Son of Man in the Person of Jesus Christ, He brought salvation to the children of Israel, based on the *everlasting* covenant *Yehôvaḣ* established with Abraham. When Jesus Christ died on the cross at Calvary, He confirmed (ratified) the *first* covenant *Yehôvaḣ* established through His servant Moses with all twelve tribes of the children of Israel at the base of Mount Sinai.

Again, this *first* covenant details the terms and conditions of us "walking" in a covenant relationship with our heavenly Father, which applies to those who were not there on *that* particular day long ago.

JESUS CHRIST IS THE "MEDIATOR" OF THE NEW COVENANT WHERE GOD'S LAWS ARE IN OUR MIND AND WRITTEN ON THE TABLET OF OUR HEART BECAUSE OUR "LAWGIVER" NOW LIVES IN US

Jesus Christ became the "mediator" of the New Covenant where God has now put His laws in our mind and written them on the tablets of our hearts, rather than on two tablets of stone.

As such, the Book of the Covenant Moses read to all the children of Israel, who *unanimously* consented to this "Covenant of Marriage," now lives inside of us—on the "altar" of our hearts.

So, we are without excuse for not walking according to all the words the Lord has said we should "do" to "walk" in a covenant relationship with Him.

Especially since we now have the Holy Spirit living on the inside of us, who gives us God's grace and power to obey His laws, which Jesus did not abolish!

464

In fact, Jesus substantiates this truth in Matthew 5:17–18, which says the following:

> *"DO NOT THINK I have COME to ABOLISH* [5]
> *[G2647: kataluo: disintegrate, demolish, or dissolve]*
> *the LAW* [6] *[G3551: nomos: regulation; specifically of
> Moses, including the volume and the gospel] or the
> PROPHETS; I have NOT COME to ABOLISH* [5]
> *THEM [the law, or the prophets] but to FULFILL* [7]
> [8] *[G4137: pleroo: consummate, execute, and ratify]
> THEM [the law, or the prophets]. For truly I tell you,
> until HEAVEN and EARTH DISAPPEAR, NOT the
> SMALLEST LETTER, NOR the LEAST STROKE of a
> PEN, will by ANY MEANS DISAPPEAR from the LAW*
> [6] *until EVERYTHING is ACCOMPLISHED."* (Matt.
> 5:17–18, NKJV) (emphasis added).

Has heaven and earth disappeared? No! Then not the smallest letter, or the least stroke of a pen, has by any means disappeared from the law until everything spoken from the mouth of the "Prophets of Old" is accomplished (fulfilled), which shall happen at the second coming of Jesus Christ.

I cover the full significance of what Jesus is saying to us in Matthew 5:17–18, in Chapter 47 of Book 3, because it is critical for God's people to fully understand "how," and in "what" ways, this statement is relevant to New Covenant believers.

In fact, this "erroneous" belief by many in the body of Christ that Jesus has "abolished" the law, and the Old Covenant is now "obsolete," is leading many of God's people astray!

465

Again, there is *only* one Scripture in the entire Word of God that refers to the *first* covenant as the "old" covenant. This is based on what the apostle Paul says in Hebrews 8:13. Yet this is referring to the *order of the Priesthood* now being obsolete, God established in the Old Testament. It is not referring to the *first* covenant, *Yehôvâh* established through His servant Moses, with all twelve tribes of the children of Israel, being obsolete.

Therefore, this "erroneous" belief by many in the body of Christ that Jesus "abolished" the law, and the Old Covenant is now "obsolete," is because this is what is being taught by the false prophets and the false teachers in the body of Christ.

It is for this very reason, I devote Chapter 40 of Book 3, to expose, uproot, and tear down this false teaching.

On the cross Jesus joined both "houses" of Israel—the Jews from the House of Judah, and those of us who were formerly Gentiles from the House of Israel (Jacob/Joseph/Ephraim) into One New Man, *spiritually* speaking. As such, we are now "one" house, "one" kingdom, and "one" body of Christ. This is made possible by our faith in Jesus Christ period!

THE EXODUS OF THE HEBREW PEOPLE FROM EGYPT WAS BECAUSE GOD "REMEMBERED" HIS COVENANT WITH ABRAHAM

The exodus of the Hebrew people from their bondage in Egypt, and their enslavement by Pharaoh, the *King of Egypt*, into the

Promised Land, was the result of one of the promises God gave to Abraham when He established the *Abrahamic* Covenant with him. This is substantiated in Genesis 15:12–21, which says the following:

> *"Now when the sun was going down, a deep sleep fell upon Abram; and behold, horror and great darkness fell upon him. Then He said to Abram: 'Know certainly that YOUR DESCENDANTS will be STRANGERS in a LAND that is not THEIRS, and will SERVE them, and they will AFFLICT them FOUR HUNDRED YEARS* [This is talking about the Hebrew people's enslavement to Pharaoh, *King of Egypt*]. *And also the nation whom they serve I will JUDGE; afterward THEY SHALL COME OUT WITH GREAT POSSESSIONS. Now as for you* [Abraham], *you shall go to your fathers in peace; you shall be buried at a good old age. But in the FOURTH GENERATION they* [Abraham's descendants—the children of Israel] *shall RETURN HERE, for the INIQUITY of the AMORITES is NOT YET COMPLETE.'"* (Gen. 15:12–16, NKJV) (emphasis added).

> *"And it came to pass, when the sun went down and it was dark, that behold, there appeared a smoking oven and a burning torch that passed between those pieces. On the SAME DAY the LORD made a **COVENANT*** [9] [H1285: *bᵉrîyth*: a *compact* (made by passing between *pieces* of flesh)] *with ABRAM, saying: 'To YOUR DESCENDANTS I have GIVEN this LAND, from the river of Egypt to the great river, the River Euphrates—*

> the Kenites, the Kenezzites, the Kadmonites, the
> Hittites, the Perizzites, the Rephaim, the Amorites,
> the Canaanites, the Girgashites, and the Jebusites.'"
> (Gen. 15:17–21, NKJV) (emphasis added).

Also, take note of Genesis 15:14, which says, *"And also the NATION whom they serve I will JUDGE; afterward they shall COME OUT with GREAT POSSESSIONS..."* (NKJV) (emphasis added).

This is referring to the exodus of the Hebrew people after God poured out His judgment on Pharaoh and the Egyptians. This exodus included a great wealth transfer from the *wicked* to the *righteous* based on Exodus 3:22, Exodus 11:2, and Psalm 105:37 to list a few passages of Scripture, which will be fulfilled in the end times, as it was in the beginning.

This will happen when God releases His judgment on all the nations of the world during the tribulation period. I cover this subject of the great wealth transfer we can anticipate to take place in the days ahead in-depth in Chapter 35 of Book 2.

GOD'S "COVENANT" PROMISES CAN ONLY BE "LEGITIMATELY" CLAIMED FOR THOSE WHO "WALK" IN A "COVENANT" RELATIONSHIP WITH GOD, WHICH WILL BE EVIDENCED BY OUR OBEDIENCE

We must understand "what" our inheritance is because we are "heirs" of the promises God gave to Abraham and his descendants.

These promises are based on the *everlasting* covenant God established with Abraham due to his demonstrated obedience. And, so it is with us, Jesus' disciples.

God's "covenant" promises He gave to Abraham and his descendants, can *only* be "legitimately" claimed for those who "walk" in a "covenant" relationship with our heavenly Father, and our Lord and Savior Jesus Christ. This will be evidenced by us being obedient to His Voice, and His Word, *after* we become saved.

Yet this does not mean we will live perfectly "obedient" lives after we become saved. Nor, does our relationship with the Lord guarantee we will never sin for this reason: We all fall short of the glory of God. This is why we are told in First John 1:9, *if* we "confess" our sins, He is faithful, and just, to forgive us our sins, and to cleanse us from all unrighteousness.

As such, we must heed and practice this critical truth: God's people should take an inventory of our "walk" with the Lord on a daily basis, and be willing to repent at all times when we realize we have not walked according to the Spirit, and we have transgressed His laws.

GOD'S "COVENANT" PROMISES CONCERNING THE "LAND" HE PROMISED TO ABRAHAM AND HIS DESCENDANTS

The "covenant" promises of God—specifically concerning the "land" He promised Abraham and his descendants, was based on

Who is Israel? Discovering our True Identity in Jesus Christ and Why it Matters! The Foundation

Abraham's faith, trust, devotion, and obedience to God period! This would fulfill that which was spoken by the patriarch Jacob, and God's servant Moses, in Genesis 48:21–22, and Deuteronomy 31:2–4.

The truth is, the Israelites did not receive the "land" because of their "righteousness." This is clearly substantiated by Moses in Deuteronomy 9:4–6. In this Scripture, Moses is talking to the Israelites, just before they are finally ready to cross over the Jordan River, to take possession of the Promised Land. This land belonged to nations which were much greater and more powerful than they were. Nevertheless, this "land" was their inheritance based on one of the promises God swore by Himself, to give to Abraham, Isaac, and Jacob (Israel), and their descendants. Deuteronomy 9:4–6, says the following:

> "Do not THINK in YOUR HEART, after the LORD your God has CAST THEM OUT before you, saying, 'BECAUSE of MY RIGHTEOUSNESS the LORD has brought me in to POSSESS this LAND;' but it is BECAUSE of the WICKEDNESS of these NATIONS that the LORD is DRIVING THEM OUT FROM BEFORE YOU. It is not BECAUSE of YOUR RIGHTEOUSNESS or the UPRIGHTNESS of your HEART that you GO IN to POSSESS their land, BUT BECAUSE of the WICKEDNESS of these NATIONS that the LORD your God DRIVES THEM OUT from before you, and that He may FULFILL the WORD which the LORD SWORE to YOUR FATHERS, to ABRAHAM, ISAAC, and JACOB. Therefore

470

understand that the LORD your God is not GIVING YOU this GOOD LAND to POSSESS because of YOUR RIGHTEOUSNESS, for you are a STIFF-NECKED PEOPLE." (Deut. 9:4–6, NKJV) (emphasis added).

WHAT IS OUR RESPONSIBILITY TO KEEP THE TERMS AND CONDITIONS OF THE "MARRIAGE COVENANT" ONCE WE BECOME SAVED?

Since a "covenant" is a written compact, or contract, between God and His people, then as disciples of Jesus Christ we are expected to know the terms and conditions of "walking" in a covenant relationship with our heavenly Father, *Yehovah,* once we come to the saving knowledge of His only *begotten* Son, Jesus Christ, *after* we become saved.

Again, these terms and conditions of the "Covenant of Marriage" were written by God's servant Moses. Therefore, based on what Moses told the Israelites in Deuteronomy 10:12–13, this still applies to God's people today who are all "spiritual" descendants of Abraham, the "Father of Many Nations." Deuteronomy 10:12–13, says the following:

> *"And now, ISRAEL, what does the LORD your God REQUIRE of YOU, but to FEAR the LORD your God, to WALK in all His WAYS and to LOVE Him, to SERVE the LORD your God with all YOUR HEART and with all YOUR SOUL, and to KEEP the*

COMMANDMENTS (10) [H4687: *mitsvâh*: a command, whether human, or divine, (collectively the Law); (which was) commanded (-ment), law, ordinance, precept] *of the LORD and His* **STATUTES** (11) [H2708: *chûqqâh*: appointed *custom, manner,* or *ordinance*] *which I command you TODAY for your GOOD?"* (Deut. 10:12–13, NKJV) (emphasis added).

To reiterate, what does the Lord our God, require of us based on Deuteronomy 10:12–13?

1. To have the *reverential* fear of Him, which by the way, is the beginning of wisdom and knowledge based on Psalm 111:10, Proverbs 1:7, and Proverbs 9:10.

2. To WALK in all, not some, of His ways to the best of our ability with the help of His Holy Spirit, as we "learn" to crucify our flesh, submit to God, and resist the devil.

3. To LOVE Him with all our heart, with all our soul, and with all our mind.

4. To SERVE Him with all our heart, with all our soul, and with all our mind.

5. To KEEP His **commandments** (a divine command [collectively the law], which is a commandment, law, ordinance, and precept) and His **statutes** (appointed "custom," "manner," or "ordinance" [i.e., His seven holy convocations based on Leviticus 23, which are all *everlasting* statutes]).

Also, do we realize "tithes" and "offerings" are an *everlasting* ordinance based on Malachi 3:7–9?

Then Moses goes on to say the following: The Lord, our God, chose our ancestors, and their descendants, as the objects of His love *above* all the people on the earth, as it is to *this* very day. This is substantiated in Deuteronomy 10:14–16. The words of God's servant Moses still speaks to us beyond the grave, according to God's *eternal* Word, which is telling us to "circumcise" the foreskin of our hearts, and for us not to be *stiff-necked* any longer! Deuteronomy 10:14–16, says the following:

> *"Indeed heaven and the highest heavens belong to the LORD your God, also the earth with all that is in it. The LORD DELIGHTED ONLY in YOUR FATHERS, to LOVE THEM; and He CHOSE THEIR DESCENDANTS after THEM, you ABOVE ALL PEOPLES, as it is THIS DAY. Therefore CIRCUMCISE the FORESKIN of YOUR HEART, and be STIFF-NECKED no LONGER."* (Deut. 10:14–16, NKJV) (emphasis added).

Moses finishes this passage of Scripture by reiterating this indisputable truth: God's people must have the *reverential* fear of the Lord. And, as we serve Him, hold fast to Him, and take oaths in His Name, He deserves our praise, because of all the great and awesome things He has done. This passage of Scripture in Deuteronomy 10:20–22, is referring to all the "spiritual" descendants of Abraham, which started out with only seventy people who went down to Egypt. Deuteronomy 10:20–22, proclaims the following:

> *"You shall FEAR the* LORD *your God; you shall SERVE Him, and to Him you shall HOLD FAST, and TAKE OATHS in His NAME. He is YOUR PRAISE, and He is YOUR GOD, who has DONE FOR YOU these GREAT and AWESOME THINGS which your EYES have SEEN. Your FATHERS went DOWN to EGYPT with SEVENTY PERSONS, and NOW the* LORD *your God has MADE YOU as the STARS of HEAVEN in MULTITUDE."* (Deut. 10:20–22, NKJV) (emphasis added).

Abraham's descendants are now as numerous as the *stars of heaven* in multitude, because God is faithful, and He is a covenant-keeping God!

Just as our fathers went down to Egypt with seventy people, Jesus appointed and sent out seventy people into *every* "city" and "place," where He was about to go. This is substantiated in Luke 10:1–3, which says, *"After these things the Lord appointed SEVENTY others also, and SENT THEM TWO BY TWO before His face into every CITY and PLACE where He Himself was about to GO. Then He said to them, 'The harvest truly is great, but the laborers are few; therefore pray the Lord of the harvest to send out laborers into His harvest. Go your way; behold, I send you out as lambs among wolves.'"* (NKJV) (emphasis added).

In addition, when Moses led this *great* multitude of God's people out of Egypt during the exodus to begin their journey to the Promised Land, God's Word says there were approximately six hundred thousand men on foot, besides children. This is based on Exodus 12:37–38, which says the following:

> *"Then the children of Israel journeyed from Rameses to Succoth, about six hundred thousand* [600,000] *MEN on foot, besides children. A **MIXED** (12)* [H6154: *'êreb:* a *mixture,* (or *mongrel* race); Arabia, mingled people, mixed (multitude), woof] ***MULTITUDE*** (13) [H7227: *rab:* abundant (in quantity, size, age, number, rank, quality)] *WENT UP with THEM also, and flocks and herds—a great deal of livestock."* (Exod. 12:37–38, NKJV) (emphasis added).

While this "mixed" multitude was in the wilderness, and they feasted on the manna God provided them, it is interesting to note God's Word specifically refers to this "mixed" multitude as the House of Israel. This is based on Exodus 16:31, which says, *"And the HOUSE of ISRAEL called its name Manna. And it was like white coriander seed, and the taste of it was like wafers made with honey."* (NKJV) (emphasis added).

GOD HAS "MULTIPLIED" ABRAHAM'S "SPIRITUAL" AND "PHYSICAL" DESCENDANTS AS THE *STARS OF HEAVEN* AND THE *SAND WHICH IS ON THE SEASHORE*

Now over four thousand years later, based on the promises God made to Abraham, as substantiated in the Scriptures listed on the following page, God has indeed "multiplied" Abraham's "spiritual" and "physical" descendants as the *stars of heaven* and the *sand which is on the seashore*! It is for this very reason; God told Moses in Exodus 3:6, *"...I am the God of YOUR FATHER—the GOD of ABRAHAM..."* (NKJV) (emphasis added).

> *"And I will make your* [Abraham's] *DESCENDANTS multiply as the stars of heaven; I will GIVE to YOUR DESCENDANTS all these LANDS; and in YOUR SEED all the NATIONS of the EARTH shall be BLESSED; because Abraham OBEYED My **VOICE*** (14) [H6963: *qôl:* to *call* aloud; a *voice* or *sound;* proclamation, thundering voice + yell] *and KEPT My **CHARGE*** (15) [H4931: *mishmereth: watch*, that is, the act (*custody*) or (concretely) the *sentry*, the *post;* objectively *preservation,* or (concretely) *safe;* figuratively *observance,* that is, (abstractly) *duty*], *My **COMMANDMENTS*** (10) [H4687: *mitsvâh:* a *command*, whether human, or divine (collectively the Law); (which was) commanded (-ment), law, ordinance, precept], *My **STATUTES*** (11) [H2708: *chûqqâh:* appointed *custom, manner,* or *ordinance*], *and My **LAWS*** (16) [H8451: *tôrâh:* a *precept* or *statute,* especially the *Decalogue* or *Pentateuch:* direction, or instruction based on the *Mosaic* or *Deuteronomic* Law]. *" (Gen. 26:4–5, NKJV) (emphasis added).

> *"Then the Angel of the LORD called to Abraham a second time OUT of HEAVEN, and said: 'BY MYSELF I HAVE SWORN,' says the LORD, 'BECAUSE you* [Abraham] *have DONE this THING, and have not*

476

*WITHHELD YOUR SON, YOUR ONLY SON—
BLESSING I will BLESS you, and MULTIPLYING I
will MULTIPLY your DESCENDANTS as the stars of
the heaven and as the sand which is on the seashore;
and YOUR DESCENDANTS shall POSSESS the GATE
of their ENEMIES. In YOUR SEED all the NATIONS
of THE EARTH shall be BLESSED, BECAUSE you
[Abraham] have OBEYED My VOICE.'"* (Gen. 22:15–
18, NKJV) (emphasis added).

In Genesis 26:4–5, we are clearly told this truth: God blessed
Abraham; because Abraham "obeyed" God's Voice, and "kept" His
charge, His commandments, His statutes, and His laws.

This was way before God's laws were given to the children of Israel
after He brought them out of Egypt because God promised
Abraham He would.

Based on Genesis 22:15–18, we are specifically told this indisputable
truth: *Yehôvah* swore by Himself, because He could swear by no one
higher than Himself, He would uphold, protect, and defend this
everlasting covenant He established with Abraham and his
descendants, forevermore!

Again, *Yehôvah* pledged His own throne to keep His end of this
everlasting covenant with Abraham, because of Abraham's
obedience alone.

Therefore, this *everlasting* covenant was not based on the
"collective" behavior of the children of Israel. So, it is with us, Jesus'
disciples.

477

THOSE WHO ARE OF FAITH WILL BE BLESSED WITH "BELIEVING" ABRAHAM WHO "OBEYED" GOD'S VOICE AND "KEPT" HIS CHARGE, HIS COMMANDMENTS, HIS STATUTES, AND HIS LAWS

The apostle Paul tells us in Galatians 3:8–10, those who are of faith will be blessed with "believing" Abraham who "obeyed" God's Voice, and "kept" His charge, His commandments, His statutes, and His laws. Abraham did this because he "believed" in the Word of the Lord, and God accounted it to him for righteousness.

Therefore, if we want to be blessed with "believing" Abraham, and inherit the covenant promises God gave to Abraham and his descendants, then we should also "obey" God's Voice, and "keep" His charge, His commandments, His statutes, and His laws.

Again, *if* we should fail to "obey" God's Voice, and "keep" His charge, His commandments, His statutes, and His laws, then we simply repent, ask God for His forgiveness, and keep traversing the "narrow" path which leads to life.

We continue to work out our own salvation with fear and trembling by doing the following: We cast down arguments and every high thing that exalts itself against the knowledge of God, bringing every thought into captivity to the obedience of Christ. As we do this, then the Lord will account it to us as "practicing" righteousness, because we love the One who has "justified" us with His precious blood.

And last, but certainly not least, God promised Abraham, in his "seed" all the nations of the earth shall be blessed. This was accomplished through our Lord and Savior Jesus Christ, whose genealogy begins with Abraham, Isaac, and Jacob because God "remembered" His *everlasting* covenant with them.

In the next chapter of this book, we will discover why the rebirth of the nation of Israel on May 14, 1948, is one of the main "signs" of God's prophetic end-time clock. Moreover, this fulfillment of what the "Prophets of Old" prophesied, from a *historical* perspective alone, authenticates the Word of God is true.

Moreover, God has declared the end from the beginning, and from "ancient" times things that are not yet done, saying His counsel shall stand, and He will do all His pleasure. Therefore, His Word which He sent forth from His mouth shall not return to Him void, and it shall accomplish what He pleases, because *"it is written…"*

CHAPTER 18

THE REBIRTH OF THE STATE OF ISRAEL ON MAY 14, 1948, IS ONE OF THE MAIN SIGNS OF GOD'S PROPHETIC TIME CLOCK AND AUTHENTICATES GOD'S WORD!

In the subsequent chapters, I have clearly substantiated how a new "spiritual" nation who would produce the proper "fruit" was birthed by God, and it is called the body of Christ, His Ekklēsía, or more commonly referred to as the Church.

Moreover, in Chapter 14 of this book, I covered in detail why America was "raised up" by God as a "physical" nation on the earth who would produce the proper "fruit," until the prophecy in Isaiah 66:8 came to pass. This resulted in the nation of Israel being "reborn" on May 14, 1948.

The rebirth of the nation of Israel would fulfill that which was spoken by the prophet in Amos 9:14–15 below:

> *"'I will bring BACK the CAPTIVES of My people ISRAEL; They shall BUILD the WASTE CITIES and INHABIT them; They shall PLANT VINEYARDS and DRINK WINE from them; They shall also MAKE GARDENS and EAT FRUIT from them. I will PLANT THEM in their LAND, And no LONGER shall they be PULLED UP from the LAND I have GIVEN them,' Says the LORD your God."* (Amos 9:14–15, NKJV) (emphasis added).

Who is Israel? Discovering our True Identity in Jesus Christ and Why it Matters! The Foundation

Until the nation of Israel was "reborn" on May 14, 1948, God's chosen people, the Israelites, consisting of all twelve tribes of Israel, were scattered all over the world when both the temple and Jerusalem, were destroyed in the year AD 70.

Therefore, America was birthed for God's purposes and glory to prevail from the very beginning, to be His "physical" nation, or vineyard, until the *fullness of the Gentiles* is fulfilled.

After the *gospel of the kingdom* is preached in the entire world as a witness unto all the nations, *Yehovah* will turn His full attention back to the physical nation of Israel which is located in the Middle East, and to the Jewish people from the House of Judah.

When the *fullness of the Gentiles* is at hand, *Yehovah* will remove the scales off of the eyes of the Orthodox Jews from the House of Judah, who are still *spiritually* blinded by *Yehovah*. As such, they will have the opportunity to be offered salvation, and come to the saving knowledge of Jesus Christ, as their Lord and Savior.

In fact, based on news reports coming out of Israel by Sid Roth, and others, this is already happening. And, as a result, many Orthodox Jews are receiving this revelation: Jesus Christ is the Messiah they have been waiting for all this time.

In Chapter 37 of Book 3, I will substantiate this truth: God has not forsaken the Jews from the House of Judah, due to their "disobedience" and "unbelief" based on Romans Chapter 11. Because if God has forsaken the Jews from the House of Judah,

482

then what would this mean for the rest of us who were formerly Gentiles, who received God's "mercy" and "grace" by our faith in His only *begotten* Son, Jesus Christ? This is despite our "unbelief," and our "disobedience" to His Voice, and His Word!

In addition, why do you think *Yehôvah* is having many of His true prophets and watchmen sound the trumpet throughout Zion? God is beseeching His people to repent and turn from our wicked ways, back to Him, before it is too late to make a course correction for all eternity.

In this hour, *Yehôvah* is calling His people to come out of *spiritual,* or *mystery,* Babylon, before we share in her sins, and receive her plagues, for this reason: The hour is very late based on all the "signs" we are seeing come to pass on a global basis, which lines up with end-time prophecy.

THE "REBIRTH" OF THE NATION OF ISRAEL ON MAY 14, 1948, IS THE INDISPUTABLE TESTIMONY OF THE AUTHENTICITY OF GOD'S WORD

The rebirth of the nation of Israel on May 14, 1948, despite all odds, from a "historical" perspective alone, should give believers, and unbelievers, the testimony of the authenticity of God's Word. It should prove to any onlooker this indisputable fact: Everything God has spoken by the mouths of His holy prophets throughout the *synergy of the ages* shall come to pass, because *"it is written..."*

If you did not get the opportunity to watch the recently televised documentary entitled, *The Miracle of Israel*, I strongly recommend you buy the DVD and watch it with your family. [1]

THE "REBIRTH" OF THE NATION OF ISRAEL IS A "KEY" PROPHETIC "SIGN" OF MANY OF THE "SIGNS" JESUS TOLD US TO WATCH FOR

Why should the rebirth of the physical nation of Israel, warrant our undivided attention, and authenticate God's Word, for all the scoffers and naysayers who are saying we are not in the end-times? Because beginning in Matthew Chapter 24, Jesus gives us *some*, but not all, of the "signs" to watch for signaling the *end of the age* of man's "rule" and "reign" on the earth. One "key" passage of Scripture for us to pay close attention to is in Matthew 24:32–35 below:

> *"Now LEARN this PARABLE from the FIG TREE: When its branch has already become tender and puts forth leaves, you know that summer is near. So you also, when you SEE all THESE THINGS, know that it [the coming of the Son of Man based on Matthew 24:29–31] is NEAR—at the doors! Assuredly, I say to you, this GENERATION will by NO MEANS PASS AWAY till ALL these THINGS take PLACE. HEAVEN and EARTH will PASS AWAY, but My WORDS will by NO MEANS PASS AWAY."* (Matt. 24:32–35, NKJV) (emphasis added).

If you take the time to watch the documentary, *The Miracle of Israel*, you will quickly realize this truth: Heaven and earth will shortly pass away, but God's Word will by no means pass away! Why? It is ETERNAL!

One of the meanings of the *Parable of The Fig Tree* concerns Israel becoming a nation again on May 14, 1948.

The rebirth of the nation of Israel restarted God's prophetic time clock, which shall usher in end-time events spoken by the "Prophets of Old."

These end-time events, which shall come to pass, will quickly accelerate the second coming of Jesus Christ.

The *physical* rebirth of the nation of Israel is a "key" *prophetic* "sign" Jesus told us to watch for. Jesus tells us to watch first, then to pray.

This is based on Luke 21:36, where Jesus says to us, *"WATCH therefore, and PRAY ALWAYS that you may be COUNTED WORTHY to ESCAPE all THESE THINGS that will COME to PASS, and TO STAND before the SON of MAN."* (NKJV) (emphasis added).

Based on what Jesus says to us in Luke 21:36, we are admonished to WATCH first, so we will not be caught off guard, so we will know the "Day of the Lord" is fast approaching. We must stay in *constant* prayer, so we *may* be "counted worthy" to escape all these things, which shall come to pass, because *"it is written…"*

NO OTHER GENERATION HAS WITNESSED THE FULFILLMENT OF PIVOTAL "KEY" EVENTS COMING TO PASS CONCERNING ISRAEL

We are *this* generation who will see all the things Jesus told us in advance to watch for come to pass, even though there are many people who think this message applies to *every* generation since Jesus first spoke these words. However, no other generation has witnessed the following pivotal "key" events:

ISRAEL BEING BORN IN ONE DAY

> *"Who has heard such a thing? Who has seen such things? Shall the EARTH be made to give BIRTH in ONE DAY? Or shall a NATION be BORN at ONCE? For as soon as ZION was in LABOR, She gave BIRTH to her CHILDREN."* (Isa. 66:8, NKJV) (emphasis added).

JERUSALEM BECAME THE CAPITAL OF ISRAEL IN 1967

> *"I have set WATCHMEN on your WALLS, O JERUSALEM: They shall NEVER HOLD their PEACE DAY or NIGHT. You who MAKE MENTION OF THE LORD, DO not KEEP SILENT, And GIVE HIM no REST till He ESTABLISHES And till He makes JERUSALEM a PRAISE in the EARTH."* (Isa. 62:6–7, NKJV) (emphasis added).

486

GOD'S PEOPLE, THE CHILDREN OF ISRAEL, WILL COME BACK TO THEIR HOMELAND ON THE MOUNTAINS IN ISRAEL FROM BEING SCATTERED ALL OVER THE WORLD

We are currently witnessing this promise based on Ezekiel 37:21–22, being fulfilled as the Jews, who were scattered all over the world, are returning to the state of Israel as one nation, *physically* speaking. Ezekiel 37:21–22 says the following:

> *"Then say to them, 'Thus says the Lord GOD: 'Surely I will TAKE the CHILDREN of ISRAEL from AMONG the NATIONS, WHEREVER THEY HAVE GONE, and will GATHER THEM from EVERY SIDE and BRING THEM into their OWN LAND; and I will make them ONE NATION in the LAND, on the MOUNTAINS of ISRAEL; and ONE KING shall be KING over them ALL; they shall no LONGER be two NATIONS, nor shall they ever be DIVIDED into two KINGDOMS again.'"* (Ezek. 37:21–22, NKJV) (emphasis added).

Moreover, now more than ever before, those of us who were formerly Gentiles from the House of Israel are making pilgrimages to the nation of Israel as God is wooing us back—if only for a visit at this time.

However, Ezekiel 37:21–22, will be *totally* fulfilled when God dispatches His angels to gather all His people. Those who comprise His *spiritual* nation—the body of Christ, will be gathered from the four corners of the earth onto the *mountains of Israel* as one *holy* nation. They will come to the land God promised Abraham and his descendants—*Mount Zion*, located in the *heavenly* Jerusalem. This will happen after Jesus Christ our King appears the second time.

Then we will *never* be divided into two kingdoms again! This is, *spiritually* speaking, for there will no longer be a *kingdom of darkness*; there will only be the *kingdom of light* under the "rule" and "reign" of only one King—the *King of kings and the Lord of lords*—Jesus Christ.

Spiritually speaking, all the "remnant" of Israel will be in the *kingdom of light* forevermore as we cross over into the Promised Land of "eternal" life in the *kingdom of heaven*.

The total fulfillment of this promise in Ezekiel 37:21–22, *physically* speaking, will take place *after* the one-thousand-year millennium is over. Then the *wife of Christ*, the *holy* Jerusalem, will descend out of heaven from God based on Revelation Chapter 21.

THE LAND IN ISRAEL WILL BLOOM

When I was in Israel for ten days in November 2010, and again for fifteen days in September 2015, it was amazing to see this prophecy based on Isaiah 35:1–2, being fulfilled.

No matter what part of Israel we were in, the land was fertile and overflowing with crops, and trees, bearing every kind of fruit imaginable. This is because of God's blessings on the land, and their state-of-the-art irrigation system.

Moreover, the contrasting landscape between Israel and her neighbors was quite apparent as well.

On Israel's side of the border, the vegetation was green and lush, producing many different types of food, and fruit trees. In contrast, the landscape on the side of Syria, Lebanon, and Jordan was comprised of only rocks and sand.

Therefore, on the border, there was a distinct visual "green line" clearly distinguishing where Israel's boundaries ended, and her neighboring Arab countries began, which is the fulfillment of Isaiah 35:1–2 below:

> *"The WILDERNESS and the WASTELAND shall be glad for them, And the DESERT shall REJOICE and BLOSSOM as the rose; it shall BLOSSOM ABUNDANTLY and REJOICE, Even with joy and singing. The glory of Lebanon shall be given to it, The excellence of Carmel and Sharon. They shall see the glory of the LORD, The Excellency of our God."* (Isa. 35:1–2, NKJV) (emphasis added).

All these Scriptures I have listed in this section, substantiates this fact: Those of us who were born into *this* generation have witnessed what the "Prophets of Old" prophesied concerning the "fig tree" nation of Israel, which have come to pass.

Jesus told us to watch for so many "signs" which are being fulfilled on a global basis, it would take another book to convey them all.

However, we are "the" generation who will witness the fulfillment of

489

all things, which shall take place before Jesus returns. In addition, there are many other prophetic "signs" which shall come to pass, before Jesus comes for His bride.

This is why in the *Parable of the Fig Tree*, Jesus says to us in Matthew 24:34, the following:

> *"Assuredly, I say to you, this GENERATION will by NO MEANS PASS AWAY till all THINGS take PLACE."* (Matt. 24:34, NKJV) (emphasis added).

Do not dismiss the significance that Jesus says all, not some; things must take place.

The bottom line is this: Jesus is coming back soon!

Yet I am sure many of you get weary of hearing people say the hour is later than most people realize.

This is based on the fact we are seeing many of the "signs" Jesus told us to watch for come to pass on a global basis.

Therefore, let's embark on a journey to discover how close the "time frame" of the return of Jesus Christ really is, based on what God's Word reveals to us concerning this matter.

However, we must remember that Jesus tells us in Matthew 24:22, *"And UNLESS THOSE DAYS WERE SHORTENED, NO FLESH would be SAVED; but for the ELECT'S SAKE those DAYS will be SHORTENED."* (NKJV) (emphasis added).

490

Donna M. Rogers

GOD'S WORD SUBSTANTIATES THE "TIME FRAME" WHICH SHALL USHER IN THE RETURN OF JESUS CHRIST

Again, the rebirth of the *physical* nation of Israel in 1948, restarted God's prophetic time clock, based on what Jesus said in Matthew 24:34. In addition, we must take into account what we are told in Daniel 9:25, which says the following:

> *"Know therefore and understand, That from the GOING FORTH of the COMMAND to restore and build JERUSALEM until Messiah the PRINCE, there shall be SEVEN WEEKS* (2) (3) **[H7620: shăbûa':** literally *sevened,* that is, a *week* (specifically of years); seven, a week. **H7651: Sheba':** a primitive cardinal number, seven (as the sacred *full* one, seven *times;* by implication a *week;* specifically a period of a total of 70 Feast of Weeks]* and SIXTY-TWO WEEKS;* (2) (3) *The street shall be built again, and the wall, Even in troublesome times."* (Dan. 9:25, NKJV) (emphasis added).

This prophecy spoken by Daniel was *partially* fulfilled in history, and this decree to "restore" and "build" Jerusalem was issued as detailed in Nehemiah 2:1–8.

This decree to "restore" and "build" Jerusalem occurred on the 1st of the Hebrew month of Nisan (sometimes spelled Nissan), on March 14, BC 445, in the 20th year of King Artaxerxes' reign. What Daniel was prophesying was when the *first* coming of Jesus Christ would take place, which was calculated based on when the decree to "restore" and "build" Jerusalem was first issued.

As such, the decree to "restore" and "build" Jerusalem when it was *first* issued was on March 14, 445 BC, which is based on the calculations provided by Daniel in Daniel 9:25, and points to the date of the 10th of Nisan (April 6, AD 32).

What significant event happened on this date? [4] This is the date that Jesus' "triumphant entry" into Jerusalem occurred, which fulfilled Zechariah 9:9 and Luke 19:28–44.

Like so many of the prophecies spoken by the mouth of the "Prophets of Old," this prophecy from Daniel, which is based on Daniel 9:25, is a dual fulfillment prophecy. What this means is this: This prophecy will have a total fulfillment in the future, even though part of the prophecy was fulfilled in the past.

Hence, this prophecy from Daniel based on Daniel 9:25, will have a total fulfillment at the end of the *synergy of the ages*. And, it also reveals the "time frame" of when Jesus Christ, our Messiah, will return the *second* time. And, it is for this very reason; I do not believe the tribulation period will be for a total of seven years.

Therefore, we need to take a closer look at Daniel 9:25. As such, the Hebrew meaning of the word "weeks" as used in Daniel 9:25, refers specifically to the Feast of Weeks (*Shavuot* or *Pentecost*), which occurs on a yearly basis until the return of *Messiah the Prince* (Jesus Christ).

492

THE SECOND COMING OF JESUS CHRIST CAN ONLY HAPPEN ONCE THE GOING FORTH OF THE "COMMAND" TO "RESTORE" AND "BUILD" JERUSALEM OCCURS AT THE END OF THE *SYNERGY OF THE AGES*

History always repeats itself, and based on Ecclesiastes 3:15, we are specifically told that which is, has already been, and what is to be, has already been, because God requires an account of what is past. Therefore, the *second* coming of Jesus Christ can only happen once the going forth of the **command** to "restore" and "build" Jerusalem occurs once again at the end of the *synergy of the ages*.

For the **total** fulfillment of Daniel 9:25 to take place, this **command** to "restore" and "build" Jerusalem, *must* be issued once again at the end of the *synergy of the ages*. This must happen for Israel, the "fig tree" nation, to shoot forth her branches which would ultimately result in "restoring" and "building" Jerusalem, even in troublesome times. This could not occur until Israel was *physically* "reborn" as a nation once again.

As such, this **command** which would ultimately result in Jerusalem being "restored" and "built" again was issued **when** the *Balfour Declaration* was **decreed** on November 2, 1917.

Without the *Balfour Declaration* being issued, the nation of Israel could not have been "reborn" *despite* all odds on May 14, 1948. As a matter of fact, on May 14, 2017, the nation of Israel will celebrate her 69th birthday. Therefore, this **command** for Israel, the "fig tree" nation, to shoot forth her branches as a result of the *Balfour*

493

Declaration, was issued by the United Nations on November 29, 1947. This was when the United Nations General Assembly passed a resolution calling for Palestine to be partitioned between Arabs and Jews, allowing for the formation of the Jewish state of Israel.

They did this, so Jerusalem would belong to the world, and be under "international" control. Thus, it is not a coincidence the United Nations, and others they are in collusion with, are trying to do the same thing once again.

However, God rendered their plan "null" and "void" as a result of the miraculous *Six-Day War,* when on June 7, 1967, Jerusalem came back under the control of Israel, based on the *everlasting* covenant God established with Abraham and his descendants.

Even now God will have the final say in this matter, and His will shall prevail for this reason: He "remembers" the *everlasting* covenant He established with Abraham, that He swore to Himself, because He could swear no higher than Himself, to protect, defend, and uphold forevermore!

TWO "KEY" PIVOTAL EVENTS TOOK PLACE CONCERNING THE "PHYSICAL" NATION OF ISRAEL WHICH "REACTIVATED" GOD'S PROPHETIC END-TIME CLOCK

This **command** to "restore" and "build" Jerusalem, until the *second* coming of *Messiah the Prince* (who is Jesus Christ), could not have come to pass at the *end of the ages* until two pivotal "key" events were fulfilled. They are as follows:

1. Israel was "reborn" as a nation in 1948.

2. The nation of Israel acquired Jerusalem as their capital in 1967 as a result of the miraculous *Six-Day War.*

As such, these two "key" pivotal events which have come to pass, is what "reactivated" God's prophetic end time clock.

These two "key" events are what "qualifies" or "defines" the generation, which will by *no* means pass away until all these things Jesus spoke about in Matthew Chapter 24 take place, which will usher in His second coming. Therefore, we need to allow God's Word to define what a generation is.

WHAT IS A "GENERATION" ACCORDING TO THE BIBLE?

A generation, according to the Bible, is one hundred years. We base this on what God told Abraham in Genesis 15:13–16, about the children of Israel being in Egypt for four hundred years.

Four hundred years equates to four generations before God would bring them out from their slavery at the hands of Pharaoh, the *King of Egypt,* who knew not Joseph so that they could worship God under the leadership of His servant Moses.

This is substantiated in Genesis 15:13–16, which says the following:

> *"Then He said to Abram: 'Know certainly that YOUR DESCENDANTS will be STRANGERS in a LAND that is not theirs, and will serve them, and they will AFFLICT them FOUR HUNDRED YEARS. And also the nation whom they serve I will judge; afterward they shall come out with great possessions. Now as for you, you shall go to your fathers in peace; you shall be buried at a good old age. But in the FOURTH GENERATION they shall return here, for the iniquity of the Amorites is not yet complete.'"* (Gen. 15:13–16, NKJV) (emphasis added).

Again, this was based on one of God's promises made to Abraham and his descendants, based on the *everlasting* covenant God established with Abraham.

In Exodus 2:23–25, we learn the following: God heard the children of Israel groan, because of their bondage, as they cried out because God "remembered" His covenant with Abraham, Isaac, and Jacob (Israel). Hence, God looked upon the children of Israel and acknowledged them. And, as a result, He sent Moses to deliver His Hebrew people out of their bondage in the land of Egypt.

So we clearly see that God's Word is saying the children of Israel would be in Egypt for four hundred years. Then in the fourth generation, they would return to the land God promised Abraham his descendants would take possession of as their inheritance.

Therefore, this defines a generation according to the Bible as one hundred years.

JESUS TELLS US "THIS" GENERATION WHO SAW THE "REBIRTH" OF THE NATION OF ISRAEL, WOULD BY NO MEANS "PASS AWAY" UNTIL ALL THESE THINGS TAKE PLACE

Based on what Jesus said in Matthew 24:34, He said **this** generation who saw the rebirth of Israel in 1948, would by **no** means pass away until **all** these things take place.

These "things" are concerning the "signs of the times" and "the end of the age," Jesus elaborates on in Chapter 24 of the Book of Matthew.

Now let's refocus our attention of the "rebirth" of the nation of Israel.

Without the *Balfour Declaration* being issued there would be no Israel to "restore" and "build" Jerusalem, even in troublesome times, until Jerusalem would come back under their control as their capital.

So, if you add one hundred years, representing one generation based on Genesis 15:13–16, to the year 1917 when the *Balfour Declaration* was issued, then *this* generation who witnessed Israel being "reborn" again as a nation will pass away around 2017, which is the Hebrew Year of 5777.

In addition, if you add seventy years, which represents the number of Feast of Weeks (*Shavuot* or *Pentecost*) which have transpired *after* the **command** (resolution) was issued (passed) by the UN, which would result in the Jewish state of Israel being reborn, and the **command** to "restore" and "build" Jerusalem would be issued based on Daniel 9:25, then you would get the following:

1947 (UN passed resolution resulting in the formation of the Jewish state of Israel) + 70 (Feast of Weeks, which equates to 70 years) = 2017, which is the Hebrew Year of 5777.

It is also the **total** culmination of the seventy weeks of Daniel, which is based on Daniel 9:24, which says the following:

> *"SEVENTY **WEEKS** [2] [3]* [H7620: *shābúa*: literally *sevened,* that is, a *week* (specifically of YEARS); seven, a week. H7651: *Sheba*: a primitive cardinal number, seven (as the sacred *full* one, seven *times;* by implication a *week;* specifically a period of a total of 70 Feast of Weeks] *are DETERMINED For YOUR PEOPLE and for YOUR HOLY CITY, To finish the TRANSGRESSION, To **make an end** of SINS, To **make reconciliation** for INIQUITY, To **bring in** EVERLASTING RIGHTEOUSNESS, To **seal up** VISION and PROPHECY, And **to anoint** the MOST HOLY."* (Dan. 9:24, NKJV) (emphasis added).

Moreover, the Jewish people sounded the trumpet in the Year of Jubilee which occurred in 1967 according to a video featuring Jonathan Cahn talking about the Shemitah year, which begins at 2:40 in the video which I have provided the link to in the appendix at the back of this book. [5] Furthermore, please note the title of this video is somewhat erroneous, and it appears they are saying the

498

Year of Jubilee will happen on September 23, 2015. This date is talking about the Day of Atonement, depending on the sighting of the New Moon by two, or more witnesses, in Jerusalem, which will officially start the Feast of Trumpets based on God's calendar. This is not talking about the Jubilee year.

In this video, Jonathan Cahn specifically says the sound of the shofar was sounded in 1967 when Jerusalem once again came back to Israel as their possession and their inheritance. As such, it was on June 7, 1967, Jerusalem came back into the hands of its rightful owners as a result of the *Six-Day War.*

According to the Word of God, a Jubilee is forty-nine years based on Leviticus 25:8, which says, *"And you shall count seven SABBATHS of YEARS for yourself, SEVEN TIMES SEVEN YEARS; and the time of the SEVEN SABBATHS of YEARS shall be to you FORTY-NINE YEARS."* (NKJV) (emphasis added).

However, the Year of Jubilee is every fifty years. This is based on Leviticus 25:11–12 below.

> *"That FIFTIETH YEAR shall be a JUBILEE to you; in it you shall neither sow nor reap what grows of its own accord, nor gather the grapes of your untended vine. For it is the JUBILEE; it shall be holy to you; you shall eat its produce from the field."* (Lev. 25:11–12, NKJV) (emphasis added).

Therefore, if you add 50 (the number which signifies the Year of Jubilee) to 1967 (when Jerusalem became the capital of Israel again), you would get 2017, which is the Hebrew Year of 5777.

THE SIGNIFICANCE OF THE HEBREW YEAR OF 5777 (2017)

The Hebrew year of 5777 refers to the "time frame" of when *this* "generation" who witnessed the "rebirth" of the nation of Israel shall pass away.

We are told in Deuteronomy 19:15, God requires the testimony of two, or three, witnesses for a matter to be established. Therefore, I present to you the "time frame," not the "day," or the "hour," which will usher in Jesus Christ's second coming based on the following facts:

❖ When you add seventy years (which represents the number of the Feast of Weeks that has transpired) after the **command** (resolution) was issued (passed) by the United Nations General Assembly on November 29, 1947, calling for Palestine to be partitioned between Arabs and Jews, allowing for the formation of the Jewish state of Israel. This would result in "restoring" and "building" Jerusalem once again, even in troublesome times, you would get the following:

1947 (UN passed resolution resulting in the formation of the Jewish state of Israel) + 70 (Feast of Weeks, which equates to 70 years) = 2017, which is the Hebrew Year of 5777.

❖ Furthermore, since we already know the Year of Jubilee is every fifty years based on Leviticus 25:11–12, if you add 50 (the number which signifies a Jubilee year) to 1967, the last known "Year of Jubilee" held in the land of Israel, which occurred when Israel took possession of Jerusalem as their capital as a result of the *Six-Day War*, you would get the following:

1967 (Jerusalem became the capital of Israel again) + 50 (Year of Jubilee) = 2017, which is the Hebrew Year of 5777.

❖ In addition, if you add one hundred years, which represents one generation based on what God told Abraham in Genesis 15:13–16, to the year 1917 when the *Balfour Declaration* was issued, without which, there would be no Israel.

And, Jerusalem would not have been under Israeli control as their capital so that they could rebuild again, even in troublesome times.

Hence, what this tells us is *this* generation who witnessed Israel being "reborn" again as a nation will pass away around 2017, which is the Hebrew Year of 5777. This is based on the following:

1917 (the *Balfour Declaration*) + 100 years (one generation) = 2017, which is the Hebrew Year of 5777.

Based on the three examples I have listed, it is not a coincidence all these pivotal events concerning the nation of Israel, and Jerusalem culminates in the Hebrew year of 5777 (2017)!

In fact, "triple" seven, is based on the number seven being God's number of *spiritual* "perfection," or "completion." The number five in the Bible represents God's grace. In other words, the biblical numeric meaning of 5777 is referring to God's grace which is made perfect, or complete.

There will be another pivotal event which shall coincide with the Hebrew year of 5777. On September 23, 2017, a major "sign" in the heavens will occur that *supposedly* only happens every 7,000 years. This great "sign" will *literally* depict that which is spoken of by the apostle John in Revelation 12:1–6.[6]

Another interesting side-note is this fact: Based on Genesis 5:31, we are told Lamech, the father of Noah, died when he was seven hundred and seventy-seven (777) years old. What is the significance of this? Lamech was the last patriarch to die *before* the flood occurred, which resulted in a New Beginning.

We are specifically told by Jesus in Matthew 24:37, and Luke 17:26, *"But as the DAYS of NOAH were, so also will the COMING of the SON of MAN be."* (NKJV) (emphasis added).

Therefore, I believe the climax of the *synergy of the ages* may happen during the seventieth (70th) year of Israel becoming a *literal* physical nation once again which shall occur after the Hebrew year of 5777 (2017) which is the Year of Jubilee.

We know that 2017 is the Year of Jubilee based on this fact: In 1967 was the last known Year of Jubilee which was celebrated in Israel, and we know that fifty (50) years is the Year of Jubilee based on Leviticus 25:11–12. Therefore, if you add 50 to the year 1967, it would equate to 2017 which is the next Year of Jubilee.

Again, on May 14, 2017, the nation of Israel will celebrate her 69th birthday since she became a *literal* (physical) nation again on May 14, 1948.

As such, on May 14, 2018, this will be the 70th anniversary (birthday) of Israel being "reborn" as a *literal* physical nation on the earth.

And, it will also be the **total** fulfillment of Daniel 9:24. In this Scripture, we are specifically told that seventy weeks (70 Feast of Weeks [*Shavuot* or *Pentecost*]) are determined for God's people, and His holy city (*spiritual* Jerusalem—the body of Christ), to fulfill the following six things:

1.   To **finish** the TRANSGRESSION.
2.   To make an **end** of SINS.
3.   To make **reconciliation** for INIQUITY.
4.   To **bring in** EVERLASTING RIGHTEOUSNESS.
5.   To **seal up** VISION and PROPHECY.
6.   To **anoint** the MOST HOLY.

After the fulfillment of **all** the things spoken by the mouths of the "Prophets of Old" is finished, this will usher in the second coming of Jesus Christ.

However, I want to be absolutely clear concerning this indisputable truth: God's Word tells us NO ONE, not even the angels of heaven, will know the "day," or the "hour," Jesus Christ will return.

Jesus tells us this truth in Matthew 24:36, when He says, *"But of that DAY and HOUR **no** one KNOWS, not even the angels of heaven, but My Father only."* (NKJV) (emphasis added).

PREPARE YE THE WAY OF THE LORD

Only our heavenly Father knows the "day," or the "hour," Jesus will return. Nevertheless, the Lord has told me to prepare His people for His return, and to tell His people He is coming back soon.

Therefore, based on the relevance of the Hebrew Year 5777, and what many have been saying about this being a Joel 2 moment, which shall usher in the final Great Awakening, please take the time to read all of Joel 2 on your own.

As you carefully examine this passage of Scripture, you will discover it is talking about what shall take place ushering in the "Day of the Lord" as God is in the process of "raising up" His end-time army which is His triumphant reserve—His militant bride.

Also, I need to share with you three visions I was given by the Lord. On March 2, 2015, while I was at a prayer gathering with other prayer leaders, during our prayer time on that day, the Lord showed me the following three visions:

- ❖ In the first vision: Jesus had both His hands held close together with both palms facing up with an all-consuming fire in the center of the palm of His hands.

- ❖ In the second vision: Jesus still had His hands held out with His palms facing up. Instead of the all-consuming fire, I had seen earlier; I now saw a globe of the earth where the fire had been.

- ❖ In the third vision: Jesus lifted up His hands and released a

504

dove, which represented the Holy Spirit, and all I saw was bright, brilliant, white light everywhere.

As I will cover in Book 3, *this* earth will be totally "depopulated" and "consumed" by fire at the second coming of Jesus Christ. However, preceding the "Day of the Lord" we are told by the prophet Joel in Joel 2:28, God will pour out His Spirit on all flesh. In addition, we are told by the apostle Paul; we shall all be "changed" in a moment, in the *twinkling of an eye* at the last trump.

Therefore, I believe these three visions I was given by the Lord is foreshadowing what is to come at God's "appointed" time, and not before.

The truth of the matter is this: It should not matter when the Lord will return, because we are admonished to be like the "wise" virgins in *The Parable of the Wise and Foolish Virgins,* and be ready at all times for our bridegroom's return. Especially based on the fact that none of us are promised tomorrow!

In Chapter 67 of Book 3, I will go into detail concerning the "time frame" of when the last trump the apostle Paul speaks of will take place on the last day of planet earth when the dead in Christ will be raised. I will also convey how all this coincides with the timing of our heavenly Father's fall holy convocations based on Leviticus Chapter 23 occurring, which has everything to do with when we will be "reborn" again, *physically* speaking.

In the meanwhile, only *Yehovah,* our heavenly Father, knows for sure the "day" and the "hour" Jesus will return in His *second* coming. However, He expects His people to be like the sons of

Issachar, men who understood the "times" and "seasons."

As such, God's people should know the "times" and the "seasons" we are in based on when God's seven holy convocations occur which are in alignment with our Creator's calendar, rather than the Jewish calendar, or our pagan calendars.

Following God's appointed "times" and "seasons," based on our Creator's calendar, requires God's people to watch and pay attention to when the Hebrew months occur, based on the sighting of the New Moon over Jerusalem, by two, or more, witnesses. The timing is also based on other factors, only our heavenly Father controls. I will cover this subject in-depth in Book 3.

In addition, God's Word details many other "signs" Jesus tells us to watch for in advance. We are admonished by Him always to be WATCHING, and PRAYING unceasingly, while we are busy doing the will of our heavenly Father.

Furthermore, the apostle Paul tells us in 1 Thessalonians 5:1–11, concerning God's "times" and "seasons," we have no need that he should write to us for this reason: Jesus, His early disciples, including the apostle Paul, kept and observed all of God's holy convocations based on Leviticus 23. As such, they knew about God's "times" and "seasons," and when they occurred, each week (the Sabbath day), and every year (the feasts).

Then the apostle Paul specifically states, the "Day of the Lord" will come as a *thief in the night,* for those who are in darkness, and they shall not escape.

506

Yet the apostle Paul specifically says, concerning disciples of Jesus Christ, we are **not** in darkness, for we are sons of light, and sons of day. Therefore, the "Day of the Lord' should not overtake disciples of Jesus Christ as a *thief in the night!*

Next, the apostle Paul admonishes us not to remain asleep, as the five "unwise" virgins did in *The Parable of the Wise and Foolish Virgins,* Jesus tells us about in the Book of Matthew in Chapter 25. In this parable, all the virgins fell asleep, yet when the Watchmen blew the trumpet, the "wise" virgins woke up and prepared themselves for their bridegroom's return.

Last, but certainly not least, the apostle Paul tells us to WATCH and be sober, so we will know when the "Day of the Lord" is fast approaching.

And, let's us not forget this truth: Jesus said all these things must take place before *this* generation who witnessed the rebirth of the nation of Israel, and the rebuilding of Jerusalem come to fruition, will pass away.

These things Jesus is talking about can be categorized into five main prophetic "signs" happening on a global basis we are to take notice of as we watch and pray. They are as follows:

1.   Signs which are impacting the nation of Israel.
2.   Signs in nature, and in the heavens.
3.   Signs in society (both positive and negative).
4.   Signs which are impacting world politics.
5.   Signs relating to technology.

Therefore, I am amazed many believers do not understand we are in the last days based on the "signs" we see happening on a global basis, Jesus told us to watch for and pray about without ceasing. But then again, we are told this would be the case based on Second Peter 3:1–4 below:

> *"Beloved, I now write to you this second epistle (in both of which I stir up your pure minds by way of reminder), that you may be mindful of the words which were spoken before by the holy prophets, and of the commandment of us, the apostles of the Lord and Savior, KNOWING this first: that SCOFFERS will COME in the LAST DAYS, walking according to their own lusts, and saying, 'WHERE is the PROMISE of His COMING? For since the fathers fell asleep, all THINGS continue as they were from the BEGINNING of CREATION.'"* (2 Pet. 3:1–4, NKJV) (emphasis added).

Speaking of the need for us to understand the promise of Jesus' first, and second coming, since our fathers fell asleep, in which all things will continue as they were from the beginning of creation.

It is for this very reason; our heavenly Father has placed it upon my heart to include in this series of books exactly what the *Abrahamic* Covenant is, and how it is still applicable for New Covenant believers, which I will cover in detail in Book 2.

Because without us knowing about this *everlasting* covenant *Yehôvah* established with Abraham, the father of our faith, we

508

cannot fully understand why all disciples of Jesus Christ are Israel, and know beyond a shadow of a doubt this truth: As New Covenant believers, we are heirs according to the promises God gave to Abraham and his descendants long ago as it is to *this* very day!

WHO IS ISRAEL? ACCORDING TO THE WHOLE COUNSEL OF GOD'S WORD—ISRAEL IS...

1. *Yehovah* (Yahweh [YHWH]); the God of Abraham, Isaac, and Jacob (Israel) who is our heavenly Father, and God, our Creator, (Maker) who is the Holy One of Israel based on the following Scriptures:

   Second Kings 19:22; Psalm 71:22, 78:41, 89:18; Isaiah 1:4, 5:19, 5:24, 10:20, 12:6, 17:7, 29:19, 29:23, 30:11, 30:12, 30:15, 30:29 31:1, 37:23, 41:14, 41:16, 41:20, 43:3, 43:14, 43:15, 47:4, 48:17, 49:7, 54:5, 55:5, 60:9, 60:14; Jeremiah 50:29, 51:5; Ezekiel 39:7; Hosea 11:12

2. Jesus Christ, God's *firstborn* Son over all creation, based on the following Scriptures:

   > "Then you shall say to Pharaoh, 'Thus says the LORD: 'Israel is My SON, My FIRSTBORN.'"
   > (NKJV) (emphasis added).

   > "I am the Lord, your Holy One, the **CREATOR** [**H1254**: *bara*: to *create*; qualify, to select or to choose] of **ISRAEL** [**H3478**: *Yisra'el*: he will

509

rule as *God, Jisrael*, a symbolical name of Jacob; also (typically) of his posterity (descendants)], *your KING* [H4428: *melek*: a royal king; H4427: *mâlak*: to *rule* and *reign*; inceptively to *ascend the throne*; induct into royalty; hence to take counsel]. " (Isa. 43:15, NKJV) (emphasis added).

"As for our REDEEMER, the LORD of HOSTS is His NAME, The HOLY ONE of ISRAEL." (Isa. 47:4, NKJV) (emphasis added).

"He [the Word] *is the image of the invisible GOD* [G2316: *theos*: a *deity*; the Supreme Divinity or magistrate], *the FIRSTBORN* [G4416: *prōtotokos*: firstborn G4413: *prōtos*: foremost (in time, place, order or importance): beginning, before, best] *over all CREATION."* (Col. 1:15, NKJV) (emphasis added).

"When ISRAEL [H3478: *Yisrā"ēl*: he will rule as God; a symbolical name of Jacob; also (typically) of his posterity; God prevails] *was a CHILD, I loved him, And out of Egypt I called My SON* [H1121: *bên*: a son (as a *builder* of the family name); including *grandson, subject, nation, quality* or *condition*, etc.; anointed

one, appointed to, branch, *firstborn*, mighty; whelp, worthy]. " (Hos. 11:1, NKJV) (emphasis added).

3. The symbolic name that was given to Jacob, Abraham's grandson, after he wrestled with God at Peniel, and prevailed, based on Genesis 32:28 and Genesis 32:30 below:

    "And He said, 'Your name shall NO longer be called JACOB [H3290: *Ya'aqŏb: heel catcher* (that is, Supplanter); Jaakob, the *Israelitish* patriarch], *but ISRAEL* [H3478: *Yisrā'ēl: he will rule as God; Jisrael,* a symbolical name of Jacob; also (typically) of his posterity (descendants)]; *for you have struggled with God and with men, and have prevailed.'"* (Gen. 32:28, NKJV) (emphasis added).

    "So Jacob called the name of the place PENIEL [H6439: *P'nîy'ēl: the face of God;* and is a place East of Jordan]: *'For I have seen God FACE to FACE, and MY LIFE is PRESERVED.'"* (Gen. 32:30, NKJV) (emphasis added).

4. The "spiritual" descendants of Abraham, Isaac, and Jacob (Israel), based on the *everlasting* covenant God established with Abraham—the "Father of Many Nations."

This also includes the "spiritual" descendants of King David based on the *everlasting* covenant God established with King

David. This is based on the following Scriptures: Psalm 89:35–37; Isaiah 9:6–7; Jeremiah 23:5–6; and 33:19–26.

Again, this is why Matthew 1:1, starts off the genealogy of Jesus Christ by proclaiming, *"The Book of the Genealogy of Jesus Christ, the Son of David, the Son of Abraham..."* (NKJV)

5. Israel is the symbolic name given to the descendants of Jacob, from all twelve tribes of Israel, referred to as the Israelites, or the children of Israel, which includes both the Jews from the House of Judah and those of us who were formerly Gentiles from the House of Israel.

These terms are also found in the New Testament as well because New Covenant believers are God's covenant children by our faith in Jesus Christ. As such, we have been grafted into the commonwealth of Israel.

The term "the Israelites" is referenced only fifteen times in the entire Word of God.

Following are the New Testament Scriptures referencing the term "the Israelites":

Romans 9:4; Second Corinthians 11:22

The term "children of Israel" is referenced 619 times in the Word of God.

Following are the New Testament Scriptures referencing the term "children of Israel":

> Matthew 27:9; Luke 1:16; Acts 5:21; 7:23; 7:37; 9:15; 10:36; Romans 9:27; Second Corinthians 3:7; 3:13; Hebrews 11:22; Revelation 2:14; 7:4; 21:12

The term "House of Israel" is referenced 291 times in the entire Word of God.

Following are the New Testament Scriptures referencing the term "House of Israel":

> Matthew 10:6; 15:24; Acts 2:36; 7:42; Hebrews 8:8; 8:10

The term "House of Judah" is referenced 123 times in the entire Word of God.

The term "House of Judah" is referenced in the New Testament only in one Scripture: Hebrews 8:8, which talks about the New Covenant, God has established with both the House of Judah and the House of Israel.

6. A physical nation on the earth located in the Middle East, which was God's first vineyard He picked out for His chosen people to take possession of as their inheritance.

This is based on one of the promises He made to Abraham

when He established the *everlasting* covenant with him, and his descendants.

Even though God made the promise to Abram when the Canaanites were still in the land, it would be Abraham's descendants from the House of Jacob (all twelve tribes of Israel), who would eventually take possession of this land as their inheritance.

This is substantiated in Genesis 12:4–7, Genesis 15:17–21, and Ezekiel 20:5–6, which says the following:

> *"So Abram departed as the LORD had spoken to him, and Lot went with him. And Abram was seventy-five years old when he departed from Haran. Then Abram took Sarai his wife and Lot his brother's son, and all their possessions that they had gathered, and the people whom they had acquired in Haran, and they DEPARTED to GO to the LAND of CANAAN. So they CAME to the LAND of CANAAN. Abram PASSED THROUGH the land to the place of Shechem, as far as the terebinth tree of Moreh. And the Canaanites were then in the land. THEN the LORD APPEARED to Abram and said, 'To YOUR DESCENDANTS I will GIVE this LAND.' And there he built an altar to the LORD, who had*

Donna M. Rogers

appeared to him." (Gen. 12:4–7, NKJV)
(emphasis added).

*"And it came to pass, when the sun went down
and it was dark, that behold, there APPEARED
a smoking oven and a burning torch that
PASSED between those pieces. On the same
DAY the LORD made a COVENANT with
Abram, saying: 'To YOUR DESCENDANTS I
have GIVEN this LAND, from the river of
Egypt to the great river, the River Euphrates—
the Kenites, the Kenezzites, the Kadmonites,
the Hittites, the Perizzites, the Rephaim, the
Amorites, the Canaanites, the Girgashites, and
the Jebusites.'"* (Gen. 15:17–21, NKJV)
(emphasis added).

*"Say to them, 'Thus says the Lord GOD: 'On
the DAY when I CHOSE Israel and RAISED My
HAND in an OATH to the DESCENDANTS of
the HOUSE of JACOB, and made Myself
KNOWN to them in the LAND of EGYPT, I
RAISED My HAND in an OATH to them,
saying, I am the LORD your GOD. On that
DAY I RAISED My HAND in an OATH to
them, to bring them OUT of the LAND of
EGYPT into a LAND that I had SEARCHED
OUT for them, flowing with milk and honey,
the GLORY of all LANDS.'"* (Ezek. 20:5–6,
NKJV) (emphasis added).

7. Since Israel is Jesus Christ, and our heavenly Father, *Yehôváh,* (Yahweh [YHWH]), is the Holy One of Israel, then all *true* disciples of Jesus Christ are:

- ❖ His *saints*
- ❖ His *elect*
- ❖ His *Royal* Priesthood
- ❖ His *Holy* Nation
- ❖ The body of Christ —His Ekklēsia
- ❖ The children of Israel—the twelve tribes of Israel
- ❖ The *Hebrew* children
- ❖ The Israelites
- ❖ His *chosen* people
- ❖ The *bride of Christ*
- ❖ The *Apple of His Eye*
- ❖ His *faithful* remnant

WE ARE ISRAEL!

Donna M. Rogers

EPILOGUE

Since we now know who Israel is, then for the House of Israel to continue to believe that everything that is written to the children of Israel, or to the Jews from the House of Judah, such as the Old Testament, or God's laws, no longer applies to New Covenant believers is heresy!

In fact, the apostle Paul proclaims to us in Galatians 1:8, *"But even if we, or an angel from heaven, PREACH ANY OTHER GOSPEL to you THAN WHAT WE HAVE PREACHED TO YOU, LET HIM BE ACCURSED* [excommunicated, cursed]*."* (NKJV) (emphasis added).

Also, the apostle Paul tells us in Romans 3:27–31, *Yehoṽah* is the God of both the Jews, and those of us who were formerly Gentiles, for there is only one God who will "justify" the circumcised by faith, and the uncircumcised, through faith.

Moreover, in this same passage of Scripture, the apostle Paul asks, *"Do we then make VOID the LAW through FAITH?"* To which he responds, *"CERTAINLY NOT! On the contrary, we ESTABLISH the LAW!"*

Our heavenly Father's instructions which are in the Torah is the same law our heavenly Father, *Yehoṽah,* has now put in our mind and written on our hearts under the New Covenant because our Lawgiver now lives in us through His Holy Spirit.

Again, since those of us who were formerly Gentiles from the House of Israel, are "citizens of Israel," what this means is this: The *same*

517

"laws," and the *same* "customs," God gave to the children of Israel, applies to all His people, not just to the Jews from the House of Judah.

This is based on the fact our heavenly Father established a New Covenant with both houses, and He has *only* one "law," and one "custom," for all His people. This is substantiated in Exodus 12:49; Leviticus 24:22; and Numbers 15:15–16.

The "faithful" remnant is the bride of Christ. Therefore, even though many are called—few are chosen. The bride of Christ is those who "believe" in and "obey" the God of Abraham, Isaac, and Jacob (Israel) whose name is *Yehôváh* (Yahweh [YHWH]), not Allah. God's "faithful" remnant are those believers who have placed their spiritual well-being and trust in His only *begotten* Son, Jesus Christ.

Our heavenly Father's law written in the Torah is His written instructions for all His people to live by, which were penned by His servant Moses. The "testimony" of God's law is found in the first five books of our Bible. *Yehôváh's* law (the Torah), is also referred to as the Law of Moses, or the Mosaic Law.

Therefore, our heavenly Father, *Yehôváh,* really wants His people to get the following indisputable truths, which are based on the whole counsel of His *eternal* Word:

❖ We have "one" heavenly Father, *Yehôváh* (Yahweh [YHWH]), whose name is *E'lōhim,* because He is "the" Creator of the heavens and the earth, and everything in it, including us, His created. He is also called *El Elyon* (the *Most High God*), and *El Olam* (the *Everlasting God*), whom Abraham called upon and served. It is for this very reason; He is called the God of Abraham, Isaac, and Jacob (Israel).

❖ We have "one" Redeemer, who is God's only *begotten* Son, Jesus Christ, whom *Yehovah* sent to the earth the first time as the Son of Man for this primary reason: To die for our sins so we could be "reconciled" and "restored" back to "walking" in a covenant relationship with our heavenly Father, *Yehovah,* (Yahweh [YHWH]).

Hence, by His blood, Jesus Christ, became the "mediator" of the New Covenant, where our heavenly Father has now put His laws in our mind and has written them on our hearts, instead of on two tablets of stone, by His Holy Spirit who lives in us.

❖ Moreover, Jesus Christ "confirmed" (ratified) the New Covenant with His precious blood for the forgiveness of our sins, to "restore" and "reconcile" both houses, back into "walking" in a covenant relationship with our heavenly Father, *Yehovah.*

This is based on the terms and conditions of the *first* Covenant, He established through His servant Moses—the law (the Torah), and it is also based on the *gospel of the kingdom,* that was preached by Jesus Christ, and His early disciples.

Also, the *first* Covenant was established with the children of Israel as a result of the *everlasting* covenant *Yehovah* established with Abraham, Isaac, and Jacob (Israel), we in Christendom refer to as the *Abrahamic* Covenant or the "Covenant of Circumcision."

However, as I have said before, but it bears repeating, all of God's *everlasting* covenants (plural), He has established with mankind, and all creation, throughout the *synergy of the ages,* are still in effect.

They all build on one another, and they were all "confirmed" by blood. The blood that was used to "ratify" these covenants was shed from either animals or human beings, until the "final" sacrifice of Jesus Christ's precious blood He shed on the cross at Calvary, was "the" only blood which has "redeemed" all creation, for all time, forevermore.

When I state some covenants are "confirmed" with the blood of humans, I am not talking about human sacrifices. I am referring to the "Covenant of Marriage" which is "confirmed" by blood.

How is the "Covenant of Marriage" confirmed by blood? When the man who has "circumcised" his foreskin (which sheds blood), and the woman who is supposed to be a "virgin" when she marries, joins as one flesh, the woman's hymen breaks, usually shedding blood, which signifies she is a virgin. As such, this was God's plan for "confirming" a "Covenant of Marriage" between a husband, and a wife, when they join as one flesh, and "consummate" their marriage.

520

Now let's refocus our attention on God's covenants (plural), He has established with mankind, and creation, throughout the *synergy of the ages*. Again, even though each covenant God established were for different purposes, and established through different individuals throughout the *synergy of the ages*, together, they solidify *Yehovah's* "eternal" purposes which shall come to pass, because He has determined the end from the beginning!

His "eternal" plan will unfold according to the good pleasure of His will to the praise of His glory of His grace which He made us accepted in His beloved, Son, Jesus Christ.

❖ Therefore, both the Jews from the House of Judah and those of us who were formerly Gentiles from the House of Israel (Jacob/Joseph/Ephraim), *only* have "one" book of instruction—the Bible.

This includes all sixty-six books of the Bible, beginning in the Book of Genesis to the Book of Revelation.

As such, God does not have a separate set of instructions for the Jews from the House of Judah, and those of us who were formerly Gentiles from the House of Israel (Jacob/Joseph/Ephraim).

Furthermore, as I have already stated, Jesus Christ will not come back until all the "faithful" remnant of Israel becomes "restored" and "reconciled" to our heavenly Father, *Yehovah*, under the headship of Jesus Christ, and we *literally* "become" One New Man in the earthly *physical* realm.

521

Also, this includes us "walking" and "living" according to the doctrine of Christ, which is based on our heavenly Father's instructions found in the Torah, and the gospels!

And last, but certainly not least, based on what the apostle Paul says to us in Ephesians 4:4–6, there is *only*:

1. One Body

2. One Spirit

3. One Hope

4. One Lord

5. One Faith

6. One Baptism

7. One God and Father of ALL who is above ALL and through ALL and in us ALL!

We are "one" body of Christ by our faith in Jesus Christ, and as such, God's people are to worship our heavenly Father, *Yehovah,* both in Spirit, and in truth, based on the whole counsel of His Word, including the volume of Moses, and the gospel. Especially *if* we want to be "heirs" according to the *everlasting* covenant God established with Abraham and his descendants, which is the topic of Book 2, I will be releasing as soon as possible.

Until we continue our journey together in Book 2, receive this blessing in the mighty "matchless" name of our Lord and Savior Jesus Christ, who is the Holy One of Israel, and the "tree of life"...

May the God of our Lord Jesus Christ, the Father of Glory, grant you the spirit of "wisdom" and "revelation" in the knowledge of Him, because "knowing" the only true God, and Jesus Christ whom He sent on a personal, intimate basis, is "eternal" life.

May His Holy Spirit unveil your true identity as His son, or His daughter, so the eyes of your heart will be enlightened so you will "know," on a personal, intimate basis, the HOPE of His calling on your life, and the legacy you will leave behind for all eternity.

May you answer the call of God for your life, He predestined you for before one of your days on this earth ever came to be, so you will fulfill your destiny, and do the will of your heavenly Father before you pass into eternity.

May you "know" and "experience" the riches of the glory of His inheritance in the saints, and what is the <u>exceeding</u> greatness of His POWER toward us who believe.

May you be driven by eternity, rather than the temporal things of this world which shall shortly pass away.

May you receive the revelation, God has already blessed you with every spiritual blessing and given you spiritual weapons, so you will "walk" in the fulness of His resurrection power and authority, and be victorious over all the ploys of the enemy.

May you learn to host His manifest presence by abiding continually in His love and light, so your lamp will have plenty of

523

oil—and your light, and love for the Word, will never be extinguished.

May you lay hold of, and possess your inheritance as His son or daughter so that you will overcome until the end. May you finish this race which is set before you with the victorious battle cry of Gideon of old.

May you "walk" in the fullness of your divine calling, as you love the Lord your God, with all your mind, heart, soul, and strength.

May the God of peace Himself sanctify you completely; and may your whole spirit, soul, and body be preserved blameless at the coming of our Lord Jesus Christ.

I pray this blessing for you in the name of the Father, the Son, and the Holy Spirit. Amen.

REFERENCES

INTRODUCTION

(1) Avram Yehoshua, "Yahshua, Jesus, or Yeshua?"
http://www.seedofabraham.net/jesusyeshua.html.

(2) "The Names of the Father and the Son."
http://christianitybeliefs.org/the-falling-away/the-names-of-the-father-and-the-son.

(3) "The Names of God in the Old Testament."
https://www.blueletterbible.org/study/misc/name_god.cfm.

(4) According to *Strong's Greek Lexicon* #**G1484**, the word **Gentiles** is the Greek word **ethnos** (pronounced **"eth'-nos"**), which is probably from G1486: a *race* (as of the same *habit*), that is, a *tribe*; specifically a *foreign* (*non-Jewish*) one (usually by implication *pagan*): - Gentile, heathen, nation, people.

(5) According to *Strong's Greek Lexicon* #**G4174**, the word **commonwealth** is the Greek word **politeia** (pronounced **"pol-ee-ti'-ah"**), which is from G4177 ("polity"): *citizenship*; concretely a *community:* - commonwealth, freedom.

(6) According to *Strong's Greek Lexicon* #**G1242**, the word **covenants** is synonymous with the word **testament** and is the Greek word **diathēkē** (pronounced **"dee-ath-ay'-kay"**), which is from G1303: properly a *disposition*, that is, (specifically) a *contract* (especially a devisory *will*): - covenant, testament.

(7)According to *Strong's Greek Lexicon* #**G3340**, the word **repent** is the Greek word **metanoeō** (pronounced "**met-an-o-eh'-o**"), which is from G3326 and G3539: to think differently or afterwards, that is, reconsider (morally to feel compunction): - repent.

(8)According to *Strong's Greek Lexicon* #**G1994**, the word **converted** is the Greek word **epistrephō** (pronounced "**ep-ee-stref'-o**"), which is from G1909 and G4762: to *revert* (literally, figuratively or morally): - come (go) again, convert, (re-) turn (about, again).

(9) According to *Strong's Greek Lexicon* #**G1519**, the word **in** is the Greek word **eis** (pronounced "**ice**"), which is a primary preposition; to or into (indicating the point reached or entered), of place, time, or (figuratively) purpose (result, etc.).

(10)According to *Strong's Greek Lexicon* #**G859**, the word **remission** is the Greek word **aphesis** (pronounced "**af'-es-is**"), which is from G863: *freedom*; (figuratively) *pardon* - deliverance, forgiveness, liberty, remission.

CHAPTER 1

(1)According to *Strong's Hebrew Lexicon* #**H6951**, the word **multitude** is the Hebrew word **qâhâl** (pronounced "**kaw-hawl**"), which means an assembly, company, or congregation.

(2)According to *Strong's Hebrew Lexicon* #**H5769**, the word **everlasting**, which is synonymous with the word **forever** is the Hebrew word **'ôlâm** (pronounced "**o-lawm'**"), which is from H5956: properly *concealed*, that is, the *vanishing* point; generally time *out* *of mind* (past or future), that is, (practically) *eternity*; frequentative adverbially (especially with prepositional prefix) *always*: - always (-s), ancient (time), any more, continuance, eternal, (for, [n-]) ever (-lasting, -more, of old), lasting, long (time), (of) old (time), perpetual, at any time, (beginning of the) world (+ without end). Compare H5331, H5703.

[3] According to *Strong's Hebrew Lexicon* #**H4393**, the word *multitude* is the Hebrew word *melo'* (pronounced "mel-o'"), which is from H4390: *fulness* (literally or figuratively): - X all along, X all that is (there-) in, fill, (X that whereof . . . was) full, fulness, [hand-] full, multitude.

[4] According to *Strong's Hebrew Lexicon* #**H1471**, the word *nations* is the Hebrew word *gôy* pronounced ("go'ee"): (in the sense of *massing*); a foreign *nation*; hence a *Gentile*; also (figuratively) a *troop* of animals, or a *flight* of locusts and in the KJV usage: Gentile, heathen, nation, people.

[5] According to *Strong's Hebrew Lexicon* #**H7886**, the word *Shiloh* is the Hebrew word *shîylôh* (pronounced "shee-lo'"), which is from H7951: *tranquil* (that is, *secure* or *successful*:—be happy, prosper, be in safety) *Shiloh*, an epithet of the Messiah: - Shiloh.

CHAPTER 2

[1] According to *Strong's Greek Lexicon* #**G1445**, the word *Hebrews* is the Greek word *Hebraios* (pronounced "heb-rah'-yos"), which is from G1443: a *Hebraean* (that is, Hebrew) or *Jew:* - Hebrew.

[2] According to *Strong's Greek Lexicon* #**G1443**, the word *Hebrews*

is the Greek word **Eber** (pronounced **"eb-er'"**), of Hebrew origin, H5677: *Eber*, a patriarch: - Eber.

[3] According to *Strong's Greek Lexicon* #**G2475**, the word **Israelites** is the Greek word **Israēlitēs** (pronounced **"Is-rah-ale-ee'-tace"**) from G2474: an "Israelite", that is, descendant of Israel (literally or figuratively): - Israelite.

[4] According to *Strong's Greek Lexicon* #**G2474**, the word **Israelites** is the Greek word **Israēl** (pronounced **"Is-rah-ale'"**), and is of Hebrew origin, H3478: *Israel* (that is, *Jisrael*), the adopted name of Jacob, including his descendants (literally or figuratively): - Israel.

[5] F. F. Bosworth, "The Bible Distinction between 'the House of Israel' and 'the House of Judah,'"

http://www.biblebelievers.org.au/nl479.htm.

[6] According to *Strong's Hebrew Lexicon* #**H1285**, the word **covenant** is the Hebrew word **b'rîyth** (pronounced **"ber-eeth'"**), which is from H1262: (in the sense of *cutting* [like h1254]); a *compact* (because made by passing between *pieces* of flesh): - confederacy, [con-]feder[-ate], covenant, league.

[7] According to *Strong's Hebrew Lexicon* #**H2708**, the word **statute** or **statutes** is the Hebrew word **chûqqâh** (pronounced **"khook-kaw'"**), and is the feminine of H2706: meaning substantially the same: - appointed, custom, manner, ordinance, site, statute.

[8] According to *Strong's Hebrew Lexicon* #**H4941**, the word **judgments** is synonymous with the word **justice** and is the Hebrew

word *mishpât* (pronounced **"mish-pawt'"**), which is from H8199: properly a *verdict* (favorable or unfavorable) pronounced judicially, especially a *sentence* or formal decree (human or (particularly) divine *law,* individual or collectively), including the act, the place, the suit, the crime, and the penalty; abstractly *justice,* including a particular *right,* or *privilege* (statutory or customary), or even a *style:* - + adversary, ceremony, charge, X crime, custom, desert, determination, discretion, disposing, due, fashion, form, to be judged, judgment, just (-ice, -ly), (manner of) law (-ful), manner, measure, (due) order, ordinance, right, sentence, usest, X worthy, + wrong.

[(9)]According to *Strong's Hebrew Lexicon* **#H4687**, the word **commandments** is the Hebrew word *mitsvâh* (pronounced **"mits-vaw'"**), which is from H6680: a *command,* whether human or divine (collectively the *Law*) : - (which was) commanded (-ment), law, ordinance, precept.

[(10)] According to *Strong's Hebrew Lexicon* **#H5769**, the word **perpetual,** which is synonymous with the word **forever** or **everlasting** and is the Hebrew word *'ôlâm* (pronounced **"o-lawm'"**), is from H5956: properly *concealed,* that is, the *vanishing* point; generally time *out of mind* (past or future), that is, (practically) *eternity;* frequentative adverbially (especially with prepositional prefix) *always.* - always (-s), ancient (time), any more, continuance, eternal, (for, [n-]) ever (-lasting, -more, of old), lasting, long (time), (of) old (time), perpetual, at any time, (beginning of the) world (+ without end). Compare H5331, H5703.

[(11)]According to *Strong's Hebrew Lexicon* **#H5771**, the word *iniquity* or *iniquities* is the Hebrew word *'âvôn* (pronounced "aw-vone'"), which is from H5753: *perversity*, that is, (moral) *evil:* - fault, iniquity, mischief, punishment (of iniquity), sin.

CHAPTER 3

[1]According to *Strong's Hebrew Lexicon* #H342, the word *enmity* is the Hebrew word *'êybâh* (pronounced "ay-baw'"), which is from H340: *hostility:* - enmity, hatred.

[2]According to *Strong's Hebrew Lexicon* #H7886, the word *Shiloh* is the Hebrew word *shîylôh* (pronounced "shee-lo'"), which is from H7951: *tranquil; Shiloh*, an epithet of the Messiah: - Shiloh.

[3]According to *Strong's Greek Lexicon* #G165, the word *ages* or *eternal* is the Greek word *aiōn* (pronounced "ahee-ohn'"), which is the same as G104: properly an *age*; by extension *perpetuity* (also past); by implication the *world*; specifically (Jewish) a Messianic period (present or future): - age, course, eternal, (for) ever (-more), [n-]ever, (beginning of the, while the) world (began, without end). Compare G5550.

[4]According to *Strong's Greek Lexicon* #G2936, the word *created* is the Greek word *ktizō* (pronounced "ktid'-zo"), which is probably akin to G2932: (through the idea of the *proprietorship* of the *manufacturer*); to *fabricate*, that is, *found* (*form* originally): - create, Creator, make.

[5]According to *Strong's Greek Lexicon* #G1577, the word *Church* is the Greek word *ekklēsia* pronounced ("ek-klay-see'-ah"), which is a

compound of G1537 and a derivative of G2564: a *calling out*, that is, (concretely) a popular *meeting*, especially a religious *congregation* (Jewish *synagogue*, or Christian community of members on earth or saints in heaven or both): - assembly, Church.

CHAPTER 4

[1]According to *Strong's Hebrew Lexicon* #H8121, the word **sun** is the Hebrew word **shemesh** (pronounced **"sheh'-mesh"**), which is from an unused root meaning to be *brilliant*; the *sun*; by implication the *east*; figuratively a *ray*, that is, (architecturally) a notched *battlement*. - + east side (-ward), sun ([rising]), + west (-ward), window. See also H1053.

[2]According to *Strong's Hebrew Lexicon* #H3394, the word **moon** is the Hebrew word **yârêach** (pronounced **"yaw-ray'-akh"**), which is the same as H3391: the *moon*: - moon.

[3]According to *Strong's Hebrew Lexicon* #H3391, the word **moon** is the Hebrew word **yerach** pronounced **"yeh'-rakh"** which is from an unused root of uncertain signification; a *lunation*, that is, *month*: - month, the moon.

[4]According to *Strong's Hebrew Lexicon* #H3556, the word **stars** is the Hebrew word **kôkâb** (pronounced **"ko-kawb'"**), which is probably the same as H3522 (in the sense of *rolling*) or H3554 (in the sense of *blazing*): a *star* (as *round* or as *shining*); figuratively a *prince*: - star ([-gazer]).

[5]According to *Strong's Greek Lexicon* #G1135, the word **woman** is the Greek word **gunē** (pronounced **"goo-nay'"**), which is probably

from the base of G1096: a *woman*; specifically a *wife:* - wife, woman.

(6)According to *Strong's Greek Lexicon* #G2246, the word **sun** is the Greek word **hēlios** (pronounced **"hay'-lee-os"**), which is from ἕλη helē̄: (a *ray*; perhaps akin to the alternate of G138); the *sun*; by implication *light:* - + east, sun.

(7)According to *Strong's Greek Lexicon* #G138, the word **sun** is the Greek word **aihreomai** (pronounced **"hahee-reh'-om-ahee"**), which is probably akin to G142: to *take for oneself*, that is, to *prefer*. Some of the forms are borrowed from a cognate (ἕλλομαι hellomai), which is otherwise obsolete: - choose. Some of the forms are borrowed from a cognate hellomai, hel-lom-ahee; which is otherwise obsolete.

(8)According to *Strong's Greek Lexicon* #G4582, the word **moon** is the Greek word **selēnē̄** (pronounced **"sel-ay'-nay"**), which is from σέλας selas: (*brilliancy*; probably akin to the alternate of G138, through the idea of *attractiveness*); the *moon:* - moon.

(9)According to *Strong's Greek Lexicon* #G138, the word **moon** is the Greek word **aihreomai** (pronounced **"hahee-reh'-om-ahee"**), which is probably akin to G142: to *take for oneself*, that is, to *prefer*. Some of the forms are borrowed from a cognate (ἕλλομαι hellomai), which is otherwise obsolete: - choose. Some of the forms are borrowed from a cognate hellomai, hel-lom-ahee, which is otherwise obsolete.

(10)According to *Strong's Greek Lexicon* #G4228, the word **feet** is the Greek word **pous** (pronounced **"pooce"**). A primary word; a "foot" (figuratively or literally): - foot (-stool).

(11) According to *Strong's Greek Lexicon* #**G2776**, the word **head** is the Greek word **kephalē** (pronounced **"kef-al-ay'"**), which is probably from the primary word κάπτω **kaptō** (in the sense of *seizing*): the *head* (as the part most readily *taken* hold of), literally or figuratively: - head.

(12) According to *Strong's Greek Lexicon* #**G4735**, the word **garland** is synonymous with the word **crown** and is the Greek word **stephanos** (pronounced **"stef-an-os"**), and is from an apparently primary **stepho** (to *twine* or *wreathe*): a *chaplet* (as a badge of royalty, a prize in the public games or a symbol of honor generally; but more conspicuous and elaborate than the simple *fillet*, G1238), literally or figuratively: - crown.

(13) According to *Strong's Greek Lexicon* #**G792**, the word **stars** is the Greek word **astēr** (pronounced **"as-tare'"**), which is probably from the base of G4766: a *star* (as *strown* over the sky), literally or figuratively: - star.

(14) "Allah Moon God," http://www.billionbibles.org/sharia/allah-moon-god.html.

(15) According to *Strong's Hebrew Lexicon* #**H3290**, the name **Jacob** is the Hebrew name **Ya'ăqôb** (pronounced **"yah-ak-obe'"**), which is from H6117: *heel catcher* (that is, supplanter); *Jaakob*, the *Israelitish* patriarch: - Jacob.

(16) According to *Strong's Hebrew Lexicon* #**H3478**, the name **Israel** is the Hebrew name **Yisrâ'êl** (pronounced **"Yis-raw-ale'"**), from

H8280 and H410: *he will rule* as *God*; *Jisrael*, a symbolical name of Jacob; also (typically) of his posterity: - Israel.

(17)According to *Strong's Hebrew Lexicon* #**H1008**, the name **Bethel** is the Hebrew name **Bêyth-'êl** (pronounced **"bayth-ale'"**), which is from H1004 and H410: *house of God*; *Beth-El*, a place in Palestine: - Beth-el.

(18) According to *Strong's Greek Lexicon* #**G833**, the word *fold* is the Greek word **aulē** (pronounced **"ow-lay'"**), which is from the same as G109: a *yard* (as open to the *wind*); by implication a *mansion:* - court, (sheep-) fold, hall, palace.

CHAPTER 5

(1)According to *Strong's Hebrew Lexicon* #**H5680**, the word **Hebrew** is the Hebrew word **'ibrîy** (pronounced **"ib-ree'"**), which means an *Eberite* (that is, Hebrew) or descendant of Eber.

(2) "What is a Hebrew?" http://yhvh.name/?w=1307.

(3)According to *Strong's Hebrew Lexicon* #**H3478**, the word **Israel** is the Hebrew word **Yisrâ'êl** (pronounced **"yis-raw-ale'"**), and is from H8280 and H410: *he will rule* as *God*; *Jisrael*, a symbolical name of Jacob; also (typically) of his posterity: - Israel.

(4)According to *Strong's Hebrew Lexicon* #**H3290**, the name **Jacob** is the Hebrew name **Ya'ăqôb** (pronounced **"yah-ak-obe'"**), which is from H6117: *heel catcher* (that is, supplanter); *Jaakob*, the Israelitish patriarch: - Jacob.

534

[5]According to *Strong's Hebrew Lexicon* #**H6439**, the word *Peniel* is the Hebrew word *P'nîy'êl* (pronounced "**pen-ee-ale'**"), which is from H6437 and H410: *face of God; Penuel* or *Peniel*, a place East of Jordan; also (as Penuel) the name of two Israelites: - Peniel, Penuel.

[6] "Two Houses of Israel"
http://www.yeshivahanateev.org/twohouses.html.

[7]According to *Strong's Greek Lexicon* #**G4309**, the word *predestined* is the Greek word *proorizo* (pronounced "**pro-or-id'-zo**"), which is from G4253 and G3724: to *limit in advance*, that is, (figuratively) *predetermine:* - determine before, ordain, predestinate.

[8]According to *Strong's Greek Lexicon* #**G3724**, the word *predestined* is the Greek word *proorizo* based on the Greek word *horizo* (pronounced "**hor-id'-zo**"), which is from G3725: to *mark* out or *bound* ("horizon"), that is, (figuratively) to *appoint, decree, specify:* - declare, determine, limit, ordain.

CHAPTER 6

No references

CHAPTER 7

[1]According to *Strong's Greek Lexicon* #**G3056**, the phrase *the Word* is the Greek word *logos* (pronounced "**log'-os**"), and is from G3004: something *said* (including the *thought*); by implication a *topic* (subject of discourse), also *reasoning* (the mental faculty) or *motive;* by extension a *computation;* specifically (with the article in

535

John) the Divine *Expression* (that is, *Christ*): - account, cause, communication, X concerning, doctrine, fame, X have to do, intent, matter, mouth, preaching, question, reason, + reckon, remove, say (-ing), shew, X speaker, speech, talk, thing, + none of these things move me, tidings, treatise, utterance, word, work.

(2)According to *Strong's Greek Lexicon* #**G3004**, the phrase ***the Word*** is the Greek word *legō* (pronounced **"leg'-o"**), which is a primary verb: properly to "lay" forth, that is, (figuratively) *relate* (in words [usually of systematic or set *discourse*; whereas G2036 and G5346 generally refer to an *individual* expression or speech respectively; while G4483 is properly to *break silence* merely, and G2980 means an *extended* or random harangue]); by implication to *mean:* - ask, bid, boast, call, describe, give out, name, put forth, say (-ing, on), shew, speak, tell, utter.

(3)According to *Strong's Hebrew Lexicon* #**H1254**, the word ***Creator*** is the Hebrew word *bârâ'* (pronounced **"baw-raw'"**), which is a primitive root: (absolutely) to *create*; (qualified) to select or to choose.

(4) According to *Strong's Hebrew Lexicon* #**H3478**, the name ***Israel*** is the Hebrew word *Yisrâ'êl* and is from H8280 and H410: *he will rule as God; Jisrael*, a symbolical name of Jacob; also (typically) of his posterity. KJV usage: Israel. Also, according to *Brown-Driver-Briggs' Hebrew Definitions*, it means *"God prevails."*

(5)According to *Strong's Hebrew Lexicon* #**H4428**, the word ***king*** is the Hebrew word *melek* (pronounced **"meh'-lek"**), which is from H4427: a *king:* -king, royal.

536

⁽⁶⁾According to *Strong's Hebrew Lexicon* #**H4427**, the word *king* is the Hebrew word *mâlak* (pronounced **"maw-lak'"**), which is a primitive root: to *reign*; inceptively to *ascend the throne*; causatively to *induct* into royalty; hence (by implication) to *take counsel:* - consult, X indeed, be (make, set a, set up) king, be (make) queen, (begin to, make to) reign (-ing), rule, X surely.

⁽⁷⁾According to *Strong's Hebrew Lexicon* #**H3068**, the word *LORD* is the Hebrew word *Yᵉhôvâh* (pronounced **"yeh-ho-vaw'"**), which is from H1961: (the) *self-existent* or eternal; *Jehovah*, Jewish national name of God: - Jehovah, the Lord. Compare H3050, H3069.

⁽⁸⁾According to *Strong's Hebrew Lexicon* #**H7069**, the word *possessed* is the Hebrew word *qânâh* (pronounced **"kaw-naw'"**), which is a primitive root: to *erect*, that is, *create*; *by extension to procure, especially by purchase* (causatively *sell*); by implication to *own.* KJV usage: *attain, buy (-er), teach to keep cattle, get, provoke to jealousy, possess (-or), purchase, recover, redeem, X surely, X verily.*

⁽⁹⁾According to *Strong's Hebrew Lexicon* #**H1870**, the word *way* is the Hebrew word *derek* (pronounced **"deh'-rek"**), which is from H1869: a *road* (as *trodden*); figuratively a *course* of life or *mode* of action, often adverbially: - along, away, because of, + by, conversation, custom, (east-) ward, journey, manner, passenger, toward, (high-) (path-) way (-side), whither (-soever).

⁽¹⁰⁾According to *Strong's Hebrew Lexicon* #**H1869**, the word *way* is from the root Hebrew word *dârak* (pronounced **"daw-rak'"**), which is a primitive root: to *tread*; by implication to *walk*; also to *string* a

bow (by treading on it in bending): - archer, bend, come, draw, go (over), guide, lead (forth), thresh, tread (down), walk.

[11]According to *Strong's Hebrew Lexicon* #**H5258**, the word **established** is the phrase **set up** in the KJV and is the Hebrew word **nâsak** (pronounced **"naw-sak'"**), which is a primitive root: to *pour* out, especially a libation, or to *cast* (metal); by analogy to *anoint* a king: - cover, melt, offer, (cause to) pour (out), set (up).

[12]According to *Strong's Hebrew Lexicon* #**H5769**, the word **everlasting** is the Hebrew word *'ôlâm* (pronounced **"o-lawm'"**), which is from H5956: properly *concealed*, that is, the *vanishing* point; generally time *out of mind* (past or future), that is, (practically) *eternity*; frequentative adverbially (especially with prepositional prefix) *always*: - always (-s), ancient (time), any more, continuance, eternal, (for, [n-]) ever (-lasting, -more, of old), lasting, long (time), (of) old (time), perpetual, at any time, (beginning of the) world (+ without end). Compare H5331, H5703.

[13] "Matthew Henry's Commentary on Proverbs 8:22–31," http://www.blueletterbible.org/Comm/mhc/Pro/Pro_008.cfm

[14] "Bosom," http://biblehub.com/topical/b/bosom.htm.

[15] "The Power and Wisdom of the Elect One," "The Fount of Righteousness," "The Son of Man," "The Stay of the Righteous: Judgment of the Kings and the Mighty," in The Book of Enoch, http://www.sacred-texts.com/bib/boe.

[16] According to *Strong's Greek Lexicon* #**G3346**, the word ***translated*** is the Greek word ***metatithēmi*** (pronounced **"met-at-ith'-ay-mee"**), which is from G3326 and G5087: to *transfer*, that is, (literally) *transport*, (by implication) *exchange*, (reflexively) *change sides*, or (figuratively) *pervert:* - carry over, change, remove, translate, turn.

[17] According to *Thayer's Greek–English Lexicon*, the word ***translated*** means: to transpose (two things, one of which is put in place of the other) (1) to transfer, (2) to change, (3) to transfer one's self or suffer one's self to be transferred, (3a) to go or pass over, (3b) to fall away or desert from one person or thing to another.

[18] According to *Strong's Greek Lexicon* #**G1492**, the word ***see*** is the Greek word ***eidō*** (pronounced **"i'-do"**), which is a primary verb used only in certain past tenses, the others being borrowed from the equivalent G3700 and G3708: properly to *see* (literally or figuratively); by implication (in the perfect only) to *know:* - be aware, behold, X can (+ not tell), consider, (have) known (-ledge), look (on), perceive, see, be sure, tell, understand, wist, wot. Compare G3700.

[19] According to *Thayer's Greek–English Lexicon*, the word ***see*** means: to see (1) to perceive with the eyes; (2) to perceive by any of the senses; (3) to perceive, notice, discern, discover; (4) to see (4a) (i.e., to turn the eyes, the mind, the attention to anything), (4b) to pay attention, observe (4c) to see about something (i.e., to ascertain what must be done about it) (4d) to inspect, examine (4e) to look at, behold; (5) to experience any state or condition.

539

[20]According to *Strong's Greek Lexicon* #**G3339**, the word *transfigured* is the Greek word *metamorphoō* (pronounced "met-am-or-fo'-o"), which is from G3326 and G3445: to *transform* (literally or figuratively "metamorphose"): - change, transfigure, transform.

[21]According to *Strong's Greek Lexicon* #**G3445**, the word *transfigured* is the root of the Greek word *morphoō* (pronounced "mor-fo'-o"), which is from the same as G3444: to *fashion* (figuratively): - form.

[22]According to *Strong's Greek Lexicon* #**G4633**, the word *Tabernacles* is the Greek word *skēnē* (pronounced "skay-nay'"), which is apparently akin to G4632 and G4639: a *tent* or cloth hut (literally or figuratively): - habitation, tabernacle.

[23]According to *Strong's Greek Lexicon* #**G1097**, the word *know* is the Greek word *ginōskō* (pronounced "ghin-oce'-ko"), which is a prolonged form of a primary verb: to "know" (absolutely), in a great variety of applications and with many implications (as shown at left, with others not thus clearly expressed): - allow, be aware (of), feel, (have) known (-ledge), perceive, be resolved, can speak, be sure, understand.

[24]According to *Strong's Greek Lexicon* #**G2316**, the word *God* is the Greek word *Theos* (pronounced "theh'-os"), which is of uncertain affinity; a *deity*, especially (with G3588) *the* supreme *Divinity*; figuratively a *magistrate*; by Hebraism *very:* - X exceeding, God, god (-ly, -ward).

540

⁽²⁵⁾According to *Strong's Greek Lexicon* #**G4416**, the word *firstborn* is the Greek word **prōtotokos** (pronounced "**pro-tot-ok'-os**"), which is from G4413 and the alternate of G5088: *first born* (usually as noun, literally or figuratively): - firstbegotten (-born).

⁽²⁶⁾According to *Strong's Greek Lexicon* #**G4413**, the word *firstborn* is from the root Greek *word* **prōtos** (pronounced "**pro'-tos**"), which is contracted superlative of G4253: *foremost* (in time, place, order or importance): - before, beginning, best, chief (-est), first (of all), former.

⁽²⁷⁾According to *Strong's Hebrew Lexicon* #**H430**, the word *God* is the Hebrew word *'Elôhîym* (pronounced "**el-o-heem'**"), which is plural of H433: *gods* in the ordinary sense; but specifically used (in the plural thus, especially with the article) of the supreme *God*; occasionally applied by way of deference to *magistrates*; and sometimes as a superlative: - angels, X exceeding, God (gods) (-dess, -ly), X (very) great, judges, X mighty.

⁽²⁸⁾According to *Strong's Hebrew Lexicon* #**H1254**, the word *created* is the Hebrew word **bârâ'** (pronounced "**baw-raw'**"), which is a primitive root: (absolutely) to *create*; (qualified) to *cut* down (a wood), *select, feed* (as formative processes): - choose, create (creator), cut down, dispatch, do, make (fat).

⁽²⁹⁾According to *Strong's Hebrew Lexicon* #**H7307**, the word *Spirit* is the Hebrew word **rûach** (pronounced "**roo'-akh**"), which is from H7306: *wind*; by resemblance *breath*, that is, a sensible (or even

541

violent) exhalation; figuratively *life, anger, unsubstantiality,* by extension a *region* of the sky; by resemblance *spirit,* but only of a rational being (including its expression and functions): - air, anger, blast, breath, X cool, courage, mind, X quarter, X side, spirit ([-ual]), tempest, X vain, ([whirl-]) wind (-y).

(30)According to *Strong's Hebrew Lexicon* #**H215**, the word ***light*** is the Hebrew word *'ôr* (pronounced **"ore"**), which is a primitive root: *to be* (causatively *make*) *luminous* (literally and metaphorically): - X break of day, glorious, kindle, (be, en-, give, show) light (-en, -ened), set on fire, shine.

(31)According to *Strong's Hebrew Lexicon* #**H216**, the word ***light*** is the Hebrew word *'ôr* (pronounced **"ore"**), which is from H215: *illumination* or (concretely) *luminary* (in every sense, including *lightning, happiness,* etc.): - bright, clear, + day, light (-ning), morning, sun.

(32)According to *Strong's Greek Lexicon* #**G3962**, the word ***Father*** is the Greek word ***patēr*** (pronounced **"pat-ayr'"**), which is apparently a primary word: a "father" (literally or figuratively, near or more remote): - father, parent.

(33)According to *Strong's Greek Lexicon* #**G3056**, the phrase ***the Word*** is the Greek word ***logos*** (pronounced **"log'-os"**), and is from G3004: something *said* (including the *thought*); by implication a *topic* (subject of discourse), also *reasoning* (the mental faculty) or *motive;* by extension a *computation;* specifically (with the article in John) the Divine *Expression* (that is, *Christ*): - account, cause, communication, X concerning, doctrine, fame, X have to do, intent, matter, mouth, preaching, question, reason, + reckon, remove, say (-ing), shew, X speaker, speech, talk, thing, + none of these things move me, tidings, treatise, utterance, word, work.

[34] According to *Strong's Greek Lexicon* #**G3004**, the phrase *the Word* is the Greek word *legō* (pronounced **"leg'-o"**), which is a primary verb: properly to "lay" forth, that is, (figuratively) *relate* (in words [usually of systematic or set *discourse*; whereas G2036 and G5346 generally refer to an *individual* expression or speech respectively; while G4483 is properly to *break silence* merely, and G2980 means an *extended* or random harangue]); by implication to *mean:* - ask, bid, boast, call, describe, give out, name, put forth, say (-ing, on), shew, speak, tell, utter.

[35] According to *Strong's Greek Lexicon* #**G40**, the word *holy* is the Greek word *hagios* (pronounced **"hag'-ee-os"**), which is from ἅγος hagos (an *awful* thing), compare G53, H2282: *sacred* (physically *pure*, morally *blameless* or *religious*, ceremonially *consecrated*) : - (most) holy (one, thing), saint.

[36] According to *Strong's Greek Lexicon* #**G4151**, the word *spirit* is the word *ghost* in the KJV and is the Greek word *pneuma* (pronounced **"pnyoo'-mah"**), which is from G4154: a *current* of air, that is, *breath* (*blast*) or a *breeze*; by analogy or figuratively a *spirit*, that is, (human) the rational *soul*, (by implication) *vital principle*, mental *disposition*, etc., or (superhuman) an *angel, daemon*, or (divine) God, Christ's *spirit*, the Holy *Spirit*: - ghost, life, spirit (-ual, -ually), mind. Compare G5590.

[37] According to *Strong's Greek Lexicon* #**G2222**, the word *life* is the

Greek word **zōē** (pronounced **"dzo-ay'"**), which is from G2198: *life* (literally or figuratively): - life (-time). Compare G5590.

(38)According to *Strong's Greek Lexicon* #**G5457**, the word **light** is the Greek word **phōs** (pronounced **"foce"**), which is from an obsolete φάω phaō̄ (to *shine* or make *manifest*, especially by *rays*; compare G5316 and G5346); *luminousness* (in the widest application, natural or artificial, abstract or concrete, literal or figurative): - fire, light.

(39)According to *Strong's Greek Lexicon* #**G1391**, the word **glory** is the Greek word **doxa** (pronounced **"dox'-ah"**), which is from the base of G1380: *glory* (as very *apparent*), in a wide application (literally or figuratively, objectively or subjectively): - dignity, glory (-ious), honour, praise, worship.

(40) According to *Strong's Greek Lexicon* #**G1271**, the word **mind** as used in this passage of Scripture is the Greek word **dianoia** (pronounced **"dee-an'-oy-ah"**), which means the following: (1) the mind as a faculty of understanding, feeling, desiring; (2) understanding; (3) mind (i.e. spirit, way of thinking and feeling); (4) thoughts, either good or bad.

(41) According to *Strong's Greek Lexicon* #**G2588**, the word **heart** as used in this passage of Scripture is the Greek word **kardia** (pronounced **"kar-dee'-ah"**), which means the following: (1) the heart, (a) that organ in the animal body, which is the centre of the circulation of the blood, and hence was regarded as the seat of

physical life, (b) denotes the centre of all physical and spiritual life, (c) the vigour and sense of physical life; (2) the centre and seat of spiritual life a) the soul or mind, as it is the fountain and seat of the thoughts, passions, desires, appetites, affections, purposes, endeavors, (a) of the understanding, the faculty and seat of the intelligence, (b) of the will and character, (c) of the soul so far as it is affected and stirred in a bad way or good, or of the soul as the seat of the sensibilities, affections, emotions, desires, appetites, passions, (d) of the middle or central or inmost part of anything, even though inanimate.

(42) According to *Strong's Greek Lexicon* #**G5590**, the word *soul* as used in this passage of Scripture is the Greek word *psuche* (pronounced **"psoo-khay'"**), and according to *Thayer's Greek-English Lexicon*, the Greek word *soul* means the following: (1) breath, (1A) the breath of life, (1Ai) the vital force which animates the body and shows itself in breathing, (1Aia) of animals, (1Aib) of men, (1B) life, (1C) that in which there is life, (1Ci) a living being, a living soul; (2) the soul, (2A) the seat of the feelings, desires, affections, aversions (our heart, soul, etc.), (2B) the (human) soul in so far as it is constituted that by the right use of the aids offered it by God it can attain its highest end and secure eternal blessedness, the soul regarded as a moral being designed for *everlasting* life, (2C) the soul as an essence which differs from the body and is not dissolved by death (distinguished from other parts of the body).

(43) According to *Strong's Hebrew Lexicon* #**H7069**, the word *possessed* is the Hebrew word *qânâh* (pronounced **"kaw-naw'"**), which is a primitive root: to erect, that is, create; by extension to procure, especially by purchase (causatively sell); by implication to

own KJV usage: attain, buy (-er), teach to keep cattle, get, provoke to jealousy, possess (-or), purchase, recover, redeem, X surely, X verily.

(44) According to *Strong's Hebrew Lexicon* #H3629, the word **reins** is the Hebrew word *kilyâh* (pronounced "kil-yaw'"), and is a kidney (as an essential organ); figuratively the mind (as the interior self).

(45) According to *Strong's Hebrew Lexicon* #H5526, the word *covered* is the Hebrew word *sâkak* (pronounced "saw-kak'"), which is a primitive root: properly to entwine as a screen; by implication to fence in, cover over, figuratively) protect KJV usage: cover, defense, defend, hedge in, join together, set, shut up.

(46) According to *Strong's Hebrew Lexicon* #H5315, the word **soul** is the Hebrew word *nephesh* (pronounced "neh'-fesh"), which means a breathing creature, that is, animal or (abstractly) vitality; used very widely in a literal, accommodated or figurative sense (bodily or mental).

According to *Brown-Driver-Brigg's Hebrew Lexicon*, **nephesh** נֶפֶשׁ means: 1) soul, self, life, creature, person, appetite, mind, living being, desire, emotion, passion 1a) that which breathes, the breathing substance or being, soul, the inner being of man 1b) living being 1c) living being (with life in the blood) 1d) the man himself, self, person or individual 1e) seat of the appetites 1f) seat of emotions and passions 1g) activity of mind 1g1) dubious 1h) activity of the will 1h1) dubious 1i) activity of the character 1i1) dubious.

(47) According to *Strong's Hebrew Lexicon* #H6108, the word **substance** is the Hebrew word *ôtsem* (pronounced "o'-tsem"), which means power; hence, body.

(48) According to *Strong's Hebrew Lexicon* #H5643, the word **secret** is the Hebrew word *sêther* (pronounced "say'-ther"), which means: covering, shelter, hiding place, secrecy; shelter, protection.

(49) According to *Strong's Hebrew Lexicon* #H7551, the word **wrought** is the Hebrew word *raqam* (pronounced "raw-kam'"), which according to the *Brown-Driver-Briggs' (Old Testament Hebrew-English Lexicon)* is a primitive root, which means to variegate color, that is, embroider; by implication to fabricate.

(50) According to *Strong's Hebrew Lexicon* #H8482, the term **lowest parts** is the Hebrew word *tachtîy* (pronounced "takh-tee'"), which means: lowermost; as noun (feminine plural) the depths (figuratively a *pit*, the womb).

(51) According to *Strong's Hebrew Lexicon* #H1564, the word **unperfect** is the Hebrew word *golem* (pronounced "go'-lem"), which is from H1563: a *wrapped* (and unformed *mass*, that is, as the *embryo*): - substance yet being unperfect; embryo, fetus.

(52) According to *Strong's Hebrew Lexicon* #H3335, the word *fashioned* is the Hebrew word *yâtsar* (pronounced "yaw-tsar'"), which is probably identical to H3334: (through the *squeezing* into shape); (compare H3331); to *mould* into a form; especially as a *potter*; figuratively to *determine* (that is, form a resolution): - X earthen, fashion, form, frame, make (-r), potter, purpose.

547

[53]According to the *Brown-Driver-Briggs' Hebrew Lexicon* the word *fashioned* is the Hebrew word *yâtsar or* יצר (pronounced "yaw-tsar'"), which means the following: 1) to form, fashion, frame 1a) (Qal) to form, fashion 1a1) of human activity 1a2) of divine activity 1a2a) of creation 1a2a1) of original creation 1a2a2) of individuals at conception 1a2a3) of Israel as a people 1a2b) to frame, pre-ordain, plan (figuratively of divine) purpose of a situation) 1b) (Niphal) to be formed, be created 1c) (Pual) to be predetermined, be preordained 1d) (Hophal) to be formed.

[54] According to *Strong's Hebrew Lexicon* #H4908, the word *tabernacle* is the Hebrew word *mishkân* (pronounced "mish-kawn'"), and is from H7931: a *residence* (including a shepherd's *hut*, the *lair* of animals, figuratively the *grave*; also the *Temple*); specifically the *Tabernacle* (properly its wooden walls): - dwelleth, dwelling (place), habitation, tabernacle, and tent.

CHAPTER 8

[1]According to *Strong's Greek Lexicon* #G2305, the word *Godhead* is the Greek word *theiotēs* (pronounced "thi-ot'-ace"), which is from G2304 and means divinity (abstractly): - godhead.

[2]According to *Strong's Greek Lexicon* #G2304, the word *Godhead* is the Greek word *theios* (pronounced "thi'-os"), which is from G2316: *godlike* (neuter as a noun, *divinity*): - divine, godhead.

[3]According to *Strong's Greek Lexicon* #G2316, the word *Godhead* or the word *God* is the Greek word *theos* (pronounced "theh'-os"): of uncertain affinity; a *deity*, especially (with G3588) *the* supreme

548

Divinity; figuratively a *magistrate*; by Hebraism *very:* - X exceeding, God, god (-ly, -ward).

According to *Thayer's Greek Dictionary*, the word **Godhead** or **God** can also mean the following: (1) a god or goddess, a general name of deities or divinities; (2) the Godhead, trinity, (2a) God the Father, the first person in the Trinity, (2b) Christ, the second Person of the Trinity, (2c) Holy Spirit, the third Person of the Trinity; (3) spoken of the only and true God, (3a) refers to the things of God.

[4]According to *Strong's Greek Lexicon* #**G2320**, the word **Godhead** is the Greek word **theotē̄s** (pronounced **"theh-ot'-ace"**), which is from G2316: *divinity* (abstractly): - godhead.

[5] *King James Version of the New Testament Greek Lexicon*, http://www.biblestudytools.com/lexicons/greek/kjv/theos.html.

[6] According to *Strong's Greek Lexicon* #**G3444**, the word **form** is the Greek word **morphē̄** (pronounced **"mor-fay'"**), which is perhaps from the base of G3313: (through the idea of *adjustment* of parts); *shape*; figuratively *nature:* - form.

[7]According to *Strong's Greek Lexicon* #**G3313**, the word **form** is the Greek root word **meros** (pronounced **"mer'-os"**), which is an obsolete but more primary form of μείρομαι meiromai: (to *get* as a *section* or *allotment*); a *division* or *share* (literally or figuratively, in a wide application): - behalf, coast, course, craft, particular (+ -ly), part (+ -ly), piece, portion, respect, side, some sort (-what).

549

(8)According to *Strong's Greek Lexicon* #**G2758**, the word **reputation** is the Greek word **kenoō** (pronounced **"ken-o'-o"**), which is from G2756: to *make empty*, that is, (figuratively) to *abase, neutralize, falsify:* - make (of none effect, of no reputation, void), be in vain.

(9)According to *Strong's Greek Lexicon* #**G1096**, the word **made** is the Greek word **ginomai** (pronounced **"ghin'-om-ahee"**), which is a prolonged and middle form of a primary verb: to cause to be ("gen" -erate), that is, (reflexively) to become (*come into being*), used with great latitude (literally, figuratively, intensively, etc.): - arise be assembled, be (come, -fall, -have self), be brought (to pass), (be) come (to pass), continue, be divided, be done, draw, be ended, fall, be finished, follow, be found, be fulfilled, + God forbid, grow, happen, have, be kept, be made, be married, be ordained to be, partake, pass, be performed, be published, require, seem, to be shown, X soon as it was, sound, be taken, be turned, use, wax, will, would, be wrought.

(10) According to *Strong's Greek Lexicon* #**G4976**, the word **fashion** *is the Greek word* **schēma** (pronounced **"skhay'-mah"**), which is from the alternate of G2192: a *figure* (as a *mode* or *circumstance*), that is, (by implication) external condition: - fashion.

(11)According to *Strong's Greek Lexicon* #**G5013**, the word **humbled** is the Greek word **tapeinoō** (pronounced **"tap-i-no'-o"**), which is from G5011: to *depress,* figuratively to *humiliate* (in condition or heart): - abase, bring low, humble (self).

(12) According to *Strong's Greek Lexicon* #**G5255**, the word **obedient** is the Greek word **hupēkoos** (pronounced "**hoop-ay'-ko-os**"), which is from G5219: *attentively listening*, that is, (by implication) *submissive:* - obedient.

(13) According to *Strong's Greek Lexicon* #**G5219**, the word **obedient** is the Greek root word **hupakouō** (pronounced "**hoop-ak-oo'-o**"), which is from G5259 and G191: to *hear under* (as a *subordinate*), that is, to *listen attentively*; by implication to *heed* or *conform* to a command or authority: - hearken, be obedient to, obey.

(14) According to *Strong's Hebrew Lexicon* #**H430**, the word **God** is the Hebrew word **'Elôhîym** (pronounced "**el-o-heem'**"), which is the plural of H433: *gods* in the ordinary sense; but specifically used (in the plural thus, especially with the article) of the supreme *God*; occasionally applied by way of deference to *magistrates*; and sometimes as a superlative: - angels, X exceeding, God (gods) (-dess, -ly), X (very) great, judges, X mighty.

(15) According to *Strong's Hebrew Lexicon* #**H433**, the word **God** is the Hebrew root word **'elôahh** (pronounced "**el-o'-ah**") (the second form is rare): probably prolonged (emphatically) from H410; a *deity* or the *deity*: - God, god. See H430.

(16) According to *Strong's Hebrew Lexicon* #**H259**, the word **one** is the Hebrew word **'echâd** (pronounced "**ekh-awd'**") and a numeral from H258: properly *united*, that is, *one*; or (as an ordinal) *first:* - a, alike, alone, altogether, and, any (-thing), apiece, a certain [dai-] ly,

each (one), + eleven, every, few, first, + highway, a man, once, one, only, other, some, together.

(17) The word **Memra** is an Aramaic word, which means the following: the Word of God by which the universe was created. The term *memra* occurs in the *Targum* literature with similar connotations to the Greek term *logos*, understood by *Philo* to mean the mind of God as revealed in creation (http://www.encyclopedia.com/doc/1O101-Memra.html).

(18) According to *Strong's Greek Lexicon* #**G2937**, the word **creation** in the KJV is **creature** and is the Greek word **ktisis** (pronounced "ktis'-is"), which is from G2936: original *formation* (properly the act; by implication the thing, literally or figuratively): - building, creation, creature, ordinance.

(19) According to *Strong's Greek Lexicon* #**G2936**, the word **created** is the Greek word **ktizō** (pronounced "ktid'-zo"), which is probably akin to G2932: (through the idea of the *proprietorship* of the *manufacturer*); to *fabricate*, that is, *found* (*form* originally): - create, Creator, make.

(20) According to *Strong's Greek Lexicon* #**G2424**, the name **Jesus** is the Greek word **Iēsous** (pronounced "ee-ay-sooce'"), which is of Hebrew origin H3091: *Jesus* (that is, *Jehoshua*), the name of our Lord and two (three) other Israelites: - Jesus. See Jesus' Hebrew name **Yêshûa'** based on *Strong's Hebrew Lexicon* #**H3442**.

⁽²¹⁾ According to *Strong's Hebrew Lexicon* #H3091, the name *Jesus* or **Lord** is the Hebrew name **Yĕhowshuwa`** (pronounced "yeh-hō-shü'-ah"), which is from H3068 and H3467.

⁽²²⁾ According to *Strong's Hebrew Lexicon* #H3068, the name *Jesus* or **Lord** is the Hebrew name **Y͏ͤhôvâh** (pronounced "yeh-ho-vaw'"), which is from H1961: (the) *self-Existent* or eternal; *Jehovah*, Jewish national name of God: - Jehovah, the Lord. Compare H3050.

⁽²³⁾ According to *Strong's Hebrew Lexicon* #H3467, the name *Jesus* or **Lord** is the Hebrew name **Yâsha'** (pronounced "yaw-shah'"), which is a primitive root: properly to *be open, wide* or *free*, that is, (by implication) to *be safe*; causatively to free or *succor*: - X at all, avenging, defend, deliver (-er), help, preserve, rescue, be safe, bring (having) salvation, save (-iour), get victory.

⁽²⁴⁾ According to *Strong's Hebrew Lexicon* #H3442, the name *Jesus* is the Hebrew name **Yêshûa'** (pronounced "yah-shoo'-ah") for H3091: He will save; *Jeshua*, the name of two Israelites, also of a place in Palestine: - Jeshua.

⁽²⁵⁾ According to *Strong's Hebrew Lexicon* #H3050, the name *Jesus* is the Hebrew name **Yâhh** (pronounced "yaw"), which is contracted for H3068: the same; *Jah*, the sacred name: - Jah, the Lord, most vehement. Cp. names in "-iah," "-jah."

⁽²⁶⁾ According to *Strong's Hebrew Lexicon* #H1961, the name *Jesus* is the Hebrew name **hâyâh** (pronounced "haw-yaw'"), which is a primitive root (compare H1933): to exist, that is, be or become, come to pass (always emphatic, and not a mere copula or auxiliary):

- beacon, X altogether, be (-come, accomplished, committed, like), break, cause, come (to pass), continue, do, faint, fall, + follow, happen, X have, last, pertain, quit (one-) self, require, X use.

(27) According to *Strong's Hebrew Lexicon* #**H1933**, the name *Jesus* is the Hebrew name *hâvâ'* or *hâvâh* (pronounced **"haw-vaw'"**), which is a primitive root (compare H183, H1961) supposed to mean properly to breathe; to be (in the sense of existence): - be, X have.

(28) According to *Strong's Greek Lexicon* #**G5310**, the word *Highest* is the Greek word *hupsistos* (pronounced **"hoop'-sis-tos"**), superlative from the base of G5311: *highest*, that is, (masculine singular) the Supreme (God), or (neuter plural) the *heavens:* - most high, highest.

(29) According to *Strong's Greek Lexicon* #**G1097**, the word *know* is the Greek word *ginōskō* (pronounced **"ghin-oce'-ko"**), and in this context, is the Jewish idiom for sexual intercourse between a man and a woman.

(30) According to *Strong's Greek Lexicon* #**G40**, the word *Holy* is the Greek word *hagios* (pronounced **"hag'-ee-os"**) and means sacred (physically pure, morally blameless or religious, ceremonially consecrated) : - (most) holy (one, thing), a saint.

(31) According to *Strong's Greek Lexicon* #**G4151**, the word *spirit* is synonymous with *ghost* as used in the KJV and is the Greek word *pneuma* (pronounced **"pnyoo'-mah"**), which is from G4154: a *current* of air, that is, *breath* (*blast*) or a *breeze;* by analogy or

554

figuratively a *spirit*, that is, (human) the rational *soul*, (by implication) *vital principle*, mental *disposition*, etc., or (superhuman) an *angel*, *daemon*, or (divine) God, Christ's *Spirit*, the Holy *Spirit*. - ghost, life, spirit (-ual, -ually), mind. Compare G5590.

(32) According to *Strong's Greek Lexicon* #G1411, the word ***power*** is the Greek word ***dunamis*** (pronounced **"doo'-nam-is"**), which is defined as follows: 1) strength power, ability; 1a) inherent power, power residing in a thing by virtue of its nature, or which a person or thing exerts and puts forth; 1b) power for performing miracles; 1c) moral power and excellence of soul; 1d) the power and influence which belong to riches and wealth; 1e) power and resources arising from numbers.

(33) According to *Strong's Greek Lexicon* #G1982, the word ***overshadow*** is the Greek word ***episkiazō*** (pronounced **"ep-ee-skee-ad'-zo"**), which is from G1909 and a derivative of G4639: to *cast a shade upon*, that is, (by analogy) to *envelop* in a haze of brilliancy; figuratively to *invest* with preternatural influence: - overshadow.

(34) According to *Strong's Greek Lexicon* #G5207, the word ***Son*** is the Greek word ***uihos*** (pronounced **"hwee-os'"**), which is apparently a primary word: a "son" (sometimes of animals), used very widely of immediate, remote or figurative kinship: - child, foal, son.

(35) According to *Strong's Hebrew Lexicon* #H4428, the word ***king*** is the Hebrew word ***melek*** (pronounced **"meh'-lek"**), which is from H4427: a *king:* - king, royal.

(36) According to *Strong's Hebrew Lexicon* #H4427, the word ***king*** is

the Hebrew word *mâlak* (pronounced **"maw-lak'"**), which is a primitive root: to *reign*; inceptively to *ascend the throne*; causatively to *induct* into royalty; hence (by implication) to *take counsel*: - consult, X indeed, be (make, set a, set up) king, be (make) queen, (begin to, make to) reign (-ing), rule, X surely.

(37)According to *Strong's Hebrew Lexicon* #**H6635**, the word *hosts* is the Hebrew word *tsâbâ'* (pronounced **"tsaw-baw'"**), which is from H6633: a *mass* of persons (or figurative things), especially regularly organized for war (an *army*); by implication a *campaign*, literally or figuratively (specifically *hardship, worship*): - appointed time, (+) army, (+) battle, company, host, service, soldiers, waiting upon, war (-fare).

(38)According to *Strong's Greek Lexicon* #**G2962**, the word **Lord** is the Greek word *kurios* (pronounced **"koo'-ree-os"**), which is from κῦρος kuros (*supremacy*); supreme in authority, that is, (as noun) *controller*; by implication *Mr.* (as a respectful title): - God, Lord, master, Sir.

(39)According to *Strong's Hebrew Lexicon* #**H5945**, the word **High** as in the title the **Most High God** is the Hebrew word *'Elyôn* (pronounced **"el-yone'"**), which is from H5927: an *elevation*, that is, (adjectively) *lofty* (comparatively); as title, the *Supreme*: - (Most, on) high (-er, -est), upper (-most).

(40) *The Book of Enoch*
http://book-ofenoch.com/chapter-48.

556

CHAPTER 9

(1)According to *Strong's Greek Lexicon* #**G2962**, the word **Lord** is the Greek word **kurios** (pronounced **"koo'-ree-os"**), which is from κῦρος kuros (*supremacy*); supreme in authority, that is, (as noun) *controller*; by implication *Mr.* (as a respectful title): - God, Lord, master, Sir.

(2)According to *Strong's Greek Lexicon* #**G3841**, the word **Almighty** is the Greek word **pantokratōr** (pronounced **"pan-tok-rat'-ore"**), which is from G3956 and G2904: the *all ruling*, that is, *God* (as absolute and universal *sovereign*): - Almighty, Omnipotent.

(3)According to *Strong's Hebrew Lexicon* #**H3068**, the word **LORD** is the Hebrew word **Yehôvâh** (pronounced **"yeh-ho-vaw'"**), which is from H1961: (the) *self-Existent* or eternal; *Jehovah*, Jewish national name of God: - Jehovah, the Lord. Compare H3050, H3069.

(4)According to *Strong's Hebrew Lexicon* #**H410**, the word **God** is the Hebrew word **'El** (pronounced **"ale"**), which is shortened from H352: *strength*; as adjective *mighty*; especially the *Almighty* (but used also of any *deity*): - God (god), X goodly, X great, idol, might (-y one), power, strong. Compare names in "-el."

(5)According to *Strong's Hebrew Lexicon* #**H3335** the word **formed** is the Hebrew word **yâtsar** (pronounced **"yaw-tsar'"**), and is probably identical with H3334: (through the *squeezing* into shape);

557

(compare H3331); to *mould* into a form; especially as a *potter;* figuratively to *determine* (that is, form a resolution): - X earthen, fashion, form, frame, make (-r), potter, purpose.

[6] According to *Strong's Hebrew Lexicon* #**H3467**, the word **Savior** is the Hebrew word **yâsha'** (pronounced **"yaw-shah'"**), a primitive root: properly to *be open, wide* or *free,* that is, (by implication) to *be safe;* causatively to *free* or *succor:* - X at all, avenging, defend, deliver (-er), help, preserve, rescue, be safe, bring (having) salvation, save (-iour), get victory.

[7] According to *Strong's Hebrew Lexicon* #**H4428**, the word **king** is the Hebrew word **melek** (pronounced **"meh'-lek"**), which is from H4427; a *king:* - king, royal.

[8] According to *Strong's Hebrew Lexicon* #**H4427**, the word **king** is the Hebrew word **mâlak** (pronounced **"maw-lak'"**), which is a primitive root; to *reign;* inceptively to *ascend the throne;* causatively to *induct* into royalty; hence (by implication) to *take counsel:* - consult, X indeed, be (make, set a, set up) king, be (make) queen, (begin to, make to) reign (-ing), rule, X surely.

[9] According to *Strong's Hebrew Lexicon* #**H1350**, the word **Redeemer** is the Hebrew word **gâ'al** (pronounced **"gaw-al'"**), which is a primitive root, to *redeem* (according to the Oriental law of kinship), that is, to *be the next of kin* (and as such to *buy back* a relative's property, *marry* his widow, etc.): - X in any wise, X at all, avenger, deliver, (do, perform the part of near, next) kinsfolk (-man), purchase, ransom, redeem (-er), revenger.

Donna M. Rogers

(10)According to *Strong's Hebrew Lexicon* #**H6635**, the word *hosts* is the Hebrew word *tsebâ'âh* (pronounced "tseb-aw-aw'"), which is from H6633:a *mass* of persons (or figurative things), especially regularly organized for war (an *army*); by implication a *campaign*, literally or figuratively (specifically *hardship, worship*): - appointed time, (+) army, (+) battle, company, host, service, soldiers, waiting upon, war (-fare).

(11)According to *Strong's Hebrew Lexicon* #**H430** the word *God* is the Hebrew word *'Elôhîym* (pronounced "el-o-heem'"), which is plural of H433: *gods* in the ordinary sense; but specifically used (in the plural thus, especially with the article) of the supreme *God*; occasionally applied by way of deference to *magistrates*; and sometimes as a superlative: - angels, X exceeding, God (gods) (-dess, -ly), X (very) great, judges, X mighty.

(12)According to *Strong's Greek Lexicon* #**G935**, the word *King* is the Greek word *basileus* (pronounced "bas-il-yooce'"), which is probably from G939: (through the notion of a *foundation* of power); a *sovereign* (abstractly, relatively or figuratively): - king.

(13)According to *Strong's Greek Lexicon* #**G939**, the word *King* is from the root of the Greek word *basis* (pronounced "bas'-ece"), which is from βαίνω bainō (to *walk*); a *pace* ("base"), that is, (by implication) the *foot*: - foot.

(14)According to *Strong's Greek Lexicon* #**G165**, the word *eternal* is synonymous with the word *forever* and is the Greek word *aiōn*

559

(pronounced **"ahee-ohn'"**), which is from the same as G104:properly an *age*; by extension *perpetuity* (also past); by implication the *world*; specifically (Jewish) a Messianic period (present or future): - age, course, eternal, (for) ever (-more), [n-]ever, (beginning of the, while the) world (began, without end). Compare G5550.

(15) According to *Strong's Greek Lexicon* #**G862**, the word *immortal* is synonymous with *incorruptible* or *incorruption* and is the Greek word **aphthartos** (pronounced **"af'-thar-tos"**), which means *undecaying* (in essence or continuance): incorruption, incorruptible.

(16) According to *Strong's Greek Lexicon* #**G517**, the word *invisible* is the Greek word **aoratos** (pronounced **"ah-or'-at-os"**), which is from G1 (as a negative particle) and G3707; *invisible:* - invisible (thing).

(17) According to *Strong's Greek Lexicon* #**G2316**, the word *God* is the Greek word **Theos** (pronounced **"theh'-os"**), which is of uncertain affinity; a *deity*, especially (with G3588) *the* supreme *Divinity*; figuratively a *magistrate*; by Hebraism *very:* - X exceeding, God, god (-ly, -ward).

(18) According to *Strong's Greek Lexicon* #**G1413**, the word **Potentate** is the Greek word **dunastēs** (pronounced **"doo-nas'-tace"**), which means Lord, master, or ruler of great and mighty authority.

(19) According to *Strong's Greek Lexicon* #**G110**, the word

immortality is the Greek word ***athanasia*** (pronounced **"ath-an-as-ee'-ah"**), which is a compound of G1 (as a negative particle) and G2288; *deathlessness:* - immortality.

[20] According to *Strong's Hebrew Lexicon* #**H7307**, the word ***Spirit*** is the Hebrew word ***rûach*** (pronounced **"roo'-akh"**), which is from H7306: *wind*; by resemblance *breath*, that is, a sensible (or even violent) exhalation; figuratively *life, anger, unsubstantiality*; by extension a *region* of the sky; by resemblance *spirit*, but only of a rational being (including its expression and functions): - air, anger, blast, breath, X cool, courage, mind, X quarter, X side, spirit ([-ual]), tempest, X vain, ([whirl-]) wind (-y).

[21] According to *Strong's Hebrew Lexicon* #**H5397**, the word ***breath*** is the Hebrew word ***nᵉshâmâh*** (pronounced **"nesh-aw-maw'"**), and is from H5395: a *puff*, that is, *wind*, angry or vital *breath*, divine *inspiration, intellect* or (concretely) an *animal:* - blast, (that) breath (-eth), inspiration, soul, spirit.

[22] According to *Strong's Hebrew Lexicon* #**H2421**, the word ***life*** is the Hebrew word ***châyâh*** (pronounced **"khaw-yaw'"**), which is a prim root (compare H2331, H2424): to *live*, whether literally or figuratively; causatively to *revive:* - keep (leave, make) alive, X certainly, give (promise) life, (let, suffer to) live, nourish up, preserve (alive), quicken, recover, repair, restore (to life), revive, (X God) save (alive, life, lives), X surely, be whole.

CHAPTER 10

[1] According to *Strong's Hebrew Lexicon* #**H430**, the word ***God*** is

the Hebrew word *'Ĕlŏhîym* (pronounced **"el-o-heem'"**), which is plural of H433: *gods* in the ordinary sense; but specifically used (in the plural thus, especially with the article) of the supreme *God;* occasionally applied by way of deference to *magistrates;* and sometimes as a superlative: - angels, X exceeding, God (gods) (-dess, -ly), X (very) great, judges, X mighty.

[2] According to *Strong's Hebrew Lexicon* #**H1254**, the word ***created*** in the Hebrew is the word ***bârâ'*** (pronounced **"baw-raw'"**), which is a *primitive root; (absolutely)* to create*; (qualified)* to cut down (a wood)*,* select, *feed* (as formative processes).

[3] According to *Strong's Hebrew Lexicon* #**H7307**, the word ***Spirit*** is the Hebrew word ***rûach*** (pronounced **"roo'-akh"**), which is from H7306: *wind;* by resemblance *breath*, that is, a sensible (or even violent) exhalation; figuratively *life, anger, unsubstantiality;* by extension a *region* of the sky; by resemblance *spirit*, but only of a rational being (including its expression and functions): - air, anger, blast, breath, X cool, courage, mind, X quarter, X side, spirit ([-ual]), tempest, X vain, ([whirl-]) wind (-y).

[4] According to *Strong's Greek Lexicon* #**G3056**, the phrase ***the Word*** is the Greek word ***logos*** (pronounced **"log'-os"**), and is from G3004: something *said* (including the *thought*); by implication a *topic* (subject of discourse), also *reasoning* (the mental faculty) or *motive;* by extension a *computation;* specifically (with the article in John) the Divine *Expression* (that is, *Christ*): - account, cause, communication, X concerning, doctrine, fame, X have to do, intent, matter, mouth, preaching, question, reason, + reckon, remove, say (-ing), shew, X speaker, speech, talk, thing, + none of

these things move me, tidings, treatise, utterance, word, work.

(5)According to *Strong's Greek Lexicon* #**G3004** the phrase *the Word* is the Greek word *legō* (pronounced **"leg'-o"**), which is a primary verb; properly to *"lay"* forth, that is, (figuratively) *relate* (in words [usually of systematic or set *discourse*; whereas G2036 and G5346 generally refer to an *individual* expression or speech respectively; while G4483 is properly to *break silence* merely, and G2980 means an *extended* or random harangue]); by implication to *mean:* - ask, bid, boast, call, describe, give out, name, put forth, say (-ing, on), shew, speak, tell, utter.

(6)According to *Strong's Greek Lexicon* #**G2316**, the word *God* is the Greek word *Theos* (pronounced **"theh'-os"**), which is of uncertain affinity; a *deity*, especially (with G3588) *the* supreme *Divinity*; figuratively a *magistrate*; by Hebraism *very:* - X exceeding, God, god (-ly, -ward).

(7)According to *Strong's Hebrew Lexicon* #**H559**, the word *said* is the Hebrew word *'âmar* (pronounced **"aw-mar'"**), which is a primitive root; to *say* (used with great latitude): - answer, appoint, avouch, bid, boast self, call, certify, challenge, charge, + (at the, give) command (ment), commune, consider, declare, demand, X desire, determine, X expressly, X indeed, X intend, name, X plainly, promise, publish, report, require, say, speak (against, of), X still, X suppose, talk, tell, term, X that is, X think, use [speech], utter, X verily, X yet.

(8)According to *Strong's Hebrew Lexicon* #**H215**, the word *light* is the Hebrew word *'ôr* (pronounced **"ore"**), which is a primitive root;

563

to be (causatively *make*) *luminous* (literally and metaphorically): -
X break of day, glorious, kindle, (be, en-, give, show) light (-en, -
ened), set on fire, shine.

(9)According to *Strong's Hebrew Lexicon* #**H216**, the word **light** is
the Hebrew word *'ôr* (pronounced **"ore"**), which is from H215;
illumination or (concretely) *luminary* (in every sense, including
lightning, happiness, etc.): - bright, clear, + day, light (-ning),
morning, sun.

(10)According to *Strong's Greek Lexicon* #**G5457**, the word **light** is
the Greek word **phōs** (pronounced **"foce"**), which is from an
obsoleteφάω phaō¯ (to *shine* or make *manifest*, especially by *rays*;
compare G5316 and G5346); *luminousness* (in the widest
application, natural or artificial, abstract or concrete, literal or
figurative): - fire, light.

(11)According to *Strong's Greek Lexicon* #**G2222**, the word **life** is the
Greek word **zōē¯** (pronounced **"dzo-ay'"**), which is from G2198; *life*
(literally or figuratively): - life (-time). Compare G5590.

(12)According to *Strong's Greek Lexicon* #**G5461**, the word **light** is
the Greek word **phōtizō¯** (pronounced **"fo-tid'-zo"**), which is from
G5457; to *shed rays*, that is, to *shine* or (transitively) to *brighten* up
(literally or figuratively): - enlighten, illuminate, (bring to, give)
light, make to see.

(13)According to *Strong's Hebrew Lexicon* #**H1697** the word **Word**
or **Words** is the Hebrew word **dâbâr** (pronounced **"daw-bawr'"**),

564

which is from H1696; a *word*, by implication a *matter* (as *spoken* of) of *thing*; adverbially a *cause:* - act, advice, affair, answer, X any such (thing), + because of, book, business, care, case, cause, certain rate, + chronicles, commandment, X commune (-ication), + concern [-ing], + confer, counsel, + dearth, decree, deed, X disease, due, duty, effect, + eloquent, errand, [evil favoured-] ness, + glory, + harm, hurt, + iniquity, + judgment, language, + lying, manner, matter, message, [no] thing, oracle, X ought, X parts, + pertaining, + please, portion, + power, promise, provision, purpose, question, rate, reason, report, request, X (as hast) said, sake, saying, sentence, + sign, + so, some [uncleanness], somewhat to say, + song, speech, X spoken, talk, task, + that, X there done, thing (concerning), thought, + thus, tidings, what [-soever], + wherewith, which, word, work.

(14) According to *Strong's Hebrew Lexicon* #H5216, the word *lamp* is the Hebrew word *nêrâh* (pronounced **"nay-raw'"**), which is from a primitive root (see H5214 and H5135) properly meaning to *glisten*; a *lamp* (that is, the burner) or *light* (literally or figuratively): - candle, lamp, light.

(15) According to *Strong's Hebrew Lexicon* #H4687, the word **commandment** is the Hebrew word *mitsvâh* (pronounced **"mits-vaw'"**), which is from H6680; a *command*, whether human or divine (collectively the *Law*) : - (which was) commanded (-ment), law, ordinance, precept.

(16) According to *Strong's Hebrew Lexicon* #H8451, the word *law* is Hebrew word *tôrâh* (pronounced **"to-raw'"**), which is from H3384; a *precept* or *statute*, especially the *Decalogue* or *Pentateuch:* - law.

565

[17]According to *Strong's Hebrew Lexicon* #**H2416**, the word *life* is the Hebrew word **chay** (pronounced **"khah'ee"**), which is from H2421; *alive*; hence *raw* (flesh); *fresh* (plant, water, year), *strong*; also (as noun, especially in the feminine singular and masculine plural) *life* (or living thing), whether literally or figuratively: - + age, alive, appetite, (wild) beast, company, congregation, life (-time), live (-ly), living (creature, thing), maintenance, + merry, multitude, + (be) old, quick, raw, running, springing, troop.

[18]According to *Strong's Hebrew Lexicon* #**H2421**, the word *life* is the Hebrew root word **châyâh** (pronounced **"khaw-yaw'"**), which is a prim root (compare H2331, H2424); to *live*, whether literally or figuratively; causatively to *revive:* - keep (leave, make) alive, X certainly, give (promise) life, (let, suffer to) live, nourish up, preserve (alive), quicken, recover, repair, restore (to life), revive, (X God) save (alive, life, lives), X surely, be whole.

[19]According to *Strong's Hebrew Lexicon* #**H4941**, the word *justice* is the Hebrew word **mishpât** (pronounced **"mish-pawt'"**), which is from H8199; properly a *verdict* (favorable or unfavorable) pronounced judicially, especially a *sentence* or formal decree (human or (particularly) divine *law*, individual or collectively), including the act, the place, the suit, the crime, and the penalty; abstractly justice, including a particular *right*, or *privilege* (statutory or customary), or even a *style:* - + adversary, ceremony, charge, X crime, custom, desert, determination, discretion, disposing, due, fashion, form, to be judged, judgment, just (-ice, -ly), (manner of) law (-ful), manner, measure, (due) order, ordinance, right,

sentence, usest, X worthy, + wrong.

(20)According to *Strong's Hebrew Lexicon* #**H8584**, the word **testimony** is the Hebrew *word t'ûdâh* (pronounced **"teh-oo-daw'"**), which is from H5749; *attestation*, that is, a *precept, usage:* - testimony.

(21)According to *Strong's Hebrew Lexicon* #**H8549**, the word **perfect** is the Hebrew word *tâmîym* (pronounced **"taw-meem'"**), which is from H8552; *entire* (literally, figuratively or morally); also (as noun) *integrity, truth:* - without blemish, complete, full, perfect, sincerely (-ity), sound, without spot, undefiled, upright (-ly), whole.

(22)According to *Strong's Hebrew Lexicon* #**H7725**, the word **converting** is the Hebrew word *shûb* (pronounced **"shoob"**), which is a primitive root; to *turn* back (hence, away) transitively or intransitively, literally or figuratively (not necessarily with the idea of *return* to the starting point); generally to *retreat*; often adverbially *again:* - ([break, build, circumcise, dig, do anything, do evil, feed, lay down, lie down, lodge, make, rejoice, send, take, weep]) X again, (cause to) answer (+ again), X in any case (wise), X at all, averse, bring (again, back, home again), call [to mind], carry again (back), cease, X certainly, come again (back) X consider, + continually, convert, deliver (again), + deny, draw back, fetch home again, X fro, get [oneself] (back) again, X give (again), go again (back, home), [go] out, hinder, let, [see] more, X needs, be past, X pay, pervert, pull in again, put (again, up again), recall, recompense, recover, refresh, relieve, render (again), X repent, requite, rescue, restore, retrieve, (cause to, make to) return, reverse, reward, + say nay, send back, set again, slide back, still, X

567

surely, take back (off), (cause to, make to) turn (again, self again, away, back, back again, backward, from, off), withdraw.

(23) According to *Strong's Hebrew Lexicon* #**H5715**, the word **testimony** is the Hebrew word *'êdûth* (pronounced **"ay-dooth'"**), which is feminine of H5707; *testimony:* - testimony, witness.

(24) According to *Strong's Hebrew Lexicon* #**H5707**, the word **testimony** is the from the root Hebrew word *'êd* (pronounced **"ayd"**), which is from H5749 contracted; concretely *a witness*; abstractly *testimony*; specifically a *recorder*, that is, *prince:* - witness.

(25) According to *Strong's Hebrew Lexicon* #**H5749**, the word **testimony** is also from the root Hebrew word *'ûd* (pronounced **"ood"**), which is a primitive root that means to *duplicate* or *repeat*; by implication to *protest, testify* (as by reiteration); intensively to *encompass, restore* (as a sort of reduplication): - admonish, charge, earnestly, lift up, protest, call (take) to record, relieve, rob, solemnly, stand upright, testify, give warning, (bear, call to, give, take to) witness.

(26) According to *Strong's Hebrew Lexicon* #**H6490**, the word **statutes** is the Hebrew word *piqqûd* (pronounced **"pik-kood'"**), which is from H6485; properly *appointed*, that is, a *mandate* (of God; plural only, collectively for the *Law*): - commandment, precept, statute.

(27) According to *Strong's Hebrew Lexicon* #**H3374**, the word **fear** is the Hebrew word *yir'âh* (pronounced **"yir-aw'"**), which is feminine of H3373; *fear* (also used as infinitive); morally *reverence:* - X dreadful, X exceedingly, fear (-fulness).

568

(28)According to *Strong's Hebrew Lexicon* #H4941, the word *judgments* is synonymous with the word *law* and is the Hebrew word *mishpât* (pronounced "mish-pawt'"), which is from H8199; properly a verdict (favorable or unfavorable) pronounced judicially, especially a sentence or formal decree (human or (particularly) divine law, individual or collectively), including the act, the place, the suit, the crime, and the penalty; abstractly justice, including a particular *right*, or *privilege* (statutory or customary), or even a *style:* - + adversary, ceremony, charge, X crime, custom, desert, determination, discretion, disposing, due, fashion, form, to be judged, judgment, just (-ice, -ly), (manner of) law (-ful), manner, measure, (due) order, ordinance, right, sentence, usest, X worthy, + wrong.

(29)According to *Strong's Hebrew Lexicon* #H8085, the word *hearing* is the Hebrew word *shâma'* (pronounced "shaw-mah'"), which is a primitive root; to *hear* intelligently (often with implication of attention, obedience, etc.; causatively to *tell*, etc.): - X attentively, call (gather) together, X carefully, X certainly, consent, consider, be content, declare, X diligently, discern, give ear, (cause to, let, make to) hear (-ken, tell), X indeed, listen, make (a) noise, (be) obedient, obey, perceive, (make a) proclaim (-ation), publish, regard, report, shew (forth), (make a) sound, X surely, tell, understand, whosoever [heareth], witness.

(30)According to *Strong's Hebrew Lexicon* #H8441, the word *abomination* is the Hebrew word *to'êbah* (pronounced "to-ay-baw'"), which is feminine active participle of H8581; properly something *disgusting* (morally), that is, (as noun) an *abhorrence*; especially *idolatry* or (concretely) an *idol:* - abominable (custom, thing), abomination.

(31)According to *Strong's Hebrew Lexicon* #**H3068**, the word ***LORD*** is the Hebrew word ***Yhôvâh*** (pronounced **"yeh-ho-vaw'"**), which is from H1961; (the) *self-Existent* or eternal; *Jehovah*, Jewish national name of God: - Jehovah, the Lord. Compare H3050, H3069.

(32)According to *Strong's Greek Lexicon* #**G2962**, the word ***Lord*** is the Greek word ***kurios*** (pronounced **"koo'-ree-os"**), which is from κῦρος kuros (*supremacy*); supreme in authority, that is, (as noun) *controller*; by implication *Mr.* (as a respectful title): - God, Lord, master, Sir.

(33)According to *Strong's Greek Lexicon* #**G5462**, the word ***light*** is the Greek word ***phōtismos*** (pronounced **"fo-tis-mos'"**), which is from G5461; *illumination* (figurative): - light.

(34)According to *Strong's Greek Lexicon* #**G5458**, the word ***lights*** is the Greek word ***phōstēr*** (pronounced **"foce-tare'"**), which is from G5457; an *illuminator*, that is, (concretely) a *luminary*, or (abstractly) *brilliancy:* - light.

(35)According to *Strong's Greek Lexicon* #**G3142**, the word ***testimony*** is the Greek word ***marturion*** (pronounced **"mar-too'-ree-on"**), which is a neuter of a presumed derivative of G3144; something *evidential*, that is, (generally) *evidence* given or (specifically) the *Decalogue* (in the sacred Tabernacle): - to be testified, testimony, witness.

570

(36)According to *Strong's Greek Lexicon* #**G861**, the word ***immortality*** is the Greek word ***aphtharsia*** (pronounced "**af-thar-see'-ah**"), which is from G862; *incorruptibility*; generally *unending existence*; (figuratively) *genuineness:* - immortality, incorruption, sincerity.

(37)According to *Strong's Greek Lexicon* #**G536**, the word ***firstfruits*** is the Greek word ***aparchē*** (pronounced "**ap-ar-khay'**"), which is from a compound of G575 and G756; a *beginning* of sacrifice, that is, the (Jewish) *first fruit* (figuratively): - first-fruits.

(38)According to *Strong's Greek Lexicon* #**G756**, the word ***firstfruits*** comes from the root of the Greek word ***archomai*** (pronounced "**ar'-khom-ahee**"), which is the middle voice of G757 (through the implication of *precedence*); to *commence* (in order of time): - rehearse from the) begin (-ning).

(39)According to *Strong's Greek Lexicon* #**G2938**, the word ***creatures*** is the Greek word ***ktisma*** (pronounced "**ktis'-mah**"), which is from G2936; an original *formation* (concretely), that is, *product* (created thing): - creature.

CHAPTER 11

(1) According to *Strong's Hebrew Lexicon* #**H6213**, the word ***make*** in the Hebrew is the word ***'asah*** (pronounced "**aw-saw'**"), which is a primitive root; to *do* or *make*, in the broadest sense and widest application: - accomplish, advance, appoint, apt, be at, become, bear, bestow, bring forth, bruise, be busy, X certainly, have the charge of, commit, deal (with), deck, + displease, do, (ready) dress

(-ed), (put in) execute (-ion), exercise, fashion, + feast, [fight-] ing man, + finish, fit, fly, follow, fulfil, furnish, gather, get, go about, govern, grant, great, + hinder, hold ([a feast]), X indeed, + be industrious, + journey, keep, labour, maintain, make, be meet, observe, be occupied, offer, + officer, pare, bring (come) to pass, perform, practise, prepare, procure, provide, put, requite, X sacrifice, serve, set, shew, X sin, spend, X surely, take, X thoroughly, trim, X very, + vex, be [warr-] ior, work (-man), yield, use.

(2) According to *Strong's Hebrew Lexicon* #H6754, the word *image* in the Hebrew is the word *tselem* (pronounced "tseh'-lem"), which is from an unused root meaning *to shade; a phantom, that is, (figuratively) illusion, resemblance; hence a representative figure, especially an idol.*

(3) According to *Strong's Hebrew Lexicon* #H1823, the word *likeness* in the Hebrew is the word *dᵉmûth* (pronounced "dem-ooth'"), which means: resemblance; concretely model, shape; *adverbially like.* KJV Usage: fashion, like (-ness, as), manner, similitude.

(4) According to *Strong's Hebrew Lexicon* #H7287, the word *dominion* in the Hebrew is the word *râdâh* (pronounced "raw-daw'"), as used in the KJV version of the Bible it means: come to, make to) have dominion, prevail against, reign, (bear, make to) rule, (-r, over), take.

(5) According to *Brown-Driver-Briggs' Hebrew Lexicon*, the word *dominion* is the Hebrew word *râdâh*, which means the following: (1) to rule, have dominion, dominate, tread down (1a) (Qal) to

572

have dominion, rule, subjugate (1b) (Hiphil) to cause to dominate (2) To scrape out (2a) (Qal) to scrape, scrape out.

[6]According to *Strong's Hebrew Lexicon* #H1254, the word **created** in the Hebrew is the word **bârâ'** (pronounced *"baw-raw'"*), means: A primitive root; (absolutely) to create; (qualified) to cut down (a wood), select, *feed* (as *formative* processes).

[7] According to *Strong's Hebrew Lexicon* #H3533, the word **subdue** or **subdues** in the Hebrew is the word **kâbash** (pronounced *"kaw-bash'"*) which means: as used in the KJV version of the Bible, it means to: bring into bondage, force, keep under, subdue, and bring into subjection.

[8]According to *Brown-Driver-Briggs' Hebrew Dictionary*, the word **subdue** is the Hebrew word **kâbash** (pronounced "kaw-bash'"), which means the following: To subdue and bring into bondage by force to make subservient, to dominate1. To subject, subdue, force, keep under, and bring into bondage a. (Qal) 1. To bring into bondage, make subservient 2. To subdue, force, violate 3. To subdue, dominate, tread down b. (Niphal) to be subdued c. (Piel) to subdue d. (Hiphil) to bring into bondage.

[9]According to *Strong's Hebrew Lexicon* #H3335, the word **formed** is the Hebrew word **yâtsar** (pronounced "yaw-tsar'") which is probably identical with H3334 (through the *squeezing* into shape); (compare H3331); to mould into a form; especially as a potter; figuratively to determine (that is, form a resolution) KJV Usage: X earthen, fashion, form, frame, make (-r), potter, purpose.

[10]According to *Strong's Hebrew Lexicon* #H6635, the word **host** is

573

the Hebrew word *tsâbâ* (pronounced **"tsaw-baw'"**), which is from H6633; a mass of persons (or figurative things), especially regularly organized for war (an *army*); by implication a *campaign*, literally or figuratively (specifically *hardship, worship*): - appointed time, (+) army, (+) battle, company, host, service, soldiers, waiting upon, war (-fare).

(11) According to *Strong's Hebrew Lexicon* #**H7673**, the word **rested** is the Hebrew word *shâbath* (pronounced **"shaw-bath'"**), which is a primitive root; to repose, that is, desist from exertion; used in many implied relations (causatively, figuratively or specifically): - (cause to, let, make to) cease, celebrate, cause (make) to fail, keep (Sabbath), suffer to be lacking, leave, put away (down), (make to) rest, rid, still, take away.

(12) According to *Strong's Hebrew Lexicon* #**H1288**, the word **blessed** is the Hebrew word *bârak* (pronounced **"baw-rak'"**), which is a primitive root; to kneel; by implication to bless god (as an act of adoration), and (vice-versa) man (as a benefit); also (by euphemism) to *curse* (God or the king, as treason): - X abundantly, X altogether, X at all, blaspheme, bless, congratulate, curse, X greatly, X indeed, kneel (down), praise, salute, X still, thank.

(13) According to *Strong's Hebrew Lexicon* #**H6942**, the word **sanctified** is the Hebrew word *qâdash* (pronounced **"kaw-dash'"**), which is a primitive root; to *be* (causatively *make, pronounce* or *observe* as) *clean* (ceremonially or morally): - appoint, bid, consecrate, dedicate, defile, hallow, (be, keep) holy (-er, place), keep, prepare, proclaim, purify, sanctify (-ied one, self), X.

(14) According to *Strong's Hebrew Lexicon* **#H8435**, the word **history** is synonymous with the word **generations** as used in the KJV which is the Hebrew word **tol̂dâh** (pronounced **"to-led-aw'"**), and from H3205; (plural only) *descent,* that is, *family;* (figuratively) *history:* - birth, generations.

(15) According to *Strong's Hebrew Lexicon* **#H5315**, the word **being** is synonymous with the word **soul** as used in the KJV and is the Hebrew word **nephesh** (pronounced **"neh'-fesh"**), which means a breathing creature, that is, animal or (abstractly) vitality; used very widely in a literal, accommodated or figurative sense (bodily or mental).

(16) According to *Brown-Driver-Brigg's Hebrew Definition* the word **being** or **soul** is the Hebrew word **nephesh** נפשׁ and means: 1. soul, self, life, creature, person, appetite, mind, living being, desire, emotion, passion; 1a) that which breathes, the breathing substance or being, soul, the inner being of man; 1b) living being; 1c) living being (with life in the blood); 1d) the man himself, self, person or individual; 1e) seat of the appetites; 1f) seat of emotions and passions; 1g) activity mind dubious; 1h) activity of the will 2. Dubious: activity of the character.

(17) *NAS New Testament Greek Lexicon* meaning of Ekklēsia: http://www.biblestudytools.com/lexicons/greek/nas/ekklesia.html

(18) According to *Strong's Greek Lexicon* **#G1577**, the word **congregation** is synonymous with the word **Church** as used in the KJV and is the Greek word **ekklēsia** (pronounced **"ek-klay-see'-ah"**), and is from a compound of G1537 and a derivative of G2564; a *calling out,* that is, (concretely) a popular *meeting,* especially a

religious *congregation* (Jewish *synagogue,* or Christian community of members on earth or saints in heaven or both): - assembly, Church.

[19]According to *Strong's Greek Lexicon* #**G4982**, the word **save** is the Greek word **sōzō** (pronounced **"sode'-zo"**), which means to save, that is, deliver or protect (literally or figuratively): - heal, preserve, save (self), do well, be (make) whole.

[20]According to *Strong's Greek Lexicon* #**G622**, the word **lost** is the Greek word **apollumi** (pronounced **"ap-ol'-loo-mee"**), which is from G575 and the base of G3639; to *destroy* fully (reflexively to *perish,* or *lose*), literally or figuratively: - destroy, die, lose, mar, perish.

[21]According to *Strong's Greek Lexicon* #**G2540**, the word **time** is synonymous with the word **seasons** and is the Greek word **kairos** (pronounced **"kahee-ros'"**), which is of uncertain affinity; an occasion, that is, set or proper time: - X always, opportunity, (convenient, due) season, (due, short, while) time, a while. Compare G5550.

[22] According to *Strong's Greek Lexicon* #**G4137**, the word **fulfilled** is the Greek word **plēroō** (pronounced **"play-ro'-o"**), which is from G4134; to *make replete,* that is, (literally) to *cram* (a net), *level* up (a hollow), or (figuratively) to *furnish* (or *imbue, diffuse, influence*), *satisfy, execute* (an office), *finish* (a period or task), *verify* (or *coincide* with a prediction), etc.: - accomplish, X after, (be) complete, end, expire, fill (up), fulfil, (be, make) full (come),

fully preach, perfect, supply.

[23]According to *Thayer's Greek Dictionary*, the word **fulfilled** means: (1) to make full, to fill up (i.e., to fill to the full); (1a) to cause to abound, to furnish or supply liberally, (1b) abound, am liberally supplied; (2) to render full (i.e., to complete); (2a) to fill to the top: so that nothing shall be wanting to full measure, fill to the brim; (2b) to consummate: a number; (2c) to make complete in every particular, to render perfect; (2d) to carry through to the end, to accomplish, carry out (some undertaking); (2e) to carry into effect, bring to realization, realize; (2f) of matters of duty: to perform, execute; (2g) of sayings, promises, prophecies, to bring to pass, ratify, accomplish; (2h) to fulfill (i.e., to cause God's will (as made known in the law) to be obeyed as it should be, and God's promises (given through the prophets) to receive fulfillment.

[24] According to *Strong's Greek Lexicon* #**G932**, the word **kingdom** is the Greek word **basileia** (pronounced **"bas-il-i'-ah"**), which is from G935; properly *royalty*, that is, (abstractly) *rule*, or (concretely) a *realm* (literally or figuratively): - kingdom, + reign.

[25]According to *Strong's Greek Lexicon* #**G1448**, the word **hand** is the Greek word **eggizō** (pronounced **"eng-id'-zo"**), which is from G1451; to make *near*, that is, (reflexively) *approach:* - approach, be at hand, come (draw) near, be (come, draw) nigh.

[26]According to *Strong's Greek Lexicon* #**G3340**, the word **repent** is the Greek word **metanoeō** (pronounced **"met-an-o-eh'-o"**), which is

from G3326 and G3539; to think differently or afterwards, that is, reconsider (morally to feel compunction): - repent.

[27] According to *Strong's Greek Lexicon* #**G4100**, the word **believe** is the Greek word **pisteuō** (pronounced **"pist-yoo'-o"**), which is from G4102; to *have faith* (in, upon, or with respect to, a person or thing), that is, *credit*, by implication to *entrust* (especially one's spiritual well-being to Christ): - believe (-r), commit (to trust), put in trust with.

[28] According to *Strong's Greek Lexicon* #**G2098** the word **gospel** is the Greek word **euaggelion** (pronounced **"yoo-ang-ghel'-ee-on"**), which is from the same as G2097; a *good message*, that is, the *gospel:* - gospel.

[29] According to *Strong's Greek Lexicon* #**G2097**, the word **gospel** is from the root Greek word **euaggelizō** (pronounced **"yoo-ang-ghel-id'-zo"**), which is from G2095 and G32; to *announce good* news ("evangelize") especially the gospel: - declare, bring (declare, show) glad (good) tidings, preach (the gospel).

[30] According to *Strong's Greek Lexicon* #**G936**, the word **reigned** or **reign** is the Greek word **basileuō** (pronounced **"bas-il-yoo'-o"**), which is from G935; to *rule* (literally or figuratively): - king, reign.

[31] According to *Strong's Greek Lexicon* #**G2631**, the word **condemnation** is the Greek word **katakrima** (pronounced **"kat-ak'-ree-mah"**), which is from G2632; an *adverse sentence* (the verdict): -

condemnation.

(32) According to *Strong's Greek Lexicon* #**G2632**, the word **condemnation** is from the root Greek word **katakrino** (pronounced **"kat-ak-ree'-no"**), which is from G2596 and G2919; to *judge against*, that is, *sentence:* - condemn, damn.

(33) According to *Strong's Greek Lexicon* #**G1345**, the word **righteous** is the Greek word **dikaiōma** (pronounced **"dik-ah'-yo-mah"**), which is from G1344; an *equitable deed*, by implication a *statute* or *decision:* - judgment, justification, ordinance, righteousness.

(34) According to *Strong's Greek Lexicon* #**G1347**, the word **justification** is the Greek word **dikaiōsis** (pronounced **"dik-ah'-yo-sis"**), which is from G1344; *acquittal* (for Christ's sake): - justification.

(35) According to *Strong's Greek Lexicon* #**G2222**, the word **life** is the Greek word **zōē** (pronounced **"dzo-ay'"**), which means (1) life (1a) the state of one who is possessed of vitality or is animate (1b) every living soul (2) life (2a) of the absolute fulness of life, both essential and ethical, which belongs to god, and through him both to the hypostatic "logos" and to Christ in whom the "logos" put on human nature (2b) life real and genuine, a life active and vigorous, devoted to god, blessed, in the portion even in this world of those who put their trust in Christ, but after the resurrection to be consummated by new accessions (among them a more perfect body), and to last forever.

(36) According to *Strong's Greek Lexicon* #**G1342**, the word

righteous is the Greek word *dikaios* (pronounced **"dik'-ah-yos"**), which is from G1349; *equitable* (in character or act); by implication *innocent, holy* (absolutely or relatively): - just, meet, right (-eous).

(37) According to *Strong's Greek Lexicon* #**G2631**, the word *condemnation* is the Greek word *katakrima* (pronounced **"kat-ak'-ree-mah"**), which is from G2632; an *adverse sentence* (the verdict): - condemnation.

(38) According to *Strong's Greek Lexicon* #**G2632**, the word *condemnation* is the Greek word *katakrino* (pronounced **"kat-ak-ree'-no"**), which is from G2596 and G2919; to *judge against*, that is, *sentence:* - condemn, damn.

CHAPTER 12

(1) According to *Strong's Hebrew Lexicon* #**H1396,** the word *confirm* as is the Hebrew word *gâbar* (pronounced *"gaw-bar'"*), which is a primitive root; which means to *Be strong*; by implication to *prevail, act insolently:* - exceed, confirm, be great, be mighty, prevail, put to more [strength], strengthen, be stronger, be valiant.

(2) According to *Strong's Hebrew Lexicon* #**H1285,** the word *covenant* as used in Daniel 9:27 is the Hebrew word *b'rîyth* (pronounced *"ber-eeth'"*), which is from H1262 (in the sense of *cutting* (like h1254); a *compact* (because made by passing between *pieces* of flesh): - confederacy, [con-]feder[-ate], covenant, league.

(3) According to *Strong's Greek Lexicon* #**G1242**, the word *testament* or *covenant* is the Greek word *diathēkē* (pronounced **"dee-ath-ay'-**

kay"), which is from G1303; properly a *disposition*, that is, (specifically) a *contract* (especially a devisory *will*): - covenant, testament.

[4] According to *Strong's Greek Lexicon* #G1303, the word *testator* is the Greek word *diatithemai* (pronounced "dee-at-ith'-em-ahee"), which means (1) to arrange, dispose of, one's own affairs (1a) of something that belongs to one 1b) to dispose of by will, make a testament (2) to make a covenant, enter into a covenant, with one.

[5] According to *Strong's Greek Lexicon* #G949, the word *force* is the Greek word *bebaios* (pronounced "beb'-ah-yos"), which is from the base of G939 (through the idea of *basality*); *stable* (literally or figuratively): - firm, of force, steadfast, sure.

CHAPTER 13

[1] According to *Strong's Hebrew Lexicon* #H4940, the word *families* is the Hebrew word *mishpâchâh* (pronounced "mish-paw-khaw'"), which is from H8192 (compare H8198); a *family*, that is, circle of relatives; figuratively a *class* (of persons), a *species* (of animals) or *sort* (of things); by extension a *tribe* or *people:* - family, kind (-red).

[2] According to *Strong's Hebrew Lexicon* #H1471, the usage of the word *nation* or *nations* is translated from the Hebrew word *gôy* (pronounced "go'ee"), which is apparently from the same root as H1465 (in the sense of *massing*); a foreign *nation*; hence a *Gentile*; also (figuratively) a *troop* of animals, or a *flight* of locusts. Or, it means a nation of non-Hebrew people which are 1) descendants of Abraham and of Israel. As used in KJV: Gentile, heathen, nation, or people. Therefore, the word *Gentile* is referring to heathen people

or nations that practice or follow pagan rituals or false gods. In other words, they are not in covenant with *Yehôvah*.

(3)According to *Strong's Hebrew Lexicon* #**H2708**, the word **ordinances** is the Hebrew word **chûqqâh** (pronounced "**khook-kaw'**"), and is the feminine of H2706, and meaning substantially the same: - appointed, custom, manner, ordinance, site, statute.

(4)According to *Strong's Hebrew Lexicon* #**H1035**, the word **Bethlehem** is the Hebrew word **bêyth lechem** (pronounced "**bayth leh'-khem**"), which is from H1004 and H3899; *house of bread*; *Beth-Lechem*, a place in Palestine: - Beth-lehem.

(5)According to *Strong's Hebrew Lexicon* #**H672**, the word **Ephrathah** is the Hebrew word **'ephrâth** (pronounced "**ef-rawth'**"), which is from H6509; *fruitfulness*; *Ephrath*, another name for Bethlehem; once used in Psa_132:6 perhaps for *Ephraim*; also of an Israelitish woman: - Ephrath, Ephratah.

(6) According to *Strong's Hebrew Lexicon* #**H3478**, the name **Israel** in the Hebrew is **Yisrâ'êl** (pronounced *"yis-raw-ale'"*), and is from H8280 and H410; He will rule as God; *Jisrael*, a symbolical name of Jacob; also (typically) of his posterity. KJV Usage: Israel. Also, according to *Brown-Driver-Briggs' Hebrew Lexicon* it, means, "God prevails.*"

(7) According to *Strong's Hebrew Lexicon* #**H1121**, the word **Son** is the Hebrew word **bên** (pronounced "**bane**"), and is from H1129; a

son (as a *builder* of the family name), in the widest sense (of literal and figurative relationship, including *grandson, subject, nation, quality* or *condition*, etc., (like H1, H251, etc.): - + afflicted, age, [Ahoh-] [Ammon-] [Hachmon-] [Lev-]ite, [anoint-]ed one, appointed to, (+) arrow, [Assyr-] [Babylon-] [Egypt-] [Grec-]ian, one born, bough, branch, breed, + (young) bullock, + (young) calf, X came up in, child, colt, X common, X corn, daughter, X of first, + firstborn, foal, + very fruitful, + postage, X in, + kid, + lamb, (+) man, meet, + mighty, + nephew, old, (+) people, + rebel, + robber, X servant born, X soldier, son, + spark, + steward, + stranger, X surely, them of, + tumultuous one, + valiant[-est], whelp, worthy, young (one), youth.

[8]According to *Strong's Hebrew Lexicon* #H1697, the word **Word** is the Hebrew word *dâbâr* (pronounced **"daw-bawr'"**), from H1696; a word; by implication a matter (as *spoken* of) of thing; adverbially a *cause:* - act, advice, affair, answer, X any such (thing), + because of, book, business, care, case, cause, certain rate, + chronicles, commandment, X commune (-ication), + concern [-ing], + confer, counsel, + dearth, decree, deed, X disease, due, duty, effect, + eloquent, errand, [evil favoured-] ness, + glory, + harm, hurt, + iniquity, + judgment, language, + lying, manner, matter, message, [no] thing, oracle, X ought, X parts, + pertaining, + please, portion, + power, promise, provision, purpose, question, rate, reason, report, request, X (as hast) said, sake, saying, sentence, + sign, + so, some [uncleanness], somewhat to say, + song, speech, X spoken, talk, task, + that, X there done, thing (concerning), thought, + thus, tidings, what [-soever], + wherewith, which, word, work.

(9) According to *Strong's Hebrew Lexicon* #**H3772**, the word **covenanted** is the Hebrew word **kârath** (pronounced **"kaw-rath'"**), and is a primitive root; to *cut* (off, down or asunder); by implication to *destroy* or *consume*; specifically to *covenant* (that is, make an alliance or bargain, originally by cutting flesh and passing between the pieces): - be chewed, be con- [feder-] ate, covenant, cut (down, off), destroy, fail, feller, be freed, hew (down), make a league ([covenant]), X lose, perish, X utterly, X want.

(10) According to *Strong's Hebrew Lexicon* #**H7307**, the word **Spirit** is the Hebrew word **rûach** (pronounced **"roo'-akh"**), which is from H7306; *wind*; by resemblance *breath*, that is, a sensible (or even violent) exhalation; figuratively *life, anger, unsubstantiality*; by extension a *region* of the sky; by resemblance *spirit*, but only of a rational being (including its expression and functions): - air, anger, blast, breath, X cool, courage, mind, X quarter, X side, spirit ([-ual]), tempest, X vain, ([whirl-]) wind (-y).

(11) According to *Strong's Hebrew Lexicon* #**H3068**, the word **LORD** is the Hebrew word **Yhôvâh** (pronounced **"yeh-ho-vaw'"**), and is from H1961; (the) *self-Existent* or eternal; *Jehovah*, Jewish national name of God: - Jehovah, the Lord.

(12) According to *Strong's Hebrew Lexicon* #**H215**, the word **light** is the Hebrew word **'ôr** (pronounced **"ore"**), which is a primitive root; *to be* (causatively *make*) *luminous* (literally and metaphorically): - X break of day, glorious, kindle, (be, en-, give, show) light (-en, -ened), set on fire, shine.

584

(13)According to *Strong's Hebrew Lexicon* #**H216**, the word *light* is the Hebrew word *'ôr* (pronounced **"ore"**), which is from H215; *illumination* or (concretely) *luminary* (in every sense, including *lightning, happiness,* etc.): - bright, clear, + day, light (-ning), morning, sun.

CHAPTER 14

(1)According to *Strong's Greek Lexicon* #**G5056**, the word *end* is the Greek word *telos* (pronounced **"tel'-os"**), which is from a primary word τέλλω tellō (to *set out* for a definite point or *goal*); properly the point aimed at as a *limit*, that is, (by implication) the *conclusion* of an act or state (*termination* [literally, figuratively or indefinitely], *result* [immediate, ultimate or prophetic], *purpose*); specifically an *impost* or *levy* (as *paid*): - + continual, custom, end (-ing), finally, uttermost. Compare G5411. The word *end* also means the following: 1) end: termination, the limit at which a thing ceases to be (always of the end of some act or state, but not of the end of a period of time) 2) the end: the last in any succession or series 3) eternal: that by which a thing is finished, its close, issued) the end to which all things relate, the aim, purpose.

(2)According to *Strong's Greek Lexicon* #**G2098**, the word *gospel* is the Greek word *euaggelion* (pronounced **"yoo-ang-ghel'-ee-on"**), which means the following: (1) a reward for good tidings (2) good tidings (2a) the glad tidings of the kingdom of God soon to be set up, and subsequently also of Jesus the Messiah, the founder of this kingdom. After the death of Christ, the term comprises also the preaching of (concerning) Jesus Christ as having suffered death on the cross to procure eternal salvation for the men in the kingdom of

God, but as restored to life and exalted to the right hand of God in heaven, thence to return in majesty to consummate the kingdom of God (2b) the glad tidings of salvation through Christ (2c) the proclamation of the grace of God manifest and pledged in Christ (2d) the gospel (2e) as the messianic rank of Jesus was proved by his words, his deeds, and his death, the narrative of the sayings, deeds, and death of Jesus Christ came to be called the gospel or glad tidings.

[3] According to *Strong's Greek Lexicon* #**G1589**, the word **election** is the Greek word **eklogē** (pronounced **"ek-log-ay'"**), which means (1) the act of picking out, choosing (1a) of the act of God's free will by which before the foundation of the world he decreed his blessings to certain persons 1b) the decree made from choice by which he determined to bless certain persons through Christ by grace alone (2) a thing or person chosen (2a) of persons: God's elect.

[4] "The Mayflower Compact," Wikipedia: The Free Encyclopedia, https://en.wikipedia.org/wiki/Mayflower_Compact.

[5] **Dismantling Political Correctness**
http://www1.cbn.com/video/I7C032217_LanceWallnau/dismantling-political-correctness

CHAPTER 15

[1] According to *Strong's Greek Lexicon* #**G1343**, the word **righteousness** is the Greek word **dikaiosunē** (pronounced **"dik-ah-**

yos-oo'-nay"), which is from G1342; *equity* (of character or act); specifically (Christian) *justification:* - righteousness.

[2]According to *Strong's Greek Lexicon* #G4102, the word **faith** is the Greek word ***pistis*** (pronounced "pis'-tis"), which is from G3982; persuasion, that is, credence; moral conviction (of religious truth, or the truthfulness of God or a religious teacher), especially reliance upon Christ for salvation; abstract *constancy* in such profession; by extension the system of religious (gospel) *truth* itself: - assurance, belief, believe, faith, fidelity.

[3]According to *Strong's Greek Lexicon* #G4100, the word **believe** is the Greek word ***pisteuo*** (pronounced "pist-yoo'-o"), which is from G4102; to *have faith* (in, upon, or with respect to, a person or thing), that is, credit; by implication to entrust (especially one's spiritual well-being to Christ): - believe (-r), commit (to trust), put in trust with.

[4]According to *Strong's Greek Lexicon* #G1344, the word **justified** is the Greek word ***dikaioo*** (pronounced "dik-ah-yo'-o"), which is from G1342; to render (that is, show or regard as) just or innocent: - free, justify (-ier), be righteous.

[5]According to *Strong's Greek Lexicon* #G5485, the word **grace** is the Greek word ***charis*** (pronounced "khar'-ece"), which is from G5463; *graciousness* (as *gratifying*), of manner or act (abstract or concrete; literal, figurative or spiritual; especially the divine influence upon the heart, and its reflection in the life; including gratitude): - acceptable, benefit, favour, gift, grace (-ious), joy

liberality, pleasure, thank (-s, -worthy).

(6) According to *Strong's Greek Lexicon* #**G629**, the word ***redemption*** is the Greek word ***apolutrōsis*** (pronounced "**ap-ol-oo'-tro-sis**"), which is from a compound of G575 and G3083; (the act) ransom in full, that is, (figuratively) riddance, or (specifically) Christian salvation: - deliverance, redemption.

(7) According to *Strong's Greek Lexicon* #**G2435**, the word ***propitiation*** is the Greek word ***hilastērion*** (pronounced "**hil-as-tay'-ree-on**"), which means an *expiatory* (place or thing), that is, (concretely) an atoning victim, or (specifically) the lid of the ark (in the Temple): - mercy seat, propitiation.

Thayer's definition is as follows: (1) relating to an appeasing or expiating, having placating or expiating force, expiatory; a means of appeasing or expiating, a propitiation (1a) used of the cover of the ark of the covenant in the Holy of Holies, which was sprinkled with the blood of the expiatory victim on the annual day of atonement (this rite signifying that the life of the people, the loss of which they had merited by their sins, was offered to God in the blood as the life of the victim, and that God by this ceremony was appeased and their sins expiated); hence the lid of expiation, the propitiatory (1b) an expiatory sacrifice (1c) a expiatory victim.

CHAPTER 16

(1) According to *Strong's Greek Lexicon* #**G3100**, the word ***disciple is*** synonymous with the word ***teach*** as used in the KJV and is the Greek word ***mathēteuō*** (pronounced "**math-ayt-yoo'-o**"), which is

from G3101; intransitively to *become a pupil*; transitively to *disciple*, that is, enrol as scholar: - be disciple, instruct, teach.

CHAPTER 17

(1) According to *Strong's Hebrew Lexicon* #**H3091**, the name *Joshua* is the Hebrew word **Yᵉhôshûa'** (pronounced "**yeh-ho-shoo'-ah**"), which is from H3068 and H3467; Jehovah-saved; *Jehoshua* (that is, Joshua), the Jewish leader: - Jehoshua, Jehoshuah, Joshua. Compare H1954, H3442.

(2) According to *Strong's Hebrew Lexicon* #**H3068**, the name *Joshua* is the Hebrew name **Yᵉhôvâh** (pronounced "**yeh-ho-vaw'**"), from H1961; (the) self-existent or eternal; Jehovah, Jewish national name of God.

(3) According to *Strong's Hebrew Lexicon* #**H3467**, the name *Joshua* is the Hebrew name **Yâsha'** (pronounced "**yaw-shah'**"), a primitive root; properly to *be open, wide* or *free*, that is, (by implication) to *be safe*; causatively to *free* or *succor*. The KJV Usage: X at all, avenging, defend, deliver (-er), help, preserve, rescue, be safe, bring (having) salvation, save (-iour), get victory.

(4) "Yahshua (Name)," Wikipedia: The Free Encyclopedia, http://en.wikipedia.org/wiki/ Yahshua_ (name).

(5) According to *Strong's Greek Lexicon* #**G2647**, the word **abolish** is synonymous with the word **destroy** as used in the KJV and is the Greek word **kataluō** (pronounced "**kat-al-oo'-o**"), which is from G2596 and G3089; to *loosen down* (disintegrate), that is, (by implication) to demolish (literally or figuratively); specifically

(compare G2646) to *halt* for the night: - destroy, dissolve, be guest, lodge, come to naught, overthrow, throw down.

[6] According to *Strong's Greek Lexicon* #**G3551**, the word *law* is the Greek word **nomos** (pronounced **"nom'-os"**), which is from a primary word νέμω nemō̄ (to *parcel* out, especially *food* or *grazing* to animals); *law* (through the idea of prescriptive *usage*), generally (*regulation*), specifically (of Moses [including the volume]; also of the gospel), or figuratively (a *principle*): - law.

[7] According to *Strong's Greek Lexicon* #**G4137**, the word *fulfill* is the Greek word **plēroō̄** pronounced (**"play-ro'-o"**), which is from G4134; to *make replete*, that is, (literally) to *cram* (a net), *level* up (a hollow), or (figuratively) to *furnish* (or *imbue, diffuse, influence*), *satisfy, execute* (an office), *finish* (a period or task), *verify* (or *coincide* with a prediction), etc.: - accomplish, X after, (be) complete, end, expire, fill (up), fulfil, (be, make) full (come), fully preach, perfect, supply.

[8]According to *Thayer's Greek-English Lexicon of the New Testament* the word *fulfill* means: 1) to make full, to fill up, i.e. to fill to the full 1a) to cause to abound, to furnish or supply liberally 1a1) I abound, I am liberally supplied 2) to render full, i.e. to complete 2a) to fill to the top: so that nothing shall be wanting to full measure, fill to the brim 2b) to consummate: a number 2b1) to make complete in every particular, to render perfect 2b2) to carry through to the end, to accomplish, carry out, (some undertaking) 2c) to carry into effect, bring to realization, realize 2c1) of matters

of duty: to perform, execute 2c2) of sayings, promises, prophecies, to bring to pass, ratify, accomplish 2c3) to fulfill, i.e. to cause God's will (as made known in the law) to be obeyed as it should be, and god's promises (given through the prophets) to receive fulfillment.

[9]According to *Strong's Hebrew Lexicon* #**H1285**, the word **covenant** is the Hebrew word is **berîyth** (pronounced "**ber-eeth'**"), and is from H1262 (in the sense of *cutting* (like H1254); a compact (because made by passing between *pieces* of flesh): - confederacy, [con-]feder[-ate], covenant, league.

[10]According to *Strong's Hebrew Lexicon* #**H4687**, the word **commandments** is the Hebrew word **mitsvâh** (pronounced "**mits-vaw'**"), and is from H6680; a *command*, whether human or divine (collectively the *Law*) : - (which was) commanded (-ment), law, ordinance, precept.

[11]According to *Strong's Hebrew Lexicon* #**H2708**, the word **statutes** is the Hebrew word **chûqqâh** (pronounced "**khook-kaw'**"), and is the feminine of H2706, and meaning substantially the same: - appointed, custom, manner, ordinance, site, statute.

[12]According to *Strong's Hebrew Lexicon* #**H6154**, the word **mixed** is the Hebrew word **'êreb** (pronounced "**eh'-reb**"), which means: a *web* (or transverse threads of cloth); also a mixture, (or *mongrel* race): - Arabia, mingled people, mixed (multitude), woof.

[13] According to *Strong's Hebrew Lexicon* #**H7227**, the word **multitude** is the Hebrew word **rab** (pronounced "**rab**"), by contraction from H7231; *abundant* (in quantity, size, age, number, rank, quality): - (in) abound (-undance, -ant, -antly), captain, elder,

enough, exceedingly, full, great (-ly, man, one), increase, long (enough, [time]), (do, have) many (-ifold, things, a time), ([ship-]) master, mighty, more, (too, very) much, multiply (-tude), officer, often [-times], plenteous, populous, prince, process [of time], suffice (-ient).

[14] According to *Strong's Hebrew Lexicon* #**H6963**, the word **voice** is the Hebrew word *qôl* (pronounced "**kole**"), which is from an unused root meaning to *call* aloud; a *voice* or *sound:* - + aloud, bleating, crackling, cry (+ out), fame, lightness, lowing, noise, + hold peace, [pro-] claim, proclamation, + sing, sound, + spark, thunder (-ing), voice, + yell.

[15] According to *Strong's Hebrew Lexicon* #**H4931**, the word **charge** is the Hebrew word *mishmereth* (pronounced "**mish-meh'-reth**"), which is Feminine of H4929; *watch,* that is, the Act (*custody*) or (concretely) the *sentry,* the *post;* objectively *preservation,* or (concretely) *safe;* figuratively *observance,* that is, (abstractly) *duty,* or (objectively) a *usage* or *party:* - charge, keep, to be kept, office, ordinance, safeguard, ward, watch.

[16] According to *Strong's Hebrew Lexicon* #**H8451**, the word **laws** is the Hebrew word *tôrâh* (pronounced "**to-raw'**"), which is from H3384; a *precept* or *statute,* especially the Decalogue or Pentateuch: - law.

CHAPTER 18

[1] *The Miracle of Israel,* DVD, 2014, Arizona: The Miracle of Israel Foundation.

http://superstore.wnd.com/The-Miracle-of-Israel-Narrated-by-Leonard-Nimoy-Movie

[2] According to *Strong's Hebrew Lexicon* #**H7620**, the word **weeks** is the Hebrew word **shâbûa'** (pronounced "shaw-boo'-ah"), which is properly passive participle of H7650 as a denominative of H7651; literally *sevened*, that is, a *week* (specifically of years): - seven, week. The biblical usage is as follows: (1) seven, period of seven (days or years), heptad, week (2) period of seven days, a week: Feast of Weeks (3) heptad, seven (of years).

[3] According to *Strong's Hebrew Lexicon* #**H7651**, the word **weeks** is the Hebrew word **shâbûa'**, and it comes from the root Hebrew word **Sheba'** (pronounced "sheh'-bah"), which is from H7650; a primitive cardinal number; *seven* (as the sacred *full* one); also (adverbially) *seven times*; by implication a *week*; by extension an *indefinite* number: - (+ by) seven ([-fold], -s, [-teen, -teenth], -th, times). Compare H7658.

[4] *The Coming Prince: The Marvelous Prophecy of Daniel's Seventy Weeks Concerning the Antichrist* by Sir Robert Anderson.

[5] "Time to Wake up the Year of Jubilee Is Upon Us September 23, 2015!!!" Video, 2015, YouTube. https://www.youtube.com/watch?v=PPaTbsQZHhM

[6] The Sign of His Coming Revealed http://signofhiscoming.blogspot.com/2016/12/923-9-months-to-day-conception.html

Who is Israel? Discovering our True Identity in Jesus Christ and Why it Matters! The Foundation

CONNECT WITH THE AUTHOR

I hope and pray you have been greatly blessed and enlightened by this book. And, as a result of reading it, may you walk in a deeper relationship with our heavenly Father, and our Lord and Savior, Jesus Christ.

If this book has blessed you, please tell those in your circle of influence about it. Also, you can assist me in getting the word out about this book by following me via Facebook, and like my page, I set up for this book, by accessing the link below:

https://www.facebook.com/bella4Jesus/

Please share my posts concerning this series, with your family and friends. I thank you in advance for posting your recommendation of this book as well.

You may also connect with me via Instagram under the following username:

bella4jesus777

In addition, if you purchased this book from Amazon, please bless me with a favorable review under the Customer Review section.

Last, but certainly not least, I would love to hear from you! I may be contacted via my website by accessing the following link:

http://www.angeloffaith777.com/contact-me.html

I have many more teachings which can be accessed via my website at the following link:

http://www.angeloffaith777.com/

Thank you in advance for your feedback and for your help with sharing this critical message with your family and friends. Together we CAN make a difference for His Kingdom and America!

ABOUT THE AUTHOR

Donna Rogers is an ordained minister of the gospel and is the founder of Angel of Love & Light Ministries. Her website can be accessed at www.angeloffaith777.com.

In 2004, Donna wrote her first book titled, *Shattered Dreams— Wake Up America Before It Is Too Late!* It was at this time; she started a Bible study out of her home for seven years.

Three years later, on October 7, 2007, the Lord closed the door on her secular career as an international Critical Issues Manager and led her to begin her prophetic ministry.

Currently, Donna serves as a servant of Jesus Christ in her role as the state of Florida coordinator for the Black Robe Regiment, and she is Director, for the State of Florida Tea Party Command Center.

In addition, she has strategically partnered her ministry with many different ministries, and grassroots organizations, in the state of Florida, and on a national level.

Donna was commissioned by Reinhard Bonnke, founder of Christ for All Nations, and is a graduate of Reinhard Bonnke's School of Evangelism located in Orlando, Florida.

She was ordained by Pastors Jerry and Anne Marie Mallory, founders of Kingdom Life Builders Int'l Ministries.

Donna lives in Florida with her husband Jimmy, and they have three children; Kristen 30, Samantha 26, and Dylan age 17.

Made in the USA
Middletown, DE
17 July 2018